F. N. Jordan
New York 11-74

IDEALISM

A CRITICAL SURVEY

IDEALISM
A Critical Survey

by
A. C. EWING

LONDON
METHUEN & CO LTD
BARNES & NOBLE BOOKS
NEW YORK

First published in 1934
This edition reprinted 1974 by
Methuen & Co Ltd
11 New Fetter Lane
London EC4P 4EE
and Barnes & Noble Books, New York
10 East 53rd Street
New York NY 10022
(a division of Harper & Row Inc.)
Printed in Great Britain by
Whitstable Litho, Straker Brothers Ltd

Methuen SBN 416 80950 2
Barnes & Noble SBN 06 472028 4

PREFACE

THE purpose of this book is made as plain as I can make it in the introductory chapter. It will surely be clear in any case that an attempt to assess the contribution to philosophy of the idealist school by one who is not a member of this school but yet in deep sympathy with it constitutes on principle an enterprise which is worth undertaking and, as the course of the book will show, is by no means irrelevant to modern controversies. Whether it has proved worth undertaking in practice as well as in principle is for my readers to judge. When I try to reach philosophical conclusions of my own through a critical examination of idealism, as I do in this book, I find myself led in a direction which is in sharp opposition to the strongest philosophical influences of the present day; but in philosophy at least the only way of salvation is through thinking for oneself undeterred by authority, so I have not hesitated to criticize my betters. Nor do I regard this divergence as wholly a disadvantage. For it is the less and not the more popular views that most need sympathetic exposition, since the errors of the latter are liable to consist just in overlooking the element of truth contained in the former, while there is from the nature of the case little danger that people will overlook what truth is contained in the latter.

I am under a deep obligation in particular to Professor G. E. Moore and Mr. H. H. Price, both because of what I have learnt from them in oral discussion on many occasions and for the really great sacrifice of well-earned leisure which they must have made in order to read and comment in much detail on the large portions of my book which I submitted to them. Their criticism was rendered all the more valuable by the fact that there was and still, I fear, is a very serious divergence between some of the views presented here and views held by Professor Moore at least. I also tender my heartfelt thanks to Professor W. R. Sorley, Professor N. Kemp Smith, and

Messrs. H. B. Acton, R. B. Braithwaite, J. D. Mabbott and J. O. Wisdom for having read and very helpfully commented on shorter portions of the book which I submitted to their consideration. I am indebted to the editors of *Mind* and of *The Proceedings of the Aristotelian Society* for permission to make use in a more or less revised form of articles published in these periodicals. Last but not least I have to thank my father and mother for having relieved me of the most tedious part of the work involved in the production of the book, namely, that of proof reading.

A. C. EWING

TRINITY HALL
  CAMBRIDGE
    October, 1933

NOTE TO THE THIRD EDITION

The asterisks in the text refer to the Notes at the end.

CONTENTS

CHAP.		PAGE
I	INTRODUCTORY	1
II	EPISTEMOLOGICAL IDEALISM	11
	§ I. THE MAIN EPISTEMOLOGICAL ARGUMENT FOR IDEALISM	11
	§ II. THE ARGUMENT FROM MENTAL CONSTRUCTION	23
	§ III. IS THE OBJECT OF KNOWLEDGE INDEPENDENT OF BEING KNOWN? THE REALIST EPISTEMOLOGY	30
	§ IV. THE EPISTEMOLOGICAL ARGUMENT FROM INTERNAL RELATIONS	43
	§ V. ROYCE'S ARGUMENT	49
	§ VI. A CONCESSION TO IDEALISM	56
	§ VII. HEGELIANISM AND EPISTEMOLOGICAL IDEALISM	59
III	KANTIAN IDEALISM	63
	§ I. INTRODUCTORY	63
	§ II. KANT'S SOLUTION OF THE PROBLEM OF SYNTHETIC *A Priori* KNOWLEDGE. WHY KANT WAS AN IDEALIST	64
	§ III. ARE SPACE AND TIME MERE APPEARANCES?	84
	§ IV. KANT'S ATTEMPT TO ESTABLISH EMPIRICAL REALISM WITHIN IDEALISM	93
	§ V. THE THING-IN-ITSELF	101
	§ VI. KANT'S CHIEF CONTRIBUTIONS TO THE IDEALIST MOVEMENT	111
IV	THE THEORY OF INTERNAL RELATIONS	117
	§ I. AN ANALYSIS OF 'INTERNAL' AND 'EXTERNAL'	117
	§ II. VARIOUS IDEALIST ARGUMENTS FOR THE THEORY OF INTERNAL RELATIONS	142
	§ III. CAUSALITY AND THE PROBLEM OF INTERNAL RELATIONS	151
	§ IV. CONCLUSIONS	187

CHAP.		PAGE
V	THE COHERENCE THEORY	195
	§ I. The Objections to the Correspondence Theory	195
	§ II. Degrees of Truth	208
	§ III. Coherence as an Account of the Nature of the World	228
	§ IV. Coherence as the Criterion of Truth	236
	§ V. Rationalism v. Empiricism	250
VI	IDEALISM AND THE THEORY OF PERCEPTION	261
	§ I. Introductory Explanation of Terms	261
	§ II. Different Senses of 'Direct Awareness' and their Philosophical Significance	264
	§ III. The Representative v. the Direct Theory of Perception	273
VII	PHYSICAL OBJECTS	290
	§ I. The Argument from Common-Sense and the Analysis of Propositions about Physical Objects	290
	§ II. Is there any Justification for the Belief in Independent Physical Objects?	316
	§ III. The Nature of Physical Objects	355
VIII	IDEALIST METAPHYSICS	383
	§ I. Theistic Idealism	383
	§ II. Does Matter Imply an Experience for which it Exists	395
	§ III. The Absolute	403
	§ IV. Panpsychism	410
	§ V. The Argument from Universals and Moral Values	416
	§ VI. Idealism and Values	427
	SUMMARY OF MAIN CONCLUSIONS	440
	INDEX	443

IDEALISM: A CRITICAL SURVEY

CHAPTER I

INTRODUCTORY

THIS work is not a history and does not seek to compete with any histories of idealism; it is an attempt to reach an independent conclusion on certain philosophical problems by means of criticism of what others have said. Its subject does not require apology, however much the treatment of it may, since, whatever our sympathies, there is no doubt that historically the most influential movement in modern philosophy has been that known by the name of idealism. The time has perhaps arrived when one may hope better to evaluate the rights and wrongs of this great movement than would have been possible either when its dominance was, comparatively speaking, unquestioned or when it was confessedly the centre of the chief philosophical controversy of the day. The need for such an evaluation of idealism is all the greater because so many prominent philosophers of other schools now seem to think that there is nothing to be learnt from it and despise and ignore it in a way which of itself suggests to a discreet observer that the reaction may have gone too far. Such philosophers must themselves realise that it is most unlikely that the school which dominated thought in this country for so long and still numbers so many adherents has nothing to give that its opponents have overlooked, and it is at least worth inquiring whether this is so. There are two reasons which in the light of my personal views seem to me to make such an inquiry especially pertinent at the present time. The first is that what started twenty-five or thirty years ago as a well-justified realist reaction at Cambridge seems like most reactions to have gone too far, and to suffer just through overlooking that side of the truth which the 'absolute idealists' whom it first attacked brought out, while bringing out admirably the side which they overlooked.

The second is that in spite of all this many philosophers, including some who are generally associated with the left wing of that very movement of which I have just spoken, have now relapsed into what I consider the chief idealist error, namely, that of refusing to separate the *esse* of a physical object from its *percipi*. But there is a further reason independent of my personal views: it is that at the present time there is great danger of the philosophers of this country falling asunder into two groups who do not understand each other's language and are quite incapable of appreciating each other's arguments, namely, the so-called Cambridge school on the one hand and on the other the school more in sympathy with what might be named the classical rationalist tradition in philosophy. Since I think on the whole that the former argues better but that the latter arrives at wiser conclusions, it seems to me very important that some of the contentions of the latter should be restated more clearly than was possible before the former had done its work of criticism. Perhaps the fact that I am not definitely a member of either the one party or the other may increase my chances of making some slight contribution in this direction that will be of help to the more moderate members of both.

The term, idealism, has been used in many different senses, but nevertheless there is a school—or, better, several schools —of philosophy to which the name would be universally applied. It would be generally agreed that Berkeley, Kant, Fichte, Schopenhauer, Lotze, T. H. Green, Bradley, McTaggart, Croce and Gentile, for instance, however much they differ among themselves, can all reasonably be described as 'idealists'. This is not to say that the definition of the term idealism in its philosophical sense is an easy matter or one about which there is general agreement. Professor Kemp Smith defines the term as covering 'all those philosophies which agree in maintaining that spiritual values have a determining voice in the ordering of the universe',[1] and there is much to be said for the view that it would have been more satisfactory if the term had been generally used in some such way as this. But, if we were to use it

---

[1] *Prolegomena to an Idealist Theory of Knowledge*, p. 1. The alternative position which he contrasts with idealism is called by him naturalism and defined as the view 'that these values emerge and begin to vindicate their reality only at some late stage in a process of evolution'.

thus now, its denotation would be far wider than is usually the case, for we should have to describe all believers in God as idealists (including most philosophers who lived before what is usually called the idealist movement began, all Christian theologians and some of the advocates of philosophical realism[1]).

At any rate what I wish to discuss in this book is not the view that 'spiritual values have a determining voice in the ordering of the universe', but only a certain line of thought that has sometimes been used to support such a conclusion. For there are many arguments, whether good or bad, for theism which are not idealist in character in the sense in which that term has most commonly been employed, e.g. the three traditional proofs of God criticised by Kant and most arguments based on ethics and on 'religious experience', and there may also be non-idealist arguments which support forms of the said view about values other than theism. There is certainly a narrower sense of idealism in common use among philosophers such that it is quite possible and usual to hold that the universe is in some way 'ordered' or 'dominated' by 'spiritual values' without being an idealist. What this narrower sense is can be roughly indicated by saying that it is the one in which the philosophers enumerated above can all be said to be idealists. What have all these philosophers in common? They have in common the view that there can be no physical objects existing apart from some experience,[2] and this might perhaps be taken as the definition of idealism, provided we regard thinking as a part of experience and do not imply by 'experience' passivity, and provided we include under experience not only human experience but the so-called 'Absolute Experience' or the experience of a God such as Berkeley postulates. By 'existence apart from

[1] E.g. Cook Wilson, *Statement and Inference*, vol. II, ad fin. On the other hand the term would not cover, e.g. Schopenhauer.

[2] Cf. the definition given by Professor Watts Cunningham: 'Idealism is that philosophical doctrine which undertakes to show that, in order to think matter or the spatio-temporal order of events in its ultimate nature, we are logically compelled to think mind or spirit along with it as in some sense foundational to it'. (*The Idealistic Argument in Recent British and American Philosophy*, pp. 338–9.) I for some time hesitated whether to use 'mind' or 'experience' in my definition but decided in favour of the latter as more comprehensive and less vague. The definition quoted, as well as mine, also seems to require further reservations, not given by its author, to make clear the distinction between idealism and theism.

experience' I mean existence [1] as unperceived. If we took as our definition of idealism the view that nothing can exist apart from experience we should exclude Kant, but we do not if we take as our definition the view that no physical thing can, understanding 'physical thing' to cover objects like stones, chairs, tables, etc., for, whatever we mean by these words, we certainly do not, as Kant recognised, mean by them unknown things-in-themselves. Further complications arise because anyone who believes in a God that created the world must believe that physical things could not exist apart from God, unless he supposes that God merely created them in the beginning and that they can now go on just as well without God, like a watch which had been wound up once for all; and if he, as is most usual, also supposes God to be omniscient, he must suppose that physical things could not exist apart from a mind which knows them and to which they are therefore in some way present.[2] Yet it is certainly not customary to call all who believe in this idealists. The point of difference is that, while others would be led to this conclusion indirectly, if at all, the idealist holds that the nature of physical things, in the only sense in which he will admit their existence, directly involves this relation to experience, so that their existence is logically inconceivable apart from experience. 'Idealism' as thus used will cover alike views which proceed from this premiss to the conclusion that physical objects depend on God or the Absolute, or are themselves psychical in character, and views which are content with making them abstractions from collective human experience.

It must be admitted, however, that even now our definition is not at all precise, and cannot be so at least till a precise definition of 'physical object' be given, a very difficult task. The reader knows the sort of thing meant by the latter term, he knows what trees, stones, mountains, tables, etc., are like, and therefore he can understand what kind of view I mean to cover by my definition of idealism; but to frame a formula which would include all the shades of opinion that have, more

---

[1] There is a further complication as to the meaning of existence (v. below p. 298). I am using the term in a primary literal sense and not in a sense in which 'A exists' means merely that anybody who e.g. looked in a certain direction under certain conditions would see A.

[2] He might hesitate to speak of the 'experience' of God, because the word suggests a certain passivity and dependence on 'sense-data' not usually attributed to God.

often than not, been described as idealist and exclude all those that have been, more often than not, described as realist is almost or quite beyond human capacity. For instance, while my definition seems to me fairly easily applicable in distinguishing the philosophies of the past since Berkeley, there are certain philosophers of the present day who hold views about physical objects covered by it and yet would resent and would not in practice usually be given the title of idealist because they are so much out of sympathy with other tendencies associated with the school. But then is it ever possible to define a movement adequately by a short formula which is quite unambiguous and precise? My view is that the term will soon die out except as a name for a past movement, since most philosophers of the present day seem to feel that it is better not to label themselves expressly as idealists or realists, while they still draw on the resources of either or, better, both schools.

The idealist may hold the view about physical things indicated either (*a*) because of a general theory of knowledge which implies that no object can exist apart from a knowing mind, or (*b*) because he holds that the particular characteristics of matter logically imply an experiencing or thinking mind, or (*c*) because he holds that physical objects, while not implying a mind on which they depend, are themselves of the nature of experience or are psychical entities of some kind. The first type of argument is discussed mainly in Chapter II, the last two in Chapter VIII. One of the reasons urged for the first view is a certain theory of relations, the doctrine of internal relations, which is specially associated with the idealist movement and should lead to very important metaphysical conclusions if it is true, and this theory necessitates a special discussion in Chapter IV. Further, the form of idealism maintained by Kant seems to require discussion in a separate chapter, as does the so-called coherence theory. However, among the chief arguments used by idealists have been negative ones based on our supposed inability to justify the belief in physical objects realistically conceived, and consequently, though it is not quite clear whether the term idealist as ordinarily understood in philosophy covers anyone who merely denies that we can defend the belief in unexperienced physical objects without asserting that such things are logically impossible, these negative arguments bulk so largely in the idealist controversy that a discussion of them is absolutely essential. This brings us to the theory of perception and the question in what sense we are justified in asserting the existence of physical things.

It seems to me that all these topics have a certain unity and are not only definitely associated with the great idealist movement of the last century but are appropriately discussed under the heading of idealism. But, if anyone thinks that I have used the term improperly, this is only a matter of words. I have a right to choose these topics for discussion if I wish, and the title is quite a minor consideration. It may be that some would have preferred me to speak of ' mentalism ' or ' subjectivism ' rather than ' idealism ', but there is one fatal objection to this course. ' Mentalism ' and ' subjectivism ' have been employed almost entirely as a kind of terms of abuse, and consequently to call any theory by these names is to set most people against the theory at the start. This I wish to avoid at all costs : the theories I am discussing may be quite untenable, but they have at any rate been held by many thinkers of the highest distinction and have constituted one of the most important currents in modern thought. This being so it is incredible that they can be mere folly, and this book is an attempt to separate the good and evil in them. Fairness is the quality most essential to the critic, and it would be hindered by the mere application of such a title. Besides, I wish to discuss some topics such as the coherence theory which certainly could not be brought under these terms. Many people will also feel a not unjustifiable objection to the use of labels in philosophy, but after all we are speaking of a distinctive school with a great deal in common and, if he likes, the reader may simply regard the term idealism as shorthand for the belief that physical objects cannot exist apart from some experience or mind. In practice I have found the term extremely useful merely as shorthand to avoid such cumbrous expressions.

It is important for the reader to be clear that the rejection of the type of view under discussion in this book would not necessarily imply the adoption of what is usually called naturalism or even the denial of the dominance of mind or spirit in the real world, provided one allowed a secondary, though perhaps dependent, reality to matter. Even if idealism is rejected three alternatives remain open, and I shall not attempt to judge between them. (*a*) The ' naturalist ' view may be adopted as the more likely, and it may be held that mind is a mere product or even a mere quality of matter. (*b*) An agnostic view may be taken, and the problem of the ultimate relation of mind and matter dismissed as one which, at least at present, is quite beyond our power of solution. (*c*) That mind or 'spirit' is dominant in reality may be held for reasons other than those discussed under the heading of Idealism. In particular, while idealism has very commonly, though not always, been associated with and used in defence of what may for short be called a 'religious view of the world', the rejection of idealism must not be understood necessarily to involve the rejection of such a view. It may well be the case, as is very often held, that while the belief in God or in the dominance of values cannot be established by argument, there is a mode of cognition, not mainly dependent on inference, associated with 'religious experience' which provides adequate justification for such a view; but even as regards philosophical arguments for theism and against naturalism the greater number, whether valid or invalid, would at any rate be unaffected by the rejection of idealism. Certainly of those who have held such religious beliefs the vast majority, including all philosophers prior to Berkeley and most theologians and many philosophers afterwards, have not held them for reasons dependent on idealism in the philosophical sense.

As I have said already, this book is not intended to be a historical account of idealism but a criticism of it and an attempt to discover how far any of the distinctive doctrines specially associated with this name are tenable. No attempt has been made to complete it by including all the chief historical figures of the idealist school, and as will be seen the order of the chapters ignores chronology altogether. I am trying to consider certain arguments and determine their validity or otherwise, not to describe how the theories in question developed or to act as interpreter of particular thinkers except as a means of fulfilling my main purpose.

One serious omission may be charged against me, namely, my neglect of Hegel. For this the justification is twofold. In the first place it is doubtful whether Hegel was or was not an idealist in the sense in which I am using the term, and if and in so far as he was the views held by him are better discussed as they occur in other philosophers who have stated them less obscurely. Secondly, it would be quite impossible to deal with Hegel without introducing a long and difficult discussion of the different possible interpretations of his work, thus overloading my book with historical controversy and exegesis. My object throughout is not to decide what different thinkers meant as an end-in-itself, but to work out my own conclusions regarding the strength and weakness of the case for a certain type of view, and to seek to determine what view others held only as a means to the fulfilment of this end. But to do so in the case of Hegel would involve so long a discussion that we should lose sight of the end in the means and should probably also attain no decisive result after all our trouble. Hegel was one of the greatest of philosophers, but his greatness did not lie in his idealism, even if he was an idealist. Similar reasons excuse me from discussing 'phenomenology'.

The twentieth century has seen a violent and widespread reaction against the idealism of the later nineteenth, and with this reaction I have much sympathy. Its leaders have in particular rendered three services of inestimable value to philosophy. In the first place they have shown up the true nature of cognition as something much more akin to finding than to making and refuted the misconceptions and dogmatic assumptions which prevent philosophers from seeing this clear truth. Secondly, they have shown that the theory of a physical world existing independently of any experience, while incapable of strict proof and still open to many difficulties, is at least reasonably arguable by philosophers, and in doing so have effectively discussed many problems such as those covered by 'the theory of perception', which idealists had highhandedly dismissed as settled without adequate detailed consideration or in their haste to reach conclusions about the whole of reality completely ignored through lack of interest. But the third service is of even more importance: they have insisted on the need for clear statement and careful analysis, and by setting a new standard in this respect have shown how gravely even the greatest philosophers of the past and in particular the leading idealists have fallen short here of what could reasonably be expected. But this is not to say that they and the representatives of the new logic generally have learnt all the lessons taught by these idealists. And admiration for the skill in analysis shown by members of this new school of thought certainly need not imply agreement with their philosophical outlook or with the view expressed by some of the more daring of them that philosophy consists solely in the analysis of the meaning of 'common-sense' statements. There is no reason why a philosopher might not have the clarity and precision of the logical analysts without their philosophy.

There seems to be besides the difference in views a difference in temperament and in style between idealists and realists such as to prove an almost insuperable bar to mutual understanding and appreciation. We must recognise that there is at least some excuse for Professor Broad's remark that 'the writings of too many eminent Absolutists seem to start from no discoverable premises; to proceed by means of puns, metaphors, and ambiguities; and to resemble in their literary style glue thickened with sawdust',[1] but I must add that, even when the style of an absolute idealist seems most troubled by obscurity and confusion, I am often subject to an uneasy feeling that this is partly due to my own failure to see something extremely well worth seeing which he sees dimly and so describes obscurely but which his critics do not see at all. It is a grave fault in a philosopher to be content with a confused account where he could give a clear one, but it is also a fault to dismiss either a rival philosopher's contentions or a particular conception as not worth consideration because they are incapable of really clear statement.[2] Owing to the weakness of human intelligence and the defects of human language it may well be the case that none of the points most worth considering in philosophy are capable of being grasped with anything like complete clearness or stated with anything like complete precision at present, and to give our philosophy clearness and precision at the expense of excluding from consideration or even dogmatically denying whatever we cannot make clear and precise may be to render our work worse for this and not better than the work of those who see something beyond our ken and do not, because the task can only be partially fulfilled, shrink from trying to communicate and justify their vision. Did not one of the ablest representatives of the new logic himself say:—'The chief danger to our philosophy, apart from laziness and woolliness, is *scholasticism*, the essence of which is treating what is vague as if it were precise and trying to fit it into an exact logical category'.[3] On the other hand I am certainly not

[1] *Examination of McTaggart's Philosophy*, vol. I, p. lii. Dr. McTaggart, he insists, is not himself in the least subject to these deficiencies.
[2] I do not mean to suggest that Professor Broad is guilty of this fault.
[3] Ramsey, *Foundations of Mathematics and Other Essays*, p. 269.

prepared to admit that idealists have usually done the utmost possible to make what did not admit of complete precision at least as precise as possible or even at all approached this ideal.

CHAPTER II

EPISTEMOLOGICAL IDEALISM [1]

§ I. THE MAIN EPISTEMOLOGICAL ARGUMENT FOR IDEALISM

THE present chapter is intended to deal with those idealist arguments which are based on the theory of knowledge and not on the more specific problem of the physical world. It does not, therefore, include any arguments derived from the characteristics or supposed characteristics of physical objects, or from the theory of perception and the difficulties which must be faced by any attempt to give a consistent account of the physical world on realist lines or to provide reasons based on the facts of perception adequate to justify our belief in such a world. It <u>only includes those arguments which are based on the nature of cognition as such.</u> Nor does it discuss the doctrines of any famous idealist thinkers in general, but rather an isolated set of arguments some of which are used in one form or other by most philosophical idealists. In practice the arguments in question have almost always been supplemented by others drawn from different sources, and no doubt if my object were to write a history I should adopt a different scheme of arrangement altogether But, since my purpose is not to give an account of the historical development of idealism but to evaluate idealist arguments, little will be gained and a great deal may be lost by mingling arguments with a different logical basis. In my opinion idealist writers have often committed the error of confusing reasoning based on epistemology with reasoning arising out of the particular problems of perception and the physical world.

[1] This chapter deals with theories which are in most quarters now considered to be out of date and perhaps also obviously absurd, but it is necessary because the theories have played such a large part in idealist thought. But in my opinion the chapter is the dullest of the book, and therefore it is perhaps only fair to warn readers that, if so inclined, they can omit it without very grave harm to the understanding of what follows.

Further, I am dealing in this chapter not with the agnostical form of idealism held by Kant, though this was based partly on epistemological considerations, since it is more convenient to handle this famous doctrine in a chapter by itself, but with the form of idealism which maintains that it has reached a positive conclusion as to the nature of reality. Such a doctrine has a short way with the thing-in-itself. If we are to form any idea of the thing-in-itself whatever, if we are to think it at all even as an unknown x, we must bring it into relation to mind, therefore, it is urged, we cannot assert its existence except in relation to mind. And so, according to many thinkers, the mere fact of knowledge and thought proves that nothing is conceivable and therefore nothing can exist unless it is the object of a knowing and thinking mind.

Fortunately a number of the arguments of this type can be treated together since they involve a common fallacy and lead to a common dilemma. When Berkeley wishes to clinch the question he asks his opponent to try to imagine a single physical object existing outside the mind, and then points out that in the very act of imagining it he is thinking of it as perceived by himself and therefore as relative to his own mind. To quote from the dialogue between Hylas and Philonous[1]:

Philonous. (To pass by all that hath been hitherto said, and reckon it for nothing, if you will have it so.) I am content to put the whole upon this issue. If you can conceive it possible for any mixture or combination of qualities, or any sensible object whatever, to exist without the mind, then I will grant it actually to be so.

Hylas. If it comes to that, the point will soon be decided. What more easy than to conceive a tree or house existing by itself, independent of, and unperceived by any mind whatsoever ? I do at this present time conceive them existing after that manner.

Philonous. How say you, Hylas, can you see a thing which is at the same time unseen ?

Hylas. No, that were a contradiction.

Philonous. Is it not as great a contradiction to talk of *conceiving* a thing which is *unconceived* ?

Hylas. It is.

Philonous. The tree or house therefore which you think of, is conceived by you.

Hylas. How should it be otherwise ?

Philonous. And what is conceived is surely in the mind.

Hylas. Without question, that which is conceived is in the mind.

[1] Everyman edition, p. 232.

Similarly the modern idealist, Signor Gentile, says that Berkeley is right in holding that

> 'Reality is conceivable only in so far as the reality conceived is in relation to the activity which conceives it, and in that relation it is not only a possible object of knowledge, it is a present and actual one. To conceive a reality is to conceive, at the same time and as one with it, the mind in which that reality is represented, and therefore the conception of a material reality is absurd.' [1]

Similar views are maintained by Signor Croce.

It is easy to object to Berkeley that the fact that something which is seen or conceived by me cannot exist unseen or unconceived at the time I see or conceive it does not prove that it could not have existed unseen or unconceived *before* I saw or conceived it; but the reason why the argument carried conviction was obviously because Berkeley thought of conception as implying that the object conceived was 'in the mind' and therefore could not be external to the conceiver. Similarly Signor Gentile is maintaining that the reality conceived is inseparable from and logically implies the act of conceiving it. Other arguments leading to a similar conclusion are that knowing is a kind of mental construction or at least involves such construction (constructing), this being taken to imply that we make the objects we know; that object and subject are essentially relative to each other and therefore cannot be separated; that what we know must fall within consciousness and cannot be conceived as existing outside it; that I can only know objects by means of my own ideas and therefore cannot go beyond 'ideas'.

In discussing this type of argument philosophers fall into two very sharply divided camps: to one their truth seems self-evident, to the other they appear mere trivial verbal fallacies. We may certainly concede at least that their plausibility has been very much increased by verbal fallacies. Berkeley may be charged with having confused two different usages of the word 'conceive'. We may be said to conceive thoughts, and in that case what we conceive is in our mind if anything can be said to be so; but we can, in conformity with the ordinary use of language, also say 'conceive that' where the that-clause stands for a fact, a truth, a reality as opposed to our thoughts of this reality. When used in that sense the object of the verb bears a relation to the conceiving quite different from that

[1] *Theory of Mind as Pure Act*, trl. by Wildon Carr, p. 1.

which it does in the first instance. In the one case it stands for the same thing as the conceiving regarded from a different point of view and so made a substantive instead of a verb; in the other case it is regarded as something objective.

Likewise 'concept' is sometimes used to stand for a thought or belief and sometimes, though loosely, for a reality or feature of reality. A similar ambiguity may be traced in words like relate, which one would expect to mean 'put into relation' by changing the relative position of objects but which usually means 'recognise as already related'. Again knowledge, perception, sensation, imagination may all stand either for the knowing, perceiving, etc., or for what is known, perceived, sensed, and it is easy to fall into the error of asserting that, because they stand for something mental when used in the first sense, they also stand for something mental when used in the second. Berkeley is not the only philosopher the apparent force of whose arguments has been much increased by these verbal ambiguities.

The phrase, 'in the mind', also has a double or rather a threefold meaning. It may mean either (1) a part of our mental process, or (2) dependent on the mind, or (3) apprehended by the mind,[1] and we cannot possibly argue that because everything we know is 'in our mind' in the third sense at the time we know it, it is therefore 'in our mind' in either of the first two (and similarly with the phrase 'in consciousness'). The ambiguity, as has often been pointed out, is rendered worse by an inadequate spatial metaphor.

Further, the idealist case acquires a fictitious strength from the fact that the word object implies subject as its correlative. But it does not follow that whatever is the object of thought cannot exist without a thinking subject; it only follows that it cannot be *an object* without a thinking subject. No author would argue that he had saved his readers' lives on the ground that without him as author they could not have existed as readers of his book. True, without a subject nothing could acquire the relational characteristic of being object, just as nobody could be a reader of this book if I had not written it, but the thing might, for anything this argument proves to the contrary, still have all the other qualities that we now ascribe to it.

Again I obviously cannot 'know that S is or was P without my knowing it' if the last words are taken as qualifying the

[1] Cf. the colloquial phrase 'I will keep this in mind'.

main verb, know; to say I can is self-contradictory. But if 'without my knowing it' is taken with 'S is P' in the subordinate clause the contradiction disappears altogether. It has been held in general that the idealist argument rests on a confusion between the truism that I cannot know (or think) anything to exist without its being known (or thought) by me and the falsehood that it cannot exist without being known (or thought) by me. If I know X, X obviously must be in relation to my mind at the time I know it, and again at any other time also it must bear the relation to my mind of 'going to be known by me [1] after such and such a lapse of time' or 'having been known by me so many hours, months or years ago', but it does not follow that the relation is essential to X or that X could not exist without being in that relation.

The idealist would retort that the mere attempt to think X as being out of relation to mind would bring it into relation to my mind and therefore only serve to establish his case. However, if we consider what the relation is, the difficulty seems to diminish. The relation in which X stands to me is not 'being known by me all the time', but 'such as to be known by me at some particular time', and therefore the argument does not prove e.g. that matter could not exist independently of mind.[2] I could not know (or form an opinion concerning) any fact about a material object unless the object were such as to allow me to know (or form the opinion about) the fact at some time in my life, but for all that the fact might have been a fact long before I came to know it or think of it in any way whatever, though I was in the future going to think about or know it. Anything that is ever known must always have been such that it could eventually come to be known, but it may nevertheless have gone through the greater part of its existence unknown, or again it may be known consciously at times and then exist for a long period without anybody's being conscious of it at all. It must indeed be admitted that any fact which ever comes to be known must be in that respect related to the knowing of it and the knower; but this is saying very little, for the relation may be altogether unimportant to

[1] Or at least of being capable of being known by me, if the former wording is rejected as involving determinism.
[2] We must remember, however, throughout that these arguments, if valid at all, would apply not only to matter but to all objects of cognition.

the fact known. After all, everything is related in some way to everything else, but there could be no science or rational action if we could not ignore as irrelevant most of these relations. The argument therefore is far from proving that whatever we know depends for its existence on our or some other mind's knowing it, nor does it even prove that everything existent is knowable or known, but only that everything known is known. It is, however, rendered more formidable by being combined with a certain theory of relations, the so-called internal theory; but this view of relations and its bearing on the question will be discussed later.

But <u>one reservation</u> must be added to what I have just said. <u>We can know some propositions of a formal type which are true of everything</u>, and consequently everything whatever, whether we call it knowable or unknowable, must be included in a class of things about which we can think as a class and of which we know some universal properties, i.e. the class of all real things, and in so far anything whatever as belonging to this class will be a member of a whole which is thought, though very indefinitely, and partially, though very imperfectly, known by us; but there may still be very many things all the more specific properties of which are and will be for ever unknown to mind. We cannot know everything about anything, but <u>we can know something about everything, so that the term unknown becomes relative.</u> Thus the opponents of the thing-in-itself were right when they said that no real thing could be absolutely unknown, only we must hasten to add that what we know of something may be very unimportant compared to what we do not know. Further knowledge is primarily of facts and only secondarily of things, and of facts a great many still may be and, it would seem, obviously are quite unknown, at least to human beings.

Nevertheless, despite the obvious reply to it the epistemological argument for idealism still appears to retain its self-evident character for many; and nothing that I have yet said is necessarily incompatible with the conclusions of such idealists, but only with their attempts to prove them by reasoning. It may still be the case that there is a necessary connection between existence in any form and being known, such that it is self-evident to those who understand these terms adequately that nothing can exist without being known, although it is impossible to prove this by any series of steps to those who are lacking in the immediate insight required, and although actual attempts to prove it have been commonly vitiated by fallacies depending on verbal ambiguity.

The most formidable objection to epistemological idealism is, however, to be found in the utterly impossible consequences to which it leads. For the same epistemological argument which is held to prove physical things to be dependent on us would prove equally that all human beings other than the person who asserts this doctrine and all facts about such beings were dependent on his knowledge or thought of them; that there is no past or at any rate that he cannot be justified in asserting the occurrence of any past events, so that memory is a complete delusion or may be such for anything he can tell; that all the laws of logic are valid only when he thinks them, and that he has no right whatever to affirm the truth of the very principles which led to his conclusion.

For if he holds any of the views mentioned above, if he holds that cognition [1] is or involves the making of its object, if he holds that he cannot transcend his own ideas, if he holds that the object cognised must be dependent on or inseparable from the cognition of it so that it cannot have being or that he has no right to assert that it has except as and when cognised, he must apply this not only to the physical world but to other human minds, to past events, to universal laws, to the very principles which he has himself asserted.[2] If these characteristics or any of them are implied [3] in the nature of cognition, they must be asserted of all cases of cognition without exception. Now among any man's objects of cognition are other human beings, therefore it would follow from the premises

[1] I use the term, cognition, rather than knowing so as to cover both certain knowledge and justified opinion. The idealist certainly means his argument to apply not only to the former but to the latter also. For this use of the term cf. Stout, *Studies in Philosophy and Psychology*, p. 307.

[2] The attempt to escape these difficulties by a distinction between absolute and finite knowing will be discussed shortly.

[3] In this book I never use 'imply' in the sense invented by Mr. Russell according to which 'p implies q' means 'it is not the case that p is true and q is false', but in the sense in which the word was most commonly used by philosophers prior to the introduction of this new usage and is still used by them outside 'mathematical logic'. In this sense p is said to imply q whenever it is possible to infer q from p, either because it is logically entailed by, i.e. follows with logical necessity from p, or because of some causal connection established by inductive evidence, or because some other proposition or propositions (often not specified) are known or held to be true which when combined with p logically entail q.

that they must be merely ideas of his, made by him, incapable of existence except as and when thought by him, or at least that he has no right to assert their existence in any other sense than this. Again among the objects of a present act of cognition by him are <u>events in his past life</u>, therefore by the same argument these only exist as cognised by him now and never existed before (or at least he is not entitled to assert, even as a probable opinion, that they existed before). Thirdly, the same applies to <u>all universal laws.</u> The laws of logic and mathematics, he will have to admit, only hold because he thinks them and when he thinks them. Finally he cannot even assert <u>the validity of the idealist arguments themselves</u> unless he assumes that they are valid independently of his thinking them and not merely because he thinks them. If their validity is inseparable from his thinking them, they only hold now at the moment he thinks them and do not hold at all when he is not thinking them. If this reasoning is correct it follows that <u>the epistemological arguments lead directly either to a complete scepticism as to everything beyond the individual's momentary experience or to a positive denial of its existence.</u> The theory brought forward to explain cognition is now seen to make most cognition totally impossible.

Idealists often meet the argument concerning solipsism by rejoining that <u>all minds are really one and the same mind</u> and that therefore to know others is only to know oneself. But this provides no real escape, for even if the metaphysical doctrine about the unity of all minds be true the experiences of other human beings are at least separable from my act of cognising them, just as my own past is separable from my present act of knowing it. The difficulty of solipsism arises because we do not have an immediate perception of any series of experiences except one which we call our own, and the truth, if indeed it be a truth, that the different human minds are at bottom the same mind cannot alter this, it cannot give us the immediate perception of others' experiences which we do not in fact possess. Whether what we call other minds are identical with our minds or not, we cannot have knowledge or even right opinion about them without transcending our own present experience, and this transcendence the form of idealism in question denies.

But the usual way of escape for the idealist from the difficulties mentioned is by <u>the distinction between particular minds and Mind.</u> Idealists issue the warning that what they say about cognition only applies to Mind *qua* mind or to the universal Mind or to the Absolute on which all truth depends. By this means it is possible for them to hold that other human minds, the past, the universal laws I know, depend not on my coming to know them as an event in experience but on the universal Mind's knowing them. This answer may take two alternative forms according as the universal mind is regarded as immanent or transcendent. The former answer is on the whole the more popular among idealists, but it seems to me the more difficult to defend. For, if the universal mind is merely immanent it only knows in and through acts of knowing by finite minds; and therefore the account given of its knowledge will apply to our own acts of knowing, and thus be still subject to all the objections mentioned above. If knowing is making at all, I make whatever I know, including other human minds or the facts I know about them, also past events and universal laws; if the object of knowledge cannot be separated from the knowing of it, then no particular fact which I know can be separated from my knowing of it, and I therefore have no right to assert that it is a fact except as an object of my consciousness.

If, however, the universal mind is conceived as transcendent, this difficulty is avoided because we need not then apply these extraordinary views to our knowing, only to the knowing of the Absolute. Other human minds, past experiences, physical objects and universal laws may still be quite independent of my knowing, though not of the knowing exercised by the Absolute. In this form idealism remains proof against the *reductio ad absurdum* I have just outlined, but it has only avoided the attack directed on its consequences by sacrificing its premisses and leaving itself without any adequate foundation. The idealist epistemology is now not an assertion about our knowing but about the Absolute's knowing. But what basis, it may be urged, can we have for making assertions about the Absolute's knowing except our own knowing? For this is the only kind of knowing of which we have experience. But our own knowing, as the idealist who takes up this position has already admitted, clearly does not possess the characteristic of making its objects but rather presupposes the prior existence of the objects which it knows, therefore we have no right, at least on these grounds, to ascribe such characteristics to the Absolute's knowing. If the Absolute's knowing is not analogous to our knowing, we have no right to make any positive assertions about its nature on the basis of our knowing; if it is analogous to our knowing then it does not make or create the objects known, although this does not rule out the possibility that they might still be created by Mind in some other capacity than *qua* knower, as is held by ordinary theism. I cannot first assert that knowing makes its object, then admit that this is incompatible with facts, and conclude that Absolute knowing but not my knowing makes its object. If the first premiss is accepted *my* knowing makes its objects; if it is denied the argument disappears altogether.

It might indeed conceivably be possible to argue from what my knowing implied at its best to the nature of the Absolute's knowing, though this was different in kind from my knowing, as it has been held that we can from imperfect human morality reach the notion of a perfection different in kind from our partial goodness; but then at its very best human cognition does not approach any closer to making its object than at its worst, indeed much less close. In so far as it reaches truth at all it is always a finding of something independent of and other than itself. The goal of our knowledge is neither identity nor creation, and the more its ideal is attained the more is it at variance with the creative character ascribed to the Absolute's knowing.

If the Absolute Mind is taken to be both immanent and transcendent, either we must say that its knowing is creative in both cases and then we are impaled on the first horn of our dilemma, or we must say that it is creative as transcendent but not creative as immanent, and then there is a difference between its two modes of knowing so radical that they ought not both to be regarded as knowing; and, what is worse, there can be no justification for an argument that its transcendent knowing must be creative if that argument is based, as it claims to be, on the characteristics of our knowing.

This argument is fatal to some but not by any means to all forms of epistemological idealism, for epistemological idealism need not be based directly on the nature of our knowing. If it were based instead on the nature of all known or knowable objects and it could be shown by a consideration of their nature that it is impossible for them to exist without a mind which knows them, we might be able to prove an Absolute Mind by a method which would not be open to the objections in question. For in that case our premiss would be the nature of the objects known and not the nature of our knowing, and so the conclusion would not be inconsistent with the premises. It would still be strange that the knowing of the Absolute Mind had this property while ours had not, but on any view the Absolute Mind and absolute knowing must be very different from our minds and our knowing. Or the argument might have the effect of showing that they must be present to some consciousness in order to exist, without implying that that consciousness (whether Absolute or finite) created them by *knowing* them. Such an argument might still be epistemological in that it proceeded by showing that they could not otherwise be known by us. It seems to be the type of argument employed by Caird and Green. We are not confined to our own ideas in that case, but we can only know what is dependent on or inseparable from some consciousness, not necessarily our own, and this such thinkers seek to establish by epistemological arguments without supposing that we make the objects of our knowledge, only that these objects must depend on some mind if they are to be known.

Can such an argument be drawn from the common characteristics of all known and knowable objects? It seems clear that all such objects must be thought by us in relation to a consciousness, but that consciousness is our own, and so far the argument would not seem to prove more than that anything thought by us is, when we think it, related to our thinking, an almost or quite tautologous conclusion. We may, however, I think, go a little further than this and admit that we can only think an object existing independently of our consciousness by thinking it as it *would* be *if* it were present to a mind. For example, if we are really to understand what is meant by talking of the state of the earth prior to man we must imagine some mind as contemplating it at the time, when no human mind was in fact contemplating it, and think it as it would have been for that mind. We can make correct verbal statements about it without doing this, but this is the only way in which we can picture to ourselves what the statements really mean. Similarly I can only realise other facts by picturing them as they would be for a knowing mind.[1] It may even be contended that the only way in which I can think an *a priori* universal truth to be necessarily valid is by thinking it as such that any mind must necessarily accept it as true if it understands it.

[1] A similar argument may be applied to mental states and processes which I have not actually introspected.

A form of epistemological idealism may thus perhaps be justified as an *als ob* fiction. Even if matter has qualities of its own independently of all minds, in order to think such independent qualities we must think them as they would be for an apprehending mind. This does not prove that they really exist only for such a mind, but it seems obvious that it at any rate heightens whatever probability there be in the view that matter is dependent on mind, unless such a view can be shown to be logically impossible, which is clearly not the case. If we have, as a matter of method, to think physical objects as if they were for a knowing mind in order to determine their nature, this seems clearly to add to the probability that they always really are for a mind.

Philosophers eager to prove sweeping conclusions about reality have been apt in the past to despise a mere increase in probability, but in the more sceptical atmosphere of the present day they can hardly afford to adopt this attitude. The extent to which this argument increases the probability of the conclusion in question will be very differently estimated by different men and will undoubtedly be held by many to be very small indeed. I myself would estimate it much higher if it were not for the fact that in taking the standpoint in question we always seem, to ourselves at any rate, to be taking it merely as a means of discovering what the thing or fact contemplated is apart from a knowing mind.[1] This may be a mistaken notion, and the circumstance may easily be explained by saying that we must abstract from what the object is for any particular human mind but not from what the object is for some human mind or other, but as far as I can tell the fiction seems to carry its instrumental character on its face. As we use it in ordinary life we are never led by it into thinking that physical objects really only exist when some mind, whether human or divine, is conscious of them. The case would be much stronger if we not only had to use this method in our thought but when using it always felt impelled to believe that idealism was true and had only progressed in knowledge by means of this belief, but this is not so. The plain man seems perfectly well able to use this method without slipping into the view that matter only exists for consciousness.

But, while the realist interpretation of the phenomenon

---

[1] If what I have said is true it is a self-defeating enterprise to try ' to discover apart from a knowing mind what the thing is ' but not to try ' to discover what the thing is apart from a knowing mind '.

seems to me more likely, the idealist interpretation is also quite possible, and this possibility strengthens whatever antecedent probability there may be in the view that matter depends on mind. If the Absolute Mind be regarded as transcendent, this view is not incompatible with holding that physical objects are quite independent of our minds. Since it is not based on propositions about the creative or constructive character of our knowing, it is not open to the objections usually urged against epistemological idealism. It may be the case, however, that the argument would be stronger if put in terms of experience than in terms of knowledge, and stronger if based on the specific case of matter than if based on the nature of all knowable objects.

§ II. The Argument from Mental Construction

Perhaps the most valuable contribution of idealist epistemology is that it has called attention to the active character of our cognitive processes and the extent to which we use 'mental construction' as a means to judgment. The active character of cognition has been stressed extremely by Sign. Croce and Gentile. But all this active 'constructing' may equally well be regarded as a way of putting ourselves in touch with something independent of our activity in construction and cognition. Not that I regard 'mental construction' as a suitable title for the process in question. It is at the best a metaphor taken from our experience of making external objects, and in several respects it conveys a misleading impression. We have to ask what it is that we make, and when one answers 'concepts', difficulties are at once raised by the ambiguous character of the word, which bears at least three quite different meanings. (*a*) Sometimes it is used to mean universals, but these are independent of our thinking them and are seen to be so in the very act of grasping their validity. (*b*) It may be used to mean propositions, or groups of propositions about a common object.[1] Now if we conceive propositions as subsistent entities independent of our judging them, we can still never be said to make propositions; but if we deny such entities and analyse 'propositions' in terms of judgments[2] and supposals, as I suggest elsewhere,[3] or at any rate regard

---

[1] I am inclined to think that this is the basic sense, and that the word is only used in the other two senses given owing to confusions.
[2] I.e. judgings. [3] V. below, pp. 202–3.

them as something that only has a being as it is judged or supposed, we can in a sense do so, and this would no doubt be the usual view of idealists. It must be admitted that it would sound queer to speak of ' making propositions ', because propositions are on neither view of their nature existents in the full sense, but at any rate they are constituted by an act of mind on our part if, as I think rightly, the first-mentioned objective view of them is rejected. Or (c) we may mean by ' concept ' <u>the mental act of conceiving</u>. It is none too clear what ' conceiving ' itself means, but I imagine that it includes both judging and (where the concept is a fiction) ' supposing '.

We can now see that <u>the analogy of physical making breaks down.</u> For physical objects made by us continue to exist independently of us once they have been made. But this is not the case with ' concepts '. For the word ' concepts ' stands either for something that is not made by us at all or for something that has being only in the very act by which we make it, if we can be said to make it. We must not fall into the old error of regarding ' concepts ' as a kind of things in the mind which copy real external things and though non-sensuous are otherwise parallel in character to images. For the assumption of such entities there is no psychological or logical warrant at all. The act of judging or supposing constructs nothing other than itself and the characteristics of itself, so that it is very difficult to see how we can legitimately even call it an act of construction. But in any case it seems clear that the evidence concerning the activity of our mind in cognition <u>will not help the idealist case unless it can be shown that at the same time this activity involves a moulding or making of the object of knowledge and not merely of our ' concepts ' of it. To say that the two are inseparable presupposes that the idealist case has already been established.</u>

It does, however, seem that, if our judgments are the result of an elaborate mental process, we have travelled further from given reality than we are apt to think, and it may be objected that if we have gone through such a process we have no guarantee that its results are true of reality conceived as independent of us. We seem to have tampered with the data given to us and so with the evidence on which our beliefs ought logically to depend. This is perhaps the chief reason why Kant denied knowledge of reality,[1] but most modern thinkers who use the argument have employed it as a basis

[1] V. below, ch. III, sect. 2.

not for agnosticism but for what Kant would have called 'dogmatic idealism'. If cognition either is or involves a process of this kind, then, it is thought, we can only know what mind in us has made, and must choose between an agnosticism according to which we can only know our own ideas and an idealism according to which all reality is constituted by the universal Mind which is partially manifested in our finite minds. To quote from an argument much in vogue, if reality is given fact we can never know it, because what we know is never pure fact without any admixture of theory, is never taken just as it is given; but if it is not mere given fact, if it is, so to speak, 'infected' by theory and therefore by mind, it is partly at least a mental construct, and since we can never reach mere unquestioned fact, unsystematised by thought, we can never distinguish any element in reality as existing in the realist sense independent of a knower or thinker.[1]

But the argument still breaks down before the distinction between the assertion that I come to apprehend the nature of an object [2] by elaborate thought-processes and the assertion that I make the object by the thought-processes. As against the views generally attributed to the British 'empiricists' (whether rightly or wrongly), it has been shown that we are active in cognition and never arrive at a fact merely by sensation or by passively receiving data but always understand it in terms of preconceived, though not usually explicitly formulated, theories; but this, although it adds to the difficulty of arriving at the facts, does not prove that we never arrive at them, unless we assume that all theories are necessarily wrong. The argument may be valid against the views of some realists, but not against all realism. Theories of knowledge may have to do better justice in the future to this characteristic of our cognitive processes than they have often done in the past; but to say this is not necessarily to contradict realism, since the real may be apprehensible not only by sense but also by thought. We cannot, it must be admitted, apprehend the real without thought, but the real need not for all that be itself dependent on thought.

There is indeed an ambiguity in the terms, fact and theory,

---

[1] V. e.g. Bradley, *Essays on Truth and Reality*, p. 108. Some Pragmatists also use this argument.

[2] Using 'object' in the widest sense as a general term for whatever is cognised by us.

as used in these and similar arguments. 'Fact' should signify what really is apart from our way of knowing it, but in conjunction with the adjective, given, it is used to signify whatever reality is known in a particular way, i.e. given to sense without being reached by a more or less 'problematic' process of inference. 'Theory,' on the other hand, is a term which does not, like 'fact,' apply primarily to reality but rather to our views about reality. Therefore, if it is argued that because no facts we reach are apprehended as merely given we only know theories not facts, or only facts infected with theory, the argument has acquired a subjectivist turn that is not warranted by the premisses. For <u>it does not follow that because we can cognise no *given* facts we therefore can cognise no facts at all but only theories.</u>

It may still be asked how we can be justified in assuming that reality must necessarily conform to our thought, but the question implies that in cognition we are primarily aware not of the laws of reality but of the laws of our thought. This is false : what we know primarily in knowing the law of non-contradiction, for instance, is not that we cannot think self-contradictions but that nothing can be self-contradictory. If knowledge is from the beginning an awareness of the reality about which we are thinking and not merely an awareness of how we think, the question does not arise. When I see the necessity or even the probability of a conclusion, what I see is not anything psychological, a law of my mind, but a law of reality.

Idealists seem often to have been influenced by <u>the assumption that knowledge involves identity between the knower and the known,</u> but if <u>a process of cognition cannot transcend itself it becomes impossible even to know oneself.</u> The cognition of a characteristic of myself is itself numerically different from the characteristic which I cognise, and the cognition of a general law governing my mind is different from the law cognised, so that I could not be aware even of facts about myself if cognition did not transcend itself. Since the law that this transcendence is impossible, if it were a law, would be different from my awareness of it, I could not know or even think this law without the very transcendence which it contradicts. And if processes of cognition transcend themselves at all, I do not see how we can set limits *a priori* to the degree of the transcendence.

It is sometimes argued <u>that mind can only know what is like itself</u>, namely mind, and that therefore reality must be mental, but we may note that even those who hold such a view admit knowledge of something generically different from minds, namely, universal laws. Nor do they succeed in showing that cognition [1] is compatible with the degree of unlikeness that prevails between different minds but incompatible with any greater degree of unlikeness. An argument to this effect might be based on the premiss that the presence of a relation implies that its terms have a determinable in common, in respect of determinate values of which the relation holds, (as seems to be the case with most or, some would say, all relations), and conclude that what knows and what is known must be of the same genus if this condition is to be fulfilled. But it is difficult to be clear either that this follows logically from the nature of a relation as such and not only from the nature of most of the particular kinds of relation we know, or that mind and its object could not have a determinable in common without the object being mental; and further the argument would seem to be equally incompatible with knowledge of universal qualities and laws, which are not even existent entities.

To know is to know something, and this something cannot be just our knowing it. To ask whether we are justified in assuming that reality must be as we must think it is equivalent to asking whether what has been proved or really seen to be self-evident is true of reality. If it is not true of reality, it cannot be really self-evident or have been really proved. That reality must conform to our thought, in so far as there is no intrinsic error in the latter, is not, strictly speaking, an assumption but something that is involved in the very conception of correct thinking. Universal doubt is indeed possible as long as we are not contemplating any particular argument which we see to be valid, but to see any argument to be valid is itself to see that scepticism is logically untenable. This does not mean that we can refute the sceptic when we play the game according to his own rules (or rather absence of rule), for he will refuse to admit any proofs as valid, but this he can only do as long as he merely treats proofs in general and does not think out the well-established proofs, e.g. of mathematics, that is, as long as he does not consider the proofs properly on their own merits. The question—how can we know that reality must conform to the laws of thought (mean-

[1] Many realists would agree that knowledge in the strictest sense is not possible either of physical things or of minds other than one's own.

ing by this the laws of logic [1])—is one that cannot legitimately be asked, and if it is once asked can never be solved by either a realist or an idealist philosophy.

If we admit on the one hand that we in some sense make concepts and on the other that these are not identical with but true of reality, we may seem to be involved in some form of the 'correspondence' theory with all its difficulties. This is, however, a point the discussion of which must be postponed to a later chapter.[2] In regard to the physical world somewhat similar considerations seem to me fatal to the direct theory of perception, but I shall try to show later that a representative theory of perception does not necessarily carry with it a representative theory of cognition.[3]

However, what is usually meant by the idealist seems to be that our knowing is not the original making of the objects known but a kind of remaking after the pattern of the Absolute's knowing. This would avoid the objections in question and there seems to be a good deal of truth in the theory, at least as applied to certain objects of cognition. To understand another human being we must to some extent relive his life in imagination ourselves [4]; and certainly, if there is an Absolute Mind or God, our knowing (in so far as it is genuine knowing and not error) will be either (on the pantheistic or immanent view) a part of God's thoughts, or else (on the transcendent view) a very imperfect reproduction of some aspect of them. Further, even apart from any metaphysical assumptions of this kind, it is difficult to see how I can really cognise an object of sense not actually present to my senses at the moment except by picturing it to myself and so 'remaking' it in the shape of an image.[5] Possibly it may even be legitimate to regard my action as a kind of 'remaking' if I do not try to picture the object in a sensual form but rethink the mathematical formulae which govern its motion, though I am not sure whether this conception can be applied

---

[1] I, however, deplore this usage of the term 'laws of thought', just because it suggests that we know the laws of logic primarily as laws of our thinking.

[2] Ch. V, sect. 1.   [3] Ch. VI, sect. 2.

[4] I do not mean picture it in sensuous images. This is the way in which we 'remake' objects of sense, but not the way in which we 'remake' human experiences.

[5] I can accept and understand many propositions about it expressed in words without doing this, but in the last resort I could only represent the meaning of the words to myself in this way.

at all profitably when we come to universals, or anywhere except in regard to experiences and objects of sense. (Signor Gentile argues that in order to understand geometry we must construct figures, whether on paper or in our imagination,[1] in order to advance in the sciences which give knowledge of the physical world we must make situations by experiment, in order to appreciate history we must reproduce in ourselves the spiritual activity which is human history.)

This is a point of view which may perhaps in some sense be included in, even if transcended by, any sound realism; but the admission that the making involved in knowing is a *remaking* renders the doctrine incapable of serving as an argument for idealism, though it may fit in well enough with an idealist system accepted on other grounds. For it is now admitted that it is possible to know by 'remaking' what we have not ourselves made, and the 'remaking' becomes a means of cognising what is independent of our process of cognition.[2] Further, it is quite clear that the making is not itself the cognition. If I relived in imagination a man's experience without being conscious that he had had that experience, if e.g. in writing a novel by an accidental coincidence I made one of my characters like a real man whom I had never met, I should not be knowing him or his life nor even having true beliefs about him. To cognise something I must not only remake it in my mind but realise that my remaking of it is patterned on an object which is independent of the act of cognition in question.

The remaking theory regards our cognition as a copying of something in reality, and so shares many of the defects of 'the copying theory of knowledge', against which idealists have inveighed so fiercely. It is alleged against the latter theory (a) that our ideas cannot be like reality and therefore cannot copy reality; (b) that, even if they did copy reality, the mere possession of ideas which copied a real fact would not constitute knowledge of that fact; (c) that we could never know whether our ideas did copy reality unless we already had a direct apprehension of reality, and that this apprehension could not

---

[1] This view of geometry, also maintained by Kant, would be contradicted by most modern mathematicians and philosophers who deal with mathematics.

[2] It might be argued sophistically that 'remaking' implies a being who was the original maker of what we remake, but clearly, unless the existence of such a being has been independently proved, this argument is merely verbal.

itself be regarded as a case of copying reality. The 'remaking' theory avoids the first objection by assuming that all reality is of the nature of thought and effects the great improvement of substituting for ideas conceived as static entities an active process of thinking, but if it be taken as a complete account [1] of cognition it falls a victim to the other two objections.

§ III. Is the Object of Knowledge Independent of Being Known? The Realist Epistemology

The argument that, because I can only know what is in relation to mind, I have no right to assert and good reason to deny the existence of anything independent of mind, may be regarded in the main [2] either as inductive [3] or as *a priori* in character. In the former case it resembles [4] an inference by incomplete enumeration from the premiss 'all instances experienced have characteristic x' to 'all instances whatever have this characteristic', giving a conclusion which, though not certain, might seem, owing to the extraordinarily wide range of the premiss (covering not only some particular observations, as is the case with the premisses used in the establishment of any ordinary law of nature, but the whole range of our experience in the most diverse fields) to be at least as probable as any other conclusion whatever established by induction. Unfortunately, however, there is a circumstance which takes away all the evidential value of the premiss. Namely, an induction to the effect that a property belongs to all of a class based on the fact that it belongs to some of the class is only of value provided there is some reason to suppose that, if any members of the class did not possess the property, they would have been at least reasonably likely to

---

[1] I do not venture to assert that its protagonists take it as this, but at any rate they do not show that they are aware of the necessity for supplementing it in the way suggested, and its bearing on the theory of knowledge is radically changed if it is thus supplemented.

[2] Only 'in the main' because on the one hand I obviously know *a priori* in any case that I cannot know anything which does not possess the characteristic 'known by me', and again I could not so much as understand what 'knowing' means without some experience of it.

[3] I am using the word here to cover only Mr. Johnson's 'problematic induction', not intuitive induction or any other kind.

[4] I say 'resembles' not 'is' because the premiss is not here reached by enumeration but *a priori*. The transition from the premiss to the conclusion, however, is the same as in an argument by incomplete enumeration.

occur among the instances known to us. In this case, however, not only is there no such reason, but there is the strongest reason to assume the contrary. For obviously no instance that did not possess the characteristic of being known by mind could be known by us. Regarded as inductive, the argument would be on a par with inferring that, because we need microscopes to see bacteria, these bacteria cannot live without microscopes. It does show indeed that we cannot settle the question against idealism by empirical evidence, because obviously we can never experience anything of which no mind is conscious, but this is the limit of its usefulness.

So we need not wonder that the idealist argument is usually regarded as *a priori* rather than as inductive. It takes the form that *esse* implies *cognosci*,[1] or at least that it implies some relation to consciousness. This argument is difficult to refute because it is always hard to prove the negative that A does not imply B unless we have experience of instances of A occurring without B, and from the nature of the case such experience is not available here; and those idealists who regard it as self-evidently true that nothing can be without being known are unmoved by the realist's counter-assertion that he cannot see the self-evidence. Still, various lines of attack are open to the realist.

In the first place it seems perfectly clear that, though the object of consciousness has in philosophical argument often been confused with the consciousness of it, the two are in fact quite different. The object of my consciousness may be a blue patch or a mathematical ratio, but my consciousness is not therefore blue or extended in the first case, nor is it a mathematical ratio in the second. The most an idealist can reasonably maintain is not that the two are identical but that the one necessarily implies the other, so that e.g. a shape cannot exist without the consciousness of it, though it is not the same as the consciousness of it. In Kant's terminology it is not an analytic but a synthetic proposition that he is

[1] I have used the term *cognosci* rather than *percipi* because we are here considering idealist arguments based on epistemology and not on the theory of perception. As a matter of fact, it is quite inaccurate to say that the idealist holds all *esse* to be *percipi*. It is only true at the most to say that he holds the *esse* of matter to be *percipi*. The *esse* of mind is perhaps *percipere* but certainly not *percipi* for the idealist, though it may perhaps be *cognosci*. Further, I have used the word 'implies' rather than 'is,' since this is all that would be necessary to reach an idealist conclusion.

defending. This is not, however, a fatal objection to the theory unless we assume that all inference is merely analytic, which seems plausible but carries with it the awkward conclusion that we can never by inference arrive at any truths that we do not know already. It is quite possible that two things may be different and yet inseparable. Colour is not the same quality as extension, yet it implies extension; the sides of a triangle are not the same as its angles, yet its sides and its angles are inseparable. Similarly mind and non-mental objects *might* still be correlates neither of which could exist without the other existing also. Their very difference might be a reason for their interdependence, because one was needed to supplement the other. Even the well-known *Refutation of Idealism* by Professor Moore is not intended to disprove the possibility of such a relation of implication but only to remove certain 'self-contradictory errors', which the author believes to have constituted the only reason why thinkers ever supposed that there was such an implication. In so doing he rendered philosophy a great service, but I cannot share the confidence expressed in the article that an idealist would necessarily cease to think that he saw such an implication once he realised that the object of consciousness and the consciousness of it were not identical.[1]

We may note also that most of those who reject the view

[1] In view of the allegation often made against Berkeley in particular that he confused an act of sensing and what is sensed (the *sensum*), it is worth noting that in his dialogues he makes Hylas raise this very objection (*Everyman* ed., p. 226 ff., *Fraser's Selections*, p. 146 ff.), and replies through Philonous that (*a*) there cannot be an *act* of sensation or perception because we are passive in the experience and do not produce it by our will, (*b*) we should then have to make the same distinction in the case of pain, but it is obvious that pain cannot be a quality of matter. The first point is a relevant and valid objection to the common description of sensing as an 'act', but no objection to making a distinction between sensing and what is sensed. The second point raises some difficulties but cannot be a valid reason for refusing to distinguish two things which are patently different. We thus see that Berkeley did not commit the alleged confusion unwittingly but had considered the point and then, as I think wrongly, decided that the distinction was untenable. Further, in § 49 of the *Principles* he insists that the qualities of the sense-datum or image are not qualities of the mind but only qualities in the mind. Kant distinguished a mental act and its object very sharply, consciousness being for him a transcendental and the object a phenomenal factor. It also seems to me that most at least of the leading post-Kantian idealists recognised the distinction, though they did not express it so clearly as Professor Moore has done.

that an object implies consciousness seem to accept the converse proposition, namely, that consciousness implies an object.[1] But anyone who makes such an admission as this is altogether debarred from rejecting the idealist view on the ground that an object is different from the consciousness of it and therefore cannot imply the latter. The fact that A implies B does not necessarily carry with it the conclusion that B implies A, but it does carry with it the conclusion that you cannot rule out this possibility on the ground that A and B are so separate that there can be no relation of implication between them.

It is desirable here to draw a distinction between experiencing and knowing, because an idealism which is built on the view that ' to be ' directly [2] implies ' to be known ' is open to objections which an idealism built on the view that ' to be ' or at least ' to exist ' implies ' to be experienced ' escapes altogether. This second type of idealism will, however, best be discussed when I have to deal with the specific problem of the physical world.

Against the epistemological arguments the counter-assertion is made by the realist that the fact of knowing necessarily implies that the object known is altogether independent of being known.[3] On this point indeed there seems to be com-

[1] Not necessarily a physical object.

[2] I add the word, directly, because, if on non-epistemological grounds we came to the conclusion that all reality was dependent on mind, it might possibly follow that everything which was was known, but this would be different from saying that being as such implies being known. A theist, for instance, may hold that God knows everything and that therefore everything which is is known without ever having accepted or even thought of the epistemological argument in question.

[3] V. Professor Moore, *Philosophical Studies, The Refutation of Idealism*, p. 29; Professor Prichard, *Kant's Theory of Knowledge*, p. 118; Professor Pitkin, *New Realism*, p. 477. In an article in *Mind* (vol. XXXIV, N.S., no. 135, p. 309) I used an argument against this view which now seems to me fallacious. I objected that it was self-contradictory to maintain, as realists do, that the nature of knowing is such that the object known must necessarily be independent of the knowing of it. For, I said, ' the argument is that it is implied in the very nature of knowing *qua* knowing that the object of knowledge is independent of the cognitive relation in question. But, since the " independence " alleged must mean, if it is to prove the point, that the fact of knowing as such implies nothing in the object, we have the curious paradox that knowing *qua* knowing implies that nothing in the object is implied by knowing *qua* knowing. Or in other words, it follows from the very nature of knowing that the object of knowledge has a quality by

plete unanimity among realists. Now it is clear that in many cases I do know what is dependent on myself, but it may be said that in these cases it is dependent on me in other respects than *qua* knower. Thus if I did not exist I could not have toothache, yet it does not follow from this that I give myself toothache by knowing that I have it. A worse difficulty is presented by the fact that my judgment or opinion that a future event will occur may be one of the principal causes leading to its occurrence or in other cases to its prevention.[1] It may be retorted that here it is not the cognition alone but the resultant action which causes or prevents the anticipated happening, that it is caused by me *qua* practical being but not by me *qua* cognitive; but this does not seem to be an altogether satisfactory solution, for it would still be necessary to admit that the cognition was part-cause or indirect cause of the event, and even this seems to involve the sacrifice of the principle that what is cognised must be independent of the cognition of it. A further difficulty is raised by the case of introspection where I change my mental state not by practical action but simply by cognising it. An emotion may be calmed or transformed by merely introspecting it, and in general the change from a non-self-conscious to a self-conscious state of mind is a very important one.

But it may be replied, and, I think, rightly, that it is not the object of cognition which is changed in these cases but something else. If I introspect my anger and as a result cease to be angry, the object of my cognition is not my state at the end of the process of introspection but my state at the beginning, and the fact that I was angry at the beginning of

virtue of which no quality which it has follows from knowing. Is this not perilously near self-contradiction?' I now think my argument fallacious because the independence implied would be not a positive characteristic but only the absence of logical relation. Therefore to say that knowing implies the independence of the object known is not to say that it stands in the logical relation of implication to something in the object known, but to say that it excludes any such logical relation. I am indebted for this correction to Dr. S. H. Davies.

[1] I have to say indeed,' judgment' or ' opinion ', not knowledge, because we have no certain knowledge of future events (though we have of hypothetical propositions, e.g. in mathematics, which also apply to the future). But there is no reason which I can see to hold that *in this particular respect*, i.e. as regards the question of the independence of the object cognised, there is any difference between knowledge and right opinion, and the arguments of both sides seem to be meant to apply to both without distinction.

the process is not altered by any subsequent change in my condition. Similarly, if I find the room cold and light a fire, the temperature of the room is changed as a result of my knowledge, but what I knew was that the room was cold at a given time and this fact is not changed. Even in the case of anticipating future events it might be said that what I cognise is always only the probability of an event relative to certain data, and this is not altered by the factual occurrence or non-occurrence of the event anticipated or by any happenings other than those which form the data.[1] These cases therefore need not overthrow the realist principle. If there is, as some people claim, such a thing as immediate correct cognition of the future and if the cognition is ever a part-cause of the future event cognised, we have a case which seems more difficult to reconcile with the absolute independence of the object of cognition maintained by the realist. He might, however, still escape the difficulty by maintaining that the immediate object of cognition in such cases was not the future event as an actuality but only as a possibility.

Two objections may rightly be brought against many statements of the realist argument. One of the chief reasons why the argument seems valid is because it is assumed that if I did change what I knew by knowing it, I should falsify the facts and so should not *know* it. Now in the first place this already presupposes the truth of the realist view that the object known is there prior to the knowing of it, otherwise it would be meaningless to talk of changing it by knowing it. If no object can exist apart from being known, it cannot be changed by being known. The idealist may reply that we are not seeking to know things as they would be in a world in which no one knew them, but as they are in the actual world where minds do know them. Their nature depends from the beginning on their being in such a world, but this does not mean that they are changed by each particular act of knowing them.

Secondly, it is obvious that in so far as I know at all I must know things as they are, but is it impossible *a priori* that I might know S as it really was and yet change S by knowing it? Even if I did so, my cognition would still be true of S, as S was prior to the change initiated by my knowing it.

---

[1] I accept Dr. Keynes' view that the same event may have all manner of different degrees of probability, relatively to different data, and that there is no meaning in speaking about the probability of an event except relatively to certain data.

Any change caused by my knowing could arise, if at all, only after I already knew S, and therefore could not destroy the knowledge which I had already gained. Supposing the fact known to be that S is P, it would indeed be a logical absurdity to suggest that my knowing that S is P could prevent S being P at the time at which I knew it as P, but it is not therefore logically absurd to suppose that my knowing might change the fact known in the sense of leading to the substitution of a new fact in future, i.e. might prevent S from continuing to be P. As a logical possibility this must be admitted; whether it occurs in practice is an empirical question. It clearly does so in some cases of introspection. I rather suspect that realists sometimes confuse the proposition that we know things as they are with the proposition that we leave them as they are by knowing them. I must know things as they are in the sense that my knowledge must conform to their real nature and will not be knowledge if it is altered in such a way as not to conform, but this is not necessarily to say that I cannot alter the things by knowing them. A correct cognition cannot directly change our views of the thing cognised independently of the thing, but that does not rule out the logical possibility of its changing the thing. But despite this it remains true that the real object of knowing cannot be changed, for this is not that S is P but that S was P at a given time. Even if S were changed or S ceased to be P as the result of our knowing, what we knew would not be changed or falsified, for what we knew was not simply S-P but S-P at a given time. It is clear also that, whenever I come to know something, I create a new relation with and so a new relational characteristic of the fact known, namely, the relational characteristic of being known by me, but this characteristic is not included in the object of that knowing,[1] though it may be in the object of another subsequent or simultaneous act of knowing.

[1] Two possible confusions should be noted here. (*a*) Knowing in one of its senses implies actual consciousness, but the term is often used in a potential sense, so that a man is commonly said to know facts about which he may not be thinking at all at the time when the assertion is made. Now if I know X it may be truly said that I know (potentially) that X is known by me, meaning that I should know this the moment that I directed my attention to the subject. (*b*) Even when not engaged in introspection I in a sense know my mental state but I make no explicit judgments about it. I have only what Professor Broad calls an 'undiscriminating awareness' of it. When I know X it may be that I always have this undiscriminating awareness of the fact that X is known by me, this fact being part of a whole

There are left objections quite sufficient to demolish the idealist argument. In the first place, it seems quite clear that cognition is an essentially different thing from making, and that the so-called mental construction which accompanies cognition, in so far as it is anything which can with the slightest show of reason be called construction, is simply not cognition at all. No idealist arguments that I have seen go any way towards proving that cognition is making; at the very most they show that it involves making, and the difference between knowing or opining and making [1] should be plain to inspection.

Secondly, knowing clearly presupposes an object to be known, and this object is logically prior to and cannot be dependent on or made by the knowing. Knowing is a discovery of what is, and this must be there to be discovered, it cannot be the result of the discovery of itself. If we eliminate this factor in knowing, it ceases to be knowing and becomes imagining, inventing or erroneously supposing. The object known cannot indeed be always said to be temporally prior, because sometimes, as with the laws of logic or mathematics or all hypothetical propositions, it is not temporal at all, but it seems clear that it is logically presupposed by the knowing of it.[2] To say that an object depends for its existence or being

of which I am aware, but this is not to know it at all as a distinct fact. But even if I were wrong, and it were impossible for anyone to know X without also knowing in the strict sense of 'know' that X was known by him, this would not make the second act of knowing part of the first act and so disprove my argument above.

[1] Even if the object known were made by us in a given case, the making of it would not be the same as the knowing of it and the knowing would not do the making.

[2] A difficulty arises in regard to future events. The difficulty would be enhanced if the genuineness of any of the alleged cases of direct prevision of the future could be established, but in any case it might be contended that there was such a thing as knowledge of the future, for I know e.g. that all cases of 2 + 2 in the future will be cases of 4. And there undoubtedly are cases of right opinion about future events. Three possible ways of meeting the difficulty suggest themselves. In the first place it might be held that the object of knowledge or opinion was never anything future as such but either a hypothetical fact or a fact about the probability of an event relative to given data, both these kinds of fact being non-temporal. Or, secondly, we might ascribe to future events a kind of being, though a kind different from that belonging to present events. We are forced to adopt a similar view in regard to the past, since if we deny being both to past and future we have nothing real left except an infinitesimal present. This would not be to say that succession in time is unreal, but to say that its reality consists in the passage of events from one of these three classes

on the knowledge of it thus involves a vicious circle, for it must be already if it is to be known. Likewise right opinion equally presupposes an object of the opinion, which we judge to be as it really is when we form the opinion.

Thirdly, the view that objects of cognition are changed by or dependent on the cognition of them would lead to the conclusion that past facts are changed by or dependent on the present, earlier events changed by or dependent on subsequent events.[1] It is impossible to escape this paradox by interpreting the phrase 'object of cognition' as meaning the truth known and arguing that this is timeless on the ground that, if it is ever true at all that anything was at a certain time in a certain state, it will always remain true that it was in that state at that time, however much it may change afterwards. For in that case, if the act of cognition changes or makes its object, it does not indeed change or make the past but it changes or makes the timeless, which seems more absurd still. It is no argument to say, as idealists and pragmatists sometimes do, that we must in any case admit that the past is capable of being changed by subsequent events because it acquires new relations to these events, for the relation between a past and a present or future event is not itself past. The paradox of being to another. An event would always have being, but it would first have the kind of being appertaining to future events, then it would acquire the more complete type of being belonging to the present, and be left, thirdly, with the kind of being peculiar to past events. Or, *finally*, we might adopt still another alternative and suppose that the future as such did not have a being but that possibilities (or some of them) did so, and that in prediction these were the object of our cognition. If there should prove to be genuine cases of immediate (as opposed to inferential) cognition of the future, one of the last two alternative theories would presumably have to be adopted.

[1] Signor Gentile replies that it is not the knowing Ego but the known Ego that is in time. When we compare past and present facts about ourselves 'we are not really comparing two realities, one present and one past, but two empirical representations both equally present as the actuality of the "I" which compares and judges', equally present because, although variously assorted in the time series, all our past states are compresent in the temporalising act of the mind (*Theory of Mind as Pure Act*, trl. by Wildon Carr, p. 126 ff.). But if it is just a question of the empirical representations now present we are not judging of the past at all. Signor Gentile does not mean to deny the reality of time, but he seems here to be trying 'to eat his cake and have it', i.e. to enjoy the benefits for his argument derivable from denying the reality of time while yet asserting it. There is a good deal to be said in favour of the view that time is unreal, though I do not agree with the doctrine (*v*. below ch. III, sect. 3), but our **acts**

can only be removed by the idealist if he regards everything as dependent on the Absolute's knowing but holds a realistic theory of *our* knowing.

Fourthly, similar difficulties arise in regard to universal laws. It is clear that we as finite knowers do not make them valid by thinking them, and if we ascribe this to an Absolute Mind we must hold a realist view concerning our own cognition of them.

Fifthly, it seems clear that even of the characteristics of our own experience some are not known. My experience always includes a great diversity of organic sensations and of sense-impressions due to my surroundings, but when my attention is concentrated on some object, e.g. on writing this book, I am only aware of these, if at all, as a confused whole and do not know them in detail. I might know some of their characteristics by a simple act of attention, but I do not know them in fact since I am attending to something else. 'To be experienced' does not necessarily imply 'to be known'. Since nobody practises introspection all the time, it seems perfectly clear that there are a great many transitory elements in our experience of whose existence we never come to know. Even the lower animals presumably have felt experiences, but it does not necessarily follow that they practise introspection and know these experiences as such. Again, young children are generally supposed incapable of introspection, and certainly of discovering all the complex facts which a psychologist would discover if he had the power to observe directly their mental states. Even for trained adults it is very difficult to introspect effectively, and there is so much dispute among psychologists as to what goes on in our minds that, even apart from any theories as to the 'unconscious', it seems perfectly clear that there is a great deal in our experience which we do not know. It is useless for the idealist to reply that all our experience is known as a whole, being (to borrow Professor Broad's phrase) the object of 'undiscriminating awareness', because that still leaves certain facts unknown, namely, the detailed facts about the parts of the whole. And in a great number of other respects the hypothesis that there are elements

of cognition as observed by us empirically undoubtedly occur in time, so that if time is real they cannot be regarded as non-temporal, while, if time is unreal, their reality is so different from their appearance that we cannot determine the nature of the former from the latter or make any statements about our real knowing.

in our experience of which we are not explicitly or discriminatively aware, i.e. which we do not know as such, is found to be indispensable if we are to give any satisfactory account of our experience at all.

Sixthly, by the same ordinary processes by which we cognise anything we commonly arrive at the conclusion that what we cognise is altogether independent of our cognition. We undoubtedly do so in the case of past events and other human minds, and our conclusions here seem to be accepted as valid even by idealists. We do also in the case of all *a priori* knowledge, for when we know a law *a priori* we know it as universally valid and therefore as valid independently of our knowing it. The only way in which the epistemological idealist can meet this objection is by maintaining that what we know, though independent of our knowing, is not independent of all knowing. Now we cannot rule it out in advance as impossible that I might be aware that an object necessarily possessed the property of being known and yet also be aware that it was independent of my knowing; but it is exceedingly difficult to see how I could ever come to this conclusion when in the only cases of cognition (whether knowledge or opinion) of which I have immediate experience I commonly find that, so far from the object being inseparable from my cognition of it, the very cognition itself forces on me the conclusion that the object cognised exists or subsists, as the case may be, independently of my cognising it. A universal proposition about cognition, like any other universal proposition, must be ultimately based not indeed necessarily on empirical evidence of particular cases but, if not on that, at any rate on an insight that the universal connection holds in particular cases; yet in the particular instances of cognition which we experience, so far from seeing that the nature of the object or the fact that it has being implies that it must be known, we often at least see the opposite, i.e. that the being of the object does not imply but is independent of the only knowing of which we have experience, namely, our own. All these considerations seem to me to render at least very unplausible the view that being implies being known and to disprove conclusively the view that the object of cognition is made, changed by or dependent on the cognition of it.

Some idealists urge against the view of the object of knowledge as independent of being known that it would make change or novelty impossible. Knowing, it is said, would cease to be anything of value and become a mere copying of what is already there, a mere redundant repetition; and reality, since it would have to be there already for us to know, would be already fixed and determinate and so would exclude the possibility either of change in the world or of activity on our part, whether practical or theoretical. For activity must consist in changing and moulding, not in accepting what is already given. Such arguments are urged by Signor Gentile not only against realism but also against any idealism which is not purely immanent.[1]

This objection does not, however, seem to me at all formidable. Knowing may be something genuinely new even if it does not mould or transform the reality known. For it is a new experience, and any reasonable form of realism will regard the experience of human beings as a genuinely real part of reality. Knowing changes the state of the mind which knows, and this is as much a novelty as if it changed the object known. If, though new, it presupposes something old, namely, the object known, in this it only resembles all other novelties. If we hold the 'copying theory', knowledge may seem indeed a mere repetition of reality; but the copying theory is not necessary to realism and there are other considerations besides this which make it untenable. Again, if we assume that the aim of knowledge is to establish identity with its object, then knowledge seems to be nothing at all beyond the already given object. But once we have realised that the knowing of x is not and cannot be either the same as x or a mere copying of x, then this knowing may well, even in a world where x has always existed, be a genuinely new occurrence. The objection is likewise invalid against transcendent idealism, for, even if we assume that a transcendent God knows everything from the beginning, since we are finite minds our knowing will be specifically different from that of God, and so will be a genuine novelty though modelled in certain respects on that of God.

Again I quite fail to see why realism or transcendent idealism should be held to be inconsistent with change in the physical world unless we assume *a priori* that mind is the only thing which can change. Reality may change as much as you like, yet those qualities in it which we know may still not be changed by the knowing of them. All or almost all our knowledge is

[1] *Theory of Mind as Pure Activity*, trl. by Wildon Carr, pp. 4, 52 ff.

of past [1] events and timeless truths,[2] and it would seem that these must from the nature of the case be completed and unalterable. Would the past be past if it were not already posited, completed, given ? Could the timeless possibly be changed in time, must it not from the nature of the case be given once and for all ? Even if there were no epistemological considerations which pointed in that direction, it would still be quite clear that this characteristic of completeness and unalterableness belonged to universal laws and to past events.

Paradoxical though it may seem, the past may indeed change its properties in the sense that it may acquire new relations to events subsequent to itself, but a sharp distinction must be drawn between these and all its other characteristics, which cannot be changed even in the minutest degree by subsequent events. We can easily see this to be consistent with the proposition that what is past itself cannot change by noting that the relation between a past and a present event is not itself past. Neither is the relational characteristic of standing in that relation : if indeed this can be said to be temporal at all, it cannot be placed in any time earlier than the later event to which the relation holds. For example, the battle of Hastings stood to the battle of Waterloo in the relation of ' followed by ' only from the date at which the latter occurred, and therefore the relational characteristic of ' being followed by the battle of Waterloo ' cannot have been possessed by it at any time earlier than the second battle. Earlier than this the battle of Hastings may have stood to the battle of Waterloo in a different relation [3] such as ' destined to be followed by ' or ' capable of being followed by ', but with these relational characteristics our problem does not arise, for *if* the former event ever stood in such a relation to the latter it did so from the very time when it itself first occurred, and did not acquire the relation after it had ceased to exist itself, as was the case with the relation ' followed by '. So we may still maintain that nothing which is past changes, for though

---

[1] Since a process of cognition must always take time, it is difficult to see how we can ever know the present. For even if the act of knowing itself is instantaneous, the auxiliary thought-processes involved must occupy some short time-period.

[2] I am thinking of universal laws here, but as I have remarked earlier the object of knowledge may in a sense always, even in the case of particular events, be regarded as timeless.

[3] *If* it is possible to stand in any relation at all to what has not yet occurred.

past events acquire new relational characteristics these characteristics are not themselves past. This leaves us indeed with the paradox that something may have relational characteristics which are not contemporary with itself. This paradox will have to be accepted though it may disturb common-sense. But it is certainly not peculiar to epistemology. It is true that when I came to know that the battle of Hastings was lost by Harold this fact [1] acquired the new characteristic of being known by me, but it also acquired the new characteristics of being temporally and causally [2] related in a certain way to me. These relations are not indeed of any considerable historical importance, but they are real all the same.

A similar paradox arising in regard to universal laws and timeless hypotheticals may be met in a similar way. The relations of the timeless to what is in time can change but not the timeless itself. As with past facts the paradox arises both in regard to the relation 'known by' and in regard to other relations, e.g. 'exemplified by', and is therefore not peculiar to epistemology.

§ IV. The Epistemological Argument from Internal Relations

Epistemological idealism is also sometimes based on an argument from the nature of relations. It is assumed on general grounds that all relations are 'internal', and then, since knowing and its object are related, it is concluded that knowing must make a difference to its object, thus overthrowing realist epistemology. Against this view realists argue that, since the conclusion is absurd, the premiss must be false and the relation between knowing and its object must be 'external'. In this chapter I shall confine myself to showing that both sides have made a mistake in supposing that the conclusion follows from the premiss in question; the meaning and validity of the premiss will be discussed later.[3]

[1] Properly speaking, what I know is never events but facts. I only know an event in the sense of (a) knowing certain facts about it, (b) being immediately acquainted with it, a different sense of 'know' with which we are not concerned here.
[2] If the battle of Hastings had not been fought or had resulted differently, the institutions and social life of this country would in all human probability not have been the same, and what I am is partly at least due to the civilization in which I was brought up.
[3] Chap. IV.

Now we must admit that there is some relation between cognition and its object. Either they are identical or they are different facts, and if different they must be related. There is no third alternative, for surely no one would maintain that cognition and its object are both different and totally unrelated. There is always a tendency in some quarters to assert the identity of knowledge and its object, but I cannot help feeling that those who take this line have not adequately realised what their words mean. <u>Even if there is a very close connection between knowledge and its object, this does not involve identity, either qualitative or numerical.</u> Can we hold the fact that I know I had toothache five minutes ago and the fact that I had the toothache then to be one and the same fact? Can we hold that they are absolutely indistinguishable and identical, that there is not the least difference between them? Can we hold that they are completely the same in existence, quality and temporal position? Even philosophers must confess themselves incapable of such a feat of faith, and this is even more clear if we substitute a universal law such as $2 + 2 = 4$. But, if what is known and the knowing of it are not one and the same fact, they must be different and related. Bradley suggests that we ought not to speak of a relation between them because they are two inseparable aspects of the same thing, but to say this is not to escape the dilemma, if it is a dilemma, but only to say that they are related extraordinarily closely.

Nor can we avoid the admission of relation by falling back on partial identity. For <u>if my knowing and what is known were partially identical, there would still be a relation between those elements in each which were different, and further even partial identity cannot possibly be defended unless we mean the identity to be qualitative not numerical.</u> They can only be said to be partially identical, if at all, in the sense that they have qualities in common, but in this sense most things are partially identical with each other. However many qualities they may have in common,[1] they still remain numerically different but related.

It does not affect this argument if a physical world independent of us be denied, because it is equally obvious that a past experience and my present knowing of it or thought

---

[1] It is not, however, easy to see what qualities they have in common except those, if any, which everything has in common with everything else.

of it are different facts. And if my knowing and its object are different facts they must be related, since otherwise I could not know the object I know. The distinction between relations and terms may be a very inadequate way of dealing with the concrete continuum, but we seem to have at least as much justification for applying the distinction here as we have in the case of other relations. All relations may be 'phenomenal', but at any rate we must admit that judgments asserting relation must be at the very least partially and phenomenally true. Relational judgments may only give truth of a low degree, but at any rate this is the best truth that we can attain by thought since all our judgments are relational.

It is sometimes held that there is no specific cognitive relation,[1] but even if this is so cognition and its object must be connected by some other relations. If not, our knowing would have nothing to do with the object known, our judgments in knowing would not be true of it and would not be in the slightest degree dependent on it, they would be mere groundless imaginings. It cannot be legitimately objected that the past which we know is now non-existent and therefore cannot be a term of a relation now, for the past obviously in any case bears some relations to present events, e.g. causality, similarity, priority in time; therefore we must either admit that the non-existent can stand in a relation or deny that the past is non-existent.

Any two facts in the physical world must bear some relation to each other, however unimportant and indirect it may be. They must have some temporal relation, some (though perhaps a very indirect) causal connection, some similarity or difference. Further, it would seem that any cognition which yields truth must stand in some relation involving dependence on and conformity with its object.

Now it is assumed by many idealists [2] that, if any terms are in fact related by any relation, the relation could not have been different without the terms also being different in some respect or respects [3] (other than the mere absence

[1] E.g. by Professor R. W. Sellars, *Critical Realism*, p. 214.

[2] For a good example of an idealist argument which assumes and depends on the doctrine of internal relations v. Royce, *The World and the Individual*, vol. I, Lecture III.

[3] I am here having recourse to the common formulation of the view. On p. 131 I point out (the suggestion comes from Professor G. E. Moore) that, if it is to cover relations between universals, the statement must be amended.

of the characteristic of standing in the relation), and from this it is concluded that knowing must make a difference to the object known and that the realist theory of knowledge is untenable. I am not here concerned with the grounds for this view about relations (commonly called the theory of internal relations) but with the conclusion drawn from it in regard to cognition. Nor am I concerned with other senses in which relations have been or may be said to be internal. These matters will be discussed in a later chapter. All I shall try to show here is that, *even if* it be the case that cognition and its object are related internally in the sense defined, it does not necessarily follow that the object of my cognition is changed or brought into being by my cognition.

Now the view described is often expressed by using the words 'make a difference to'. This phrase, however, ordinarily means 'cause a change in', and it is this sense of the words on which turn most of the realist objections that I have mentioned. It seems absurd to suppose that my cognition can cause a change in the past or in a universal law. But does this absurd consequence really follow from the doctrine of relations in question? It would only do so if the proposition were true that, whenever any terms A and B are connected by a relation which is internal in the sense defined, the presence of the relation [1] causes a change in A and B. But this proposition is certainly false. If A is like B in respect of a certain quality or qualities there is a relation between A and B which is internal in the sense defined, namely, the relation of similarity. If A and B are similar at all, they could not have failed to be similar to each other unless they had been different in quality from what they now are. Again, if A is half of B the relation is internal, since it could not have been absent without A or B being different in size from what it now is. The relations mentioned are clearly internal in this sense if any relations are, yet with neither of them is it true that the relation causes a change in the terms related. The fact that A is similar

[1] I do not mean to maintain that knowing is simply a relation, but at any rate it implies a relation, and if an argument of the kind in question is to be possible at all it must be to the effect that the relation implied in knowing is of such a character that the object known cannot be the same as it would have been if it had not entered into the relation.

to B or half of B does not cause a change in either A or B. And it is equally obvious that this relation though internal does not create, make or bring into being either of its terms. The same is clearly true of the numerous internal relations that hold between timeless universals, as in pure mathematics. We therefore cannot possibly argue that just because knowing and its object are internally related it necessarily follows that knowing either causes a change in or brings into existence its object, for we have seen that in other cases such a conclusion does not follow from the fact that a relation is internal. To justify the conclusion in the case of knowing a further argument beyond a mere appeal to the internality of the relation would then be needed, and this argument has not been provided.

There is another internal relation the case of which is more nearly parallel to that of the relation between knowing and its object, namely, causality. For it may be argued that both the effect of a cause and an instance of knowing, in so far as it is really *knowing*, are completely dependent for their nature on the other term of the relation, i.e. respectively the cause and the object known. Now in the case of causation it is generally held that the effect could not have failed to occur unless the events which acted as cause had been different in some respect [1] from what they were, but do we therefore hold that the effect changes or modifies (causes a change in) the cause or brings into existence the cause? Certainly not. Then why should we draw this conclusion in the case of knowing, even if it be true, as we grant here for the sake of argument, that the relation involved is internal in the sense defined? Perhaps the point may be made clearer by an illustration. Suppose a man had died through his head being cut off. In that case it would certainly be true that, if the man had not died, it could not be a fact that his head had been cut off, just as idealists suppose that, where it is the case that I know S, S could not have been the same if I had not known it. But would it be right to conclude from this that the man had cut off his own head, or that by dying he had caused a change in the preceding stroke of the axe which led to his own death? Certainly not. Therefore why should we argue similarly that because, as the idealists assume, the object known would have been different if I had not known it, therefore

[1] Other than the presence or absence of a relation of causality.

my knowing changed or brought into existence the object known?[1]

It is therefore illegitimate either for idealists to argue that because all relations are internal in the sense in question idealist epistemology is true, or for realists to argue that because idealist epistemology is false the relation between knowing and its object at any rate cannot be internal; and this conclusion of ours, though only negative, is still very important in view of the use made of these arguments. We can later discuss the question whether all relations in general and the cognitive relation in particular are internal in that sense without being disturbed by any desire to establish or to overthrow epistemological idealism.

The assertion that knowing and its object are internally related in the sense defined would not make it impossible for us to know [2] what anything was like before we knew it or even before it was known by anyone; for even if it were true, it would only lead to the conclusion that, the world being what it is, minds could not have failed to know any given fact that they actually have come to know, perhaps thousands of years afterwards, unless it had been different, not to the conclusion that by knowing it they made it different from what it was before they knew it. For, although what they know may have existed before they knew it, it never existed in a world in which they were not going to know it; and to ask what it would have been like in such a world would be to ask a futile question, for we wish to know not what it would be if the world were different but what it is in this actual world. That it would have been different

---

[1] I do not mean to identify the cognitive relation with causality, far from it; but all I need to show is that the supposed fact that the relation between knowing and its object is internal would not necessarily imply that knowing changed or brought into existence its object, and for this purpose it is quite to the point to show that in the case of other internal relations this inference cannot be drawn. It would not be sufficient to show this if the argument were based on the specific nature of the relation between knowing and its object; but it is not based on that, it is based only on the premiss that the relation is internal in the sense given, and it is easy to show by contrary instances of internal relations which do not change or bring into existence their terms that this fact cannot prove what both sides apparently think that it proves.

[2] 'Know' is here, as by those who have employed the arguments discussed, used in its less strict sense. We can hardly claim to have *certain* knowledge on these subjects.

if it had been such as never to come to be known would not matter in the least, since it actually is known or is going to be known. To take an illustration, granted that a particular Englishman has had a tolerable education in history, he could not have failed to learn at some time of the battle of Hastings unless the battle had been much less far-reaching in its effects than it actually was, therefore we may say that, he being what he was, if he had not some time known that the battle of Hastings took place the battle would have had to be different from what it was; yet this certainly does not imply that the battle was dependent on or made or changed by his knowing it to have taken place. Needless to say, we have not, as yet at any rate, offered any argument to show that the relation between cognition and its object is or is not internal, but only repelled an idealist argument based on the assumption that it is internal in a given sense and removed a realist objection intended to show that it could not be internal in this sense. And here I must leave the question of internal relations for the present and pass to other epistemological arguments for idealism.

§ V. Royce's Argument

A more difficult argument to combat than any yet put forward is provided by Royce. It is based on the close connection between knowledge and purpose. Royce points out that all judgment involves purpose in two essential respects. (*a*) What it shall select as its object is fixed by the purpose of the knower. Even the realist does not deny that I can within certain limits select whatever I please as the object of my investigation or judge about whatever known truths or matters of opinion I choose, this choice being determined by my purpose, whether the purpose be a mere momentary whim or have as its object the most vital interests of the human race. (*b*) The way in which my thoughts or cognitions shall correspond to their object and so the standard by which they are to be judged is also fixed by my purpose. A map, a verbal description and a book of photographs of typical scenery all correspond to (represent) the same country in a different way and so are subject to different standards, and I can choose which I shall produce and so by which standard my production is to be judged. Similarly with any judgment its truth or falsehood must be tested by and so depends on the standard the judger sets himself. When a plank is 2·9999999999999 feet long, to say 'this line is three feet long' may be true if I am talking about carpentry and false if the context of my assertion is to be found in the subject-matter of an exact science. Again I decide whether it is more serviceable to use a mental diagram or to think in mathematical symbols, and if I adopt the latter course I cannot possibly be criticised on the ground that the shape of the symbols is not in the least like that of the real object.[1]

Now Royce thinks that the only way of reconciling these characteristics of judgment with its objectivity and with the possibility of error is by distinguishing true judgments as those which are in conformity with the purpose of the Absolute—this, since the Absolute is immanent in me, being at the same time my own real purpose. The difficulty in finding the truth, according to Royce, is the difficulty of finding what we really want ourselves; for it may be very hard to discover our needs, as recent psychology has insisted so emphatically, and as is apparent in practical life, especially in youth when it is so easily possible to go wrong through making a mistake about the career or wife the man really wants himself, as Royce points out. According to Royce, progress in knowledge consists in the advance from a less determinate to a more determinate purpose, the latter being recognised when I reach it as what I really implied and really wanted all the time if I had only known it. By the introduction of the Absolute Mind he claims to give the only intelligible account of the correspondence theory of knowledge by interpreting it in terms of correspondence with the ideal knowledge of the Absolute Mind, an ideal which is at the same time real and therefore may be regarded relatively to our knowing as objective, independent, actual fact.

By this means he also claims to solve the antinomy between the thesis that in the object of an idea there ' seems to be no essential characteristic not determined by the conscious purpose of the idea itself ' and the antithesis ' that no finite idea can predetermine its own object ',[2] and to provide a reconciliation of two leading rival tendencies in epistemology, the tendency to regard the object known as essentially independent of being known and the tendency to find knowledge in identity with object known. If we make the

---

[1] The illustrations are my own, not Royce's.
[2] *The World and the Individual*, vol. I, p. 320 ff.

Absolute Mind purely immanent we fail to do justice to the facts which support the former tendency; if we make the Absolute Mind purely transcendent we seem to neglect those which support the latter. But according to Royce I attain knowledge only in so far as I conform to an Absolute purpose which transcends mine and is not made by my seekings after it, yet this Absolute purpose is itself my own ultimate purpose, what I really want though I may not consciously realise it. Otherwise there would be no reason why I should seek to conform to the Absolute purpose, and the errors would not be my errors.

Royce's theory, developed, as it is, into a whole philosophical system, is a fine example of metaphysical thinking and one that must be judged as a whole and cannot be dismissed by disclosing a verbal fallacy or two. It remains a possible and, so far as I can see, a fairly coherent account of reality: what is more, it deserves a high place among the great metaphysical systems of the past. But it is not, as Royce actually claims in one passage, logically necessary. For, in the first place, he only disproves the realist view by exaggerating the independence which the realist is committed to claiming for his objects, and by using an argument based on internal relations which, as I have tried to show,[1] possesses no validity. Secondly, even if he has succeeded in disproving both realism and the two other views he cites (the 'mystical' and the 'critical' views), he has not shown that he has exhausted the possible alternatives to his own view.

Thirdly, the facts cited about the connection between purpose and cognition are not necessarily incompatible with realism. I may well select which of the objects that exist independently of being known I shall attend to, and I may decide by my purposes the way in which I shall seek to 'correspond' in my cognition to that object, thus determining the standards according to which my cognition shall be judged, but that does not mean that the object is dependent for its existence or content on anybody's cognition of it. All that follows is, as far as I can see, (*a*) that it could not be an object for me without my cognising it, (*b*) that I decide the way in which my cognition is to be tested but not the result of the testing. To select an object is not to determine the content of it, but to determine that I shall stand in a certain relation to it; and, further, it is difficult to see

[1] Sect. 4.

how I can select without presupposing a range of alternatives themselves independent of my purpose in selecting. Nobody would dream of using such an argument in regard to particular physical objects and contending that, because I can choose to draw a map of Africa instead of Europe, and can decide by my own choice to mark red the parts of the continent which belongs to the British Commonwealth, thus fixing a standard according to which the accuracy of my map shall be judged, my purpose decides which parts of Africa belong to the Commonwealth and which do not. No doubt Royce and those who think like him see an essential difference between the argument he has used and the absurd argument about the map, but they cannot hope to convince realists till they have made clear, as they have not yet done, the difference between the two cases. It may even be admitted that I can only reject a view as untrue because it does not conform to a certain purpose of mine,[1] namely, the purpose of attaining truth, but it can only fail to conform because the part of reality under consideration has a certain character independently of at least this purpose of mine, therefore it is far from clear how all this can justify the conclusion that it must be dependent on some purpose, let alone my real purpose.

Fourthly, there are the difficulties raised by the failures of purpose because of what seem to be recalcitrant facts. Royce holds that, whenever I think that my purpose is thwarted, it is only my purpose as it seems to me at the time and not my real purpose, but this is a very hard view,[2] and one that we could only accept if forced on us by the strongest arguments. I need not dwell on its obvious difficulties, since I have tried to show that the arguments brought forward by Royce are far from strong, but I shall just point out that one of my *real* purposes must be to attain knowledge, and this purpose at least could attain no satisfaction if it did not presuppose a reality independent of itself to satisfy

[1] Similarly I reject a map of Africa as bad because it does not conform to my purpose of giving an accurate representation of Africa.

[2] It is only possible at all if we hold : (1) that what a man *really* desires is always the good (never his own good in any sense which conflicts with that) ; (2) that, if we could see all its consequences, what happens is always what is best ; (3) that no one can ever *really* desire that it should be possible to gain the good in question *without* the pain and evil involved in the means (for, if anyone does really desire this, his desire is assuredly thwarted).

EPISTEMOLOGICAL IDEALISM

it. That this reality might be an Absolute Mind I am not disposed dogmatically to deny, but I do not see that we are brought any nearer this conclusion by the facts about the connection between knowing and purpose.

There remains the argument that Royce's theory gives the only satisfactory account of the relation of correspondence between judgment and its object. This is a point where it has perhaps a definite advantage over realist theories. If the relation of correspondence is to be further analysed or described at all, Royce's account is perhaps the most plausible I know, but we cannot accept a given analysis of something which introduces unproved assumptions simply because all other attempts at analysis have failed. The relation in question may well be unanalysable. Some concepts must be in this position, for otherwise we have a vicious infinite regress, and a relation so fundamental as that between judgments and the reality of which they are true is as likely as any to be unanalysable. I do not indeed accept as valid the argument that the relation must be incapable of being described in language on the ground that any further description would have itself to bear the relation in question to that which it described. This argument depends on the assumption that a proposition cannot contain any assertion about itself, and this seems to me false in any sense in which it would carry with it the conclusion desired. For, while it seems to be true that a proposition cannot contain any assertion about itself as a single proposition, it may and sometimes does contain an assertion about a class to which it itself belongs, and therefore indirectly about itself, e.g. 'all propositions are either affirmative or negative', 'most propositions can be analysed into subject and predicate', 'propositions are not entities separable from the thinking of them'. But while I know no way of proving that the relation is unanalysable, it is certainly not clear that it must be analysable.[1]

However, it remains true that to regard correspondence as 'thinking like the Absolute Mind' is a more intelligible way of regarding it than to look on it as copying or likeness or a one-to-one parallelism between Reality and the mysterious entities known as propositions. The realist may object that to think like the Absolute would be to believe or know the

[1] But, though I am inclined to think that it is unanalysable and indescribable in language, I do not see any reason to draw the startling conclusions from this that are sometimes drawn.

same propositions as the Absolute knows and to know a proposition is to know it to correspond to Reality, so that Royce really still leaves outside his theory the relation of correspondence which he is trying to explain, since the propositions known by the Absolute Mind would still have to bear this relation to the real facts to which they referred. Royce could and could only reply, as far as I can see, by making a fundamental distinction between our knowing and the Absolute's knowing, and saying that to attain truth is to believe or know propositions which the Absolute makes true by knowing or at least by thinking them. This is not open to the objections I raised earlier to this type of solution, in so far as the argument is based on the nature of the relation of correspondence and not on the nature of our knowing. It is difficult to see how an argument based on the nature of our knowing could give us any clue to a knowing which is so fundamentally different in kind from ours as to create its objects, but an argument based not on our knowing but on the relation of correspondence might conceivably give such a clue. And the argument is to some extent supported by the fact which I pointed out earlier that in order to understand or know anything we must think it as it would be for a knowing mind. But I do not feel that these two points provide an adequate foundation for the conclusion that all objects known actually depend on some knowing mind.

Finally, Royce would say that in all this as in any possible realist reply I was still presupposing idealism, for any argument to prove realism could do nothing but assert that 'certain ideas now present to you are valid ideas'[1]. It still moves in the realm of 'ideas'. This is in fact the most ultimate and fundamental argument for epistemological idealism. The only test of truth, it is urged, must from the nature of the case lie within the realm of 'ideas' and therefore we can never go beyond 'ideas'. But I think that enough has already been said in the course of the chapter to show that this argument is invalid. We may reply, first, that it is equally true that the only test of truth for me must lie in my 'ideas', but that this does not prove solipsism or prove that I cannot think any alternative incompatible with solipsism.

Secondly, to recognise an 'idea' as true is to regard it as applying to reality, to regard reality as qualified in a certain

[1] V. *The World and the Individual*, vol. I, p. 249.

way, and this reality is always other than the 'idea' in question. A test of truth may be a test in terms of 'ideas' and by 'ideas', but it is also, equally essentially, a test to decide whether something real other than the 'idea' in question is of a certain character. Further, by the very same cognitive processes through which I form my ideas and apply the test by ideas I come to recognise facts that are certainly not themselves at least human ideas.

Thirdly, we can only say that the test of truth lies in ideas if we mean by ideas our thoughts about reality. It is obviously false if 'ideas' means 'sensible images', and there is no evidence for a set of entities, ideas, in the mind other than thoughts about reality and sensible images. But to say that the test lies in our thoughts about reality obviously is not to say that the reality thought about is necessarily either dependent on mind or mental. If we eliminate the reality thought about, the thoughts are thoughts of nothing and the argument falls to the ground.

Fourthly, the argument assumes that we are not from the beginning aware in at least our successful cognitions of a reality independent of the cognition. If we are aware of this, a successful test by 'ideas' is always at the same time an apprehension of something which is other than the 'ideas' involved and is not itself apprehended as an 'idea'. The realist can retort to Royce that any idealist argument itself presupposes realism, for whatever is asserted as true by the idealist must from the nature of the case be asserted as true of something which is not a human 'idea' (thought). The universal principles laid down by idealists, like any other universal principles, cannot be, at least if true at all, just 'ideas'. Even if matter were reducible to laws governing our experiences such laws would be either 'universals of fact' about our experiences or causal connections between different experiences, and not merely 'ideas'. Or at least they cannot be human 'ideas'. Nothing that we have said indeed proves that these facts cannot be, as Royce held, 'ideas' for an Absolute Mind, but if we are necessarily aware in all successful cognitive processes of a reality which is not apprehended as an 'idea', the argument that every fact must be an 'idea' for an Absolute Mind because knowledge moves in the realm of 'ideas' breaks down completely. Royce's conclusion may be true, but it has not been proved by his arguments.

§ VI. A Concession to Idealism

If the attempt to prove the idealist case from epistemology must be pronounced a failure, there still remains a sense difficult to define in which our ordinary cognitive attitude to the world does include idealist elements. The ease with which ordinary language lends itself, as we have seen, in multitudinous ways to fallacious arguments for idealism is itself a strong indication that the type of view criticised in this chapter does justice to some important element of truth which is overlooked by the realist and yet is vaguely felt to be present in our ordinary cognitions. Still more significant perhaps is the tendency of modern physical science to incorporate reference to an imaginary observer in its method.

On the other hand a thorough-going idealist epistemology is quite incapable of working in any branch of knowledge at all. All particular studies—physics, biology, psychology, mathematics, economics, history alike—assume that the object studied is different from and independent of our cognitions of it. It might be objected that the moderate realism implied in this attitude is only a fiction which works, but I fail to see how we can make the slightest sense of any of these sciences without not only using the assumption as a fiction but accepting it as literal truth, whether we consider the question from a point of view within the science or from a ' higher ' philosophical standpoint.

Now we have already found an idealistic element in knowledge in the fact that in order to determine what something is we must first think what it would be for a mind fully and discriminatingly aware of it,[1] and this does a good deal to explain the strength of the idealist tendency in philosophy and science. It enables us to conclude our discussion with a treaty of peace by which we grant epistemological idealism a place within realism as a method for attaining the truth about independent reality. For to think of objects of cognition as they are or would be for a knowing mind is a method necessary if we are to attain any truth at all. By this I do not mean merely the trivial tautology that what I cognise must stand in a relation, namely, the relation of being cognised, to a conscious mind, my own. I mean that to know any fact, X, or form any intelligible opinion about X I must ultimately think X *as it would be* for a mind which was consciously

[1] V. above, p. 21 ff.

aware of it as a present fact, though there may never be or have been such a mind. That is the only way in which I can realise it to myself, imagine [1] what it is like at all. Thus ultimately we can only think of unperceived physical things in terms of a possible observer, in the sense that we must think them *as if* they were objects of actual present experience or rather of conscious perception (a species of cognition). This does not, as has often been held, necessarily imply that physical things can only exist as objects for an observer, for the method is merely a means to deciding what they are in themselves, but it may be that it is a necessary means if we are to think them as anything more than either an unknowable x or mere laws governing human experiences.

A similar contention may be put forward even in regard to 'necessary truths'. As far as I can see we can only think universal principles as true *a priori* by thinking them as in some sense necessary for any mind that accepts the premisses on which they are based, by thinking of them as such that any mind which realised their meaning would be bound to accept them as true. I certainly do not hold that logical implication is only a relation in the mind, but still we can only see that A implies B by seeing that any mind which accepts and understands A must accept B. Like the material world, universal principles have a character independent of our minds, but we cannot reach that character without thinking them as they would be for mind. Apprehension of *a priori* truth seems to have this twofold nature: on the one hand we apprehend the truth as true whether human minds know it or not, on the other hand we only attain this apprehension of its independent character by thinking of it as also being that which any mind must think. The two features are inseparable for us. Again, a conscious or unconscious element in the mind I must either treat as a mere unknowable x or conceive *as it would be* for an introspecting mind. Causal laws and facts of any other kind only have meaning for us in relation to physical or psychological events

---

[1] I do not mean 'make a sensuous picture of it'. This is only the way to realise what *some* objects (i.e. objects of sense), not all objects, are like. Nor do I mean to suggest that before we thus think it **as** it would be for a mind we must have knowledge of it of some other sort. All cognition is either a thinking what we cognise as it would be for a mind in order to find out what it is in itself, or uses symbols the meaning of which has been at some time or other grasped by a process of this kind.

or characteristics, and therefore are covered by the account I have given.

But if our cognition is thus on one side 'idealistic' it is an equally true and even more important fact that it is on the other 'realistic', for at the same time we are by the same ordinary processes of cognition aware of the things we cognise as possessing these characteristics independently of our cognition, and therefore cannot prove by this argument that they are dependent on any cognition. <u>We can only realise their character by thinking of them as they would be for a knowing mind, but this does not prove that they cannot have this character independently of any mind.</u> The same properties that present themselves to the knowing mind normally present themselves as independent of this mind, and in the absence of any special argument to the contrary must be assumed to be capable of existing (or in the case of universals subsisting) apart from any mind, especially if the very cognitive processes without which they could not be discovered at all lead at once to the conclusion that they have a being or existence independent of at least human cognition. This is the case with *a priori* knowledge, for what we see *a priori* we see to be universally and necessarily true and therefore true independently of particular acts of human cognition, dependence on which would make it intermittent and arbitrary. It is also on the usual view the case with physical objects, for perception seems *prima facie* to present them as independent of us and if we are to give a coherent account of experience we seem to need to assume that they exist when we are not perceiving them; but whether this assumption of their independence is ultimately justifiable or not will fall to be discussed in a later chapter, since the answer to the question does not depend mainly on epistemology. But at any rate it will be impossible to refute a positive answer on epistemological grounds.

Nor does the necessity of this idealistic method even prove, though to some it may strongly suggest, that every fact is dependent on the thought of an Absolute Mind. The most that can possibly be said is that the antecedent probability of such a supposition is heightened by the fact that we have to picture the realities which we conceive to be independent of human experience or cognition as if they still were facts for some mind, but this may be merely a methodological fiction and cannot prove, though it may make slightly more likely, any metaphysical conclusions. But even on the most modest view it gives an important place to the idealist standpoint in knowledge. The cognitive process is on one side idealistic, on the other realistic; it is idealistic in so far as it always involves thinking facts as they would be for a mind, as if they existed for a mind, realistic in so far as, where successful, it is always a finding of a reality independent of the cognition of it. <u>Our knowledge must be realistic, but it can only be attained by idealistic methods</u>. We have already seen that if we are idealists we can only produce a view in the least defensible by admitting realism within idealism, by admitting that at any rate our particular cognitions are directed to facts independent of these cognitions, but it is also true that if we are realists we must admit in the way just described an idealism within realism. One of the greatest difficulties of epistemology and one in face of which almost all philosophers have badly failed is to hold these two conceptions in due balance together.

§ VII. Hegelianism and Epistemological Idealism

There remains another very important sense besides the epistemological one in which reality is sometimes said to be identical with thought. The word, thought, is in ordinary language applied both to the thinking and to the content thought.[1] Now if it is used in the former sense we have a more subjective form of idealism, but if it is used in the latter what is meant may be rather that reality is thinkable or intelligible as a rational system than that it is reducible to the thoughts of any particular minds as minds or even of an absolute mind. This view is compatible with realism, and its validity turns largely on the question of internal relations and the 'coherence theory'[2] of truth, which will be discussed in Chapters IV and V. The contention is not an argument that reality is dependent on being thought by a mind, but rather an argument from the logical, systematic character of correct thought to the possession by reality of this character.

Even if an 'Absolute' be introduced and the real be declared, as by e.g. Bradley and Bosanquet, to have no content save experience, the Absolute is often conceived not as a mind

---

[1] I.e. to what objective truths are thought by us.
[2] While in some senses in which it has been taken this theory implies idealism, in others it does not do so.

in the sense of a single cognitive consciousness but as the totality of rationally connected experiences, which on the idealist view make up the universe, combined in a unity which is higher and even closer than but not identical with the unity of a single mind. To establish the conclusion that there is nothing in reality but experience, the idealists I have just mentioned did not rely on the epistemological arguments discussed in this chapter, but rather on the argument that unexperienced matter was inconceivable and the fact that all the content of our knowledge is drawn from experience.

The application of what has been said to Hegel himself is a task of extreme difficulty because of the possibility of various interpretations, and I am not prepared to join in the controversy as to his meaning, for this would involve far too vast a digression. But it is worth while pointing out that, if some accredited interpretations are correct, he certainly did not, despite the protestations to the contrary by himself and later members of the school, escape the fallacies of epistemological idealism. Thus many specific points of great significance in Hegel's doctrine, and indeed the supreme metaphysical importance ascribed to self-conscious intelligence, seem, according to both Caird's and Stace's interpretations, to be based partly on the argument that thought and reality must be identical because otherwise reality could not be known, it being still not clear whether by 'thought' is meant here acts of thinking or content thought. If the former the argument is fallacious; if the latter I do not see how it can possibly give a proof that reality is mental or spiritual,[1] or dominated in some sense by mind or spirit. According to both commentators realism, in the sense of a separation of subject and object and a belief in a reality capable *per se* of existing unknown and logically independent of and prior to the thought of it, is denied; and it is not to the point to reply, as Dr. Stace does, that Hegel asserts its independence of any human being's particular knowing. This assertion is made by almost every idealist, and with most is quite consistent with their philosophy, as in the case of Hegel. These commentators may no doubt be mistaken, but it remains true that Hegel's philosophy has gained an illegitimate appearance of additional strength

[1] It may be urged that Hegel does not mean by reality everything that is, but only what is most valuable. But in that case to assert that reality is spiritual is no more than is admitted by anyone except the grossest materialist.

from the use or supposed use by him of invalid arguments of an epistemological character.

We need not repeat what we have already said against such arguments. The fact that Hegel conceives the thought impersonally might avoid certain objections but would not make the argument cogent. It has not been proved that mind can only know that in which it itself is immanent, and in the absence of a proof of this we have no right to assert that reality, because we can know it, must be of the nature of thought or must be spiritual. Dr. Stace, however, adds that this argument is also essentially a proof of the objectivity [1] of universals; and if we are to save Hegel from these criticisms we must interpret him as meaning to insist not that all reality is reducible to concepts as mental facts, but that the logical connections between concepts [2] cannot be merely subjective but are also present in the real world, an assumption which may reasonably be defended as a necessary postulate of thought without involving any denial of realism. Hegel's principal object was undoubtedly to reveal a certain logical structure in reality. The impersonal objective reason on which he lays such great stress may then be conceived as the rational laws and logical connections in the real world. If we wished to harmonise his view with realism we could then say that he conceived reality as intelligible not in the sense that it was present to actual thinking or was itself of the nature of thinking, but in the sense that there was nothing real the general nature of which excluded *a priori* the possibility of its being thought by mind (no Kantian thing-in-itself) and that reality was a system the general principles of which at any rate were deducible *a priori*. We could say that the doctrine that the possibility of knowledge implied the identity of reality and thought meant for him not that, because minds can know reality, reality must be of the nature of mind, but that thought depends on connections of universals and that arguments based on this could not be valid of reality if there were only a logical connection between universals in our mind and not also in reality. For, as I have suggested already, in talking of thought Hegel had less in mind the thinking than the content thought, especially

---

[1] This does not mean their subsistence separately from any particulars in which they are manifested, but their reality as manifested in particulars.
[2] As I pointed out earlier, one of the meanings of 'concept' is 'universal'.

those very general universals between which he traces the connection in his *Dialectic*. We might hold that identity between subject and object only meant for Hegel a connection such that the meaning of the one term could not be understood without the other, not a connection such that nothing of which we can think as an object could in fact exist otherwise than for a subject. (We cannot argue, as Dr. Stace, if I understand him aright, is inclined to do, that because universals are ' concepts ' they are mental, unless some specific proof can be given of their mental character, for the word concept is ambiguous in the extreme. It may stand both for the conceiving and for what is conceived, and it does not follow because the former is mental that the latter is so also.) Whether Hegel can be interpreted without introducing as essential an idealist element of the kind I have mentioned is for his commentators to say, but if he is to be interpreted realistically he may be interpreted in some way like the one just outlined.

Whatever view is taken of my argument and of the merits or demerits of epistemological idealism in general, one must remember that Hegel's *Dialectic*, by which he claims to prove through a series of logical steps not founded on epistemology that the ultimate category is what he calls the ' absolute idea ', is not necessarily thereby overthrown. It *may*, for anything I have said, give a conclusive proof that reality as a whole has a character which might be described as spiritual. But such an argument is not characteristically idealist in the sense defined in Chapter I, and is therefore not covered by the present book. Even if Hegel was an idealist, his real greatness does not lie in his idealism. The view that reality is a rational system and the allied coherence theory developed under Hegelian influence constitute one of the most important products of the idealist movement and cannot be thus dismissed, but discussion of them will be postponed to Chapter V.

CHAPTER III

KANTIAN IDEALISM

§ I. Introductory

WE must now turn to the greatest of the philosophers who used arguments of the idealist type in building up his system, and the man who contributed more than any other towards making idealism the dominant philosophy that it has been. For we may follow the ordinary usage and call Kant an idealist, because by physical objects we mean the objects of everyday life and science existing in space. These objects Kant treated in a characteristically idealist fashion, reducing them to elements in human experience and leaving to the realist only the unknowable thing-in-itself. Unfortunately we have not here to consider Kant in all his greatness, but only in regard to the one aspect of his system which present-day students including myself are most disposed to consider unsatisfactory. Nevertheless this aspect must be regarded as extremely important for the history of thought, even if we deplore it.

What Professor Kemp Smith calls the subjectivist side is assuredly not the only side of Kant, but we cannot possibly gloss over that side. As Professor Kemp Smith admits, it is retained throughout the *Critique* and remains untranscended to the end of Kant's work. Kant does definitely hold that we can only know our representations (*Vorstellungen*), that space and time are only forms of our intuition and have no reality independently of us, that we can only know what we have ourselves made out of given material by an act of synthesis, and he further holds that the confinement of our knowledge within these limits is the main purpose of his system. Kant commits himself to these views as much as he commits himself to any view. They are held by him from the beginning of his critical period to his death, and though they may be supplemented are never repudiated. Even when he speaks as a realist, it is always a realism within idealism. This is shown by the fact that in his *Opus Postumum* where he develops this realism most freely he also stresses the part played by our real self in constituting phenomena even more than he does in any other of his writings and ascribes to this self as ground even more of the characteristics of phenomena. And when asked by contemporaries which of his commentators gave the best account of his meaning, Kant referred them to Schultz's paraphrase, which interprets the *Critique of Pure Reason* in a very subjectivist fashion. Yet Kant had read Schultz's manuscript and given him the benefit of his advice in all difficulties.

§ II. Kant's Solution of the Problem of Synthetic A Priori Knowledge. Why Kant was an Idealist.

Why was Kant an idealist? Four reasons may be distinguished, three of them epistemological [1] in character.

(1) In the first place Kant, persistently asked the question why objects should be held to conform to our categories and our forms of perception. Is it not gross presumption to suppose that the laws of our little minds can dictate to reality what its nature shall be? Why should reality be just what we, perhaps owing to a mere accident of our psychological constitution, must think it? For Kant the only possible solution to this difficulty is to suppose that what we know is not reality but appearance. In that case there is no difficulty in seeing why it should correspond to our laws of thought and our forms of perception, for otherwise it could not be known or experienced by us, i.e. could not appear to us, and therefore could not exist at all, since at the most it exists only as appearance.

My answer to the argument is that the question is a wrong one. In knowing something *a priori* we do not, as the form of the question assumes, know primarily how we psychologically must think, but what reality is like. It is no more and no less difficult to understand how we can do this than to understand how we can know a law of our own mind. Kant assumes and must assume if his philosophy is to stand that we can have the latter kind of knowledge, though he himself admits that there is something very strange about such knowledge. He

[1] Many of Kant's arguments should therefore theoretically fall in the previous chapter, but the distinctive character of his treatment is obviously such as to call for separate discussion.

says that it is impossible to conceive how the self can know itself as object, thus making even knowledge of the appearance-self highly mysterious, while knowledge of the real self he altogether denies. And it would surely be unreasonable, especially in view of the 'critical' principles of Kant's own philosophy, to assume that we knew enough about the relation between ourselves and other realities to rule out *a priori* as impossible knowledge of these other realities. The assumption, often recurring in philosophy, that we can really know ourselves but cannot know other things is connected with the unfounded idea of knowledge as identity with the object known. When we come to know that $7 + 5 = 12$ or that an Euclidean triangle must have the sum of its angles equal to two right angles or that 'M is P' and 'all S is M' together imply [1] that 'all S is P', it may be difficult to decide the ontological status of what we are knowing, but in any case it is certainly not a law of our psychology. When we see something to be 'inconceivable' what we see is not merely that we cannot think it but that there are different elements in the notion which are incompatible and cannot be combined in the real world. If we do not know this we know nothing at all, for mere inability to conceive is not knowledge, and our perception of this inability could not give us a universal law even about the self, for we could not know whether the inability would last. Certainly if Kant be interpreted as meaning to ask—Does reality conform to the principles which we see to be self-evident?—he is asking the absurd question whether we know what we know. To see that a principle is self-evident is just to see that it is necessarily true of reality.

As a matter of fact, however, Kant applied this argument not to logical principles but to the forms of intuition,[2] space and time, and to certain categories, such as causality, which he did not hold to be logically self-evident and thought he could only prove of appearances not of reality. The law of non-contradiction he apparently holds to be valid of things-in-themselves while insisting that it cannot by itself give us

[1] In this book I never use 'imply' in the sense introduced by Mr. Russell but only in the older sense of the term, v. p. 17 n.

[2] Intuition is of course the usual and etymologically correct translation of '*Anschauung*'. This word, however, does not, as is well known, carry with it any of the usual implications associated with 'intuition' as commonly used in English, and in fact stands for something quite different. For Kant it means practically sensuous perception, though it might conceivably take a non-sensuous form in God.

more than a merely formal and negative criterion of truth.[1] Arithmetic he probably held valid of them because, though conceptual, it can be represented in sensuous intuition. And since dreams and illusions are sufficient to show that the mere fact of our perceiving something is not enough to prove that it really exists as a physical object just as we perceive it, there is room also in this sphere for Kant's doubt. But the question is still wrongly put, for even here the object of our awareness is not a law of our mind, a form of our perceiving, but a particular content perceived, a sense-datum or sensum as it is now commonly called. That this content is mental cannot in the absence of specific proof be assumed to be the case, and unless it is mental what we are knowing is still something real other than ourselves, though not perhaps something physical in the usual sense of the word.

But it remains open to doubt whether we are justified in ascribing the characteristics of this content, now usually called a sense-datum or sensum, to physical objects, and hence Kant's argument could well be restated to the effect that while there is good reason to suppose that sensa have those characteristics which are necessary for them to be objects of experience to us, since if they were not experienced by us they could not exist, there is no good reason for ascribing such characteristics to a material cause of the sensa which *ex hypothesi* can perfectly well exist without being experienced by us. If the argument is put in this way it assumes not that sensa are mental but only that they are or, for anything we can tell, may be dependent for their existence on our experiencing them. Thus stated it resolves itself into two contentions, discussion of which will have to be postponed for the present : (*a*) we can prove the categories to be valid of objects of experience which are dependent for their existence on being experienced but of nothing else ; (*b*) we have no grounds for ascribing to their external causes any of the sensible qualities perceived by us, i.e. we must posit ' things-in-themselves ' but have no right to say anything about their qualities on the strength of experience. It was generally supposed that the latter point had already been established in regard to everything save the primary qualities ; Kant thought he had established it in regard to the primary qualities also.

These contentions will have to be discussed later, but we

[1] *Critique of Pure Reason*, B 190 ff., 268, 302, 329. (In references to this work A stands for first edition, B for second edition pages.)

may at any rate rule out now the assumption so important for Kant's philosophy that whatever is *a priori* must be contributed by the mind. This assumption led him directly to the idealist conclusion that everything we know must be made by us (out of given material), since otherwise he was unable to explain how we could know that it must conform to the *a priori* categories without which any knowledge was for him impossible. And it led him to assume that the proof that space and time were *a priori* was a proof that they were subjective.

(2) Kant was an idealist because he was in an important sense an empiricist. It is often suggested that idealists do not do justice to the empirical element in our knowledge, but for Kant it was the realist who went beyond experience. To be a realist would be to claim that we have either knowledge or at any rate justified beliefs about the character of things-in-themselves, and such knowledge or justified beliefs could only be obtained by applying beyond experience principles which we can according to Kant only show to be valid within experience. His attack on supposed transcendent knowledge, i.e. knowledge of what is not an object of actual or possible experience, is not only an attack on dogmatic theologians, it is just as much an attack on the realist. If we ask further how Kant established the view that we cannot go beyond experience, we find that it is based mainly on his view that only experience can enable us to make synthetic judgments.

Now it is most important that this problem should be discussed, both for the understanding of Kant and for the general question. The problem of synthetic judgments is the problem how inferences can follow from their premisses and yet give new knowledge not already assumed in their premisses, for though formulated in terms of judgment the question is really one about inference, i.e. the justification of judgments. Expressed in colloquial form it is—how can we get out of our premisses what is not already in them? Though Kant's formulation of it is new, it was by no means a new difficulty but had been discussed, e.g. by Plato in the *Meno*. And there is still an important school of philosophers who deny altogether, at least in words, the possibility of synthetic inference.

Kant's view was that pure thought must depend entirely on the principles of identity and contradiction, and from this he concluded that it could only yield 'analytic' judgments, which analysed and clarified concepts we already possessed but did not give any fresh knowledge. But it was patent to him that the *a priori* inferences of mathematics did yield genuinely new knowledge, and also that such a principle as causality was synthetic, for the cause is different from the effect and therefore cannot be reached by a mere analysis of the effect or *vice versa*. Hence he was driven to the conclusion that neither the truths of mathematics nor the *a priori* principles necessary for natural science could be established by pure thought without reference to experience. Yet he realised equally the impossibility of establishing either mathematical knowledge or the general principle of causality empirically, i.e. by generalising from the observation of particular cases. The problem was then to find a way of establishing them by experience otherwise than by generalisation from particular experiences. This was solved by the doctrine of *a priori* intuitions. Space and time were sensible and yet *a priori*, that is, they had the quality of being perceptual and not merely conceptual, and yet they were presupposed, in the case of space in all experience of physical objects, in the case of time in all experience whatever, in such a way that we could know *a priori* that the characteristics which we found in space and time were true of that experience in general. This enabled geometry to be both *a priori* and synthetic : synthetic because it was based on something sensuous, *a priori* because space was presupposed in all outer (physical) experience and therefore the objects of this experience had to conform to geometry if they were to be experienced at all. The justification of the *a priori* 'concepts' (the categories) though different has a certain similarity. The reason why we know these to hold of all appearance is according to Kant because they are implied in the sensible intuition of time, being deducible from the very notion of any possible experience in time. This solution, since it only justifies synthetic *a priori* judgments within experience, *ipso facto* forbids us to assert them beyond experience.

Kant's solution would find little favour nowadays with mathematicians, whose general opinion would be that the modern development of the science shows the *a priori* character of geometry, in so far as it is *a priori*, to be based on logical concepts and not on the actual sensible character of space as present in our experience, but geometry is of course only an instance of the method, though an instance which Kant makes very prominent. In general Kant's attempt to solve the problem of synthetic judgments breaks down before the following difficulty. If he is to maintain his position that the synthetic element is due not to thought but to sensuous intuition, he is logically bound to ascribe all novelty in geometry, everything that cannot be accounted for by merely analytic judgments, to the literal sensuous seeing of new qualities in our pure intuition of space.[1] He does not say this in so many words; if he had formulated it in this way he would have no doubt realised the difficulties involved. But this is the position to which he is logically committed and his statements at least imply this. He attaches the greatest importance to the fact that we can draw figures in geometry and actually see new properties in the figure. If this were a perception of one particular object among others it would not yield any *a priori* conclusions, but since it is an intuition which accompanies every experience of external objects we know according to him that whatever characteristics are given in this intuition must hold of all such objects without exception. For such objects cannot be experienced by us except in space and therefore must conform to the nature of space. But, we may object, what then becomes of the *inferences* in geometry? If Kant's solution were correct all geometrical proofs would have to be effected not by inference at all but by observation of the figure, or, better, of the pure intuition in our mind which is exemplified in the figure, the inference only serving as an analysis of what we see there. But in a geometrical proof we do not experience e.g. the angles of a triangle as actually equal to two right angles (no measurement of angles to find their empirical size occurs in the proof); we see, in the non-sensuous sense of seeing, that being a Euclidean triangle entails having angles equal to two right angles.[2] This cannot be explained

---

[1] Kant's view of space and time in the *Analytic* is not altogether compatible with that in the *Aesthetic*, and his admission that the apprehension of even time, and so presumably space, presupposes a synthesis and categories is inconsistent with the solution of the problem of mathematics discussed in these pages. But he never worked out a solution in terms of his later view, and never seems even to have realised that it was inconsistent with the account of geometry given in the *Aesthetic*.

[2] Whatever doubts may be cast on this proof, it undeniably follows if Euclid's postulates are granted, i.e. it is true as a hypothetical proposition about Euclidean triangles. But it is only mentioned as a familiar example, and not on its own account.

by sensible ' intuition ', for <u>entailment is not a sensible characteristic which can be literally sensibly seen.</u> The theory would likewise not give ' necessity ', for we could still only see in this way that the angles were actually equal, not that they were necessarily equal. Yet Kant's chief aim was just to account for the *necessity* of mathematics.

If I might venture to make such a suggestion in the case of one of the greatest philosophers of history, <u>it seems that he was misled by a confusion between two different cases of necessity</u>. Granted that the theorems of pure geometry are true of space and that external phenomena can only exist in space, it follows *necessarily* from these premises that any proposition validly proved in pure geometry is true of external phenomena, and this would, as far as it goes, solve one of Kant's problems, i.e., granted that pure geometry is valid, what right have we to apply it to concrete physical objects. But it would not solve the other problem, which he does not separate adequately from this one, namely, how is it that the proofs in pure geometry are themselves necessary, i.e. follow validly from their own specific premises or from the geometrical system as a whole irrespective of whether that system can be applied to objects or not? While his account explains the necessity of objects conforming to the conclusions of geometry, whatever these be, it does not explain the necessity by which the conclusion of a theorem in geometry follows from its premises though admittedly not contained in them. Yet this is just the problem of synthetic *a priori* judgments with which Kant had started his quest.

It would be still more difficult to defend a corresponding view in regard to other branches of mathematics, and in particular Kant has not attempted to work out a theory of arithmetic, which one would have thought essential to his purpose of justifying synthetic *a priori* judgments.[1] We may note, however, that the same objection applies to any attempt to base arithmetic on the intuition of dots on paper or on counting on one's fingers or even on some intuition of time-relations, possibilities which Kant suggested.

We must not suppose that Kant would have stated his view in the crude form in which I have stated it. My contention is not that he said that the conclusions of geometry were based simply on observation of images, e.g. of triangles,

---

[1] He definitely asserts that arithmetical judgments such as $5 + 7 = 12$ are *a priori* synthetic.

which he certainly did not, but that he could not solve the problem of synthetic *a priori* judgments by his method without really implying that this was true, though he did not realise that his method had this implication. This was veiled from him by the over-subtlety of his language and thought.

Kant speaks of reaching the conclusions of geometry by a chain of inferences guided by intuition.[1] But precisely how does intuition solve the problem? The difficulty is that we can from A infer something not included in the concept of A, but how the fact that the premisses are intuited sensibly can make it any more intelligible that they should imply something beyond themselves is not clear. To put the objection in another way, Kant is involved in the following dilemma. Either he must maintain that it is merely a case of sensible intuition, i.e. of literally seeing the new properties in the figure we have drawn or in some ideal figure, in which case it is not an inference at all, and certainly neither *a priori* nor necessary; or he must admit that over and above the intuition there is an inference, in which case the inference can only be valid if it is possible for a premiss by its own nature to imply something beyond itself, and this implication cannot be intuited sensibly and contradicts his view of pure thought as analytic.

In the case of the categories it is still clearer that the proof of them by reference to experience in time does not remove the problem of synthetic inference. Time may be sensible, but, since sensible intuition does not as such give substance and causality, there is still a synthetic inference required that succession in time implies the categories of causality and substance, and if the inference is valid its synthetic character is due to thought. What is to be explained by sensible intuition is not the inference but the premiss, the fact of succession in time. Thought alone can tell us that from this premiss there follows a further conclusion. For Kant does not mean simply that e.g. causality is found by analysis to be present in our experience (that would have enabled him to dispense with a proof of the categories); he means that they are implied in other characteristics of our experience, i.e. specially its temporal character, and that is why he can and must give a proof of them by inference. But the fatal objection to Kant's solution of the problem of synthetic *a priori* judgments is that it really leaves no room for inference at all.

[1] *Critique of Pure Reason*, B, 744-5.

Kant also suggests that a synthetic *a priori* judgment can be valid if and only if there is some third factor which includes and unites its subject and predicate.[1] This third factor is experience in time. A and B are thus linked together because they are both included in C. The doctrine might be developed in a way which approximates to the Hegelian solution, but it does not avoid the dilemma of Kant. For there are two alternatives: either A and B are just seen to be *de facto* present in C, or A is seen to imply B through the mediation of C. In the first case the connection is merely empirical; in the second case the problem of synthetic inference is only put further back by the introduction of C. No interpolation of a third term C will enable us to make a synthetic inference from A to B unless there is a synthetic inference possible from either A to C or C to B or both.

All the same I think it true that pure *a priori* judgments, i.e. judgments which contain no element given in experience,[2] are impossible. I should indeed go further in this respect than Kant does, if he did regard certain judgments belonging to the study of formal logic as purely *a priori* and conceptual, though for that very reason analytic. It does seem to me, however, that even formal logic involves an empirical element. For it presupposes at least previous experience of what thought and judgment are. If we had not had that experience, we should not understand in the least what was meant even by the formula S is P. Similarly arithmetic involves an empirical element, namely, the experience of numbered things or at least of order, not *in abstracto* but in particular cases, just as logic presupposes the experience of particular judgments and, for most branches of it, inferences. Logic may in a sense deal with form not content, but to comprehend it we must have first experienced the form in particular cases of judgment. To try to judge without using anything derived from experience would be like trying to build a house without any bricks or other building materials. Even analytic judgments would be impossible without some content, however meagre, for them to analyse, and such content must ultimately be supplied by experience.

[1] *Id.*, B, 194.
[2] Including in 'experience' perception of oneself, which is as much empirical as perception of the physical world, also experience of universals in particular instances. Without universals any recognition or perception of objects would be impossible.

On the other hand I agree with Kant that some of our concepts are non-empirical if by this is meant that we have knowledge of some universal characteristics or relations [1] which cannot be discovered by mere analysis of what is observed or be reduced to characteristics or relations thus discoverable. Some indubitable examples are the relation of logical entailment (v. Kant's 'necessity'), the fundamental ethical[2] notions and the notion of probability. Only I think that this presupposes our first detecting the presence of these characteristics or relations either in particulars empirically given or at least in universals derived by abstraction from such particulars. If I had never had a particular experience which I apprehended as good I could have no knowledge of the characteristic goodness, nor could I possibly know what logical entailment was if I had not seen instances of such a connection between universals which are present in empirical particulars, and thus made specific judgments which involve this general logical notion (e.g. that X and Y cannot both be speaking the truth because they said that Z was in different places at the same time, or that there are now seven chairs in the room since I have brought in two and there were five there before).

The *a priori* character of mathematics and logic need not consist in dealing with purely *a priori* concepts; it may consist simply in the fact that their conclusions follow *a priori* from the concepts with which they start, though these are derived from experience. Kant was wrong in saying that geometry was *a priori* because space was *a priori*; whatever be the truth about the source of our perception of space, the science can still be *a priori* if and in so far as it unfolds what the nature of space (or, on the newer views, certain kinds of order) implies logically. Even the metageometries that claim to have no reference to perceived space must presuppose some experience of some kind of order. Kant only escaped this conclusion because he regarded space and order in general

[1] By this I mean to assert both (1) that we are aware of them, know what they are; (2) that there is something of which we can truly predicate these characteristics or in regard to which we can truly assert these relations to hold. Such characteristics or relations would be discovered in the real in the first place by what Professor Broad calls 'non-perceptual intuition' (*Examination of McTaggart's Philosophy*, I, p. 51), though our knowledge which objects they belong to may subsequently be extended by inference.
[2] But on ethical concepts v. my *Second Thoughts in Moral Philosophy*, pp. 50 ff.

as due to mind and therefore as non-empirical. But, whether they are ultimately due to the mind or not, we can certainly only learn of their occurrence even in our representations empirically. The fact, if it is a fact, that something is dependent on mind does not prevent it from being given in experience. Kant tended to identify the *a priori* with the mental, but that seems to have been due to the erroneous supposition about the nature of the *a priori* criticised earlier.[1]

But if experience provides the material without which we cannot advance, the fact of inference implies that all features of the material are not logically independent of each other but that there is sometimes a logical connection between different characteristics or relations given or capable of being given in experience, and here thought comes in. It sees this connection and by virtue of it passes from one characteristic or relation to the other without needing to experience both. This synthetic connection cannot be either explained or explained away but must be accepted as a fact, for it is itself the foundation of all inference and so of all explanation. That the world should be like this may raise metaphysical difficulties, but we have no difficulty in seeing the connection in specific cases, and where this is so it is a mistake to suppose that any further explanation of it is required.

Kant again, I think, is right in holding that mere sense-experience cannot give any knowledge; in order to give knowledge or even a judgment expressing opinion the material must be to some extent organised. We cannot have content without form, and this form cannot be discovered by merely receiving sense-impressions passively.

If we concede to Kant that all judgments are partly empirical it might seem that we had abandoned all hope of knowing reality, because we could not then go beyond our experience and say what things are like when not experienced by us. At any rate the conclusion seemed obvious to Kant. But what does going beyond experience mean? It does not mean going beyond what has actually been experienced, even for Kant. If it did, all scientific prediction or inference would be impossible. Now inferences going beyond what has actually been experienced fall into two classes (*a*) causal or inductive, (*b*) *a priori*. To take the former, it is obviously not true that causal inference is on principle unable to tell us of new things (particulars) not experienced by us. What is true is that it

[1] P. 64 ff.

cannot justify the ascription to any objects of characteristics which are not either the same as or definable in terms of characteristics experienced by us. This limitation in our knowledge of matter must be admitted by the realist, but it is quite compatible with holding that we are justified by causal inference in accepting as a probable hypothesis the view that characteristics of the same kind as some immediately perceived by us qualify some objects even when unperceived. I am not contending here that this has been established, only that it cannot on Kant's grounds be ruled out *a priori* as for ever incapable of establishment by us.

Nor does the presence of an empirical element in all our judgments necessarily rule out the possibility of reaching conclusions by *a priori* inference about reality, or at least about some factors in the real world which are independent of our thinking or experiencing them. For the empirical content given may and, if inference be possible at all, must sometimes have features which lead beyond itself. We may see that A implies B in a given case and realise that this is not due to the particular features of A but to some universal which it has in common with other things, and we may then be able to see that this universal would imply B in all cases, whether experienced or not. Or, to put it in another way, we may see that what implies B in a given case is neither the particular A-ness of A nor the fact that it is an experienced and not an unexperienced A, but some generic property C, and in that case we obviously have a right to assert that C always implies B whether C is experienced or not, since being experienced is not included in the premisses of the inference. I discover by considering a particular triangle that its angles must be together equal to two right angles, and I see that in making this inference I have included in my premisses neither the particular size of the angles in this particular figure nor the fact that I or anybody else have seen the triangle, therefore the inference is valid of all triangles whether perceived or not. This does not rule out the possibility that there might be other reasons on account of which it was impossible for triangles to exist unperceived, but the fact that I have seen my conclusion to follow from premisses common to all triangles and not including the premiss that I have perceived the triangle justifies me at least in holding that, *if* triangles do exist unperceived, my conclusion must still apply to them. Yet both this triangle and the fact that its angles are equal to two right angles are essentially empirical data.[1] In this way I can even reach a conclusion about everything in reality, namely, that nothing is both triangular and possessed of angles the sum of which is greater or less than 180 degrees. Further in formal logic we see e.g. that no true judgments can be self-contradictory, and this implies that all reality must be self-consistent, though the notion of judgment itself involves empirical content.[2] We may be able to see *a priori* that a principle holds universally connecting two terms, though we could never have come to know what the terms were without in some previous instance having experienced them or elements to which they could be reduced. We may even be able to see that everything which exists must have a certain formal property, though we should not have known that property save through experiencing it in particulars, provided, when we have come to know it, we see that its absence would be logically impossible, as is the case with self-consistency. That we can arrive at many such true affirmative propositions about all that is I am not asserting, but there is no general *a priori* objection to the possibility of doing so.

It would be different if, as Kant held, no synthetic *a priori* judgments could be proved except of appearances (or seen to be self-evident without this reservation). But we have seen no reason to accept the premiss from which this conclusion follows, since, as has been argued above, the problem of synthetic judgments is not really eased by introducing a reference to experience.

It might still, however, be the case that the specific proofs of the categories given by Kant were valid only for appearances, and that it was impossible to justify the application of the categories to things-in-themselves either by a proof or by the mere realisation that they were self-evident. Kant based this view on the contention that he could prove the categories only by showing that we could have no experience of anything which did not conform to them. Such an argument was decisive in the case of appearances because appearances could

---

[1] If it be objected that only approximate and not perfect triangles exist empirically, we may take an arithmetical instance. The inference we draw to the effect that $5 + 7 = 12$ is valid also of non-experienced objects, if there are any such, because in order to make it we do not need to include in its premisses any statement about being experienced, though it does not of course prove that there are any non-experienced objects.

[2] All this is not meant as a criticism of Kant, but as an account of my own position.

not exist at all without being experienced by us and therefore must conform to the conditions without which they could not be so experienced, but it seemed to be totally devoid of cogency when applied to things-in-themselves. For what did it matter to these if we could have no experience of them? Hence Kant argued that the categories could not be proved of the real world, and that, therefore, since all our judgments presupposed the categories, we could have no knowledge or even justified probable opinion concerning reality.[1] Kant held that his idealism was required by physical science itself, since it provided the only basis on which the indispensable presuppositions of the latter could be justified.

It would then be an argument in favour of the view that we can only know appearances if this view provided the only foundation from which we could build up a proof of the categories. It would not be by any means a conclusive argument, for we cannot be sure that a theory must be true just because it would, if true, provide a premiss from which to prove something else which we think to be true but cannot prove otherwise; but it would increase the probability of the view since the impossibility of proving certain categories, especially causality, combined with the necessity of accepting them, has long been a serious difficulty for philosophers. We shall see, however, that even this cannot be admitted.

Kant's attempted proof of the categories follows two main closely connected lines, both of them intended to establish the conclusion that the categories are necessary if we are to have any knowledge [2] of events in time. The first is simply to the effect that even the most elementary judgment involves some organisation and unity, and that this organisation and unity, which must therefore be regarded as a necessary presupposition of all our knowledge, is impossible without the categories. I am inclined to think myself that the argument for causality at least, the chief of the categories, is substantially valid, but we need not here discuss its validity. All we need point out is that, if it is valid, the same argument applied to independent physical objects will also be valid for the realist;

---

[1] The only reservations which Kant makes concern certain judgments based on ethics and do not provide a loophole for the physical realist.

[2] Kant says necessary for 'experience' (*Erfahrung*), but expressly identifies *Erfahrung* with empirical knowledge (*empirische Erkenntnis*). V. *Sieben kleine Aufsätze*, I (Berl. vol. XVIII, p. 318), *Critique of Pure Reason*, B, 147, 218.

while, if it is invalid, it will obviously make no difference to the question. Kant argued that we could only know appearances, not things-in-themselves, because we could only prove the categories of the former not the latter, but this argument falls to the ground either if we cannot prove them even of the former or if we can also prove them of the latter. In any case, since it is not really possible to avoid accepting the principle of causality, at least in regard to 'phenomena', in some form which enables us to pass from observed to unobserved events (Kant's or the idealist's 'possible' as opposed to 'actual experiences'), it is reasonable to accept it also as applying to things-in-themselves unless there is some special ground for limiting it to the former, such as Kant thought he had supplied. Now Kant's line of argument does not provide any such ground, so far as I can see. If it is valid at all Kant has proved that *all* judgments about events or objects in time presuppose the categories, and in that case if judgments about physical objects existing independently of us are held to be justified on other grounds they will also presuppose the categories. This is no argument for realism, but it does show that if realism be established on other grounds Kant's proof of the categories can provide no counter-objection, even if successful, but rather a proof that if realism is true the categories apply to independent physical objects.

Secondly, Kant argued that the distinction between physical objects (at least as 'appearances') and merely subjective representations is necessary if we are to make any sense of our experience or even to be aware of it as ours, and that the notion of physical objects, thus shown to be necessary, can be interpreted idealistically (i.e. consistently with the other principles Kant thought he had proved), only if we presuppose the categories.[1] But it seems clear that, *if* on the idealist view the notion of a physical object implies the notion of a system of actual and possible experiences, and therefore the categories, the notion of a physical object on the realist view must equally imply the notion of a system of experienced and experienceable physical states, and if the one system involves the categories so will the other.

[1] (3rd ed.) I should not now agree that this second argument carries any weight for the realist, but I should also now maintain that it could not prove universal causation (or reciprocity, let alone substance) even if idealism be true. What it does show is that, if physical object propositions are analysed idealistically, the analysis must include *some* reference to causal laws if it is to supply a distinction between, *knowledge* of appearances and mere illusion (v. p. 95ff. below).

Whether Kant's admission that in order to make any sense of our experience we must introduce the conception of physical objects in distinction from merely subjective representations and treat these objects as substances, i.e. treat them at least *as if* they were independent permanent things, does not itself logically lead to realism, is a moot point. Certainly if the coherence test be accepted it must, because, if Kant is right in this, greater coherence is gained by admitting these objects, but Kant himself nevertheless continued to treat them only as working conceptions and never admitted that objects in space could exist independently of us.

Here we must digress slightly to touch on a point of very considerable importance. Kant's proofs were epistemological in character, or, as he called them, transcendental, that is, they were arguments to the effect that certain principles must hold because without them all knowledge, or at least all knowledge of the kind we have, would be impossible. Now it has commonly been assumed that such arguments presuppose idealism and are only possible for the idealist. Consequently it is usual for realists to deny that epistemological considerations can be of any importance for determining the nature of reality, except negatively as refuting the arguments of the idealists. Because they have accepted the view that reality is quite independent of our knowledge of it, they are apt to conclude that a study of the nature and conditions of our knowing cannot lead to positive conclusions about reality at all. No doubt there is some health in the realist claim that epistemology should be degraded from its position with many idealists as the fundamental philosophical discipline,[1] but it is important to realise that the rejection of idealism does not by any means put an end to the possibility of important metaphysical arguments based on epistemological considerations. It does not do so because, if we know something, A, in fact, and if we can show that it is only possible to know what possesses certain properties, it clearly follows that A must possess these properties even though it is quite independent of and unaffected by our knowing it. *Ex hypothesi* we know A, and we could not do so if it did not conform to the conditions without which knowledge would be impossible. The fact that we know it need not determine or affect its nature,

[1] V. e.g. *The New Realism*, p. 45 ff.

but yet this fact obviously and certainly implies that it must, independently of our knowing it, be of such a nature that we can know it. Therefore if any principles can really be shown to be the conditions of all knowledge and all judgment, these principles must hold also of the objects of the realist, for what I have just said obviously applies to probable opinion and to all judgments as well as to knowledge. <u>If realism is true some affirmative judgments about independent physical objects are justified, therefore any principles without which these judgments could have no validity or meaning must also be accepted as true of reality.</u> Kant said: These objects could not exist without being known by us, they could not be known by us unless they conformed to the categories, but they are known by us and so exist in the only way in which they are capable of existing, therefore they do conform to the categories. The realist could say: These objects are known by us in fact or at least are objects of justified probable judgments, they could not be objects of knowledge or of such judgments unless they did conform to the categories, but, to repeat, they either are known or are objects of such judgments, therefore they do conform to the categories. For though physical objects may exist without being known by us, they assuredly cannot be known without being known or justifiably judged probable without being so judged, and therefore any conditions which epistemology may show to be presupposed in knowledge and judgment will hold of them. It follows that epistemology may be of metaphysical importance as a clue to the nature of reality not only for the idealist but also for the realist, though its importance has been exaggerated by Kant and his adherents.

Unfortunately Kant did not realise this and assumed that the categories could only be proved if his system of idealism were accepted. He assumed incorrectly that the 'transcendental method'[1] involved 'transcendental idealism', and that we could only argue from the principles governing our cognition to the nature of the object cognised if in the course of cognition we made these objects. Here we may trace the influence of Kant's view, mentioned earlier, that to apply [2] the categories to real things independent of us was equiva-

[1] I.e. the method of proving the catagories by reference to the possibility of 'experience' (empirical knowledge).

[2] Except in a modified sense mentioned later.

lent to an arrogant assertion that reality must conform to the laws governing our minds, but in this <u>he was confusing psychological and logical necessity</u>. As I said earlier, the categories, if known at all, are known primarily not as laws of our thought but as laws of the object about which we think.

(3) <u>Kant was an idealist because he believed that knowledge involved an act of synthesis by which the mind made or put together the object known by us.</u> Like so many of his predecessors he found it impossible to conceive relations as given by sensation, and therefore he attributed them to the mind. At the same time he realised that we had no conscious experience of anything totally unrelated and unorganised, so he by implication put the act of synthesis outside our conscious life. The admission of a synthesis in this sense, however, made it impossible for him to abandon idealism. For we obviously could not synthesise things-in-themselves, and since all combination (*Verbindung*) according to him came from the mind, Nature was only a unity because we had ourselves put it together and so made it what it is. The synthesis was responsible at least for all the order in our world, therefore this order was only the work of our mind, and only phenomenal. But if so the whole of our world was in this position, for if you took away all order there would be no world left, nothing thinkable intelligibly by us but only a manifold more chaotic than the wildest dream.

This is not the whole truth about Kant's account of the synthesis, for besides being an account of the act by which we were supposed to make the phenomenal world it was also an account of our mode of consciousness of the world as it now is and an affirmation of the unity of our knowledge and the unity of the world, and in this capacity it may be of more value even to the realist. Both lines of thought are embodied in Kant's view of the synthesis, and both are regarded by him as valid. The account of the synthesis is both an account of the way in which the phenomenal world has come to exist, if we may be allowed to use the past tense about a synthesis that according to Kant is not in time at all, and an account of the world and of our knowledge of it as it now is. What he says may be true of the unity of our consciousness and of our modes of knowing as facts of experience, and yet not true of a supposed act by which we made the known world. Viewed as such an act the synthesis will be open to serious criticism from the realist. Here we have the doctrine that knowing involves making the object known in a specially difficult form.*

Unfortunately Kant does not tell us how he derived the proposition that combination can only come from the mind. It is clearly synthetic, not analytic, and as such requires justification. It is open to the further objection that, even if we can regard the categories and forms of perception as imposed by the mind, we have to account for e.g. the spatial and causal relations of particular things by reference to the given manifold, as Kant admits, and this is to say that the manifold is already at least implicitly related. But implicit relation is after all a relation, therefore in that case all relation does not come from the mind. Further, Kant does not explain why the synthesis must be regarded as a construction of the objects themselves and not merely as preparing or enabling us to come to know objects independent of it. No doubt the explanation is in the main what I gave as the first reason for his idealism, i.e. that it would be 'dogmatism' to take the latter view, for it would involve the claim that reality must conform to the laws of our thinking. The general view that knowing is a kind of making or presupposes the making of its object by us has already been criticised in the second chapter of this book, but in the form professed by Kant it is open to the further objection that the account he gives of the synthesis is quite inconsistent with his own system of philosophy. For if the synthesis is itself phenomenal it cannot be the ground of all phenomena, and if it is not phenomenal it must on Kant's own principles be unknowable by us. Yet Kant professes to give a quite definite account of its nature. He distinguishes various syntheses (or different aspects of the same synthesis) and ascribes them to certain faculties, implying that he is saying something very important when he says that e.g. the synthesis is due not only to imagination but to understanding. Besides, even if he had confined himself to the assertion that we make everything we know by a synthesis of a given manifold in which our mind applies to it the categories, an assertion absolutely necessary for his theory of knowledge, he would have committed himself to a definite view about what happens in reality quite incompatible with his principles of agnosticism.

Now I shall later have occasion to defend Kant against the well-known charge that he is inconsistent in applying the categories to reality, and I shall do so by pointing out that while he does deny all definite knowledge of things-in-themselves he does not mean to deny the possibility or legitimacy of an indeterminate formal kind of thought about them, so it might be suggested that his position in regard to the synthesis could be saved in the same way by understanding him to maintain the statements I have mentioned not as definitely established doctrines but as an indeterminate, analogical way of thinking which will yet give us some idea of the truth. But, though this line of defence is justified in regard to certain other of Kant's doctrines, in the case of the synthesis it will not hold. For Kant inserts the account of the synthesis in the middle of what he thinks to be the best-established results of the *Critique* and makes no distinction between it and the rest of the transcendental deduction, which he certainly regards as proved in the fullest sense of the term and as giving not 'regulative ideas' but definite knowledge. In A XI, while admitting that the account in the first edition of the faculties involved in the synthesis may *seem* like a hypothesis and mere opinion as opposed to knowledge, he says that it is not really so. The bold claim to certainty for the whole of his philosophy made just before [1] and repeated elsewhere is thus meant to hold for his account of the synthesis, though he admits that it is of less importance than the 'objective deduction'. No difference is ever mentioned in respect of certainty between it and the rest of Kant's philosophy, and Kant actually claimed for his philosophy a certainty like that of mathematics, thus outrunning altogether the comparative modesty of most modern philosophers. We may note further that in order to make possible his account of the synthesis sensations have to serve inconsistently both as elements in the phenomenal world and as material out of which this whole world is made by us. But the element of value in Kant's account of the synthesis can be saved by confining it to an account of the actual processes by which we come to know a reality independent of us, since this does involve a species of synthesising, though not a making of the objects known by us.

[1] A IX.

§ III. Are Space and Time mere Appearances?

The <u>fourth</u> reason for Kant's idealism is supplied by <u>the antinomies, which drove him to the conclusion that space and time, if taken as real, are riddled with contradictions</u>, since it was impossible to conceive the world in space and time as either infinite or finite. I do not propose to go into the difficulties raised about space and time. The new logic inspired by mathematics claims to have shown that these difficulties are really illusory, and this may well be the case, though I am not perfectly sure myself whether it has shown very much more than that infinity can be successfully treated mathematically. What I shall try to show is that, <u>even if the contradictions be as serious as Kant held, any attempt to solve them by making time and space appearances in Kant's sense is untenable.</u>

Kant's solution consists in saying that the alternatives given are not exhaustive, for the world is neither infinite nor finite in space and time, since it is not given as a whole in space or time at all. The natural world according to him only exists as appearance, that is, as a set of actual or possible representations in human minds. Now it is obvious that there are not an infinite number of actual representations, therefore the infinity can only apply to possible representations, but since these are never all realised the problem does not arise at all. The world is still infinite in the sense that it can be divided and extended without limit in space and time, not in the sense that there ever are or have been more than a finite number of actual events realised in it. This solution is not, in Kant's form at least, available for the realist, because the latter is driven to hold at four different points that the whole of an infinite series is actually realised. He must hold it (*a*) in regard to past events in time, since all events that are past must have already happened and these events together form an infinite series; (*b*) in regard to the extent of the physical world in space; (*c*) in regard to the divisibility of matter in space, since any physical space includes an infinite number of smaller spaces and therefore the same applies to the things which occupy space; (*d*) in regard to causation, for an event cannot occur unless all its causes have first occurred and these form an infinite series reaching backwards into the past. Points (*a*) and (*b*) give rise to the first antinomy, (*c*) to the second, (*d*) to the third and fourth.

KANTIAN IDEALISM

The solution is often criticised on the ground that Kant fails to solve the problem of infinity but only removes it to another realm since the appearances still remain infinite. But Kant would reply that this does not present the same difficulty as if independent physical things were infinite. For the difficulty lay not in the conception of infinity itself but in the actual existence of a completed infinite, and appearances do not exist as independent things but only as actual or possible objects of experience, therefore they need only be infinite in the sense that we could always find more if we continued to look for them, not in the sense that there is an infinite number actually there at any time, since an infinite number is never actually experienced. Thus, if we adopt Kant's view, we may say that all physical objects are infinitely divisible since we know we shall never reach a smallest part in dividing them beyond which it would be logically impossible to go, but we need not for all that suppose there are an infinite number of parts present in them, for the parts only exist as we experience them, and in any actual division we can only experience a finite number of parts, never an infinite. We may assert that the world is infinitely extended in space and past time [1] in the sense that, so far as the nature of space and time is concerned, the regress to remoter objects in space and earlier and earlier events in time can always be continued, not in the sense that matter actually extends to an infinite distance or that an infinite series of events has actually occurred in past time.

But the solution still seems to me to break down because, while it does not involve the infinity of the appearances, it involves the combination of a finite series of appearances with an infinite space and time, that is, just the combination Kant had rejected in the antitheses as impossible,[2] except that he has substituted for independent reality real appearances. For, while phenomena are now finite except in a potential sense, phenomenal space and time, or space and time as given in intuition, according to him are still infinite, and, if they were not, the view of Kant that any

---

[1] Kant does not think that the infinity of future time gives rise to an antinomy. Nor does he base an antinomy on the infinite divisibility of time, though he might well have done so.
[2] In the statement of the antinomies he assumes as incontestable that space and time themselves are infinite, whatever be the case with events and objects in them.

particular space or time implied the one infinite Space or Time would collapse altogether.

The difficulty is especially obvious in the case of time, at least unless we adopt the incredible view that past events never occurred at all even as appearances. It may be possible to hold that physical phenomena only exist in our 'regress' to them, but the corresponding view about the past is surely impossible. To say that the past only existed in our regress to it would be to say that the past only existed in the mind of somebody who looked back upon it in the present, in other words, that there was no past at all. It would not mean merely that events which appeared past to us had really occurred non-temporally, for according to Kant's view the nature of phenomena gives us no clue whatever to the nature of reality. There would on that view be a reality behind them, but the actual events we seem to remember or anything in the remotest degree similar to them we should have no justification for supposing in the slightest degree likely to have occurred at all. Now Kant himself does not in fact believe that there was no past at all. He evidently believes that there were, at least as real appearances, actual past experiences of human beings, but in that case he has not solved the problem. For any such series of experiences would itself have to be either finite or infinite, and either alternative Kant has already condemned as self-contradictory. If we do not admit at least some past experiences as real experiences we could have no ground for any scientific judgment, but if we admit them as real experiences the first antinomy arises again.

A similar difficulty, I think, also arises in regard to space. Everything in space or time is according to Kant appearance, and the appearances must fall into two classes, what is actually experienced and what is only an object of a possible experience. The latter class of appearances only exist in a potential sense, that is, only exist in the 'Pickwickian' sense that they would exist if certain events which did not in fact happen had happened (i.e. if there had been an observer present when in fact there was no observer). Now if the number of actually experienced appearances in space at any given time or in past time as a whole were infinite, the antinomies would not have been solved. But what happens if, as Kant held, it is finite? We must note here that Kant's objection to the view that the real world is finite was simply that space and time are in any case infinite and therefore a finite world would be surrounded and preceded respectively by an infinite empty space and time, which to him was inconceivable. Thus the antinomies would not have arisen at all if it had not been for the assumption that space and time themselves, whatever is the case with matter, are infinite. They only arose because a finite space or time seemed inconceivable except as part of a Space or Time stretching to infinity. But this assumption, if correct at all, cannot be discarded when he makes space and time appearances. Space and time are still present as real elements in our experiences, and therefore if the notions of space and time really involved infinity before they will still do so now. Kant in fact does maintain definitely in the *Aesthetic* that space and time as intuitions are infinite,[1] and he does not question this assumption here or anywhere else in the *Critique*.[2] The question is always about the infinity of the physical universe, not of space and time themselves. Hence the finite actually experienced appearances must still occur in an infinite space and time, while the potentially experienced appearances do not occur at all but only would occur under certain conditions. But if so does not the same antinomy arise once more? Kant might say that it did not because the infinite space and time are only there in a potential not in an actual sense, but in that case his original assumption that space and time must be infinite is false. To say that they are potentially infinite is not to say that they are infinite at all. At the most it would be equivalent to saying that they would be infinite under given conditions; as infinity is interpreted by Kant in regard to appearances it does not seem to mean even this, but only that, while the total experience we can have is always finite, it may always increase and can never include an experience of one particular kind, namely, the experience of an absolute limit. Hence either the original assumption of the antinomy, i.e. that space and time are infinite, is false, in which case there is no antinomy even for the realist; or the appearances occur in an actually existent though phenomenal infinite space and time, and the same difficulty arises again. If any particular space does not imply actual spaces beyond itself *ad infinitum* and similarly with time, the antithesis of the antinomy collapses; if it does imply this, the particular spaces and times which

---
[1] B, 39, 48.
[2] (3rd ed.) But v. B, 457.

occur in my representations likewise do so. If space and time must be conceived as actually infinite, the only escape from the dilemma would be to reduce space and time to the rank of mere illusion and deny that anything spatial and temporal was real even as a representation, which was certainly not Kant's intention and would plunge us in absolute or almost absolute scepticism. We should have to deny not only independent spatial objects, but even that we have spatial images or see anything spatial whatever. If, on the other hand, Kant can really avoid the difficulty by saying that it is a potentially infinite and not an actually infinite space and time which are implied in our experience, the difficulty can be in the same way avoided by the realist.

But even if these objections were invalid and the antinomies were clearly insoluble by the realist, Kant's solution as a whole would still lead to difficulties greater than those he sought to avoid. Kant maintained that we could have no knowledge of reality but that we could have real knowledge of appearances, meaning by appearances what we experience under given conditions. But if so we know something real in time, namely, our experience, and time must be accepted as real. To say that something is an appearance is at least to say that we really experience it. It is essential to Kant's philosophy to maintain both that we can have real knowledge of appearances and that we can have it *only* of appearances, but the two positions are incompatible. For what is from one point of view an appearance as only ' our representation ' is *per se* a reality equally with the physical objects of the realist, for even mere representations are real.

If we might make a digression, this brings us to the fundamental difficulty of all views which deny the reality of time in the sense in which Kant denied it.[1] Even if time be ultimately unreal it cannot be disputed that things at least really appear to us in time, but this is to say that something real, namely our experience, really is in time. We cannot rid ourselves of anything by calling it appearance ; if it is anything at all, even only an experience, it as such still falls within the real. The same applies to space, though this has

[1] Note this reservation. I am only discussing the view that space and time are mere appearances in a sense of appearance which would make appearance fall outside reality, not in the Hegelian or Bradleian sense according to which appearances are subordinate elements in a **reality imperfectly understood.**

been less frequently noticed, for even if it be the case that there are no external spatial objects existing independently of human perception it assuredly is the case that some immediate objects of our sense-experience really have spatial properties. The red patch that I see now may not exist apart from my experiencing it, but it is still real and really spatial when experienced by me. It follows that, <u>if there are self-contradictions in our notion of space and time, they cannot be removed by making space and time appearances, for appearances in their own place are real enough.</u>

Advocates of the unreality of space and time have not usually realised this fully [1]: once they realise it they must choose between giving up their arguments and maintaining frankly that we are under an illusion not only in supposing that independent physical objects are spatial and temporal but in supposing that we experience anything spatial and temporal at all. This heroic course is adopted by McTaggart. He is actually prepared explicitly to maintain that we never see anything which has shape or size and that we never have temporally successive experiences, but only seem to do so. The majority of philosophers would hold in extreme opposition to this that we can never be in error at all as to our immediate present experiences [2]; but I think that this is going too far and that McTaggart is right in contending that some 'misperception' of present experiences may occur.[3] But, while I am prepared to admit slight errors or illusions, it seems to me utterly impossible to admit that the error and illusion is as far-reaching as all this.[4] If it is, all em-

[1] Even Kant did not fully realise it. If he had done so he could not have maintained the possibility of real knowledge of appearances.
[2] And immediate objects of present experience.
[3] The difficulties of introspecting correctly should be quite sufficient to convince us of this even when we have made ample allowance for mistakes due to verbal ambiguity, faulty memory, etc.
[4] How much error and illusion it is reasonable to admit in them is a question of degree, but so are a great many other questions. It seems clear to me personally that, while there may be some degree of illusion about some matters, we cannot reasonably admit the presence of such an amazing extent of illusion as McTaggart does. We can obviously be confident or even certain that so much illusion as all that is impossible without being able to state with anything approaching exactitude what is the maximum possible degree of illusion. Nobody would contend that, because I do not know exactly the maximum number of cups of tea that I could drink per day on the average without harming myself physically, I have no right to assert that a thousand cups a day would be too much.

pirical judgments ever made are wrong to an enormous and incalculable extent in fundamental points, and this seems to me quite incredible. He claims to have proved it *a priori* by showing that there are contradictions in the notion of time, but even if I could detect no fallacy in his argument, which is not the case, it would seem to me a very much more likely supposition that there is some undetected mistake in his reasoning than that all our empirical judgments are mistaken. If his argument were accepted we must abandon science, since if we can misperceive to such an extent we can have no right to put the slightest trust in those perceptions of the objects of immediate experience on which all science outside mathematics is ultimately based. If we can perceive all or most of our sensa as spatial and all our experiences as temporal when they are not really spatial and temporal at all, then we can no longer rely on our perceptions of our own experience and sensa in any respect, and the empirical basis for any prediction or scientific generalisation has disappeared, especially as the other characteristics of sensa and experiences are inseparably bound up with their spatial and temporal character respectively and could not be in the least like what they are if these were removed.

I shall therefore claim exemption from the task of discussing at length the numerous attempts to discover contradictions in the notions of space and time. Such attempts provide interesting and important material for philosophical consideration, but I am convinced that, while it is one of the most difficult tasks of philosophy to arrive at a right understanding of the nature of space and time, the solution cannot lie merely in declaring them to be appearance. This seems to me to be fleeing from, not solving a difficulty, and it is a case where flight is futile since there is no place whither we can flee, for <u>if time and space are given any sort of being they must still keep the contradictions of which idealists complain, if they ever had them at all.</u> Were it not the case that this book is already showing a tendency to acute inflation, I should feel bound to discuss such arguments in detail, but as it is I must sacrifice them for the sake of topics which seem of greater importance for my purpose.

I shall just mention two other general considerations in reply to such arguments. In the first place, many philosophers who deny the reality of time (including Kant but not McTaggart) combine this denial with a general agnosticism as to propositions about reality,[1] and indeed if we must regard time as a mere appearance this is the most consistent course, but yet they seem to have no hesitation in accepting one set of assertions about reality, as opposed to appearances, namely, assertions about other particular human minds. They might say indeed that they did not *know* but only believed these propositions to be true; but such a philosopher has usually maintained doctrines which exclude by implication not only all certain knowledge but all justified belief about reality, as opposed to appearances,[2] and therefore he ought logically to deny that he has any justification for believing that other human beings exist at all, and assert only at the most that he himself experiences appearances which misleadingly or groundlessly suggest the existence of such beings.[3] Of course if these philosophers are satisfied with the position the objection will not touch them, but I cannot believe that they would be satisfied if they once realised that they were logically committed to such a doctrine, and I think that their satisfaction with their own view is due to their failure to see the conclusions to which it really leads them. To have knowledge of other minds is to know something about reality; to hold a justifiable belief about other minds is to hold a justifiable belief about reality—not indeed reality as a whole but some element in reality, and it follows that our knowledge or justified beliefs cannot, as many philosophers have held, be limited to appearances by the very nature of our minds. If it is retorted that we have no ground for asserting the existence of *minds*, only of *experiences* other than our own, this is not to escape metaphysical assumptions about reality, since we are still asserting that reality is not inanimate but includes a plurality of different real experiences, and we are therefore not limited either to our own 'ideas' or to the mere study of appearances.

Secondly, even supposing the alleged antinomies in the conceptions of space and time to be insoluble, it would not necessarily follow that space and time were not real at all, but only that their nature was somewhat different from what

[1] Except purely formal ones such as the principle that everything is self-consistent.
[2] This is not true of Kant without reservation, but his reservations do not cover the case I have in mind, namely, the existence of other human beings.
[3] If he is justified on his premisses in asserting even as much as this, which I should not be prepared to admit.

it seems to be, in unknown points relevant to the antinomies. The antinomies would then prove that we have a somewhat wrong idea of space and time, but not that there is no such thing as space or time at all.[1]

The view that time and everything in it is unreal in the sense under discussion sometimes claims the support of religious and mystical experience, but surely at its best religion must not negate the rich world of phenomena which provides us with training and enjoyment but include it in its blessing. Surely to say that reality as viewed by the truly religious man must be a unity quite separate from and disconnected with everything concrete which we know and value is to reduce it to mere emptiness. Surely the unity will be more worthy of worship in proportion to the diversity within itself which it transcends and harmonises.

What has just been said about time applies equally to space, *mutatis mutandis*. To many it seems easier to deny the reality of space than the reality of time because we ourselves seem to be in time in a sense in which we do not seem to be in space, but we must not forget that many of our immediate objects of experience, if not in physical space, are at least spatial in character, so that their reality would be affected by the denial. For, while it is possible to maintain that we do not directly perceive independent physical objects, it can hardly be maintained that we immediately experience nothing spatial at all. If physical objects are denied there still remain our sensa and images, many or perhaps all of which are spatial as well as temporal. It is as inconceivable that there is nothing really spatial as that there is nothing really temporal, for while a case can be made for the view that the spatial objects I immediately perceive do not exist apart from my experience of them, I in any case still really see something spatial, if only a fleeting sense-datum. I should therefore dismiss outright all those arguments for idealism which rest on alleged contradictions in space and time and claim thereby to disprove the reality of space and time, if this is understood in anything like its literal sense, in which everything that exists is real. It must not be supposed, however, that to assert the reality of space and time is necessarily to deny idealism, for the idealist may quite well hold

[1] Even if the possibility of immediate prevision of the future could be established, this would not prove that succession was mere appearance, but only at the most that the future has some kind of being.

that they only exist as elements in our experience and yet that they are real.

There are, however, other senses of unreal, difficult indeed to define, in which time and space may perhaps reasonably be said to be relatively unreal. But with these we are not concerned here. Certainly I do not imagine that any of the arguments which I have used for the reality of time would touch the contentions of philosophers such as Hegel, Bradley or Bosanquet when they say that time is appearance or that time is unreal. For them reality is a matter of degree, and to deny the reality of anything is not to say that it does not exist at all but rather to make a low estimate of its significance in the universe. For the 'appearances' do not fall outside the real but are subordinate elements in the real. The contradictions which these philosophers claim to discover in everything we know do not lead them to a total denial of the reality of the phenomena, but to the supposition that all particular things must be dependent on some larger whole in which these contradictions are reconciled in an intelligible fashion. This view has its own difficulties, especially in connection with the problem as to how the same thing can be at once self-contradictory as it stands and self-consistent from the point of view of the Absolute, but it escapes the objection that it reduces space and time to mere illusion. And, even though time is not an illusion, it may still well be the case, as Bosanquet puts it, that it is more correct to say that time is in Reality than that Reality is in time, or even perhaps in some sense that 'both in thought and in feeling to realise the unimportance of time is the gate of wisdom', to quote the words of Mr. Bertrand Russell. But such a view about time (or space) is not inconsistent with the view that physical objects exist in space and time though unperceived by any observer.

§ IV. Kant's Attempt to establish Empirical Realism within Idealism

We must now turn to Kant's attempts to safeguard the objectivity of the physical world without making it independent of our mind as does the realist. No idealist has been more anxious to achieve this end than Kant. He insists that his philosophy combines 'empirical realism' with 'transcendental idealism'. It is more difficult to see precisely in what 'empirical realism' was supposed to consist, or at least what Kant conceived the essential difference to be between himself and a thoroughgoing idealist. We might say perhaps that the difference lay more in an attitude and a policy than in a philosophical dogma; it lay especially in Kant's insistence that we must not, because physical objects are merely phenomenal, despise what science has to tell us of them but treat this scientific knowledge as real and all-important.[1] In this connection it is significant that he reduced to the level of appearance not only physical objects but even the self as known by us. He was thus able to say that physical science was in at least as good a position as any human knowledge, and did not need to exalt psychology as knowledge of reality above the physical sciences as knowledge of appearances,[2] as he thought any other form of idealism must. If the physical world in so far as it affected our experience could be known, if further it was as real as the self we knew in introspection and as much or more capable of being made an object of knowledge, then it seemed to have quite as much reality as was needed by the scientist. But according to Kant not only was transcendental idealism compatible with science; it was actually necessary to it. For his transcendental idealism seemed to him to constitute the only possible basis for a proof of the categories and a solution of the question how mathematics could give synthetic *a priori* knowledge, and the whole of science would collapse without the categories and without mathematics. He points out repeatedly that he has not denied the reality of appearances provided we add to reality the words 'in experience'[3]; and in the second edition at least of the *Critique of Pure Reason* he comes to regard the introspective consciousness of our mental states, giving the appearance-self or empirical self, as posterior to consciousness of physical objects, though the latter are also appearances.

[1] The empirical reality of time which Kant sought to maintain in the *Aesthetic* is defined as 'objective validity in respect of all objects which allow of ever being given to our senses' (B, 52), and that of space is defined similarly (B, 44), i.e. space and time are objectively real because they are of universal application within experience. We may note in this account two moments; space and time are called objective (*a*) because they are actually experienced, (*b*) because of their universality. (The translations I use are taken from that by Professor Kemp Smith.)

[2] He in fact disparages the science of psychology severely, putting it not on a level equal to but on one much lower than the physical sciences.

[3] E.g. *Critique of Pure Reason*, A, 374–5; B, 53–4, 520.

Now any form of idealism, even if it has reduced all judgments to assertions about our experience, has still to recognise the distinction between mere illusion and genuine perception, between the merely subjective and the at least relatively objective, between false and true judgments about physical objects, unless indeed it is prepared to put the best-established conclusions of natural science on the same level as the wildest fancies of children and savages. It has reduced all judgments to assertions about our experience, but this distinction must still be reinterpreted in terms of our experience. There must be some distinction between saying, I experience A, and saying, A is present in a physical object, even if physical objects be mere appearances. Kant's distinction is that in the case of genuine perception of physical objects my experience proceeds according to certain laws which determine inevitably that if I look I must have the experience in question. This constitutes Kant's proof of causality.[1] We can only distinguish between objective and subjective sequence if we regard the former as consisting in an experience in which the order is determined by necessary laws. Thus if I watch a boat going down stream (objective succession) I must see it pass the different places on the river banks in a given order, while if I look at a house (merely subjective succession) I may see either the ground-floor or the roof first, whichever I choose.[2] The distinguishing mark of cognitive awareness of the objective in appearances (and we can have no such awareness outside appearances) is that the object perceived is determined independently of the individual act of perceiving. Objectivity means for Kant necessity, and he claimed that it was his philosophy alone which secured this, for his philosophy alone was really reconcilable with the possibility of synthetic judgments carrying with them necessity.

His method of distinguishing subjective and objective is liable to two criticisms. In the first place, it may be pointed out that illusions, or at least some of them, are as much determined as any perceptions. If I look at a stick in water I am

[1] And reciprocity.
[2] The fact that the order in which we perceive coexistent objects is in the proof of causality said to be reversible in opposition to the necessary order of objective succession does not mean that perception of the coexistent is not subject to laws, since Kant proceeds in the third analogy to prove reciprocity of the coexistent by another application of the same method by which he had proved causality of the successive.

just as much determined to see it bent as I am to see it straight when it is not in water, and presumably even a man subject to hallucinations often cannot by any action in his power at the time prevent himself seeing e.g. snakes or pink rats.

Secondly, it may also be urged that our psychological states are causally determined as well as the physical objects perceived by us. Even if we are not determinists we must admit that causality plays an important if not a universal part in the self,[1] but the mere presence of causality cannot be enough to distinguish the physical from the psychological unless the latter is not subject to causality.

Kant provides no answer to these objections, but he clearly holds the appearance-self (or empirical self) to be completely determined by causality, for his whole discussion of freedom proceeds on that assumption, and we may guess how he might have answered them. Kant might have said that physical reality, in the only sense in which it could belong to appearances, entails necessity, but that necessity need not entail physical reality. The conception of a physical object entails a system involving necessity, but there are other systems by which we may order representations according to necessary laws, and these need not be the same as that treated in physical science. Thus, wherever we think of the appearance-self we are ordering our representations in a psychological system in which they may occur in quite a different order and connection from that displayed in the physical system. This psychological system includes, besides the same representations which go to make up physical objects, also others such as emotions which are not regarded as part of the physical world at all, but system it still is. Otherwise we could make no judgments about it. Similarly we could no doubt have systems of illusions, explaining these by reference to perspective, etc.; though the relation in which such systems stand to the physical world and to the appearance-self remains obscure.

The system which constitutes the physical world still possesses quite enough peculiar features to distinguish it from the object of psychology. Firstly, it approximates more to being completely systematic and is much more amenable to scientific study. Secondly, it is common to all human percipients, i.e. all percipients with our form of sensibility, and is therefore

[1] We are here talking about the self studied in psychology and revealed in introspection, which Kant regards only as appearance and not as the real self.

universal in a sense in which psychology is not. Thirdly, according to Kant, the appearance-self is not subject to the categories of substance or reciprocity, though he repeatedly states or implies that it is completely determined by causality. Fourthly, the appearance-self is not in space but only in time, and therefore psychology is without the definiteness and clearness that can only be attained by demonstration in spatial form, and further suffers seriously from our inability to apply mathematics to it. Fifthly, though both the objects of psychology and physical objects are governed by causal laws, the laws are different in the two cases.

It must be admitted, however, that Kant is inconsistent in his treatment of the appearance-self [1] (he sometimes denies by implication that the categories can be applied to it at all and mostly applies one, causality, without applying the others [2]); and, secondly, that he does not realise the full seriousness of the problem of the distinction between genuine perceptions and illusions. After all, most illusions are forced on us as much as genuine perceptions, and are also common to all normal human observers under the same conditions. All men see a straight stick in water as bent and see objects smaller as they recede, and they cannot avoid these experiences. Kant holds that the distinction between dreams and genuine perceptions must be made by means of empirical laws,[3] but we should like to have seen his views elaborated. One might think he meant that what was not determined by law did not belong to the physical world and what was determined did, but this is obviously contrary to fact and incompatible with his application of causality to the appearance-self. The point of Kant's proof of causality is that objectivity entails causal necessity, but the circumstances affecting us which are subjective from the point of view of the physical scientist are studied as objective and therefore causally determined facts by the psychologist.

The physical world is then objective in the sense that it consists of elements in our experience which are necessarily determined irrespective of our individual peculiarities, and in the sense that it is an object of science since it is governed by necessary and universal laws. Objectivity for Kant is closely

[1] V. my book on *Kant's Treatment of Causality*, ch. VI.
[2] Kant refuses to admit psychology to the rank of a science (*Berlin edition*, IV, pp. 470–1).
[3] V. *Critique of Pure Reason*, B, 520–1.

and essentially connected with necessity. This is quite compatible with physical objects in space having no existence apart from human experience. They are merely necessarily determined common elements in human experience. The conception of the physical world Kant admits to be essential if we are to systematise our experience at all, but he does not admit that we need therefore regard the physical world as independent of ourselves; it remains for him just a necessary way of ordering our experience. Kant does not hold that we are first conscious of our own representations as subjective modifications of our mental state and then from them erroneously infer independent physical objects; he holds that we cannot think at all except by systematising our experience in terms of a world of objects, and that introspective knowledge of representations is posterior not prior to this consciousness of objects. But for all that physical objects are not independent of our mind as are the things-in-themselves, but only exist as combinations of actual and possible objects of experience.

There are a very few passages, however, in which Kant seems to go further than this. In the famous second edition refutation of idealism he declares in so many words that physical objects are not representations but things outside us; in the first analogy he declares all matter to be absolutely permanent, an assertion which seems altogether incompatible with the view that it only exists in our fleeting experiences of it; and in his posthumous work he definitely shows more signs of realism than he had ever done since the beginning of his critical period. But it remains a realism within idealism, as is shown by the fact that it is just in his *Opus Postumum*, the only work where he develops this realism with any approach to completeness, that he goes further in ascribing characteristics of the physical world to acts of synthesis by the self than he does in any other book. Nowhere does he claim that scientific knowledge can refer to reality (things-in-themselves) or admit that physical objects may exist in space in a realist sense unperceived by us. Physical objects, though realistically conceived, remain appearances.

How is this reconcilable with the passages mentioned, especially the second edition refutation of idealism? In this remarkable passage Kant argues that consciousness even of my subjective representations presupposes something permanent, and that 'perception of this permanent is only possible through a *thing* outside me and not through the mere representation of a thing outside me '.[1] The passage seems flatly to contradict Kant's repeated assertion that physical objects are only our representations, and it has consequently been supposed by many commentators that he was referring here to the thing-in-itself and not to physical objects. This interpretation seems to me quite impossible, and it would assuredly never have been suggested if it had not been thought necessary to make the passage consistent with Kant's other views. The principal objection to the interpretation is perhaps that Kant speaks of the ' things outside me ' as ' objects in space '. This spatial character is essential to the argument here, and it is even more essential to Kant's philosophy that things-in-themselves should not be known to be in space. There is no doctrine which Kant reiterates more repeatedly and firmly than this, and nowhere else does it even seem to be contradicted by him. Further, in the introduction to the *Refutation of Idealism* itself he had just asserted that, if space is regarded as a property of things-in-themselves, ' space, and everything to which it serves as condition, is a non-entity (*Unding*).' It is hardly credible that Kant would have said this and then a few lines later calmly proceeded to ascribe space to things-in-themselves. We cannot in this case invoke the theory of the multiple composition of the *Critique*, since the whole *Refutation* was added in the second edition. Other objections are as follows : (*a*) Kant speaks of these objects as a permanent element in perception (*Wahrnehmung*), a phrase which would have been absurd as applied to things-in-themselves. (*b*) They are introduced for the purpose of determining time-durations, and seem to be presupposed as being themselves in time. (*c*) The argument is essentially the same as one used to prove substance in the first Analogy, yet Kant certainly intends there to prove substance only of phenomena. (*d*) In the second note added to the proof Kant tries to confirm it by the facts that we always measure time by means of changes in the relations of physical objects and that there is nothing permanent given in experience except physical matter.

[1] B, 275. Kant says in his preface to the second edition (B, xxxix n.) that the sentence should be altered to the following : ' This permanent cannot be an intuition in me. For all grounds of determination of my existence which are to be met within me are representations ; and as representations themselves require a permanent distinct from them, in relation to which their change and so my existence in the time wherein they change may be determined.'

So we must regard the refutation as an attempt of Kant at feeling his way towards a realism within idealism; and we find that it can even be rendered consistent with most of the more subjectivist passages if we adopt Professor Vaihinger's solution that Kant is here speaking from the standpoint of the appearance-self. Relatively to the appearance-self indeed physical objects simply cannot consistently be regarded as representations in our mind but only as ' things outside us '. For it cannot be that the whole phenomenal world exists only in the appearance-self, which is itself only a member of that world. But from the point of view of the real self they may still remain mere representations. Kant's realism, so far from contradicting the view that physical objects are relatively to the real transcendental self representations, is a logical deduction from that view, when combined with the view that our phenomenal or appearance-self also is only a set of representations. For if so the latter cannot itself be the cause of all our representations. If the appearance-self is conceived as only a part of the phenomenal world, to make all phenomena dependent on it would be like saying that a man had built the house in which he was born; if it is rather conceived as consisting of the whole material of outer sense viewed in a different light, it still more obviously presupposes and is not itself the constitutive condition of the physical phenomenal world. A realism relatively to the appearance-self is inconsistent with Kant's general doctrine only if it be assumed that physical phenomena presuppose for their existence not a transcendental synthesis alone but also conscious introspection with the help of ' inner sense ', for the appearance-self has no being at all except as an object of introspection.

So a Kantian idealist not only may but, if he is to be consistent, must regard the physical world both from the transcendental point of view as a set of mere representations made by us, and from the empirical point of view as a set of independent objects. What the relation is between these two aspects of the physical world Kant does not specify, but to do so would have been to go beyond the limits of knowledge laid down by himself, for it would have been to claim knowledge of the relation between things-in-themselves and appearances.[1]

---

[1] Some commentators insist that appearances are just things-in-themselves as they appear to us, while Kant's phraseology seems to me more often to suggest that appearances are treated rather as different things from the latter, but the controversy is easily solved

And he might have retorted that, if no one can say what the relation is, no one can say that it is self-contradictory or impossible to maintain that the physical world can combine these two aspects, can both be relatively independent and from the other point of view a mere appearance.

Further, it seems clear that any system of idealism which is to do justice to physical science must somehow combine within itself these two aspects, including realism within idealism. Kant's position is all the safer because he only stated the two aspects without committing himself to any definite views as to their connection. The chief difficulty left is his statement here and in the First Analogy that matter is permanent, which would naturally imply that physical objects actually exist even when not perceived, a view that may seem definitely and completely inconsistent with the rest of his philosophy and indeed is so when interpreted in the ordinary realist sense, but even this statement may be reconciled with his idealism if we suppose that what Kant thinks permanent is not anything actually perceived but certain conditions governing perception. Indeed on Kant's view the statement that a physical object exists when we are not perceiving it is perfectly intelligible and true, *provided only* it is interpreted as meaning that under certain conditions we should perceive it, so that he would feel no difficulty in ascribing permanence to physical objects which were only actually perceived intermittently.

§ V. The Thing-in-itself

So far we have not dealt with the bugbear of most of Kant's immediate followers, the thing-in-itself.[1] I cannot find any justification for the view either that Kant eventually gave up his belief in the thing-in-itself or that he came to mean by it the Whole, including appearances. Certainly he does not

if we remember that according to his own principles Kant had no right to specify what the relation was between things-in-themselves and appearances. Hence he was bound to leave it vague and could not commit himself either to the view that appearances were the identical things-in-themselves appearing or to the view that they were secondary entities separate from these.

[1] Or better perhaps things-in-themselves, though in strict consistency it is illegitimate to use either the singular or the plural, since Kant cannot have intended to commit himself to the view that the **unknowable** was either one or many.

regard appearances as partially known things-in-themselves. There is indeed an inconsistency here, since, if appearances are anything they must somehow fall within reality, but it does not seem to have been an inconsistency that Kant realised as such.

Now the doctrine of things-in-themselves is the part of Kant's philosophy which has been subjected to the severest and most frequent criticism, and it would be impossible to defend his *ipsissima verba*. But the doctrine in its general outlines seems to me much more defensible than is often supposed by critics. The chief complaint against Kant is that he has declared things-in-themselves to be absolutely unknowable and yet assumes some, though a very limited, knowledge of them. It is objected that to admit their existence is itself to claim of them some knowledge (or justified opinion, which on his view would seem equally impossible). For it would be absurd to say that things-in-themselves exist unless we mean something by the term, but if we mean anything at all by it to assert that they exist is to assert that they have the attributes included in the minimum meaning of the term. To say that we know X to exist is to say nothing at all if what we mean by X does not include some characteristic known by us, and if it does we know something about X, namely, that it has the characteristic in question. It was argued by Kant's idealist successors that the conception of the thing-in-itself is the conception of a mere empty nothing and becomes the impossible, the inconceivable, a mere blank, unknowable by us not because it is too much above our ken but because it is infinitely poorer in content than the conceptions which yield us fruit, unknowable only because it contains nothing to know. And the inconsistency seems to be intensified by the fact that Kant in the interests of religion comes round to a view which admits under another name many of the philosophical conceptions that he had previously rejected and allows, if not knowledge, well-grounded faith in the truth of some very important assertions about the nature of reality.

These objections, however, may be met by the distinction between determinate knowledge and indeterminate thought. Kant denies definite scientific knowledge of things-in-themselves, but he admits that we can form a kind of vague and indefinite but still very useful conception of something not ourselves which affects us and on which appearances are grounded. And similarly it is not logically inconsistent, on the one hand, to refuse to commit oneself to a clear-cut metaphysical theory of God, and on the other to hold, as Kant did, that our highest experience justifies us in coming to the conclusion that the least inadequate way of picturing to ourselves the nature of reality is to think of everything as controlled by an all-wise, all-good, all-powerful mind, while adding the proviso that in doing so we are not saying what it really is but only what it is in relation to us.

A similar answer may be given to the common objection that Kant after having insisted that the categories can only be applied to phenomena, proceeds inconsistently to apply them to things-in-themselves. If this is an inconsistency it is one which follows necessarily from the very conception of things-in-themselves, for to admit that there are such things at all is to ascribe to them one category at least, the category of reality (*Realität*); and moreover to think of the world we know as the appearance of unknown things-in-themselves is to base it on the latter as ground and so as cause. Ground is just the category of cause unschematised. If the things-in-themselves are not at least part-cause [1] or ground of the phenomenal world it is meaningless to say that the latter is the appearance to us of the former, so that even the very innocent-looking assertion that we know the appearance only of reality not reality itself implies that two categories at least, namely, reality and causality, are applicable to things-in-themselves. And Kant does expressly apply causality to the real world. He applies it to things-in-themselves in his doctrine of 'transcendental affection',[2] to the self in his account of freedom, and to God in his practical theology. Also we can hardly avoid thinking of the things-in-themselves as substances if we think of them at all.

The charge of inconsistency here is again met by Kant's distinction between knowing (*erkennen*) and thinking (*denken*).[3] For his philosophical system does not debar him from thinking God or things-in-themselves or the transcendental self as having some relation to appearances which, though non-temporal, is otherwise like in kind to that which phenomenal

[1] It is not true that the relation of reality to appearance = the relation of cause to effect or ground to consequent. What I am contending is that it implies that relation at least, whatever other relations it may also imply.
[2] I.e. he holds that things-in-themselves causally affect us, thus producing sensations in us.
[3] *Critique of Pure Reason*, B, xxvi–xxx, 706–7, 724–5.

causes have to phenomenal effects.[1] Kant's view is that we have no definite conception of the relation of reality to phenomena, but that we cannot help thinking this reality and we cannot think it without using our categories, though as applied to reality they are empty forms and so yield only the poorest and most inadequate of concepts. To put it colloquially, while we cannot know reality or form any proper conception of it at all, we can still 'think it in a sort of way', and this, though a very unsatisfactory result for anybody seeking scientific or theoretical satisfaction, is yet sufficient for practical needs, once we are convinced of the moral law and of the necessity that reality must be somehow ordered in conformity with this law. We have no clear conception of the relation between reality and appearances, we cannot make it a matter of knowledge, yet we cannot help thinking a reality which appears, and we have no other way in which we could think it, no other categories which we could employ. And in the case of the conceptions of God and freedom what positive content is required comes from ethics, a branch of knowledge which is according to Kant, unlike theoretical knowledge, independent of experience.

For we must distinguish between the categories as unschematised and the categories as schematised. As 'unschematised' the categories are mere logical forms, and before they can be used in everyday life or science they must be 'schematised' by the addition of time. Thus the pure category of causality is logical ground, the schematised category succession in time according to a law. Now Kant does hold (*a*) that the categories as schematised could not be applied to reality, which is indeed a truism from his point of view, since reality is timeless and the schema always involves time ; (*b*) that the categories as unschematised yield no definite conceptions and nothing that could possibly be called knowledge ; (*c*) that the categories could not be proved to hold of anything but phenomena. But these views are certainly <u>not incompatible with maintain-</u>

---

[1] In the *Prolegomena* (§ 57 *ad fin.*–58) Kant says that, when he declares that we must look upon the world as if it were the work of a supreme understanding and will, he means that the sensible world is related to the unknown in the same way as a clock, a ship or a regiment is related respectively to its maker, builder, commander, and describes this kind of knowledge as knowledge by analogy, adding that analogy means for him a complete likeness of relations though the things related may be quite different (*eine vollkommene Ähnlichkeit zweier Verhältnisse zwischen ganz unähnlichen Dingen*).

ing that the categories as unschematised may be used in indeterminate thinking about reality, though there is no theoretical proof of their validity and though the conception they give is purely formal.

Kant indeed sometimes goes further and denies that the categories have any meaning (*Bedeutung*) at all apart from sensible conditions,[1] and this, if taken in the strict sense, is incompatible with allowing even the limited application in question, for how could the application of totally meaningless names be of any help to us whatever? We might as well call the relation 'abracadabra'. But there is no need to press the literal sense of his language so far when it obviously makes nonsense of his philosophy. If we take him as signifying by meaning here clear, definite meaning we have an interpretation which can well be reconciled with his general views. No doubt in his anxiety to avoid any dogmatism Kant sometimes expressed himself too strongly, but his general position in this respect is plain, especially when we consider that the *Critique of Pure Reason* was intended from the beginning to make the ground clear for a rational faith and when we take into account also his later works. The circumstances of the time explain adequately why Kant laid such great stress on the negative side of his philosophy, for it was a time when even leading thinkers were apt to use the conception of God in order to provide a cheap solution for every intellectual difficulty and in general to treat it as if it were a scientific concept which could be made precise by *a priori* reasoning. What excesses must have been committed in this respect by lesser minds when even such great thinkers as Descartes and Leibniz misused theological conceptions as they did in their philosophies! If Kant had been writing in our own day when the main tendency is rather towards the opposite extreme of scepticism and subjectivism, he might well have worded his philosophy somewhat differently.

It must be admitted, however, that there is a difficulty in combining Kant's theological views with his theoretical agnosticism, but it does not lie in any logical inconsistency between denying 'knowledge' of reality and admitting the notion of God as a 'regulative idea'. It is perfectly possible logically that science and theoretical philosophy might give us no information about reality and yet that we might be justified in accepting a certain conception of reality as adequately

[1] E.g. *Critique of Pure Reason*, B, 308, 707, 724.

established by a consideration of our ethical knowledge. But, though possible logically, it does not seem a very likely or plausible conclusion: what I should feel is rather that if we once adopt the line of the *Critique of Pure Reason* and insist that we are not justified even in forming opinions (let alone, claiming knowledge) on theoretical grounds of anything but appearances, if by its very nature our theoretical reason is for ever shut off from the cognition of the real, if science cannot give us the slightest clue to any real characteristics of real things,[1] if we can have no theoretical knowledge or justified opinion whatever of the nature even of our real selves, if even introspection only gives the appearance of ourselves and never even a partial reality, then this distrust of our intellectual powers must extend also to whatever ethical and religious conceptions we may have formed. If we hold that the rest of our experience gives us only appearance not reality, why should we hold that our knowledge of the moral law (granted that it remains valid as a guide to action) tells us anything about what reality is? If we distrust ourselves altogether in the field of theoretical knowledge, have we any more grounds for trusting an ethical faith which Kant does not claim to have justified by a proof in the strictest sense of the term? If our theoretical faculties, which, one would think, were adapted to the discovery of the truth about reality if any part of our nature is, fail us altogether in this matter and cannot be trusted at all, is it not unreasonable to trust that those intellectual faculties whose function it is not to find truth but to regulate our practical activity will reveal to us the ultimate nature of the real? If, on the other hand, it is reasonable to have religious faith, as Kant holds, then surely it is reasonable also to hold that our theoretical and not only our ethical consciousness gives us some glimpse of the real world.

This line of criticism is important because it applies not only to Kant but to all the attempts that have been so often made to secure religion by denying truth to science and abandoning all faith in our reason. There are a few men to whom the truths of religion seem more certain than any other so that they could doubt everything else while still holding to God, but they are rare indeed, and in the absence of strict logical proof religion involves a trust that the human mind is in harmony with reality which in all consistency must, if

[1] Kant somewhat modifies this position later, especially in the *Critique of Judgment*.

admitted at all, be extended to the 'theoretical' sphere. This does not mean that we need suppose science to give us knowledge in the strict sense outside mathematics, but it does mean that if we have faith in the religious and ethical consciousness we should have faith that science at the very least can give us justified opinions containing partial truth about some characteristics of real things, if only their relations. The religious man or the philosopher is, so to speak, cutting his own throat if he maintains the opinion, popular in certain quarters nowadays, that science cannot give truth but only practical utility. Probably he usually means merely that science cannot give us 'the ultimate truth' about 'the inner nature' of reality, which science does not claim to do, or that the truths of science are less important to reality and are blended with a greater element of fiction than many scientists have thought in the past, but expressed in its more extreme form the view calls for the immediate retort that if they are forbidden to believe the scientist most men are likely to find less ground still for believing the religious man and the philosopher.

But while, as I have indicated earlier, I see no adequate reason for agreeing that reality is totally and necessarily unknowable theoretically, neither do I agree with the view of so many critics that the thing-in-itself is an inconceivable or groundless supposition. It is inevitable indeed that a thoroughgoing idealist should regard it as inconceivable if it is supposed to be independent of a knowing or experiencing mind, but this objection need not be discussed here since it will only be valid if we have first succeeded in establishing idealism. Kant did not bring any arguments to show that everything must be dependent on such a mind, but only to show that the objects of our knowledge and experience must be. Another reason why the thing-in-itself seemed inconceivable was because the conception was so empty and apparently so gratuitous. Kant gives no ground for believing in things-in-themselves, but merely asserts their existence dogmatically.

Yet despite its difficulties the conception is of great importance, and further it is essential for Kant's system. No doubt the primary reason why Kant believed in things-in-themselves was because it seemed evident to him that reality could not consist only of human minds and their representations. He had taken away from the real world all sensible qualities, but he was still left with a real world, as Locke after taking away colour and other sensible qualities was still left with the primary qualities. In fact <u>the most likely explanation of Kant's neglect to provide a proof of the existence of things-in-themselves was that he felt the doctrine to be too obvious to need a proof.</u> Had Kant denied the thing-in-itself his system would have been totally transformed. In the first place the physical objects we perceive would no longer be mere appearances since there would be no reality behind them of which they were appearances. (Kant says in one passage that there must be things-in-themselves because an appearance implies some reality which appears.[1]) In the second place he would have had to ascribe not only the form but the content of phenomena to mind, there being nothing else left to which to ascribe it, and this would have destroyed one of the most vital distinctions of his philosophy. The doctrine of the synthesis as a putting together of given material would have had to be radically changed, and, what is more important still, our knowledge would no longer be dependent on what is given us from outside and so would have lost its empirical character. Thirdly, Kant would have become what he called a dogmatic idealist, for he would have had either to substitute an Absolute Mind for the thing-in-itself or to leave no reality save finite minds and their representations.

<u>The doctrine of things-in-themselves seems to have been based mainly on the fact that we are partly passive in perception.</u> The form in what we perceive is due to the transcendental self, but what we perceive is not merely an empty form. Besides form there is content, and since he had no reason to think that this content was due either to our own or to any other mind Kant could not do anything but leave its source [2] an unknown x. He could not identify this source with God as Berkeley had done : that would have been 'dogmatic idealism'. But he was as convinced as Berkeley or as any realist of its existence, and was convinced also that it could not be in space or time and could not possess any of the ordinary perceptible qualities. All he could do was to describe it as unknowable. He did not thereby exclude the possibility that it might really be of the nature of mind or be in some sense

[1] This argument may seem merely a verbal quibble, but probably what Kant meant was that the appearances presented to us are of such a character as intrinsically to point beyond themselves to a reality which appears.

[2] He should in consistency have only asserted the thing-in-itself as a possibility on that ground, since he had not proved the categories to be true of reality and therefore could not know that the content must have any source at all, for a source is a cause.

created and completely controlled by a divine mind ; on the contrary this was his own belief, based on ' practical reason '. All he said was that we must not *qua* theorisers assert this, though we may believe it *qua* moral agents. He does not even say expressly that the source of experience could not lie wholly in human minds, but only that, since we do not know its nature, we must not make any positive assertions about it. As a matter of fact, however, he was far too much impressed by our passivity in experience and by the presence of the given element in knowledge seriously to think of this as a possibility. Combination is *the only* element which is said to come from understanding [1] not from sensibility, and sensibility is always regarded as consisting in the mere passive reception of impressions.

The doctrine of things-in-themselves thus appeared to Kant not as an ungrounded superstition but as a reasonable form of agnosticism : after limiting knowledge in the way in which he had done Kant would have had no right to deny things-in-themselves, for that would have been to lay down a ' dogmatic ' theory of the universe as entirely constituted by selves and their representations. To omit this unknown x would have been more dogmatic than to assert it, for this would have been to declare that the whole of reality was mental, which he had not proved and could not on his own principles hope ever would be proved. It might more reasonably be objected, however, that Kant would have done better if he had admitted it only as a possibility, a solution towards which he seems to incline sometimes but which he never definitely adopts. He does succeed in showing that we must think things-in-themselves as a limiting conception, but that we have to think something outside the world of experience ought not, according to Kant's own philosophy, to be regarded as a proof that this something exists, and he has at any rate only succeeded in showing that we must think it as a possibility. To admit any limitation to our experience is to *think* things-in-themselves which are not completely revealed by our experience, but it is not so easy to see how he could consistently with his other views prove their actual existence. It may be objected that, even if it is not going beyond the world of experience to assert that it may not be everything, it surely is going beyond it to assert definitely that it is not everything, i.e. that there really is something else.

[1] *Critique of Pure Reason*, B, 129–30.

Kant's answer to this criticism might be that in his doctrine of the antinomies he had shown that it was self-contradictory to regard the phenomenal world as real, because in that case we should have to regard it as either finite or infinite in space and time, and it could be neither. And even if we do not hold him to have succeeded in showing this, it may still be urged that we have certain standards as to reality to which the world of appearances does not conform, though it is not self-contradictory in the strict sense of formal logic. It is not coherent or intelligible, it seems to carry incompleteness on the face of it, it is lacking in real substantiality, owing to the infinite regress it is never given as a whole, it has no reason in itself for anything which happens within it since phenomenal causality is on Kant's view merely necessary succession, and it gives no opportunity for freedom which is yet an indispensable postulate of ethics, at least so Kant would add. Kant's 'ideas of reason' are not fully realised or realisable in it, and therefore, if it be real and all the real, we are in the position of being inevitably by the very nature of our reason led to form conceptions which are as standards essential to success in science and yet quite false. It satisfies neither the intellectual nor the ethical nor the religious consciousness, and as agents and knowers we are profoundly aware that we are more than appearances and must act as beings who altogether transcend the phenomenal world. All this may well be regarded as an adequate argument to show that the phenomenal world is not everything; and once this conclusion is established we must either assert that reality consists entirely of minds, or distinguish between the minds that we know to fall within it and the rest of reality, which we can only describe as consisting of unknown things-in-themselves since we have no right to imply that it is either physical or mental.

Only this argument is hardly reconcilable with the absolute unknowableness of reality, for the condemnation by it of the phenomenal world as unreal implies that what is real must have a certain character [1] which the phenomenal world has not. If we say of A that it cannot be real because it has not the quality *b*, we imply that we know or are justified in asserting that what is real has the quality *b*. In any case, however, the unknowableness of the thing-in-itself cannot be maintained in a strict sense, because, if we know even only how it appears to us or what experiences it helps to produce in us, we know at

[1] If only the character of self-consistency.

least some of its relational characteristics. And we might still reasonably maintain that our thought of the thing-in-itself was purely formal and empty of content. That all this was not considered by Kant incompatible with his view that the thing-in-itself was unknowable is shown by his application of the categories to the latter.[1] He has also the valuable and suggestive doctrine of 'Ideas of Reason'[2] to help him out. The term, thing-in-itself, is perhaps unfortunate as it suggests that a real thing must have a nature of its own which has no connection whatever with other things, but this is an objection rather to the phraseology than to the substance of Kant's contention.

Kant's view of the real self is more difficult to defend against the charge of inconsistency. For, firstly, his admission that there is a real self at all is much harder to reconcile with his agnosticism than is the admission of the thing-in-itself, since to say that there is a self is to say that there is something the generic character of which is known by us. Secondly, as we have seen,[3] his doctrine of the synthesis makes the inconsistency worse, for it implies considerable knowledge of the relation between the real self and appearances. Thirdly, definite knowledge of this relation is claimed implicitly in the whole of Kant's epistemology, even apart from the specific account of the synthesis, since he throughout presupposes the knowledge that the self makes phenomena. Fourthly, the assumption that he knows of the existence of other real selves besides himself is impossible to reconcile with his agnosticism about reality. If he can only know appearances, he is involved in solipsism.

Further, we have seen that Kant's view that time is unreal and that we do not perceive even our own real self in introspection involves great difficulties. And, in general, our knowledge cannot be limited to appearances to the exclusion of the real, because, if they are anything at all, appearances are themselves part of the real.

§ VI. Kant's Chief Contributions to the Idealist Movement

It may seem that I have done little but criticise Kant in this chapter and have shown no sign of appreciating his

[1] V. above, p. 103 ff.   [2] V. below, p. 114 ff.
[3] V. above, p. 82.

greatness, but I shall now proceed to give a summary of those points where in my opinion he has made specially valuable contributions towards the development of a distinctively idealist philosophy and towards the solution of any of the problems which we are discussing.

(1) Recognising the importance of the distinction between analytic and synthetic judgments, and the impossibility of identifying the *a priori* and the analytic, which had usually been confused, he failed indeed to *explain* the possibility of synthetic judgments by his theory of intuition, but developed a far more fruitful conception of the *a priori* than any which had gone before. He showed that *a priori* categories were involved in all judgment but that they could not be divorced from experience, and he connected them with the fact that to think at all we must order and organise what is given in experience. Even if Kant's particular categories are, in the form in which he stated and proved them, not finally valid, he proved that there must be some *a priori* categories in the only sense in which such a principle could be proved.

(2) Kant laid the foundations of the coherence theory of knowledge. For this theory is implicit in his doctrine that all knowledge or judgment involves systematisation, though it was developed much further by his successors. As applied to the physical world and also to the appearance-self, the doctrine if accepted carries with it a proof of universal causality.

(3) While establishing self-identity in the only sense in which it can be established by theoretical argument, he showed that this identity was unthinkable apart from the unity of objects known. In this connection he developed the idealist doctrine that subject and object are inseparable correlatives without falling into a one-sided mentalism, as have done e.g. the Italian Neo-Idealists.

(4) While it may be hard to defend the doctrine of the synthesis as an account of the origin of the phenomenal world, it at least emphasised the rôle played in cognition by an active mental combining and thus initiated an influence that has been of great importance in modern thought. We can trace it in an exaggerated form in Pragmatism and in Italian Neo-Idealism, but it also occurs e.g. in most modern non-behaviouristic psychologies of perception.[1] The realist

---

[1] The general doctrine of mental construction in cognition is discussed above (ch. II, sect. 2).

may deny hotly the proposition that the objects we know are constructed by a synthesis, but he cannot deny the part that some kind of synthesis plays in the psychology of cognition and perception. Though it does not construct its objects, it is at least necessary if we are to know them. The realist must admit that we can make no judgments about the merely given as such without any conceptual handling and any fitting together with the results of previous experience, square this with realism how he may. All perception of physical objects involves a synthesis in the sense of 'recalling and holding before the mind a number of data successively and separately presented and then recognising that they form a whole of a certain kind',[1] and the same applies, I think, to all cognitions.

(5) Kant recognised clearly that, if idealism is to stand, it must be reconcilable with physical science and must therefore reinterpret in terms of experience the distinction between illusion and genuine perception. He saw further that the minimum condition without which the reinterpretation cannot be effected is the admission of causal laws, physical objects being conceived as at least systems of experiences connected by causal laws.

(6) Though an idealist, Kant put forward what are really two strong arguments in favour of realism: (i) that our experience can only be brought into even the minimum order necessary for judgment by the use of the conception of physical objects; (ii) that self-consciousness, whether transcendental or empirical, presupposes consciousness of objects.[2] For the transcendental unity of apperception can only be realised in unifying objects, and empirical awareness of the appearance-self (introspection) presupposes awareness of physical objects. But this is held by him, rightly or wrongly, only to justify a realism within idealism, though the relative independence and objectivity of the physical world is strongly asserted.

(7) The double view of the self as knower and object known, though generally rejected in the form in which Kant stated

[1] Price, *Perception*, p. 286.
[2] I.e. for us physical objects, though this does not rule out the bare possibility that some non-human selves or we ourselves after physical death might have to deal with objects of such a different kind that they could not be described as physical. We have no right to limit the possibilities as to what the object might be, only to say that a self is to us inconceivable without objects.

it, is in some form a necessary corollary of any idealism which neither treats knowing as merely one event among others nor agrees with Berkeley in confining the creative side of knowing to a transcendent God. From one point of view the self is to be treated as any object of science; from another it is that for which in a sense all objects and all science exist. Granted the premises, we must, on the one hand, regard the self as a legitimate object of scientific study and must examine it frankly and fearlessly, not hesitating to explain by causal laws everything that can be so explained; but, on the other hand, we must recognise that there is another aspect of the self, namely, its aspect as knower and agent, and that this aspect in a sense transcends the physical world and the temporal process altogether, since otherwise the self could not know what occurs at different times and places. In this way idealism at once left psychology free to advance unencumbered by metaphysical presuppositions, and also safeguarded against naturalism what it held to be the spiritual interests of man. This does not prove its truth, but it was based on arguments which, though they win far less ready assent to-day, certainly cannot be dismissed lightly or adequately regarded as merely superficial fallacies due to a confusion between knowing and object known; and though it need not be accepted it must not be despised by a realist till he has worked out a more adequate and more coherent philosophy of mind than his opponents. But, as far as Kant is concerned, those who condemn such views as too dogmatic should remember that he protested in the strongest terms against any definite assertion as to the ultimate nature of the self or the spiritual character of reality. The knowing self to Kant can only be known in its effects, i.e. knowledge, not in its intrinsic nature.

(8) The conception of regulative principles (Ideas of Reason) is of the greatest value as helping us, more than any other logical distinction yet made can, to tread the precarious middle path between dogmatism and scepticism. Kant saw that science presupposes certain standards but he did not assert these to be established facts about reality or even about appearances, except in so far as they were the minimum condition without which we could have no knowledge at all (in which case he called them categories or concepts of understanding as opposed to ideas of reason). Neither did he dismiss them as ungrounded; he recognised their value as ideals

which might be progressively realised and at the worst can serve as a stimulus and guide for research. We must not say that the world is ultimately a thorough-going system, but we can hope that it will prove progressively more and more to be so, and we can act on the assumption that our knowledge can always be made more of a system than it is already, provided we let this serve as an encouragement for detailed research and not as a substitute or sedative. We have ideas rooted in our mind of intelligibility, system and unity which go further than anything that can be presented in our experience, and these give us a not irrational hope that they may be fulfilled in some fashion, if not in the world of experience, at any rate in a reality behind experience. We cannot prove them or turn them into definite concepts, we must not treat them as metaphysical or scientific dogmas, but they have been of supreme value to science by providing it with an ideal and a policy.

Somewhat different is Kant's treatment of those 'ideas of reason' which he regarded as essential for religion or for a philosophical ethics. These—God, freedom and immortality —Kant means not merely to hold out as hopes but definitely to assert as realities. He does not, like the '*Als Ob*' school, hold merely that we must act as if there were a God though there may be no God, nor does he mean that propositions about God are valid only as expressing our practical or our emotional attitude towards reality and not as asserting objective facts. It is on the contrary quite certain that Kant believed in God, freedom and immortality. The idea of God is for him regulative, as opposed to constitutive, only because it is not logically or scientifically provable and is not a definite, clearly intelligible concept capable of being employed in a way that will give it concrete empirical content,[1] but it is still for him an object of justifiable subjectively certain belief. Kant's protest was mainly against the attempt to employ it in order to remove scientific and metaphysical difficulties and against the assumption that it had the same kind of logical status as a scientific concept, which must be precise, clear-cut and usable in dealing with empirical data ; and the same applies to freedom and immortality. His account of the right philosophical attitude towards the fundamental concepts of religion is masterly and holds the balance admirably between the sceptic and the unreasonable dogmatist.

[1] What content it has is supplied by ethics.

Historically its effects have been very great, but few who have been influenced by it have succeeded so well in hitting the middle path, for his doctrine is liable to grave abuses both by those who make use of his theoretical agnosticism to bolster up irrational and unfounded views and those who reduce religious beliefs to mere fictions and yet think they can preserve their value for life and practice.*

CHAPTER IV
THE THEORY OF INTERNAL RELATIONS

§ I. An Analysis of 'Internal' and 'External'[1]

THE doctrine that all relations [2] are 'internal' is commonly held to entail two very important consequences. In the first place the doctrine is usually thought both by advocates and opponents to lead to some form of epistemological idealism. For if all relations are 'internal' the relation between cognition and its object will share this character, and it would seem to many to follow that the object cognised is made or changed by our cognition of it. The fallacy involved in this argument I have pointed out elsewhere,[3] though no doubt the internal relations view in some of its interpretations would entail a much closer unity between the two than would be admitted by a realist.

There is, however, another very important consequence

---

[1] My conclusions from the long and complicated argument of this section are given on pp. 136–7.

[2] It may be asked whether I regard relations as holding between substances, or between qualities or states of substances. The answer is—'sometimes one way, sometimes the other'. Substances are related to each other, and so are qualities and states of different substances or of the same substance. Further, any relation between states or qualities of two substances entails a relation between the substances, i.e. the relation of having states or qualities related in this way. This explains why e.g. causality and similarity are treated sometimes as relations between things and sometimes as relations between qualities or states of things. We say alike—this coat is similar to that (in some unspecified qualities), and the colour of the two coats is similar, or the two coats are in a similar state of disrepair, and again we speak sometimes of things and sometimes of events or qualities as the cause of a given effect in a thing. 'A causes B' implies 'A has states or qualities connected with B by the relation of causality', but to have states or qualities related in this way itself constitutes a real relation between A and B. 'A is similar to B' is equivalent to 'A has some characteristic similar to or identical with a characteristic of B'.

[3] Ch. II, sect. 4.

which, I think, really would follow from the doctrine in question, in the sense in which that doctrine is usually held, and would involve a totally different view of reality from any that could be established on another view of relations. For if it is true that all relations are internal in the sense usually given to the term by those who maintain the so-called theory of internal relations, it would seem to follow and, I think, really would follow that reality is a unity of a type something like that postulated by the coherence theory, and we are near to Bradley's conclusion that we could know no one thing fully without knowing everything else also.

But this is talking vaguely; as usual in controversy, the terms round which the dispute centres are used in several different senses, and it is necessary to distinguish these before we can proceed with the discussion. I wish myself—and I am quite certain any readers will before long wish far more strongly still—that we could have been spared this labour, but there is no doubt that the expression, internal relations, has in the course of the controversy been used in each of the different senses to be distinguished here, and I think that the idealist theory of relations has gone astray through failing to make the distinctions in question. I am most painfully aware that this section will in consequence be very complicated, but for this a large share at least of the blame must be borne by those who have used the words so ambiguously.

Now, etymologically, ' internal relations ' should mean ' relations between elements within a given whole ', and ' external relations ' should mean ' relations between that whole (or elements in that whole) and something outside the whole '. (By ' outside ' I mean not ' spatially outside ' but ' other than and not included in, whether partially or wholly '.) But this is clearly not what is meant by the distinction in the form in which it has become a subject of controversy, though some writers on the subject may have been influenced by this sense of the words. To maintain in this sense that all relations are internal would obviously be sheer nonsense unless the whole in question was everything that is, in which case it would be a tautology. No doubt particular relations may be described as internal or external in this sense relatively to a particular whole, but we can leave the sense aside for our purpose. We shall find quite enough different meanings of the terms which have been the centre of controversy without introducing a single one beyond what is absolutely necessary.

In the <u>first</u> place it is sometimes said that <u>all relations are internal in the sense that they all ' fall within the nature of the related terms '</u>. This definition, while etymologically more justifiable than most, involves many ambiguities and confusions. If we mean by the nature of a thing its full nature and do not include only its essential characteristics, this may be interpreted as including everything which is predicable of it and so all its relational characteristics without exception, however unimportant they may seem.[1] We may then say that any relation falls within the nature of both or all the terms that it relates, if by this is meant simply that, whenever r relates A to B, A has the characteristic of standing in the relation r to B and B has the characteristic of standing in the converse relation to A; but this will not carry us very far. It is an important fact about relations that no instance of a relation can occur as a self-subsistent entity, but only in conjunction with terms which possess the characteristic of standing in that relation; but <u>if by ' nature ' be meant essential nature it does not follow, at least without further argument, that relations fall within the nature of either or both</u>[2] <u>related terms. Further, it is not, strictly speaking, the relation which falls within their nature, even in the extended sense of ' nature ', but the characteristic of standing in the relation.</u> It is not true that ' between ' or ' alongside of ' is predicable of me, but only the relational characteristic of being between the table and the door or alongside of the table.

And, if the use of the terms ' nature ' and ' relation ' is misleading and ambiguous, so is the use of the spatial metaphor of ' within ' and ' without '. Spatial metaphors may indeed sometimes provide the least inconvenient way of refer-

[1] Mr. Bertrand Russell exaggeratedly says: ' The whole point of view ' (of the Hegelians) ' turns upon the notion of " the nature of the thing " which seems ' (i.e. according to the latter) ' to mean " all the truths about the thing "' (*Problems of Philosophy*, p. 224). Dr. McTaggart uses ' nature ' to mean all the qualities of a thing (*The Nature of Existence*, vol. I, p. 64), including the ' qualities ' of standing in the various relations in which it stands (id., p. 116). The latter are what I have called ' relational characteristics '.

[2] For the sake of convenience I have sometimes spoken as if all relations were dyadic, but my statements could easily be expanded so as to cover relations with more than two terms. Nor do I necessarily rule out the possibility of a term standing in some relation to itself

ring to non-spatial facts, but the present one is disqualified for this purpose by two serious faults. In the first place it suggests that a relation stands to each of its terms as part to whole, which is certainly not the case. A relation could not connect its terms, could not do its work of relating if it were not something more than part of either or severally of all its terms. If the difficulty is met by saying that it is not the relation but the characteristic of standing in the relation which falls within the nature of each term, we have still committed the error of confusing a characteristic [1] and a part. When we say that A stands in the relation *r* to B, we do not mean that 'standing in the relation *r* to B' is part of A. A characteristic of X is predicable of X, but of a whole we cannot predicate its parts, only the characteristic of having these parts.

Further, while X cannot be within A in the spatial sense without being wholly within and cannot be both within and without A, the fact that a relation 'falls within' A in the sense given does not imply that its whole nature is included in A. This description ignores the external reference which is the most essential feature of a relation, and this being so it is not even clear that in the sense in question a relation cannot be both internal and external. Even if we are speaking not of relations but of relational characteristics, it seems obvious that the whole nature of a relational characteristic is not exhausted when we have described it as characterising the term to which it belongs. For its reference to another term is also essential to it, otherwise it would not be a *relational* characteristic at all. Nor is any metaphor necessary here. To say that a relation falls within the nature of a thing is only true if it means no more than that the thing stands in that relation to something, and if this is all that is meant it is better to say so.[2]

[1] I call a characteristic of X whatever can be predicated of X, thus including under this heading both non-relational qualities and the property of standing in any specific relation, i.e. all 'relational properties'. Both classes of characteristics are in an important sense attributes of the term and so in a sense qualify it; but it is perhaps best to avoid the words, attribute and property, in this connection because of their logical and metaphysical associations, and to confine 'quality' to non-relational characteristics. (I am not using 'characterise' in Mr. Johnson's sense, in which it is opposed to 'inherence'.

[2] Under this heading comes Bradley's definition of 'internally related' as meaning that 'the element itself, and not merely something else, is qualified' by the relation (*Logic*, I, p. 127 note 14, added

The second meaning of 'internal relation' is 'a relation essential to its terms'. This sense can easily be derived from the first if we interpret 'the nature of a thing' more strictly so as to exclude all characteristics which seem superficial. The theory of 'internal relations' is consequently often criticised on the ground that, so far from all relations being essential to their terms, some relations in which a thing stands are quite unimportant to it.[1] One of the causes which have hindered the acceptance of the theory as usually understood and of the allied coherence theory has been the erroneous supposition that an advocate of such views was bound to maintain that all relations are essential to their terms, a proposition which, when applied to the relation between any particular human being and a meteor fifty million miles away or a mammoth in the Ice Ages, seemed utterly absurd. Even if everything is related to everything else, all science depends on making a distinction between the relations which are important [2] and significant and those which

in 2nd edition). That 'a relation must (at least to some extent) qualify its terms' is used by him as an argument against external relations, but he does not show how it follows from this that a relation cannot be external in the other senses of the term, for this is clearly not all that he means by external. E.g. he gives also the quite different definition of 'external' as 'making no difference to its terms.' Nor is the word 'qualify' at all appropriate. For (a) it ignores the distinction between qualities, which alone qualify, and relations, and suggests, quite inconsistently with Bradley's real intentions, that he means to reduce all relations to qualities; and (b) it confuses a relation with the characteristic of standing in that relation. Professor Joachim also asserts as an essential part of the doctrine of internal relations that a relation 'qualifies its terms' (*The Nature of Truth*, p. 11).

[1] It has been objected to my treatment that 'important' is not the natural meaning of 'essential'. It is clear, however, that one sense of 'essential' has reference to the distinction between essence and accident, and since both on my own view and on that of the idealist philosophers whose doctrine of relations I am discussing this distinction can in the case of concrete objects only be regarded as one either of degree or of convention, it resolves itself into the distinction between the more and the less important. Further, even if essential is not the same as important, it is clear that to show that a relation makes no appreciable difference to a thing is to show that it does not belong to the essence of the thing in the sense in which essence is contrasted with accident. Even if what is important is not necessarily essential in this sense, certainly what is unimportant cannot be. Another sense in which relations may be held to be essential to their terms I shall discuss later.

[2] Usually this means causally important. We call something important usually either because it produces effects which are very

are quite unimportant and superficial, and since most relations of a thing could be altered without changing the thing much it seems that most relations of a thing fall into the latter class. It seems clear also that this is often so with the relation between cognition and its object; in the case of most of the things I know it is a very unimportant fact for the thing known that it happens to be known by me, and sometimes at least it is a very unimportant fact for me that I happen to know it. This is true, but to dismiss the arguments of any considerable idealist philosopher about relations simply on these grounds is unfair; <u>we cannot say that the idealists denied that some relations are unimportant to their terms, but at the most that they did not sufficiently emphasise this fact in their exposition.</u> This was partly because it is impossible to draw a hard and fast line between relations which are important and relations which are unimportant. But the same applies to most distinctions: it holds of the qualities of a thing, for instance, as well as of its relations. But, while the coherence theory asserts that everything is relevant to everything else, it does not deny the different degrees of relevance without which science would be impossible. However the term 'essential' may be used without reference to the distinction between essence and accident and may imply not that the relation is very important in the ordinary sense but only that the terms related could not be the same if the relation were absent, and this is undoubtedly involved in the internal relations view as usually held; but it is better to express this interpretation of the view more clearly under a later heading.

<u>Thirdly</u>, some forms of the internal relations view commit the definite error of <u>implicitly reducing relations to qualities.</u> This is involved in the logical doctrine that all propositions are of the subject-predicate form, and in the theory that

numerous and extensive in range or because it produces effects to which we attribute great value, positive or negative. It is impossible precisely to define the distinction between important and unimportant any more than the distinction between great and small, but differences in degree of importance are still real, as are differences in degree of size. Again (and here the parallel with size breaks down) what is more important in one respect e.g. economically may be less important in another e.g. culturally, but that does not prevent the one being really more and the other really less important in each respect. At any rate, if some relations are not objectively more important than others, in respect at least of the difference they make to a given process, there is an end of physical science or reasonable practical action.

the subject includes all its predicates analytically, from which Leibniz deduced the non-interaction of the monads. It is all too easy to interpret the phrase 'within the nature of' in a sense which will have this effect, and to be misled by the fact that a proposition asserting a relation can be put in the verbal form 'A is related to B by relation r' or 'A has the quality of being related to B by relation r' into treating relations as if they were really simply qualities. Such a view carelessly obliterates or ignores one of the most fundamental distinctions of philosophy, and <u>at once leads to a vicious infinite regress, for we need other relations to relate the qualities</u>, and these relations being still really qualities need others *ad infinitum*. If relations are reduced to qualities they will not do their distinctive work of relating. Mr. Bertrand Russell said in 1924 that he meant by the doctrine of external relations

'primarily this, that a relational proposition is not, in general, logically equivalent formally to one or more subject-predicate propositions. Stated more precisely: Given a relational propositional function "x R y", it is not in general the case that we can find predicates α, β, γ such that, for all values of x and y, x R y is equivalent to $x\alpha$, $y\beta$, $(x,y)\gamma$ [1] (where (x,y) stands for the whole consisting of x and y) or to any one or two of these. This, and this only, is what I mean to affirm when I assert the doctrine of external relations, and this clearly is at least part of what Mr. Bradley denies when he asserts the doctrine of internal relations.' [2]

I am inclined to agree with the doctrine of external relations thus interpreted, but do not think that this is what is usually meant by it. In particular I must dissent from Mr. Russell's interpretation of Bradley, who, so far from reducing relations to qualities, makes it an essential part of his argument for the merely phenomenal character of all the objects of our thought that they cannot be thus reduced and that 'qualities are nothing without relations'.[3] It is true that Bradley regards relations as unreal, but he puts qualities in the same position.[4] Likewise Bosanquet says in so many words that 'relations cannot be reduced to qualities, nor qualities to relations'.[5] Leibniz, who did commit the error

[1] I assume that α, β, γ stand for any *non-relational* characteristics.
[2] *Contemporary British Philosophy, First Series*, p. 371 ff.
[3] *Appearance and Reality*, p. 26 ff.
[4] V. *Appearance and Reality*, pp. 20–1.
[5] *Logic*, 2nd ed., p. 279.

in question, was not a member of the school of philosophers usually associated with the theory of 'internal relations'. But in any case we shall do well to dismiss as quite untenable the view that all relations are internal in the third sense as in the second sense of the term, while voicing a strong doubt whether it is fair to accuse leading idealists of having held that all relations are internal in either of these senses.

Fourthly, the internal view of relations may be taken as simply asserting the fact that relations involve some kind of genuine unity between their terms. As Professor Laird says,[1]

'Ultimately the question is whether a relation between things can describe a genuine connection or unity between the things. If it can, there is no mystery; for the fact, *ex hypothesi*, is intelligible. If it cannot, such relations do not relate and are unintelligible if they pretend to do what they cannot do.'

Many idealist philosophers have, however, shown the tendency to leap at once from this mere assertion of some unity to the view that everything is bound up in a unity of a particularly close and intimate nature with everything else. But, because there is some connection between two related things, we must not therefore jump to the conclusion that they are as much a unity as are different states or ideas of the same mind or different qualities of the same thing. A fallacy of this type seems to me to form part of the basis of Spinoza's monism. He assumes that, because, if we define substance as something absolutely independent, there cannot be more than one substance in the world, therefore every particular thing is a mode of the same substance in a sense which gives it a merely adjectival being. But it does not follow because things are related e.g. causally that therefore they are related as closely as are different characteristics of the same substance. He and his followers have not shown that there is no middle term between no relation at all and such a close relation as that, nor refuted the common-sense view that there is a distinction between the relation which holds between different things and that which holds between different qualities of the same thing, so that the world may consist of a number of different things which are causally related but have not the intimate relation that constitutes one substance in the more usual sense of the term. Because things are causally related to each other and therefore are not separate

[1] *Knowledge, Belief and Opinion*, p. 214.

substances in the sense of being absolutely independent, it does not necessarily follow that they are mere qualities; it does not necessarily follow, as many Hegelians have held, that, because human minds depend on each other in many ways, they all constitute one single Mind.[1] When we have said that a relation entails the unity of the related terms we have said very little, for if we are asked what the degree and nature of that unity is we can only answer that it is just the kind of unity which consists in being united by that specific relation. When we have given the relation, we have already defined the unity which it involves. This may be very slight, as when the relation is mere coexistence at the same time, or very close as when it is compresence as a part of the same state of consciousness. To speak of the unity involved in all relation is of little value except as a warning against the more extreme pluralists who sometimes talk as if there were hardly any connection or unity in the universe at all, but, since everything in the physical universe is related in some way (if only by the relation of spatial distance) to everything else, relation is compatible with a high degree of separateness, unless some specific proof can be given to show that the world is really much more of a unity than it appears to be.

Professor Laird also criticises strongly a certain interpretation of the internal relations view, which we may take as our *fifth* sense.

'It is possible to assert with some confidence', he says, 'that if A has some relation *r* to B, it is not only logically conceivable that A and B retain their characters unmodified in the relation; but it is logically inconceivable that they should not do so. Relations hold *between* terms, and form or express a tie *between those very terms*. Thus, in the propositions "3 is greater than 2" and "3 is greater than 1", one and the same 3 occurs in both propositions, not a 3 modified by its relation to 2 in the first instance and a different 3 modified by its relation to 1 in the second instance. Either the whole relational way of regarding things is mythopoeic, or this identity of terms must be preserved.'[2]

Clearly he is right in holding that no tolerable view of relations can be incompatible with the fact that the same term may stand in different relations, and he is also, as I

[1] Cf. also Lotze's argument from causal connection to monism.
[2] *Knowledge, Belief and Opinion*, pp. 78–9; cf. also Cook Wilson, *Statement and Inference*, vol. I, p. 71 ff.

contend elsewhere,[1] right in holding that it cannot be true that all relations alter or modify their terms, if by this is meant that they cause a change in their terms. If A and B are to stand in a relation at all they must first have a certain character of their own, and this character is not made by the relation in question. Relations, we may say then, are all external in the sense that any relation presupposes a certain character in the terms related which is itself not due to and not modified or constituted by the relation in question. But for all that it might still well be the case that the relation was internal in the different senses, discussed later, that its character followed from the character of the terms, and that the terms could not be the same if the relation were different. The nature of the number, five, is not modified or constituted by the fact that it is the cube root of 125, for the points made by Professor Laird clearly apply in this case, yet that they stand in the relation in question follows from the nature of the terms, and five could not be what it is without being the cube root of 125. Professor Laird seems to me therefore wrong in concluding from the argument I have quoted taken alone (and he cites no other argument) that:

'It follows that, in so far as some known object O stands in the relation of being known to an ego E, it cannot be logically inferred that O is therefore different from what it would be if it were quite alone, or from what it would be if related to something that is not an ego at all.'[2]

I think the proposition is true, but to maintain that it follows from the argument given involves a confusion between two senses of 'internal relation'.

Sixthly, Bosanquet defines internal relations as '<u>relations grounded in the nature of the related terms</u>'.[3] By this must presumably be meant that their presence depends[4] on and is determined, *either causally or logically*, by characteristics of their terms. <u>This is undoubtedly true of some relations, e.g. the mathematical relations, also similarity and difference.</u> That

---

[1] Ch. II, sect. 4. [2] Id., p. 79.
[3] *Logic*, p. 277 ff., 2nd end.; cf. Taylor, *Elements of Metaphysics*, p. 141.
[4] A may be said to depend on B wholly when A could not occur without B and follows necessarily from B alone, and to depend on B partly when the presence of B is a necessary though not a sufficient condition of the presence of A.

7 is half of 14 or that something blue differs in colour from something red can undoubtedly be deduced from the intrinsic nature of the terms. But on the other hand the relation of physical contiguity between Professor Stout's *Manual* and Professor Ward's *Psychological Principles* in my bookshelf obviously does not follow from the nature of the books thus related, since an external agent, myself, placed them together and might equally well have put other books side by side instead. But even here we cannot say that the intrinsic nature of the books had nothing to do with the relation. They certainly would not have been put together on my bookshelf if they had not both been books, and, if we may include in their intrinsic nature not only their physical form but also their subject-matter, the fact that they are both psychology books is not irrelevant, for I make a habit of putting on the same shelves books dealing with similar subjects.[1] The occurrence of this relation is therefore partly due to their intrinsic nature, but not *wholly* due to this, both because my intervention as an external agent was required and because the general rule I have mentioned does not fix which particular psychology books I put side by side, so that the *Manual* might, as far as this is concerned, have equally well been neighbour to any of the other books on the subject I possess. This illustration shows how even a relation of a very 'arbitrary' kind may be and commonly is due partly to the nature of the related terms. Mere juxtaposition and distance in space are usually taken as the best examples of purely 'external' relations, yet even these depend partly on the character of the objects related. For whatever is thus related must at least be spatial itself and have an intrinsic nature compatible with that, and again it must be intrinsi-

[1] Here what dependence and determination there is is causal not logical (though it is never a relation but only its occurrence at a given time and place which can be said to be caused), but the idealists to whom we are referring are thinking of relations as 'grounded' in a very wide sense which covers both causal and logical grounding. Different as logical and causal necessity may be, it does seem clear that they have something in common which may be expressed by the words follow from, depend, determine, and that it is an important fact about relations that they are grounded in their terms in this sense. In all cases the nature of the terms is *relevant* to the relations in which they stand to each other. Anyhow the view we are discussing cannot be stated unless we are allowed to use 'dependence' and 'determination' in this wider sense. The relation between causal and logical necessity will be considered later.

cally of such a nature that it reacts upon the causes which have operated on it in such a way as to lead to, or at least be compatible with, its occupying the position it now does. For instance, the articles I mentioned above would not have occupied the position they now do if they had been too heavy for me to lift them, or liquid, or for any reason incapable of standing on a bookshelf. We can indeed go to the length of saying that <u>in all cases where terms stand in a relation this circumstance is partly dependent on and due to the nature of the terms in question</u>. The only alternative would be to hold either that the presence of some relations is altogether independent of anything else in the universe, including their own terms,[1] or that in some cases a third term C could produce a relation between A and B absolutely irrespective of the nature of A and B, which is impossible since the nature of A and B must at any rate be such as to be amenable to C's causal influence. <u>For a relation to occur at all a necessary, though not always a sufficient, condition of its occurrence must be found in the nature of its terms.</u> The qualities of a term are *relevant* to the relations in which it can stand.

In the first place a relation, if it is to be a relation at all, must unite some terms. Secondly, <u>most, if not all, kinds of relation presuppose a specific common character, usually or always of the type called by Mr. Johnson a determinable, in the related terms, without which the assertion of the specific relation would be not merely false but absurd</u> in the way in which the questions—is virtue yellow? or is the British Constitution a triangle?—are absurd to anybody who knows in the barest outline what the words mean. Spatial relations presuppose in this way the common determinable of extension, arithmetical relations the common determinable of number, the relation of similarity presupposes some common determinable in the determinate value of which the objects are said to be similar, the relations of enmity or love the common determinable of emotional capacity, the relation of causality [2] the common character of being events or con-

[1] Bradley argues that, if they were external, relations would have to be thinkable apart from any terms at all (*Essays on Truth and Reality*, pp. 238, 291).

[2] As commonly understood There may be other senses of ' causality ' in which it may connect terms one or more of which are not events or continuants in time, but that relation, if it occurs, is a different relation from the causality known to us, though analogous

tinuants in time, and perhaps membership in some specific causal system.

Further, not only do most or all relations presuppose a common determinable, but also the number and kind of relations into which anything can enter under given circumstances are at least very much limited by the determinate values of the determinables which qualify it at the time. I cannot indeed, whenever A stands in a given spatial relation to B, say that it could not have stood in that relation if its shape or weight had been different (e.g. if Ward's *Principles of Psychology* had been an ounce heavier than it is, that presumably would have made no difference to its place on my bookshelf next to Stout's *Manual*), but I can say that its shape and weight as causal conditions are most important factors in determining the spatial relations into which a thing enters. For a book to stand in my bookshelf at all its weight and size must fall within certain relatively narrow limits, and in the natural world apart from human control the positions and so the spatial relations of things seem to be determined causally mainly by the determinate values of a few determinables ('primary' qualities) which characterise the things related. Only, while we may say of a relation that its presence logically presupposes a certain determinable, we cannot say that it logically presupposes but only that it is causally determined partly by the determinate value of that determinable. This is an important distinction often slurred over too readily by idealists.

In the case of the cognitive relation it is difficult to find a determinable common to both terms which is logically presupposed by the relation, but it is still quite clear that the determinate characteristics of the terms play a large part in causally determining whether and when a given mind enters into that relation with something. Which facts I come to know is a circumstance that depends partly on the specific nature of the facts, partly on my interests and my capacity and so on my psychology. It is also clear that the cognitive relation always logically presupposes in *one* of its terms certain determinables, namely, those which are involved in being a mind.

But if we use 'determine' in a wide sense to cover both logical and causal determination, we may say that the occur-

to it. A theologian would not regard God as cause of the world in quite the same sense as one phenomenal event is regarded as cause of another.

rence of a relation is always at least partly determined by the intrinsic nature of its terms, though it is, as I have said, important to note that we can only maintain this if we include under 'determining' both the case where B is *a priori* deducible from A and the case where A is part-cause of B. With the same qualification we may say that it 'partly depends' on qualities in its terms in the sense of 'partly depend' which was defined above,[1] where I said that A might be described as depending partly on B 'when the presence of B is a necessary though not a sufficient condition of the presence of A'. In this sense it is obvious that any relation depends on qualities in its terms. It could not be present at all if its terms were not characterised by a certain determinable and if their determinate qualities within this and other subordinate determinables did not fall within certain limits, and in cases where the entry of two terms into a relation is causally conditioned some qualities of the terms always form a necessary part of its causal conditions. For A and B cannot be causally determined to enter into the relation *r* unless the nature of A and B is such that the external causes which determine them produce just these effects and none of the infinite number of other alternative effects which are logically conceivable. So far from relations being independent of their terms the qualities of their terms are most relevant to the occurrence of the relations.

Seventhly, an internal relation is often described as a relation which 'makes a difference to' its terms.[2] It might be thought that 'make a difference' meant 'cause a change in', but it is perfectly obvious that everything cannot be related in this way. I suppose, however, that what is meant is not that the relation *causes* a difference but that the terms would necessarily have been different from what they are if they had not been thus related. This formula cannot be

[1] p. 126 n. 3.
[2] E.g. Professor Taylor (*Elements of Metaphysics*, p. 147) defines external relations as 'relations which make no difference in the qualities they relate'. On p. 141 he defines them as 'relations which are independent of the special qualities of their terms' as though the two meanings were convertible. Bosanquet (*Logic*, 2nd ed., p. 277) says that what he is concerned to maintain in the doctrine of internal relations is that relations are so connected with the properties of their terms that any alteration of relations involves an alteration of properties and *vice versa*, but he adds that he prefers the expression 'relevant relations' to 'internal relations'. It might have saved a good deal of confusion if all the advocates of 'internal relations' had done so.

applied to relations between abstract universals, e.g. the relation of equality between the pure number 4 and 2 + 2, because we cannot speak of the possibility of an abstract universal being different from what it is, but only to relations between concrete terms [1]; but, since I only discuss the latter class of relations, I need not try to reword the definition so as to cover relations between universals also.

So the assertion that all relations are internal in this sense means that, where terms are related in some specific way, it is always true that they could[2] not have been what they are[3] without the relation being present.[4] This is true, e.g. of most or all quantitative relations and of the relation of similarity or difference. If P is half the size of Q or greater than Q or similar to Q in a given quality, it follows that if the relation had not been present the terms P and Q could not both have been what they in fact are.

But in all cases of relations internal only in this sense between concrete terms *one* of the terms could have been the same without the relation being present (or, to cover the case of multiple relations, let us say all but one of the terms related). If P is two and Q four cubic inches in size P must bear the relation 'half the size of' to Q, but it does not follow that P would still stand in that relation to Q if Q were different in size. There are indeed thinkers who claim to have shown that no one fact in the universe could have been different from what it is without everything else being different, but until and unless this is proved we must not assume it in our definitions. If it be established later we can draw the conclusion then. At present let us call a relation internal in this sense if it is such that *both* of the terms could not have been what they are without the relation holding between them.

[1] I have to thank Professor G. E. Moore for pointing out this limitation in the definition proposed by himself in *Philosophical Studies* (p. 283 ff.).
[2] Again we must interpret 'could' as covering both causal and logical possibility.
[3] With one reservation mentioned below (p. 132).
[4] This is the only sense in which it might be maintained with any show of reason that all relations are 'essential' to their terms, i.e. it might be said that their terms could not exist without them on the ground that, if they were at all different qualitatively, they would not be the same terms. In the other sense of 'essential' mentioned earlier (p. 121) it would be simply absurd to say that all relations are essential to their terms.

There are two fallacies to be avoided in connection with this sense of 'internal'. In the first place it is clear that if A and B are related at all they must both be different in one respect at least from what they would be in the absence of the relation, inasmuch as they both possess the characteristic, which they assuredly would not otherwise possess, of standing in this relation. But obviously this is not what is meant by the internal theory of relations, otherwise it would be a mere tautology of no value. It <u>obviously means that the terms would be different in some other respect or respects also if the relation were not present,</u> and we cannot straightway infer this from the fact that they are different in this one respect. If any persons have been led to believe or think they believe in the internal theory of relations by confusing these two propositions they have committed a fallacy.

Secondly, granted that A and B are related by the relation r and something else, C, is not related to B by the relation r, it follows necessarily *a priori* that C is not identical with A, but we cannot therefore conclude that it is impossible that A could be what it is if it did not stand in the relation r to B. That is, the propositions 'A is related to B by r' and 'C is not related to B by r' entail 'C is not A', by the same principle as governs the ordinary second figure syllogism, but it does not follow that the proposition 'C is not related to B by r' would entail 'C is not A' apart from the proposition that 'A is in fact related to B by r'. To argue that it would is like concluding that, because in the syllogism P a M, S e M, S e P, the conclusion follows from both premisses, therefore it follows from the second alone.[1] This fallacy seems to be involved in Dr. McTaggart's argument in *The Nature of Existence*[2] to the effect that 'no quality of a substance could be different while leaving the others unchanged'. For he includes under 'quality' what I have called relational characteristics, i.e. the characteristics which consist in standing in specific relations.

I do not think, however, that these two mistakes are the whole or the main cause of the prevalence of the belief that relations are internal in the seventh sense of the word.[3] That

---

[1] The fallacy is refuted at length by Professor G. E. Moore (*Philosophical Studies*, p. 289 ff.).

[2] Vol. I, § 109.

[3] I.e., in the sense in which it signifies that 'they make a difference to their terms', or that 'their terms could not both have been what they are if the relation had not been present.'

sense, the one under discussion, is perhaps the most important sense in which relations are maintained to be internal. If the 'internal' view is true in this sense, it means that all reality is an interconnected system such that a difference in one part would always involve a difference in others.

There are two main reasons which account for the wide prevalence of the view.

(*a*) The first depends on a confusion between the sixth and the seventh senses of internal or on the assumption that the sixth sense implies the seventh. It seemed impossible to conceive that a relation could really relate its terms, could, as e.g. Bradley puts it, hold its terms together if it were not somehow rooted in their nature, and we have seen already that all relations must be at least partly rooted in the nature of their terms, if by that is meant, as I suppose is the case, that they must follow from their terms or from a set of conditions including their terms as relevant and even essential parts. But if a relation was thus rooted in the nature of its terms, it seemed clear that it could not be absent without the nature of the terms being different.[1] So much indeed would follow logically from the ordinary rules of ' the hypothetical syllogism ' if it were the case that the nature of the terms constituted the *whole* condition from which the relation followed. For in that case, supposing a, b to stand for the nature of the respective terms and r for the relation, we could truly say—if ' x, y are a, b, then x and y are related by r ', and from that follows— ' if x and y were not related by r, then they would not be a, b,' i.e. if the relation were absent both the terms could not be what they are. This is clearly the case with the very numerous relations which do admittedly follow solely from the nature of their terms. If it is a fact that A is half of B or that A is similar to B in quality x we have a relation which follows solely from the nature of the related terms, and these relations could certainly not be absent without A or B being different from what they are.[2] It would not indeed be necessary for both terms to be different, but at least one must be so.

But the position is changed when we consider cases where the terms only constitute part, though an essential part, of the

---

[1] E.g. Taylor (*Elements of Metaphysics*, p. 148) insists that, unless a relation makes a difference to its terms (my seventh sense), it can have no foundation in their nature (my sixth sense).

[2] In respects other than the characteristic of standing or not standing in the relation in question.

conditions from which the relation follows. In that case we cannot say that one of the terms would have to be different if the relation were absent, for, since the relation is not due to the nature of the terms alone but to other conditions also, we can only argue that if the relation were absent *either* one of the terms *or* one or more of these other conditions would be different. Hence the seventh sense does not, as might have been thought, follow from the success of the arguments used to establish the sixth, for these only succeeded in establishing partial, not complete, determination of the relation by its terms, and the argument from the sixth to the seventh sense is valid only if the determination is complete, not partial.

(*b*) What has been perhaps even more influential in leading to the widespread adoption of this view of relations is the conception of the world as a causal system, a conception so strongly suggested and supported by physical science at the time when this doctrine of relations was at its zenith, though much less strongly to-day. But owing to its length I shall for the present defer my discussion of the argument from causality.

Now it is clear that every existent known by us is related to every other by some relation which is internal in the seventh sense. For every existent that we know is similar to every other in some respect if only in the respects of existing in time and conforming to the necessary truths of logic, and similarity is a relation of such a kind that wherever it relates two terms it is true that if it had been absent the terms could not have been the same in other respects. But this does not prove that reality is a system of the kind contemplated by the advocates of internal relations, for most relations are at least *prima facie* not of this character, e.g. the spatial relations of a thing to other things might well, it would seem, be different even though its other characteristics were the same.

It is worth noting, however, that in some instances of such relations (e.g. 'half of') we can from knowledge of one term plus the fact that it stands in the relation to something infer some determinate characteristic in the other term, while in other instances of relations which are also internal in the seventh sense, e.g. difference,[1] we can draw no such conclusion.[2]

---

[1] Where it is a relation at all.
[2] At least directly. This is not meant to exclude the possibility that knowledge of the full nature of the term would imply knowledge of everything else.

THE THEORY OF INTERNAL RELATIONS 135

We cannot tell what colour anything has from the mere knowledge that something blue is different in colour from it. This gives us then an <u>eighth</u> sense in which a relation might be internal or be held to be internal, i.e. <u>if the relation is conceived as such that from a knowledge of one term and the relation in which it stands to the other term we can infer with logical necessity that the other term possesses a certain *determinate* [1] or relatively determinate characteristic other than the characteristic of standing in the relation in question.</u> Some of the relations of every existent are internal in this sense, since every existent is similar to some others, and the relation of similarity if defined with sufficient precision is internal in the eighth sense.[2]

But we must remark here that, while it is true that in any case in which A and B really are similar or A is half the size of B the relation could not have been different without one of the terms being different, it may still also be true that A could have existed without standing in that relation at all. For B may not be essential or even relevant to A, though, granted B, A and B could not but stand in the relation. It is obvious that, if there is a particular lump of iron on Mars twice the size of a given lump of iron here, the two lumps of iron are internally related in the seventh and eighth senses, yet the existence of the one lump is in no way essential to the other's existence and does not even make it the size it is. It may be true that the first lump would have been what it is if the other had not existed at all, though granted its existence it must stand in that relation to it. But advocates of internal relations undoubtedly commonly suppose their doctrine to imply that, when two things are internally related, the one could not have existed without standing in that relation to the other. So we have a <u>ninth</u> sense of internal relation according to which <u>A is internally related to B by the</u>

---

[1] In the case of most relations we can infer from the knowledge of the relation that both terms are characterised by some value of a certain *determinable*.

[2] It might be thought that *all* things are internally related to each other in the eighth sense of internal, since, as we have seen, they are all related by similarity in some respect or other; but this does not follow, because everything is certainly not similar to everything else in any determinate characteristic (in the sense in which the term is used in Johnson's *Logic* as opposed to determinable), and I have defined the eighth sense as applying to determinate or relatively determinate qualities, not to determinables or to purely formal logical characteristics.

relation *r* when A could not exist unless B existed and was related to it by *r*.

Finally, we may distinguish between causal and logical dependence, thus giving a tenth sense of 'internal' in which one term is not only dependent but logically dependent on its relation to the other and *vice versa*. If, as has often been held, causality is or involves a species of logical entailment, this tenth sense follows from the ninth. Most advocates of the internal relations view seem to have held that any particular thing was not only causally but logically dependent on the other things to which it was related, for they insist that it is self-contradictory (i.e. logically and not only causally impossible) without them. Anybody who maintained that everything was internally related in this sense to the rest of reality would mean that reality was a system such that any one part of it would ultimately be found to be logically incoherent and self-contradictory if abstracted from the rest, but when seen in the light of the whole would be seen to follow from it by an intelligible logical nexus, and not merely coexist with the other things in the universe as a matter of fact. This view seems altogether absurd to many thinkers at the present time, but I am not by any means sure that the prevailing tendency of thought is a right one, and at any rate the important part the view has played in the history of philosophy is sufficient justification for examining it.

To sum up, we must admit that all relations are internal in the first and fourth senses, i.e. they always presuppose terms which have the characteristic of standing in the relation in question, and they involve a genuine, though perhaps very partial and limited, unity between their terms. We can positively deny that any relations are internal in the third sense because relations are not qualities, and also in the fifth sense because they presuppose some positive character in the terms related which is not itself constituted (or even modified) by the relation, the nature of no term being exhausted by any one relation. We can also deny that *all* relations are internal in the sense of essential to their terms (second sense) while admitting that some are, though we must add that the distinction between essential and unessential is in most cases one rather of degree than of kind. We can assert that every relation follows either logically or causally from the nature of its terms or from a set of conditions including as necessary factors its terms (sixth sense), but we cannot infer from this that either of the terms could not be the same in other respects if the relation were not present. In this (the *seventh*) sense we have neither proved nor disproved the proposition that all relations are internal, similarly with the *eighth*, *ninth* and *tenth* senses distinguished by me. These await further discussion. They seem to constitute what idealist philosophers have chiefly in mind when they assert that all relations are internal.

Obviously what I have said about all relations will, if true, apply to any specific relation or relations involved in cognition ; but can we say anything further about such relation or relations that does not just follow from the general nature of all relations ? Now it is very difficult to determine exactly what are the relations involved in cognition. It is sometimes contended that the object of cognition is a proposition not a reality, but in discussions concerning idealist epistemology the term ' object of cognition ' is never or hardly ever used in that sense, and it is certainly the case that if we know a proposition to be true we thereby know, in a very important sense of the word, the objective fact to which the proposition refers. What is the relation between this and the cognition of it ? If the fact is something appertaining to an event or continuant in time there will no doubt be temporal and probably causal relations between them, but *is there any relation which can be described as specifically cognitive* ? Our answer to this question will depend partly on our analysis of knowing (or our denial that it can be analysed), but in any case there is one relation (though there may be more) which must be regarded as specifically cognitive, i.e. it cannot occur except in connection with a cognition [1] and must occur in so far as the aim of a cognition is achieved.

The relation of which I am thinking is the one which always subsists between a true judgment and the fact to which it refers and never between a false judgment and anything objective, the relation which constitutes the truth of a ' judgment '. It has commonly been given the name, *correspondence*, and in the absence of another name in use I shall employ this word, though it is unfortunately a misleading expression, for the relation cannot be reduced to copying, likeness, parallelism in structure, or anything of that kind.[2] The actual relation, I think, is *unique and irreducible*. We know perfectly well

[1] I use ' cognition ' here as elsewhere as a general term to cover knowledge, judgment, belief, opinion.
[2] V. p. 201 below.

what it is, in particular cases at any rate, since we always understand what is meant by a judgment being 'true of [1] something', but I do not think it can be defined or further analysed. At any rate I have seen no definition or analysis that gives any promise of being successful. Such a relation between the non-objective and the objective sides in cognition must be admitted by anybody who allows an objective reference to cognition at all and distinguishes between judgment and its object, since they are obviously not altogether unrelated and therefore, if different at all, must be connected by some specific two-termed relation, but <u>it is not so clear what is the non-objective term of the relation.</u> That is why I could only describe it in a sentence by deliberately using 'judgment' in an ambiguous sense. Some persons would hold that the relation subsists between a proposition and something objective in the fuller sense (for 'judgment' is sometimes used to mean what Cambridge philosophers call 'proposition'), the proposition being conceived as a separate entity from either the judging of it or that to which it refers; others would regard propositions as merely a convenient fiction, but do not leave it so clear what are the terms between which the relation subsists. An alternative would be to say that the relation subsists between my judging or, better, a certain characteristic of or element in this judging and that to which my judging refers. But that there is such a relation cannot reasonably be doubted. Now it is possible to prove that this relation is internal in the seventh and eighth senses of the expression 'internal relation' [2]; and fortunately this proof is unaffected by the view we take as to the non-objective term which is related to the objective fact in this way (at least I know no view on this question which could affect it).

[1] 'True of X' = 'bearing the relation of correspondence to some fact about X.' I should have liked to substitute the expression 'true of' for 'corresponding to' to signify the relation, but, as was pointed out to me, this expression, while only definable, as above, in terms of the relation between a judgment and a fact, describes that between a judgment and a subject of attributes.

[2] I.e. in the sense in which an 'internal relation' means a 'relation the terms of which could not both have been what they are if the relation had not been present,' and the sense in which it means a 'relation such that from a knowledge of one term and the relation in which it stands to the other term we could infer with logical necessity that the other term possesses a certain determinate or relatively determinate characteristic other than the characteristic of standing in the relation in question'.

The relation is internal in the seventh sense, for it is certainly true that one of the terms would be different if the relation were lacking. The terms are the judgment that S is P and the fact S–P. In any case of a true judgment we can always rightly say that the relation of 'correspondence' could not have been absent without either the judgment or the fact judged about being different (whether we interpret the first term of the relation, the judgment, as being my judging as characterised in a certain way or as being a 'proposition'). If I judged that S is P and S really is P, the relation of 'correspondence' must necessarily subsist between the two terms in question, and it could not be absent unless either I had judged differently or facts were different in regard to S and P.

This is obviously a case of logical entailment and not merely of causal following. My judgment being what it is and S being what it is, it follows *a priori* that my judgment corresponds to the fact S–P. The premisses being what they are, there can be no more escape from this than from any logically necessary inference.

The relation is internal also in the eighth sense, for from the fact that I judge 'S is P' and the fact that this judgment 'corresponds' to something it follows logically that S really is P, and from the fact that S is P and the fact that I have judged truly about (i.e. made a judgment corresponding to) the relation between S and P, it follows logically that I have judged 'S is P'.

But, as I argued earlier, we cannot infer from all this any sweeping conclusions either in favour of or against idealism. I do not know that the proof I have given has any important metaphysical or epistemological consequences, but the fact that the relation in question is of this character is at least as well worth knowing in itself as e.g. a generalisation about a species of plant or animal in Biology that has no further obvious significance for general theory. All that I have said will apply equally if we regard the non-objective term in the relation as a subsistent proposition, or in any other possible way, as can easily be seen by substitution in the arguments. If, as is often held, knowing, as opposed to uncertain or erroneous judgments, entails a relation between mind and object known other than those I have mentioned, that relation will likewise be internal in the sense given for the same reasons, but whether there is such a further relation peculiar to knowing I am not clear.

It might be objected that, while the relation was internal in the seventh sense, it was not internal in the eighth sense because the inferences in question could never be made in practice, because I could never in fact be in a position in which I could infer that S is really P from the premisses that I judge S is P and that my judgment corresponds to fact, or from the premisses that S really is P and that I make a judgment corresponding to this fact infer that I judge S to be P. It may be argued that I can never make these inferences because I cannot know my judgment that S is P to be true without already knowing S–P to be an objective fact, and because I cannot both know S–P to be an objective fact and know myself to make a true judgment as to this fact without already knowing that I make the judgment ' S is P '. But if a logical relation of entailment subsists, the question whether it is ever actually used in inference is quite irrelevant. The postulates of Euclid entailed Pythagoras' theorem just as truly 3,000 years ago, before anyone had drawn the inference, as they do to-day, and would still entail it if the only intelligent beings in the universe had been so constituted that it was impossible from the nature of their minds that the inference ever could occur to them. Further, we may remark that, although I could not draw these inferences in my own case at the time of making the judgment, I both can and often in fact actually do draw them in regard to other people. I often infer that S–P is an objective fact because somebody has judged S to be P, and because owing to my estimate of his character, intelligence and opportunities of acquiring correct information on the subject I think that his judgment corresponds to the facts. (Any uncertainty in this inference is due not to the absence of a relation of logical entailment but to the uncertainty of the premisses, or usually the second premiss.) Again from my knowledge that S–P is a fact and my memory that I had e.g. given full marks to a candidate in an examination for his answer about S-P, thus implying that it was correct and so corresponded to the facts, or praised a man for his truthfulness in admitting a fact which was to his own disadvantage, I might easily draw the conclusion that he answered that S was P without remembering what he actually did answer. And I could make similar inferences in connection with past judgments made by myself.

That such inferences are not to be dismissed as mere tautologies seems clear to me both from the examples given, which clearly involve not merely a verbal but a real advance from the premisses to the conclusion, at least as much as other equally simple examples of *a priori* reasoning, e.g. syllogisms, can be said to do, and on general grounds. For the fact that I judge S to be P and the fact that S is P are certainly different facts, and one fact does not include the other, since I can judge S to be P without S really being P, and S may also be P without my judging it; and, if we admit, as we surely must, that between a true judgment and the fact to which it refers there is a relation which makes the judgment true, it is again obvious that the fact that the judgment stands in this relation is a different fact from either the fact that I judge S–P or the fact that S is P. This third, relational fact might perhaps be identified with the fact that the judgment is true; but that my judgment is true is obviously a different fact from either the fact that I make the judgment or the fact that S really is P, since either of these may be facts without the first being so. And if these three are different facts from each other separately, I do not see how one of them can be included in the other two taken together.[1] The view I am maintaining could only be overthrown by denying that there was a specific relation which held between every true judgment and the fact to which it refers, and this seems plainly untrue. But, as I have said, our conclusion though perhaps of some interest does not provide any argument for idealism.

But the cognitive relation cannot be regarded as internal in the ninth or tenth senses [2] unless we suppose epistemological idealism to have already been established on other grounds. *Prima facie* it seems clear that at least most facts known by me

[1] Even if we held that 'my judgment S–P is true' means simply 'I judged S–P' and 'S is really P' and nothing more, there would still be some relation of correspondence between the judgment and the fact S–P, and the fact that they are so related would still be a third fact, though this third fact would no longer be identified with the fact that the judgment is true. So we could still argue: I judged S is P, my judgment corresponds, therefore S was P, etc. It is obvious that, since the judgment and the fact S–P are at any rate different facts, they must be related, and further that there is some relation between them which holds in the case of all true judgments but never in the case of a false one.
[2] I defined the ninth sense as the sense according to which A is internally related to B by the relation *r* when A could not exist unless B existed and was related to it by *r*, and the tenth sense as the sense according to which if A is internally related to B it is *logically* dependent on B and its relation to B (pp. 135–6).

do not depend for their being on my knowing them or on my making a judgment about them which corresponds to them, and it also seems clear that my judgments do not depend for their being on the presence of facts to which they correspond, since if they did I could never make a false judgment, a disability from which I unfortunately do not suffer. I could not indeed *know* that S was P without S–P being a fact, but that is only because we should not use the term 'know' in that case, but my psychological state might be the same though the judgment was erroneous and there was no corresponding fact. And in any case no reason has been given to show that it would not be possible for my cognitive state to be dependent on its object in the ninth and tenth senses without the converse propositions being true also.

Perhaps one of the causes which has led to the adoption of epistemological idealism is that people saw that the cognitive relation was internal in the seventh and eight senses [1] and confused this with the assertion that it was internal also in the ninth and tenth senses. That this does not follow necessarily is clear from the instances given. The relations half of, exactly similar in a given quality to, opposite in sex to, are internal in the seventh and eighth but not in the ninth and tenth senses.[2]

§ II. Various Idealist Arguments for the Theory of Internal Relations*

Let us now examine some of the arguments used by the leading thinkers with whom the theory of internal relations is associated in order to see whether it is possible to establish

---

[1] I.e. in the sense in which an 'internal relation' means a relation the terms of which could not both have been what they are if the relation had not been present, and the sense in which it means a relation such that from a knowledge of one term and the relation in which it stands to the other term we could infer with logical necessity that the term possesses a certain determinate or relatively determinate characteristic other than the characteristic of standing in the relation in question.

[2] From the proposition that I am male and that I am opposite in sex to Queen Anne it can be inferred that Queen Anne is a woman, but it does not follow that I am dependent for my existence on Queen Anne or *vice versa*. Nor does this follow from the fact (seventh sense of internal) that, if the proposition 'Queen Anne and I are opposite in sex' had been false, one of us would have had to be intrinsically different from what we are.

THE THEORY OF INTERNAL RELATIONS 143

the view that all relations are internal in any or all of the last four senses.

(1) In the first place it seems to be supposed by Mr. Bradley and Professor Joachim [1] that to admit external relations is to make the relation a kind of third term separate from the other two which it is supposed to relate. Such a view by making relations a kind of *things* would deny the distinctive character of relations altogether and would quickly meet its nemesis, for the relation, having become really a term, would require other relations to connect it with the other terms and so on *ad infinitum*. But I know of no advocates of the theory of external relations who do hold this mistaken view, nor do I see any reason why anybody who denied that relations were internal in any or all of the senses [2] still under discussion should be supposed to imply such a view. Mr. Bertrand Russell's theory of types, which is certainly a most important part of his logical doctrine, quite definitely implies that relations, as belonging to a different logical type from terms, cannot be treated in the way just criticised by the idealists. Perhaps the confusion is due to the misleading effect of the spatial metaphor: we cannot say that A is external to B in the spatial sense unless it is altogether outside B, but 'external' cannot be used in the spatial sense of relations. It is quite illegitimate to pass, as Bradley apparently does, from the denial that a relation is ever external in the sense of being a sort of third term to the assertion that all relations are internal in the sense of 'making a difference to their terms'. Such are the bad effects of trying to solve the problem without first distinguishing the different senses in which a relation may be called internal or external.

(2) It is contended that we can sometimes argue from one fact to another and that this would be impossible if the two were not internally related [3] (apparently in all the last four senses of the term). This, if true, could not prove that all relations are internal or even that most or all facts are internally related in these senses. As is well known the circumstances under which

---

[1] *The Nature of Truth*, p. 11.
[2] Or in any of the others except perhaps the first, i.e. if he should deny or ignore the fact that the terms of a relation have the characteristic of standing in that relation, thus cutting relations adrift from their terms. Bradley seems to think that you can prove relations to be 'internal' in the sense of 'making a difference' by simply showing that in some loose sense they must 'qualify' their terms.
[3] E.g. Bradley, *Essays on Truth and Reality*, p. 259.

we can argue *a priori* from one or more facts to another fact are extraordinarily limited, and the features of real things in regard to which this is possible for us seem always to be of the type commonly described as formal characteristics. The argument would therefore only be valid against anyone who held that not only some but all relations were external in these senses.

(3) In regard to the relation between cognition and its object it has been argued that it is obvious that one term at any rate, the object cognised, makes a difference to the other, and that it is absurd to suppose that there could be a relation which was, so to speak, internal at one end and external at the other.[1] Such a supposition seemed absurd to me also as long as it was stated in general terms, but when I analysed it in accordance with the various senses of internal at issue now the absurdity seemed to disappear.[2] There is nothing absurd that I can see in supposing e.g. that A might be different because of its relation to B without B being different because of its relation to A, or that A might depend for its existence on B but not *vice versa*. If these propositions are absurd, at any rate their absurdity is not self-evident, and some proof is required. Till such proof is given we cannot possibly dismiss them as necessarily false, and such a proof has, so far as I know, not been attempted at all.

(4) The advocates of the internal theory of relations do succeed, I think, in showing that all relations are partly dependent on and determined by characteristics of their terms (sixth sense), and most of their endeavours seem to be directed to this end, but then they apparently forget that they have only shown the relations to be *partly* determined by their terms and erroneously assume that from this it follows that the relations are internal in the seventh sense, i.e. that the terms could not be the same if the relations were different. But the inference, as I have shown above,[3] would only be valid if the relations in which they stand could be proved to be wholly determined by the terms related. The advocates of the internal relations theory also fail to distinguish causal and logical necessity without supporting by argument their identification.

[1] Id., p. 337 n. Joachim, *The Nature of Truth*, p. 50 n.
[2] I am not concerned to deny that it might be absurd if maintained in regard to some of the earlier senses of internal about which we have come to a decision already. [3] pp. 133-4.

THE THEORY OF INTERNAL RELATIONS 145

(5) It is argued by Bradley that in feeling we have a unity which is non-relational and therefore cannot be fitted into any scheme of external relations.[1] But the fact that in feeling we do not recognise relations does not prove that there are no relations or even no external relations present either within the total feeling-state or between this state (or elements in this state) and something else. This argument only seemed conclusive because Bradley already assumed a form of idealism and refused or failed to distinguish between the true proposition that we do not know the relations of our feeling and the false proposition that it has no relations. Even if I cannot have feelings without in some sense knowing that I have them, I certainly can have them without distinguishing all their relations. There is indeed an important element of truth in Bradley's contention, namely that feeling cannot be reduced to a set of terms in relation. I think this is true of feeling as of everything else, but this does not prove that no relations are present or that all its relations are internal in the senses under discussion.

(6) Bosanquet says that 'the all-important argument' is that 'relations are true of their terms. They express their position in complexes which positions elicit their behaviour, their self-maintenance in the world of things.'[2] But we cannot pass from the fact that relations (or, more correctly, propositions ascribing relational characteristics) are true of their terms to the view that relations are internal in the full sense maintained by Bosanquet himself, and the latter part of the argument could never prove that all relations affected their terms, only that some did, which, as far as I know, no one has denied. We can only suppose that Bosanquet spoilt his case by writing this passage somewhat hastily.

(7) Bradley, as is well known, claims to discover a contradiction in the very notion of relation,[3] but while he denies ultimate validity to any judgment asserting or involving relations (i.e. to all judgments without exception) he evidently holds that it is a good deal nearer the truth to regard relations as internal than as external. This in a philosophy according to which no judgments are either wholly true or wholly false is a very important distinction. It is indeed only a distinction

[1] *Essays on Truth and Reality*, p. 237; v. also Joachim, *The Nature of Truth*, p. 26.
[2] *Logic*, 2nd ed., pp. 278–9.
[3] V. *Appearance and Reality*, chs. 2 and 3.

in degree of truth or, perhaps more accurately, of error, but then according to that philosophy it is only a distinction of degree which separates the most certain truths from the most groundless and stupid errors. And that the internal relations view, though not ultimately true for him, is regarded by him as truer than the external relations view and as being what we must accept, not indeed ultimately, but ' in our intellectual world ' seems clear.[1] While he holds that even internal relations are not free from self-contradiction, he directs his criticisms mainly against the external view. Further, if it could be shown, as he thinks he has shown, that relations are unreal, the result would be a monism similar to, if more far-reaching than, that implied by the internal view, and would provide a more promising ground for the establishment of the inseparability of objects from a mind which knows them. For, if mind and object known cannot be legitimately regarded as related, the only alternative seems to be to regard them as blended in some supra-relational unity. They are obviously not quite separate, since, if they were, knowledge would be impossible even at the phenomenal level, and therefore they must be united somehow. This at any rate is the alternative adopted by Bradley. That such a unity cannot be really thought out by us is not a fatal objection, since we may well have a faint glimpse of an ideal of thought which we cannot determine in detail and since every alternative that suggests itself has been shown according to his arguments to be self-contradictory. And such a view would, like the internal relations view as usually maintained, carry with it the implication that anything is internally incoherent when taken apart from everything else, or, to speak more correctly in terms of Bradley's philosophy, imply that the proposition that this is so is far truer than any proposition which contradicts it. So Bradley is commonly included among the supporters of internal relations. Bosanquet, whose views are similar to Bradley's, argues not that relations are unreal but that they are not external, without implying that there is any marked difference between his views and Bradley's on the subject,

---

[1] E.g. in a note added in the second edition of the *Logic* he says that in ' our intellectual world ' we must take every element as qualified internally by its relations to the whole so that everything will imply all its relations, while adding that ' our whole world as merely intellectual is not ultimately real ' ; v. also *Essays on Truth and Reality*, p. 239 ff.

though if he had differed on such an important point he could hardly have failed, when deliberately discussing Bradley's theory of relations, to say so.

Bradley's actual argument against relations I need not discuss at length because it has already been answered by several different writers,[1] and I do not think I have anything really fresh to add. The contradictions which he alleges seem to arise through supposing that a relation must be treated either as a quality or as a third term.[2] For in the former case it will qualify but not relate its terms, and in the latter case it needs a fresh relation to link it to each term and so *ad infinitum*. One might similarly argue that it was impossible to tie two things together with string because you would need another piece of string to tie the string to each object and so on for ever. The argument would be valid if each piece of string used were so defective that it broke in the middle, similarly Bradley's objection would be valid of relations if and only if they did not fulfil their function of relating. Only then would they need another relation to do the relating for them. But in that case they would not be relations. If, in A *r* B, *r* is really a relation, it relates A and B itself and does not require new relations to connect it to either, for the relational characteristic of standing in the relation is not itself a relation. To say that, because A is related to B by *r*, A must stand in the relation *r* to B, and therefore must be characterised by (i.e. stand in the relation of 'having as characteristic' to) the relational characteristic of standing in the relation *r* to B, and be characterised further by having the characteristic of being characterised by the relational characteristic of standing in the relation *r* to B, is only to say the same thing over again in different words, so that the so-called different relations which are supposed to constitute the infinite regress are really only more and more cumbrous ways of expressing the same relation.

The same fallacy in a subtler form appears in Bradley's argument that each term 'has a double character, as both supporting and as being made by the relation', so that these two aspects will be again related and so on *ad infinitum*.[3] The

---

[1] Hobhouse, *Theory of Knowledge*, ch. 12; Schiller, *Humanism*, essay XI; Stout, *Studies in Philosophy and Psychology*, ch. 9; Cook Wilson, *Statement and Inference*, vol. II, p. 692 ff.
[2] But v. below p. 443.
[3] *Appearance and Reality*, p. 31; cf. Taylor, *Elements of Metaphysics*, p. 146.

distinction, so far as I can understand it, is between A as abstracted from the relation and A as related. But what is the relation between these two aspects of A? Simply that the second includes besides the other characteristics of A the characteristic of standing in the relation, while the first does not do so. But this will not generate a second distinct relation between them and so on *ad infinitum*, unless it is assumed as before that A must have a relation to the characteristic of standing in any particular relation and that this relation must in turn be related to A by another relation.[1]

Nor do I see any vicious regress in the fact that relations presuppose qualities and qualities relations. There is a kind of 'circle' whenever it is true both that A implies B and that B implies A, but it is not vicious unless we try to prove A by B though we can only prove B by means of A, which is certainly not the case here. We have direct evidence in experience for both relations and qualities, and do not need to prove the existence of the one by reference to the other.

But, even if we could see no means of surmounting the difficulties raised by Bradley about relations, most men would still think it infinitely more likely that there was some undetected fallacy in his arguments than that there was a fatal fallacy in everybody else's arguments on every subject whatever, i.e. that all our judgments were false and self-contradictory. According to the coherence theory itself relation, being presupposed in all our judgments and in the very notion of a coherent system, must surely be accepted as a valid conception. But it is not by any means clear what Bradley meant by saying that all our judgments are partly false. His critics understand 'false' in its ordinary sense and are thus able to riddle him with objections, but it seems clear that he is not using 'false' in quite the ordinary sense of the term.[2] And it does seem to me a reasonable view to hold that all our judgments are inadequate, meaning by this not merely that they do not tell the whole truth but that

[1] If A enters into the relation in time as a result of causation and the relation changes A in other respects, then there will be a distinction between A as it was before its entry into the relation and A as it is afterwards, and a kind of infinite regress will arise as a result of the infinite divisibility of time, but this difficulty about causation does not seem to be what Bradley had in mind here, and cannot be urged against relations as such.

[2] V. below p. 209 ff.

they in some way misrepresent, convey a wrong impression of the real. The forms we use in judgment and speech do after all suggest that relations and terms are two kinds of separate things and that reality is a set of such things, whereas it is really a continuum from which the relations and the terms alike are mere abstractions. What is given to us in experience is not terms by themselves (as thinkers prior to Bradley seem often to have supposed), nor relations plus terms, nor a mere undifferentiated continuum (a 'blooming buzzing confusion' as suggested by William James in one passage), but a varied and interrelated continuum, and we have no right to suppose that the methods of abstraction we employ in order to analyse out that continuum will represent with complete adequacy even the general nature of our own experience. Relations and terms are no doubt present in the real, but they are not present as separate entities side by side, yet we can hardly think of them discursively (as opposed to experiencing them) without thinking them as thus separate by an unjustified abstraction. This is partly due to the defects of language, though I think myself it goes deeper than that. As Mr. Bertrand Russell himself points out, the fact that we have to use the same kind of symbols, namely words, for both terms and relations and that the word for a relation is as much a separate word, an entity by itself, as the word for a term inevitably conveys the impression that terms and relations have the same kind of being and that relations are to be regarded as just other terms.[1] It is difficult in practice to avoid making the assumption that every word we use stands for a separate single entity, but the assumption is unjustified. If we once view relations as terms we are involved in Bradley's infinite regress, yet in speaking about them at all we are really treating them as if they were terms. Not only is it the case that reality cannot be reduced exhaustively to a set of terms and relations but that every proposition we lay down about anything concrete suggests a separateness that is not to be found in the real. I do not say that all our judgments are therefore partly false but I do say that they are metaphysically misleading. But one thing is clear: what we have said may involve an amendment of the conception of relations but it does not involve their denial.

(8) Bradley's most important argument against relations

[1] *Contemporary British Philosophy, First Series*, pp. 369-70.

is, however, interpreted by Professor Campbell [1] as being to the effect that the assertion, A is B, is tautological if A and B are the same and self-contradictory if they are different. This self-contradiction could only be removed by thinking of them as diverse but necessary expressions of the same system, but we can only connect them externally without really seeing the logical necessity of the connection and therefore the contradiction cannot be removed by us. Now I admit that our intellect does demand such a logically connected intelligible system, but I cannot see that there is any actual contradiction in denying it. For, when we say that A is B or is related to B, we do not mean that A is identical with B but that it is qualified by B or stands in relation to B. Professor Campbell says that, if we distinguish the 'is' of predication and the 'is' of identity and thus maintain that 'A is B' really means 'A has the quality B', we have not escaped the contradiction, for 'has B' must = 'is such as to have B', so that we are now asserting the identity of A with 'such as to have B' and the same difficulty arises again, but surely if the 'is' of predication is distinct from the 'is' of identity at all it is distinct in the proposition 'A is such as to have B', and we therefore do not in this proposition assert that A is *identical* with 'such as to have B'.

Thus Professor Campbell's reply assumes that his position has already been admitted by us. It is open to him to contend that all predication presupposes system, but I do not see how this can be established by finding formal contradictions between identity and difference. And even if it be the case, as Professor Campbell thinks, that we cannot predicate B of A without assuming that A and B follow with logical necessity from the same system, the fact that we cannot see the logical necessity still would not make our assertion self-contradictory. It is not self-contradictory to say 'I know (or believe) that B follows from A though I have not the least idea why or how it does so', or 'A and B must follow necessarily from some ground though I do not know what'.

Bradley holds that differents must contradict each other except when combined in a system, but it seems to me that it would be more correct to say that they cannot contradict each other except in a system, i.e. the notion of a contra-

[1] *Scepticism and Construction*, p. 7 ff.

THE THEORY OF INTERNAL RELATIONS 151

diction between A and B presupposes some kind of system [1] with a fixed place for A which is, so to speak, invaded by B. Alive and not alive do not contradict each other *per se* but only when applied to the same subject at the same time; two contradictory colours can perfectly well exist together unless they are ascribed to the same place within the same system of space. It is not that differents contradict each other *unless* brought in a system, but that they only contradict each other when one of them is put in the wrong place in a system. But Bradley would reply that they could not be thought at all except in a system.

§ III. Causality and the Problem of Internal Relations*

We now pass on to what is perhaps the objection most strongly felt by opponents of the external relations view. It is that the view in question makes relations ' mere conjunctions ' (as Bradley puts it) and that mere conjunctions are ' irrational '. Bradley bases on this argument the view that relations must be internal in the sense of being grounded in their terms (sixth sense), and then assumes [2] that because they are internal in this sense they must also be internal in the sense of ' affecting ' the terms, i.e. our seventh sense. ' The process and its result to the terms, if they contribute nothing to it, seems really irrational throughout. But, if they contribute anything, they must surely be affected internally.' [3] He says that the point which should be emphasised in regard to the doctrine of external relations is ' that everything ordinarily covered by the word " implication " is here utterly denied '.[4] Professor Taylor likewise says : ' If no relation in the end makes any difference to its terms, and thus has no foundation in their nature, it becomes a standing miracle how or why the terms should enter into relations to which they are all the time absolutely in-

---

[1] Though not necessarily a fully intelligible system or a universal system comprising all reality.
[2] Wrongly, as I contend, v. above, pp. 133–4.
[3] *Appearance and Reality*, p. 575.
[4] *Essays on Truth and Reality*, p. 259 ; cf. Professor Campbell, *Scepticism and Construction*, p. 9 ff. ' We need make only the simplest " ideal experiment " to discover that to write differences *per se*, or simply, is abhorrent to thought. On the other hand, their union as connected expressions of a systematic identity seems not only abstractly intelligible, but also to represent plainly the goal of the intellect in actual practice.'

different.'[1] Professor Joachim [2] argues that the theory of external relations leaves all relations of things in the position of arbitrary and irrational coincidences, so that 'external relation' is not an answer to the problem how things can be related and yet not lose their independence but only 'a name for the problem to be solved'.[3] Bosanquet said in 1913 of Bradley's theory of relations: 'What he in principle refuses to accept I understand to be bare conjunction, that is, the bringing together of differents, without mediation by any analysis of their conditions satisfactory to thought', and cites in his favour the fact or supposed fact that every science 'rejects relatively bare conjunctions, that is, such conjunctions as are presented by empirical observations'. 'Is there any man of science,' he asks, 'who, in his daily work and apart from philosophical controversy, will accept a bare given conjunction as conceivably ultimate truth?'[4] It seems clear that the 'irrationality' of which these thinkers complain would only disappear if all relations could be regarded as following logically from their terms or from a whole in which their terms were included. To satisfy them relations would have to be internal in the tenth as well as in the seventh, eighth and ninth senses of the word. All this seems to assume that the connection of different things and different events is capable of a rational explanation deducible *a priori* from their nature, not indeed by our mind but at any rate by a mind which possessed real insight into this nature.

The advocate of external relations would probably reply by boldly denying that there is any such problem as that from which his opponents start. He does not see why we should suppose the relations of things to be intelligible and doubts even whether the question as to their intelligibility has meaning at all. Logical implication is for him not a relation that could hold between events in the real world. He would say that, even if it is the business of the scientist in some sense to look for causes, this is not to seek to make intelligible what has happened or reveal its logical ground, and it does not imply that the causes he finds have any internal *logical* connection with their effects but only that they always (or usually) are followed by them in fact. To this controversy the key is the concept of causality, and it will

[1] *Elements of Metaphysics*, p. 148.
[2] *The Nature of Truth*, p. 44 ff.   [3] Id., p. 49.
[4] *The Distinction between Mind and its Objects*, pp. 59–60.

THE THEORY OF INTERNAL RELATIONS 153

therefore be necessary to devote a section to the latter. The older schools of philosophy usually assumed that the connection between cause and effect was a species of that between logical ground and consequent; and from this it would follow that, since everything in the world we know is, directly or indirectly, causally related to everything else, the world is in some marked degree a logically intelligible system, and that the nature of any one thing, because logically connected with that of others, is incomplete and internally incoherent when taken by itself apart from the causal system on which it depends. On that view causation [1] implies that different things by their very essence belong together, otherwise an event in one could not stand in a relation of implication to an event in another. Against this it is now commonly asserted that there is no such thing as causation except in the sense of regular sequence.[2] On the issue between these opposing views or the compromise we adopt between them turns to a large extent the issue between the internal and external view of relations, between monism and pluralism, between a view like the coherence theory and the view that reality is a mere aggregate of intrinsically unconnected facts.

The regularity view, specially associated with Hume and Earl Russell, has become very popular today. In its simplest form it maintains that to say that C causes E ' means simply that C is a set of conditions such that [3] (a) whenever they are all fulfilled E happens, and (b) whenever E happens they have all been fulfilled '. On this view causality does not involve any connection whatever between cause and effect but that of regular sequence or concomitance. Earl Russell's statement may sound fairly innocent, but it carries with it and is undoubtedly meant to carry with it the startling implication that if, for instance, A shoots B, the shot has no more intrinsic connection with B's death than has my drinking tea or an earthquake at the other end of the world.[4] The only

[1] It is perhaps desirable to say that I use ' causation ' and ' causality ' as synonyms throughout.
[2] With a few relatively unimportant reservations.
[3] It is highly obscure what can be meant by ' such that ', if not ' such as to cause this to happen '. We might have a better statement of the view if we simply substituted the words ' of which it is true that '. This would avoid the charge that the theory is covertly reintroducing causation in the definition of it.
[4] He adds that, if his definition is to apply to the ' causes ' of ordinary speech, ' usually ' will have to be substituted for ' always '.

connection consists in the circumstance that his death in fact follows it and would always or usually do so under specificiable conditions.[1]

Other factors beside regular sequence or concomitance which are frequently supposed to be present in cases of causation by people who do not hold the regularity view are the following: (1) The effect is held to be continuous with, dependent on something in the cause, so that the two do not merely happen in regular succession but are intrinsically connected with each other. (2) The cause is held to explain the effect, to answer not only the question—how?—but the question —why?, so that the demand for causes is primarily a demand for reasons, which implies that there is a logical connection between the two like that of ground and consequent such that the cause is at least part of the reason for the effect and helps to make the occurrence of the latter intelligible.[2] (3) The cause is held actively to produce or determine the effect in a sense in which the effect cannot be said to produce or determine the cause. (4) Causality involves neces-

[1] The issue does not merely concern the meaning of the word, cause, but the question whether events commonly described as cause and effect relatively to each other are really related only in the way maintained by the regularity view or also in the way which I wish to maintain. If we could justify the view that they are related, e.g. as logical ground and consequent, then, even if anybody still insisted that the real meaning of causation was regularity, we might cheerfully make him a present of the word provided he admitted that cause and effect were connected by this relation of logical entailment as well as by the relation of regularity, which according to him constituted causation. What an advocate of the regularity view contends is that only a small part of what we usually *think* we mean by cause is in fact true of anything, for we certainly usually *think* we mean something more than regular sequence; what an opponent of the view contends is that other elements in what we think we mean are true of at least some of the events which we usually call causes and effects, and this is what I shall try to show.

[2] The distinction between the first and the second point is only provisional. I cannot myself really think them apart or define 'intrinsic connection' except in terms of logical entailment, which would give me the second view, but I must distinguish them here, because there might be different views on this point, e.g. Professor Alexander when he speaks of the cause as ' passing into ' the effect might reasonably be interpreted as asserting intrinsic connection, and yet he emphatically denies that causality involves any sort of logical entailment. In fact, I think very many people feel that cause and effect must be intrinsically connected in some way, not, as far as I know, clearly defined, and yet would shrink from assimilating it to the logical connection of ground and consequent.

sity. If there is a causal law connecting A and B, it is not only the case that B does follow A but that it *must* follow A. The explicit denial of this necessity is one of the chief points made by the advocates of the regularity view. It seems to me that all these four points are really implied in the ' common-sense view ' of cause.

On the regularity view, on the other hand, the only objective relation signified by ' causality ' is that of regular sequence or concomitance.[1] The only arguments in favour of this view that I know fall under two heads : (*a*) the difficulties involved in other views of causation, (*b*) the fact that the regularity view keeps closest to the empirical evidence. The first set of arguments cannot carry us very far, for, as Professor Broad points out,[2] the fact that we could not give a satisactory statement of what else there was in causation would not prove that there was nothing else beyond regularity. We may even be certain that there is more than regularity and yet not be clear what that more is. The same thing occurs throughout philosophy; he would be a bold man who said that he knew what justice is, yet the merest tiro in philosophy could tell that some accounts of justice, e.g. as helping your friends and harming your enemies, are inadequate or false. The advocate of the regularity view cannot find any good argument on these lines for the view that causation is only regular sequence [3] ; all he can do is to demolish

---

[1] Mr. Ramsey and Mr. Braithwaite, whom I should class as supporters of this view, strive to avoid any flagrant discrepancies with the denotation of the term cause as ordinarily used by including in their definition of causality also certain propositions to the effect that all or most people expect E to follow C (*Foundations of Mathematics*, etc., p. 240 ff. ; *Mind*, N.S. XXXVI, no. 144, p. 470). But these psychological propositions still leave regular sequence (or concomitance) as the only objective relation covered by causality. (Even if it is said that there is now a further indirect relation between cause and effect of ' being believed to be regularly followed by ', it will be evident that the presence of this relation can make no difference to any of the objections I shall bring. If ' being regularly followed by ' does not relate cause and effect adequately, ' believed to be regularly followed by ' will not.) Nor in my opinion does their account give anything that approximates to the ordinary connotation of ' cause ', even if they avoid disagreement with the common usage as regards denotation.

[2] *The Mind and its Place in Nature*, p. 454.

[3] By the words ' causation is only regular sequence ' I mean the view that the only element in the popular notion of cause which is objectively true of the real world is the assertion of ' regular sequence '.

particular accounts of the other factors in it, which course leaves open the possibility that there may be a great deal more in causation than regular sequence, though nobody has yet succeeded in giving a satisfactory account of what it is. The other factor or factors may after all be unanalysable, as some relations must be in any case, and if this be so the criticism of alternative attempts to analyse them would be no argument whatever in favour of the regularity view. But even if causation be analysable we cannot assume that a particular analysis of it must be correct and exhaustive just because other analyses have partially failed, especially when the analysis strikes us as very strange and quite different from what we thought we meant by causation. The history of philosophy shows that we are much more likely to err by accepting an analysis as complete when it is not really complete than by refusing to do so.

The main attraction of the regularity theory for me, however, lies in the fact that it seems not to admit more than the minimum necessary and therefore does not cumber itself with unproved assertions about causality. All it admits is regular sequence, which seems to be a fact indisputably given in experience, while all other views go very much beyond what can be certainly established empirically. Here, however, a dilemma awaits the advocate of the regularity theory. Is he to maintain 'regularity' in the sense that any event which occurs once will always occur under the same conditions, thus identifying causality with the Principle of the Uniformity of Nature or some similar principle? (The exact formulation of it will vary a great deal.) In that case he is himself going far beyond the evidence of experience and thus partially [1] sacrificing the chief advantage of his own as compared to other views, for while he or anybody else has only experienced observed events he is now making an assertion about events that have not been observed. Or is he to interpret the principle as simply covering only the observed regularities of the past, so that, when anybody says that C is the cause of E, the only part of his assertion which is to be accepted as giving the truth becomes the proposition that C has in all observed cases been regularly followed by E? In that case he must answer the question how induction and the sciences based on induction can be anything more than

[1] Not wholly, because he is still committed to asserting *fewer* propositions about causality which go beyond experience than his opponents.

an illusion. For induction imperatively requires some principles which go beyond what has been observed. This in the past has been regarded as one of the main objections to a philosophy of empiricism.

Recently, however, a somewhat novel attempt has been made by Mr. Ramsey to escape the difficulty raised by induction.[1] He denies the need of 'justifying' induction altogether and yet holds that it may be 'reasonable' to be influenced in our beliefs by inductive evidence, provided we distinguish between two different senses of 'reasonable'. Beliefs based on induction, conscious or unconscious, are not reasonable, he maintains, in the sense of being logically provable or deducible from empirical premisses by any steps which logic could sanction, but they are reasonable in the sense that it is a useful habit to form this kind of belief on the strength of past experience. By calling these habits useful he means that 'the opinions they lead to are for the most part true, or more often true than those which alternative habits would lead to'. He says that the fact, established as he thinks by Hume, that induction cannot be justified on logical grounds at all is no 'scandal to philosophy', any more than it is a scandal that the evidence of memory cannot be logically proved.

Does Mr. Ramsey really avoid the difficulty? In discussing this question I do not propose to deal with his highly ingenious theory of probability and his brief but equally suggestive account of general laws. Fortunately this is not necessary for my purpose. What I shall try to show is that he has not really succeeded in escaping the above-mentioned dilemma. 'Reasonable' is used by him to mean the outcome of a useful habit, and 'useful' to mean leading to opinions which are mostly true (or more often true than those which would have been reached otherwise).[2] But does he mean merely that the habit has led to these true opinions in the past or that it is likely to do so in the future also? That the habit of being influenced by inductive evidence has been useful in the past may have been proved empirically, but this does not make it reasonable to continue to indulge it unless we assume on the strength of past experience that

[1] *The Foundations of Mathematics and Other Logical Essays*, pp. 197-8.
[2] This definition of 'useful' should, in fairness to Mr. Ramsey, be noted carefully. It enables him to escape some of the objections to which the usual pragmatist solution of the difficulty seems open.

the habit will usually continue or at least is likely to continue to be useful. This assumption Mr. Ramsey makes. He means to assert as his belief that a habit which has been useful in the past in leading to true opinions will really more often than not be useful in the future in this way, not merely that it was useful in the past (or the outcome of a useful habit) to believe this. But in that case he is still involved in a dilemma. For he must admit either that he is holding a belief which has no claim whatever to be thought true, even that of utility, or that inductive evidence justifies an inference from past to future utility. He cannot escape by saying again that 'is justified' merely means 'is useful to believe'[1] (i.e. liable to lead to truth), for he has no right to say that the habit of holding beliefs on the strength of inductive evidence is any more liable than any other course to lead to truth in the future, unless he is prepared to admit that in some cases past utility in this way is an adequate ground for inferring at least the likelihood of future utility, i.e. to make a categorical judgment about the future on the strength of inductive evidence. A similar argument would apply against anyone who tried to justify induction by its useful consequences in the past, however he defined useful; but the point against Mr. Ramsey is not that he has failed to justify induction, which he never tried to do, but that he has declared that inductive conclusions are reasonable only in a sense which itself implies that if any inductive conclusions at all are reasonable in this sense at least one [2] must be reasonable not only in this sense but also in another, namely, the sense in which it has usually been held by philosophers that inductive judgments are reasonable. The introduction of his secondary sense of reasonable has thus not provided a *via media* between genuine acceptance of inductive arguments and complete scepticism as to their validity.

Since the only alternative suggested has now broken down, we must make our choice between refusing to accept any inductive evidence at all and admitting that to infer regularities in the future from regularities in the past is reason-

[1] The belief may well also be useful besides being justified in my sense, but he can have no possible right to assert that it is so unless he makes the admission in question.
[2] I.e. the judgment that what was useful in the past will (probably) be useful in the future.

able in a sense other than merely useful. Anyone who adopts the former alternative must hold e.g. that for anything we can tell it is no more likely that he will die shortly after eating a pound of arsenic than after eating a pound of bread, or that it is no more reasonable to think that he will fall to the ground if he jumps out of a window in the top storey of his house than that he will fly. Such sceptical views have not been conclusively refuted by philosophers, and if any reader accepts them I have nothing further to say to him, but I at any rate am so prejudiced, if it be a prejudice, that I cannot do so, and I suspect that most people are in this respect equally prejudiced. As a matter of fact Mr. Ramsey himself seems really to hold that induction is valid in a sense other than useful (or the outcome of a habit which has been useful in leading to true opinions in the past). For he says that 'induction is one of the ultimate sources of knowledge just as memory is',[1] and though he is evidently not using the word knowledge in its strictest sense since he does not claim certainty for the results of induction, the passage obviously implies that he supposes it to give us truth about the future, as memory does about the past.

What he does attack is the view that induction depends for its validity on being justified by logic in the sense of being formally validated by universal *a priori* principles. Now he is undoubtedly right in holding that particular inductive arguments may be legitimately accepted as valid without such a justification, and in holding that if we attempt a justification we fail hopelessly unless we assume principles which are neither deducible from formal logic nor capable of being established by observation. Again he may be right in emphasising the difference between induction and deduction more strongly than has usually been done in the past. But it does not necessarily follow that it is not incumbent on the logician to give a justification of inductive methods and that a philosophy which is incompatible with their being ever justifiable is not on that account open to the gravest objection. In induction we do not, it is true, start by seeing the universal logical principles which hold in all cases and then base our specific arguments on these. On the contrary we may and do see the validity of particular inductive arguments without having thought of or being able to state the general logical principles which they exemplify. But

[1] *Foundations of Mathematics*, etc., p. 197.

deduction is after all situated similarly. We can see the validity of particular syllogistic arguments perfectly well without knowing what a syllogism is or the general conditions under which syllogisms are valid, but it still remains true that every valid syllogism is valid only by virtue of certain general principles, which it is the aim of the logician to discover and formulate, and I should have thought that the same was true of induction.

Inductive arguments do not indeed require justification by the philosopher before they can be seen to be valid, but they would not be valid if they were not capable of such a justification, however difficult it may be in practice to find how to justify them. Deduction and induction are in the same position in this respect, I think, except that in the case of induction we have been far less successful in determining what are the principles involved. We need not wait with using syllogisms till they are justified by logic, but all the same the particular syllogisms we use are only valid in virtue of general principles that fall within the field of logic, and if a system of logic contradicted these general principles it would be at the same time implicitly denying the validity of all the syllogisms used by us. This does not mean that we should be in danger of having to give up our syllogistic arguments as logically unsound; we should rather have to abandon the system of philosophy which contradicted them, and the same holds with induction. Now if we are to avoid contradicting all our particular inductive arguments we must assume that we can pass from past to future regularities. This cannot be a case of merely empirical knowledge for the simple reason that we have never observed the future but only the past, yet if it is not sometimes justified all scientific predictions as to the future are totally groundless. And the same applies to the passage from past events which have been observed by human beings to past events which have not. Every scientific law involves such a passage. It is not merely that the regularity view in the form in which it is confined to empirically established facts cannot justify induction (it has been alleged that all systems fail in this), but that it is incompatible with the very possibility of induction being valid at all.

So we must in any case go beyond the empirical evidence and admit that we can sometimes reasonably infer with a considerable degree of probability that because a regularity has occurred in the past it will occur in the future also.[1] If we are to retain the regularity view of causation, we must then understand it so as to cover not only the fact that regularities have occurred in the past but the justifiable anticipation that they will be repeated in the future under similar conditions. 'C causes E' (or the only part of this proposition which we are justified in believing) then becomes equivalent to something like 'C is always followed by E', i.e. has been always followed by E in the past and will (or will probably) be so in the future. This version of the view is generally held to constitute the only sense of causality in which causality is necessary for induction, the other elements in the common notion of cause generally (though not, if my subsequent argument is correct, rightly) being considered superfluous for this purpose. But the advantage of being reconcilable with induction is achieved only by sacrificing the chief attraction of the other form of the regularity view, namely, that it does not go beyond the empirical evidence. Let us now turn to the positive arguments against the view.

In the first place it is not generally realised that, if the regularity view were the whole truth, all practical life would become sheer nonsense. For practical life presupposes that we can 'do things' and are moved by motives and desires, but it seems to me perfectly obvious that, whatever is meant by these statements, they cannot possibly mean merely what they could alone mean on any form of the regularity view.

If 'causality' meant regularity and if this were the only sense in which causality was true of the self, in what sense could I possibly say that something occurred because I willed it, or even just that I did something, or that my motive for a certain action was so-and-so? To say that an action was willed or was done by me is certainly not merely to say that the action was of a type which follows most or all states of mind like my own at the time under conditions of the type before me, or that my act can be analysed into a set of factors

[1] Mr. Bertrand Russell (*Knowledge of the External World*, p. 226) maintains that the *a priori* principle necessary is 'induction not causality', but what he means by the principle of 'induction' seems reducible to the principle that the same event will happen under the same conditions, which is identical with what is meant by causation on the regularity view. (The interpretation Mr. Russell gives of his principle (id., p. 225) is obviously not meant to be ultimate.) When universalised the regularity view is thus equivalent to what has been usually called the Uniformity of Nature.

each of which is always, whenever it occurs, preceded by some factor in the state which preceded my action on that occasion, or to make either of these statements together with the further statement that most people believe this to be so or that I intend to use it to arrive at opinions about future events (as would have to be the case on Mr. Braithwaite's and Mr. Ramsey's theories respectively). To say that such and such an action is due, e.g. to desire for power as a motive, is more than to say that such actions generally are preceded by desire for power or to make any of the other statements mentioned in the last sentence. It is to say that in this particular case it does not merely follow on but is determined by the desire in question. It is not generally realised that the regularity theory would make all talk about motives senseless, and that every time I speak of myself or anybody else doing anything I must imply causality in a sense other than regularity. I am not arguing that we perceive causal connection immediately in these cases, a proposition which is more doubtful, but that, whatever our ground for believing that will and motives cause action, that belief, which I, like most people, cannot reject, and which does not *necessarily* presuppose *immediate* awareness of the connection, does entail a view of causation different from the regularity view, does entail causation in the sense not of regular sequence but of genuine intrinsic connection. And that, I am surely right in holding, is a very strong argument against the regularity view from any standpoint save that of an epiphenomenalist or of a behaviourist. If the regularity theory be true all practical wisdom, which presupposes throughout that I can do things by willing them and can act from motives, becomes worthless. This does not, strictly speaking, disprove the regularity theory, but the fact that a view inconsistent with it is presupposed in all practical action and all the psychology and ethics of practical action is, if not a strict proof, a sufficiently strong argument to make our conclusion highly probable.

Memory itself, I think, presupposes causality in a sense other than any admitted by the regularity view. If we are to be aware of the past in memory we must think of the past as determining or at least causally affecting our present state in remembering it; if our state is not in any degree determined by the past event we have no genuine memory but a fancy or illusion. (I do not mean that remembering an event is the *same* as having our present state determined by the event or that the cognitive relation in question is a species of causality, but at any rate it *involves* causality.) Now that the past event I remember affects my present state obviously means more than that a similar state of mind always follows a similar past event, or that both terms can be analysed into a number of elements of which this is true. For it is not a statement about what usually happens but about a particular cognition in a particular self, and it involves a real dependence of my state in remembering on that which is remembered by me. So here again the regularity view proves totally inadequate.

'The whole foundation of Hume's scepticism is destroyed if it is once admitted that the fainter copy of an impression may be so connected with its original that in perceiving the copy we *eo ipso* know immediately not only this, but the previous existence of the impression as the original of the copy. For to admit this is to admit necessary connection in matters-of-fact.'[1]

Thirdly, if any beliefs due to inference are ever justified, the regularity theory of causation is refuted, for to say that the reason why I believe x was y implies, among other things, that a part-cause of my belief in x was my belief in y[2] in a sense in which it cannot be reduced to a proposition that all beliefs of the same kind as my belief in x follow in time or accompany beliefs of the same kind as my belief in y,[3] or any other similar proposition. If we do not admit this, none of our beliefs supposed to be grounded on inference can be rational, for in that case the intrinsic character of the reasons has nothing to do with our holding a belief to be true. All that has happened is that we hold it to be true *after* having entertained these reasons, for no other closer connection is admitted at all by the regularity view.[4]

---

[1] Stout, *Mind and Matter*, pp. 218–19.
[2] Note that the causal relation I assert is not between x and y themselves but between believing x and believing y. Nor do I say that to infer x from y is the same as to believe x because I believed y, only that the former is impossible without the latter.
[3] Nor can it be reduced to this plus the proposition that everybody does under certain conditions believe that a belief in x will always be followed by a belief in y, or any proposition or propositions of this character.
[4] I do not mean that the relation between the premisses and conclusion in an inferred belief can be reduced to one of causation or defined in terms of causation.

If there were no causal connection beyond regularity of sequence, it is difficult to see how we could ever have arrived at the notion that there was anything more. To do so we should have had, in Locke's phraseology, to create a new simple idea. The advocate of the regularity view cannot reply that it is an illegitimate extension of a concept based on the experience of willing, or, as Hume holds, on the experience of being necessarily determined by association to think in a certain way, for if we do experience ourselves as determining and determined in this fashion we have already therein directly experienced causality. In the one case the experience is of ourselves as cause; in the other case it is of a phase in ourselves as effect of something else, either also in ourselves or external to us. Either the will really is causally active, in which case there is some causation other than mere 'regularity'; or it is not, in which case the illusion is still unexplained. We may give a similar answer to Hume's attempted explanation. For us to apply necessity, as he holds, through a confusion to the external world, we must first have experienced it at least in ourselves, passively if not actively, and if so we have causality, there at any rate, in a sense other than regularity. To be conscious of ourselves as determined or constrained is not merely to be conscious of our state as succeeding certain events and to remember from experience that such a state regularly followed such events in the past; and, if it were only that, Hume would not have explained the origin of the belief that causality is something more than regular sequence. If we were only conscious of causation in ourselves in the sense of regular sequence, why should the experience of being determined to think in a certain way lead us to make the mistake, as Hume considers it, of applying causality in the fuller sense to the external world, any more than does our experience of physical events and objects?[1]

It may indeed, for anything I have yet said, be still true that causation prevails in the physical world in the sense merely of regularity, for the arguments from motives, etc., memory and rational belief apply only to the self. But a particular pro-

---

[1] (3rd ed.) It might be held that the notion of causality was derived from the application of the notion of logical necessity which we acquired through seeing one proposition to follow necessarily from another in cases where we admittedly see it to do so, whether we regard this application as an error or not.

position is sufficient to refute the contradictory universal. Further, if causation in the self involves something very different from mere regularity, the probability that this will be so too with causation in the external world is very much heightened.

Also if, as seems to be the case, we are immediately aware of ourselves as passive in perception or in facing obstacles to action, I should have thought that this must imply that we are at the same time immediately aware that something external [1] is acting or has acted causally on us in a sense which, just as much as with our awareness of ourselves, goes beyond mere sequence, however regular. Professor Whitehead has rightly, I think, insisted on the consciousness of the causal efficacy of physical objects acting on us as the primary, or at least a primary, factor in perception.

A further argument commonly employed is that causation is involved in the very notion of a physical object. The argument seems to me to be a strong one, and, if valid at all, to prove causation in a sense other than regularity, for it seems to me clear that we cannot consistently think successive states as belonging to the same thing unless we think them as connected in some way like that demanded by the critics of the doctrine of external relations or at least in a way very different from any compatible with the regularity doctrine. It seems to me that, whatever else their combination in one object involves, it must at least involve necessary connection. I do not agree with Mr. Braithwaite when he maintains in reply to an argument of this kind that ' the principle connecting into a unity the states of a substance may quite as well be a universal of fact as a universal of law '.[2] For a principle that connects them into a unity must involve some objective relation between them beyond mere temporal sequence, but the regularity principle, which constitutes a ' universal of fact ', gives no such relation. It merely adds to the assertion of temporal sequence the further assertion that what we call the effect always occurs in the relation of temporal sequence to the cause when what we call the cause is repeated. But this does not give us any new relation beyond temporal

---

[1] We need not be clear what that something is in order to have this awareness. We may be aware of our state as the effect of something, as constrained by something, without knowing what it is of which the state is the effect.

[2] *Mind*, N.S. XXXVII, no. 145, p. 70.

sequence, but merely asserts the regular occurrence of the relation of temporal sequence, and this relation is clearly not enough for the purpose. It is not merely that the later states succeed the earlier and that in all similar conditions similar states succeed and would succeed on similar; this would give no intrinsic connection at all, yet they could not be different states of the same thing without a very genuine and close connection.

It may be objected that the fact that they belong to one substance is sufficient to connect them; but this will not hold, for we cannot say that they are not intrinsically connected themselves but related merely by belonging to the same substance unless we are prepared to separate a substance from all its states and qualities, a view which seems untenable and would now generally be rejected. Unless a substance and its successive states are to be completely separated, the substance cannot retain its identity if its successive states and qualities are not intrinsically connected but merely follow according to uniform laws on each other. The qualities and states, it would seem, must be united together and grounded in the nature of the substance, and that involves causality. We need not hold that substance is reducible to causality, but we must, I think, hold that it implies the latter. And by similar arguments we can show the presence of causal connection in the self as a necessary prerequisite of its unity. Whether such an argument proves universal causality is more doubtful, but it seems at least to prove some causality other than regularity.

But I shall not lay my main stress on this argument. There remain two more which to my mind conclusively disprove the regularity view not only of the self but of the physical world, provided only we assume the validity of some of the ordinary inductive arguments used by natural science, and if we do not assume this we have no right to accept as true the conclusions of science. I do not demand that philosophers should justify induction before they accept results reached by it in science, but I demand that if they accept it in science they should not also accept views in philosophy which are totally inconsistent with the very possibility of its being valid. The arguments which I shall adduce also lead definitely to the conclusion that one of the relations included in the relation of causality is that of logical entailment. If good reason can be given for this conclusion we ought not to be deterred from admitting it by our inability to see the logical connection involved in particular laws of nature or understand why a particular cause should entail its particular effect, as we can understand why one side of a Euclidean triangle cannot be greater than the sum of the other two sides, for C may perfectly well entail E without our being able to see that it does so, and we may have general grounds for assuming the presence of a logical necessity which we cannot grasp ourselves, or at least see that this assumption is really presupposed in all our scientific reasoning.

Now, in the first place, if scientific arguments are to have any validity at all, it must be possible to argue legitimately from cause to effect, but no inference can possibly be legitimate unless the premisses really entail the conclusion. And how a conclusion can be entailed by premisses in any sense which justifies us in inferring it from the premisses if it is *logically* independent of the premisses, if it is *logically* quite possible that it should be otherwise, is quite beyond my comprehension. At least it is incumbent on anyone who dissents to give an alternative sense of 'entail' according to which we shall be justified in inferring conclusions from premisses when there is no logical connection between them, and I think I can safely defy him to do so. Any comprehensible view of the relation between cause and effect that is compatible with the fact that we can infer one from the other must admit this logical connection. Therefore, if science is to have any claim to truth, the cause must really involve, necessitate the effect, not indeed, as far as we can prove by this argument, in any sense in which the effect cannot equally necessitate the cause, but in a sense which is quite incompatible with the view that it is merely a case of regular temporal following. True, a premiss is a proposition or a set of propositions, and a cause an event; but how can there be a valid argument from a proposition or set of propositions to another proposition or set of propositions unless the content of the fact referred to in the one is really entailed by the content of the fact referred to in the other? If it is not, the argument is simply a *non sequitur*. This is overlooked in the case of causality because by the roundabout method of problematic induction, i.e. by observing instances and concluding on the strength of them that there is a connection, we are able to make the inference without seeing the connection, an achievement which would be impossible in deduction of the ordinary type; but though we cannot see such a connection we really covertly assume that there is one whenever we make any causal inference whatever. How can we possibly be justified in deducing the effect from the cause unless we suppose that it is dependent on or follows necessarily *from* the cause and does not merely follow it ? The relation of entailment present in causality is no doubt due to very different conditions from those which justify *a priori* inferences in pure mathematics and logic,[1] but entailment there must be if our inference is to be justified. We have no reason whatever for supposing that E will follow C in the future as well as in the past unless we suppose that the content of the two is so connected that, C being what it is, it *cannot* because of its intrinsic nature, and not merely always does not, occur without being followed by E.

The relation of causation shares with non-causal logical entailment at least its most important feature, namely, that it justifies inference. This is the principal reason, I imagine, why the philosophers of an earlier age generally treated cause as a species of logical ground, and this argument has in modern times, as far as I can see, been indeed overlooked but not refuted. Mr. Ramsey would no doubt have said that we have only shown that it is reasonable in some sense to form such beliefs, not that it is reasonable in the sense in which a logical conclusion is reasonable. But we have seen above [2] that his attempt to distinguish two different senses of 'reasonable' breaks down.

It does not indeed follow that the relation of causality is simply identical with or a species of the relation of logical entailment, indeed this seems to me certainly false; but it does follow that this is one of the relations which together make up the complex relation of causality. We need not and must not assume that causality is a perfectly simple relation and that the feature of it which is clearest to us must be the only import-

[1] The difference between entailment in logic or mathematics and the entailment involved in causation lies in the following circumstances on my view : (*a*) the general conditions governing and affecting it are very different in the two cases ; (*b*) the terms connected by it are also very different in the two cases ; (*c*) we cannot understand it or see its validity in the case of causality, but only assume on the strength of inductive evidence that it holds between given characteristics ; (*d*) though entailment is one relation present in causation, it is certainly not the only relation present. It would be false to say, e.g., that causation = a relation of entailment between events in time, because entailment is not the only relation included in causation. What the other relations are I am not trying to decide.

[2] p. 157 ff.

ant one, though this seems to be a fallacy which most philosophers who have dealt with the subject have committed in one way or another.

Let us now proceed to the second argument.[1] Current accounts of scientific thought make great play with the notion of establishing a generalisation by showing the extreme improbability of the repeated occurrence of instances in accordance with it if the generalisation be not in fact true. But, if the regularity view be right, all generalisations are nothing but sheer coincidences. If there is a connection between cause C and effect E so that one really explains or entails and does not just in fact precede the other, then the coincidence is indeed removed because there is now available a reason why E should always follow C, but not otherwise. On the regularity view there still just remains the brute fact that E always follows C, and that by itself is just as improbable as if an unweighted penny showed heads every time it was tossed. And indeed the strongest argument for the truth of inductively established laws is often, or even perhaps usually :—if the law in question or some law like it did not hold, it would be extraordinarily improbable (one chance in many thousands or millions) that E should in all the observed instances have followed C, therefore it is much the most likely alternative that the law (or some law like it) is true. Now read for 'law' 'fact that E always succeeds C', and the argument becomes : in the absence of any further conclusions, the chance of E succeeding C in all, say the hundred, observed instances is one in many millions, which would be a very improbable coincidence, therefore we had better suppose that E not only succeeds C in these hundred cases but also in all the thousands or millions of unobserved cases, (for that is all that a law now means), though this should according to the previous reasoning be millions of times more improbable still! The extraordinary unlikeliness of the generalisation cannot be removed unless we suppose a logical connection between C and E. If a 'law' stands for nothing but the mere fact that E always follows C, to posit such a general law because it is fulfilled in many cases is only to increase the improbability, and there can be no possibility of diminishing it unless to generalise by means of a causal law signifies something more than to assert an endless repetition of instances. If C and E be logically connected so that the

[1] For this cf. Professor Montague, *Proceedings of the Seventh International Congress of Philosophy*, p. 198 ff.

one entails the other the coincidence disappears, but otherwise how can it?

It might be objected that the notion of probability or improbability itself presupposes causation and that therefore an argument based on the improbability of a coincidence cannot be used as an argument for causation, but (*a*) if it does presuppose causation in the fuller sense, anybody who uses an argument from improbability or probability, as all inductive logicians do, has already presupposed this, and *cadit quaestio*; (*b*) if it only presupposes causation in the sense of regularity, this is no objection to using an argument from improbability to prove that causation holds in another sense also; (*c*) as Dr. Keynes has shown, probability and improbability are not notions which presuppose causation in any sense, since they are applicable where causation does not occur, e.g. to some propositions about numbers [1] or to the chances of a particular non-causal argument establishing a given conclusion. I have indeed assumed that the frequency view of probability is false, and I can hardly afford the space to examine the arguments which to my mind render this view quite untenable.[2] I will only say that, if the frequency view be true, the argument that a combination of events is highly improbable on any other ground than that such a combination has never or very rarely occurred in the past becomes nonsensical; and therefore we could never support a hypothesis by arguing that otherwise a combination of events frequently observed would be very improbable. But no modern logician who rejects causation in the older sense has constructed or could construct an inductive logic which dispenses with such arguments.

To sum up, then, I do not claim to have disproved the regularity view, but I do claim to have shown that to hold such a view is very unreasonable. Nobody has indeed succeeded in defining altogether satisfactorily what else is involved in causation, but it is no argument for accepting an unsatisfactory definition that nobody has given a satisfactory one, and we cannot exclude the possibility that causation or some factors in it are unanalysable. I reject the regularity view as

---

[1] E.g. it is very much less probable that all prime numbers between ten billion and eleven billion which have never been thought of by anybody should be one less than the square of some number than that at least one of them should.

[2] V. Keynes, *A Treatise on Probability*, ch. 8.

a complete account because it goes beyond the empirical evidence without going far enough either to reconcile itself with our intuitive convictions as to causality or to provide a basis for induction, because it would really commit us to accepting a countless host of extraordinary coincidences the probability of which is of the order of one in millions, because it is irreconcilable with any account of the self which admits willed action or motives and so with the assumptions of our whole moral and practical life, because its denial is implied in the conception of physical objects and of the self alike, and indeed in all rational action and belief. The view only seems tolerable because men have not the leisure each time they use the word cause to think out what it means afresh and therefore are apt to forget the way in which they have defined it, so that while they may accept the regularity view when they reflect on the matter abstractly they unconsciously still use the term cause on other occasions as if a contrary view were true. And if the regularity view were true, the fact that causation has ever been thought to involve the features mentioned other than regularity would be totally inexplicable.

What positive account can we now give of the nature of causation? What characteristics can we ascribe to it? In the first place, though we have rejected the regularity view as a complete account of causation, we may accept it gratefully as a partial account, and affirm that causality involves among other things uniform sequence. But every one of the objections to the regularity view given above shows the presence also of something which is extremely hard to define but may be roughly indicated by the words, intrinsic or inherent connection. Others may perhaps think this in different ways, but such a connection I can only think at all definitely by thinking cause and effect as connected by a relation of logical entailment, i.e. as internally related in the tenth sense of this term.[1] That we must admit this relation of entailment between them if we are to accept the most universally admitted inductive inferences of science seems to be definitely proved by the last two arguments in particular. This justifies the acceptance of the first two of the four features of causation mentioned [2] as implied in the ' common-sense ' view (if they can indeed be separated, which

[1] I.e. so related that one is logically dependent for its existence on the other, and that it would be logically impossible for the one to be what it is without the other existing also.
[2] V. above, p. 154.

I doubt), i.e. (1) intrinsic connection, (2) logical entailment; and the second point at least carries with it the fourth, necessity. It is an additional objection to the regularity view that it is impossible to identify 'could not be otherwise' with 'always is'. Those who find it depressing to think that the future is logically entailed by the past must remember that it is equally true that the past is logically entailed by the future. In this respect the relation of causation is symmetrical, since the cause can be inferred from the effect as well as the effect from the cause, though in other respects, as I point out in the next paragraph, it may not be so.

The third feature, commonly known in philosophical circles as 'activity', presents greater difficulties, but it is fortunately not necessary to discuss it here. The chief reason for assuming its presence is that it seems obvious that the cause produces or determines the effect in a sense in which the effect cannot be said to produce or determine the cause, but I know neither of any proof of this apparently obvious proposition nor of any satisfactory analysis of 'activity'. But that may be because the proposition is self-evident and the concept unanalysable, indeed I am rather inclined to think that this is so. But in any case, while logical entailment is a part, it is not the whole of causation. This we can see quite clearly, though what the other factors are may be very obscure. But, whatever be the whole truth about causation, it is sufficient for the argument of this book to have shown that logical entailment is present between cause and effect. We must now return to this important point and explain it somewhat further, since it is one which seems repugnant to the present generation.

The view that causation involves logical entailment has often been stated in a radically wrong way. It is often said that the effect must be contained in the cause or that there must be identity between cause and effect. These statements, taken strictly, are preposterous. The effect cannot be contained in the cause, for otherwise all causation would be simultaneous; and it cannot be identical with the cause in the proper sense of the word, for otherwise it would not be a different event. Both views would do away with change and so with causation itself. Even if it were true that the effect consists merely of a redistribution in space of the same entities as are present in the cause and that causation does not involve a change in their qualities, a conception which played an enormous part in the development of the mechanistic view of the universe,[1] the second distribution would still not be, properly speaking, either contained in or identical with the first. There is something present that was not present before, namely a new arrangement of the same things, and 'contained in' becomes only a metaphor. If there is a logical connection between cause and effect, it must still be a synthetic and not an analytic connection. If we assume all logical connection to be merely analytic, Hume's argument certainly holds against the view that causality has any kinship with such a connection.

That causality involves a relation of logical entailment between cause and effect is proved, I have contended, by the fact that we can argue from the cause to the effect, which presupposes that the former entails the latter, though we cannot understand the connection. This view is not inconsistent with the well-warranted principle that existence cannot be proved *a priori*. What was true *a priori* would still be not a categorical but a hypothetical proposition, not that a certain effect (E) exists, but that, *if* a certain cause (C) exists, a certain effect (E) must do so, or *vice versa*. At the same time it is necessary to insist that, when we have said that the cause logically entails the effect, we have not given a complete account of causation, this being both beyond the scope of the present book and beyond the author's capacity. Causation includes but is not reducible to a relation of logical entailment.

Even so my view of causation is flagrantly inconsistent with certain widely held theories of inference. If logical relations can only hold between propositions and not between facts in the real world, or if all inferences are merely 'analytic', or if inference and logic have merely to do with symbols and not with the realities to which the symbols refer, then it will be impossible to suppose that a logical connection between cause and effect could ever be perceived by any mind, even by Omniscience itself. But I feel bound on general grounds unconnected with causation to reject the

[1] Thus the idea that the cause should make the effect logically intelligible, by leading men to assume, wherever possible, that it was like the effect, has played a large part in the development even of physical science. (Cf. the insistence of scientists, till the last few years at any rate, that change must be 'continuous', and the arguments used against the interaction of body and mind.) Personally, however, I do not hold that logical entailment need involve likeness.

views of inference in question.[1] The connection between cause and effect is indeed synthetic, but so, I hold, is the logical relation of entailment, at least in some cases. 'To entail' does not mean 'to include'. At the same time rationalistic philosophers are going too far if they simply identify cause with logical ground. The relation between cause and effect includes other relations besides entailment, and is therefore not identical with the relation subsisting between logical or mathematical propositions in virtue of which one or more propositions entail another. In both cases there is the relation of entailment, but the other relations between the terms are too different to be classed together by us. The difference between the two cases was grossly slurred over by most pre-Kantian thinkers, but I doubt whether the modern reaction against this tendency has not gone even further from the truth in the opposite direction. In that case the world possesses more of the characteristics of a logical system than is now usually admitted. If I had been writing three hundred or, for that matter, thirty years ago, I should, if I had been wise enough (which would doubtless not have been the case), have insisted rather on the difference between causality and non-causal logical entailment, but this is remembered far too well nowadays to need stressing, what is forgotten is their similarity. Whether these conclusions can be used to justify some form of the coherence theory is a question I shall discuss in the next chapter.

It is not a necessary consequence of what I have said that the set of events known as the cause must be the whole logical ground of the effect, the whole reason for its occurrence. This must be found rather in the world system as a whole, one would imagine. But, whatever the ground is held to be, and even if it be held to reside ultimately in the whole or in a timeless reality of which physical events are mere appearances, *part* of it must lie in the physical cause, for what is to be explained is the sequence of an event E on another C, and the special nature of C and E must be relevant to this. Even if we were to adopt occasionalism and to regard every physical event as due to the will of God operating without the mediation of any other event or object, yet we should be bound to suppose that there was something in the apparent physical cause which made God think it suitable that it should be followed by

[1] V. below, ch. V, sect. 5.

the event which was its physical effect, for otherwise the act of God in connecting the two would be unmotived and irrational, so we should even then have to suppose a connection between cause and effect dependent partly on their intrinsic character.[1]

The principal difficulty which has led to the abandonment of the older view of causation is that we seem unable in any case to see an *a priori* connection between a cause and its effect or *vice versa*. No causal law which we can formulate is either logically self-evident or, as far as we can see, deducible *a priori* from any self-evident propositions. But this does not prove that there is no *a priori* connection. An Egyptian thinker of three thousand years ago would have no doubt denied any *a priori* connection between the different properties of triangles on the ground that he could see none. Inability to detect the presence of a connection cannot prove its absence. Obviously the properties of concrete events are far more complex than the properties of triangles, and even the advocates of the coherence theory do not and need not maintain that particular causal laws are logically necessary when taken by themselves. Their necessity on that view lies only in their relation to the whole system, which we cannot possibly be expected to understand, so that if there is an *a priori* connection there are very good reasons to explain why we cannot see it. That there might be a very large number of *a priori* connections of which we are not aware a realist should be the last person to deny. To maintain, as Hume does, that if we can see no connection between two events therefore they are quite separate and unconnected is sheer dogmatism, though it comes from one who is reputed the most sceptical of philosophers. Besides, how could we expect to see the connection when we do not know the two things between which alone it really holds, the *whole* cause and the *whole* effect?

Even though we cannot see such a connection, the assumption that there is such a one has been implicit from the earliest ages in our demand for causes and in our inductions. To ask for a cause was primarily to ask for a reason; and the usual ground why men have assumed the past to be a valid guide to the future in induction has always been because they assumed that there was a relation between cause and effect such that the former inherently involved the latter and that the latter was therefore impossible, and not merely

[1] (3rd ed.) Unless it is held, as apparently by Berkeley, that it is good there should be general laws but it does not matter what the laws are.

did not occur in fact, without the other. Thinkers and scientists looked for causes because they wished to *explain* events, and if they had seriously held from the beginning the views of causation which most realist philosophers hold to-day, half the inspiration of the scientific search for causes would have been missing and induction would never have been trusted at all. It is the opposite view, the type of view I am defending, which has led scientists to seek for causes, under the impression that the discovery of them would make the world more intelligible,[1] and to suppose that their findings had universal validity, though based on particular observations and experiments. Hence almost all philosophers prior to Hume held that there was an intelligible logical connection between facts in the physical world despite their inability to discern its nature.

Further, it seems to me that in the psychological, though not in the physical, sphere we do have faint glimmerings of such *a priori* insight.[2] It seems to me that we can see and to some extent really understand why an insult should tend to give rise to anger, why love should lead to grief if the object of one's love die or prove thoroughly unworthy, why a success should give pleasure, why the anticipation of physical pain should arouse fear. It does seem more reasonable on *other than inductive*[3] grounds to suppose that if A loves

[1] An enormous part has been played in scientific as well as philosophical controversy by the assumption that the real cause must be like the effect. This is evidently an inference, though not necessarily a correct inference, from the view that the cause explains and implies the effect. It was felt that causation by what is like is more intelligible than causation by the unlike. This assumption cannot be explained as the result of experience, because in the causal connections with which we are most familiar in experience cause and effect are often most unlike. Can there be anything much more unlike than an act of will and a movement in my body, than a vibrating piston and the noise it makes, than a physical wound and a sensation of pain, than a coloured image and certain wave-lengths, than water and hydrogen and oxygen together just before their combination into water? There is no conjunction of events which we have experienced more frequently than that of a physical event and a feeling, yet this seems of them all the least and not the most intelligible. (It may be objected that the instances mentioned never constitute the *whole* cause, but then experience never gives us that at all.)

[2] On this subject v. also Stout, *Studies in Philosophy and Psychology*, p. 77 ; Shand, *Foundations of Character*, p. 19 ; Köhler, *Gestaltpsychologie*, Engl. ed., p. 268 ff.

[3] I mean by induction here as elsewhere in this chapter non-intuitive, or, as Mr. Johnson calls it, problematic induction.

B that will tend to make him sorry when B dies than to suppose that it will make him intensely glad, or that to be told he has done something exceedingly well will be pleasant rather than unpleasant to A when he thinks that the remark is made by a man qualified to judge and is really meant.[1] It may indeed happen that by the time B dies A will have gone mad and will actually rejoice in the occurrence, or that owing to some violent quarrel the love will have changed to hate. It is again possible that A may school himself actually to rejoice in being abused as a part of his moral training or as an opportunity for the exercise of patience, and even that he may carry this to such a morbid extreme as actually to regret his own successes, but what we see, if we see anything, is not that love *must* lead to grief or that success *must* give pleasure, but that there is a causal tendency for it to do so, which will operate unless prevented by other circumstances but which *may* be counteracted. If A loves B, there is a tendency at least for him to feel grief at B's death. Nor do I suppose that men perceived this general principle to be true in advance of experience ; as with all general principles we first apprehend it in particular instances in our experience, and then by a kind of *intuitive* induction reach the general principle. I do not suggest that such a principle is self-evident in the degree in which the fundamental principles of logic are, but I am convinced on general grounds that we must admit different degrees of self-evidence.[2] In this case our insight is lacking in certainty and clearness, but it may be present for all that. We may be in a position in regard to some of the general laws of psychology analogous to that in which an unintelligent schoolboy who is just beginning to comprehend the proofs of the most elementary theorems stands in regard to geometry. He does not yet fully grasp the points involved, his notions are obscure and confused, but yet he is in a higher position than if he had a total and absolute lack of insight. Our power of insight is not marked enough to help us much in reaching conclusions as to laws, which have therefore to be based on problematic induction, but in some cases we seem to be able to see a certain intelligibility, if not necessity, in the law discovered that we do not see in any causal laws of the physical sciences. At any rate anybody who denies altogether the insight for which I am contending will have to hold that

[1] Another good instance of this is the relation between belief in the premisses of a valid argument and belief in the conclusion (v. Stout in Arist. Supp. Vol. XIV p. 50).
[2] V. below, ch. V, sect. 5, *ad fin.*

it is just as reasonable to think of love as causing intense joy at the death of the person loved, except that this does not happen in fact; and it is certainly difficult to accept such a view.

The instance in which this insight has been most commonly asserted is a less defensible one. It has been asserted in the case of the connection between volition and physical movement, but in that case it has to meet the objection that what is called the effect here is connected with the cause by many intermediate steps involved in the physiological apparatus for controlling our movements and that of the intermediate steps we have, apart from the empirical evidence of the physiologist, not the remotest idea.[1] But if we substitute for physical movement the thought willed and confine ourselves to the voluntary control of mental, not of bodily processes, our position is less open to attack. The argument that the effect does not follow in all cases, i.e. that we sometimes fail to control our thoughts as well as our bodies, may be met if we hold that what we are aware of is not that the act of will is a sufficient cause, but that there is a causal tendency in virtue of which it will *per se* make the effect in question more likely, though it may be counteracted by other causes.[2] We may note in this connection that the other instances of apparent insight I have given are instances connected with certain conative tendencies.

My argument is not overthrown by the possibility that there may exist somewhere non-human minds of a quite different psychological 'make-up' in whom these laws do not operate. For what we perceive, if anything, is not the absolute necessity of these laws but their intelligibility within the system constituted by human nature as we know it,[3] and consequently great deviations from this nature would

---

[1] I do not think the objection sufficient to refute the view completely, if it is held that what we see is only a causal *tendency*, but combined with the utter unintelligibility in general of the connection between mind and body it seems sufficient to me to make the view unreasonable.

[2] To control one's thoughts for long by an effort of will is extremely difficult, but to turn one's attention *momentarily* to a subject as a result of a volitional act is perhaps not beyond the capacity of the weakest of us. The difficulty lies in keeping our attention fixed on it.

[3] I agree with the coherence theory that the real ground of at least most inferences is the system within which they are made as a whole.

negative the connection. Further, the connection perceived is, as I have said, at the most only a causal tendency and not a law in virtue of which an effect inevitably follows.

It may be objected that there only appears to be a connection of the kind in question because we do not call a sentiment love unless it involves a tendency to feel grief at the loss of its object, or call an event a success unless it is liable to give pleasure. But this cannot be the explanation, for the characteristics of tending to arouse grief at the loss of its object and tending to arouse pleasure are certainly not the only characteristics of love and of success respectively. It is therefore not a merely verbal judgment that these characteristics tend to accompany the other characteristics of love and success. If it were, we could not say that A loved B till we knew that he had lost or thought he had lost B and that he felt grief in consequence.

The apparent intelligibility cannot be explained by repeated experience, since we have experienced many physical connections still more frequently without their seeming intelligible. If we hold to the traditional conception of what *a priori* insight is we must deny that we have any sort of *a priori* insight here, for we do not know the truth and see the logical necessity of any causal laws in advance of experience, but if we admit what I contend elsewhere [1] that some degree of *a priori* insight may occur without certainty and without yielding definite clear-cut judgments, then it does seem that such *a priori* insight occurs in the case of causal laws governing the human mind but not in the case of causal laws governing the action of matter. It was because too much was expected of the *a priori* that the slight degree of *a priori* insight we do possess in psychology passed unheeded. What insight we have does not enable us to prove causal laws in advance of all experience, but it may well be at work helping in the decision between two different hypotheses, whether in theoretical psychology or in practical life. I doubt whether the decision that one hypothesis is more likely than another because it is more in line with a particular man's character or human nature in general can be explained entirely by previous experience without some further insight into the connections involved, and this insight *may* be one of the features that distinguish the good from the bad psychologist. Anybody who denies such insight altogether should at least

[1] Ch. V, sect. 5, *ad fin.*

explain why it is that the connection between love and grief at the death of the person loved, success and joy, pain and fear, praise and self-satisfaction, seems natural and intrinsically suitable in a way in which the even more frequently experienced connections between different physical events do not.

If it be true that we can have even glimmerings of an *a priori* connection in the case of the mind, the fact that we do not have them in the case of matter need not trouble us, for we have at the most only a skeleton knowledge of the real nature of matter,[1] and therefore it would be strange indeed if we could see an *a priori* connection there. But this is not the case with mind, since we have immediate experience of one mind, our own.

It may be objected that while, if A genuinely entails B, A cannot ever be a fact without B also being so, the causal connection mentioned as holding between e.g. love and grief does not hold in all cases, and that I have therefore by speaking of 'causal tendencies' only concealed an insuperable gulf between causal connection and logical entailment. To this I should reply (i) that it is still *universally* true both, (*a*) that the love of a person makes the occurrence of grief at his death *more probable* than would otherwise be the case, and (*b*) that, *other things being equal*, the person who loves him would always feel the grief. Where he does not, this is due to other counteracting factors. (ii) I think that our premisses, as in at least many cases of non-causal logical entailment, are not just one or two isolated circumstances but these circumstances in conjunction with our rough idea of the system within which the inference takes place, here our general idea of the man's nature or of human nature in general. But the imperfections in our idea of the system adequately explain any uncertainty. Grief does not follow from love of B + B's death taken alone but from these within a causal system, and since our knowledge of the system is very imperfect there are always unknown factors to make the inference uncertain. The whole cause would universally entail, absolutely necessitate the effect, but we never know the cause as a whole. There is nothing surprising in a failure to reach conclusions which hold universally if we only know

[1] The 'primary qualities', which are the only ones generally recognised as causally effective, obviously cannot constitute the inner nature of material objects.

THE THEORY OF INTERNAL RELATIONS

part of the premisses required to establish them, and yet a knowledge of even part of the premisses may sometimes give us some rough indication of the conclusions which would be really established by fuller knowledge, or result in certain laws based on a generalisation from experience seeming intelligible and natural to us in a way in which others do not.

I have not assumed in all this that causation is universal, though in another book I have argued in favour of that view.[1] For, even if it is not universal, it is obvious that it does play at least a part in determining every event we know in the physical realm and that any mind in which causality played no part would be unthinkable to us, for it would be a mind that never acted from any motive whatever. Consequently, if I be right in my contentions as to the nature of causality, we cannot in any case reasonably refuse to the universe as far as known by us the title of a real system, though, unless causality be completely universal, it would, like many other systems, not completely determine all its members.

The question whether causality is universal or not is one which belongs quite definitely to the domain of philosophy. Any attempt to settle it by means of a special science is as much an encroachment as it would be for a philosopher to try to settle particular points in a science by metaphysical arguments. Such encroachments must be resisted, whether they be in favour of determinism, as they were till quite recently, or whether they be in favour of indeterminism, as they usually are now. Empirical evidence cannot possibly establish either alternative. We cannot argue that, because a great many events have been successfully ascribed to causes by science, therefore all events must have causes. The proportion of events of which science ever claimed to have found the causes has always been very small compared to the total number of events, and the causes even of these have only been found by assuming *a priori* some principle of causality. Nor can we argue that, because science has failed to discover the causes of some important class of events, therefore they have no cause. Science can only reach its results by mathematics, observation and causal inference, and since universal causality obviously cannot be disproved mathematically, or by observation, as we cannot observe the absence

[1] *Kant's Treatment of Causality*, ch. IV. For an attempt to reconcile this with human freedom, v. id., pp. 215–22.

of causes, a scientific disproof would have to run like this: Some events can be best explained [1] causally if we deny that they have any causes,—an argument which is obviously not of a very cogent character. For the philosopher to refuse to regard scientific evidence as relevant here is not to tamper with science but to refuse to allow the scientist illegitimately to tamper with philosophy. But this is not to deny all philosophical importance to recent discoveries. It may well be the case—though I do not profess the scientific knowledge to form a judgment as to whether it is so—that these discoveries mark the final breakdown of the whole way in which thinkers of the last three centuries have viewed physical causality. But it is obviously, to put it mildly, far too early to say that, because one type of causal explanation has failed, therefore none is possible at all.[2]

That 'mechanical' causality is a category inadequate to reality is a discovery anticipated by the despised idealists themselves. They did not indeed foretell that any such discoveries would be made within science itself, but they did emphatically maintain that, whatever its scientific value, the conception of mechanical causality was ultimately inadequate and untrue; and this very view of theirs they held as a deduction from the doctrine that reality is a thoroughly unified whole, the doctrine which it is now so widely assumed has been refuted just because the prophecies based on it seem to have come true. It may be that the conception of mechanical causality fails us not because the universe is too little of a system but because it is too much of an interconnected system for a view which uses only one narrow set of characteristics ('primary qualities') in its causal explanations to be true. It may be simply that the universe is too much of a unity for such drastic abstractions completely and ultimately to succeed. Or, if again some readers attach their preference to the suggestion that the movements of electrons cannot be determined by general laws but vary according to the individuality or spontaneity of the different electrons themselves, this need only mean that they find their cause

[1] Even if 'causally explained' is used in the 'Pickwickian' sense in which it is generally used by upholders of the 'regularity' type of view.
[2] The view that recent scientific discoveries establish indeterminism is strongly condemned by Einstein himself, and by M. Planck in *Where is Science Going?*

THE THEORY OF INTERNAL RELATIONS

in the differing internal character of the different electrons, not that they have no cause at all.

But, whether causality is universal or not, it seems clear that realist and pluralist critics have not paid sufficient attention to the fact that there is at least one all-pervasive relation which makes a difference to its terms in a very real sense and is sufficient to give to the world a unity closer than any that could be given by mere juxtaposition. For, even if I should have gone much too far in my contentions about logical entailment and causality, it is at any rate perfectly clear that causality is internal:

(a) in the sixth sense, i.e. it follows from the nature of its terms, in some sense of 'follow' other than that of regular sequence;

(b) in the seventh sense, i.e. it could not have been absent (in some sense of 'could not' distinct from 'never is') without at least one of its terms being different;

(c) in the ninth sense, i.e. neither could the cause have existed without the effect following nor the effect have existed without being preceded by the cause.

If we accept universal causation we are thus driven to the conclusion that everything in the physical universe is internally related in the sixth, seventh and ninth senses, not indeed to everything else, if by that is meant all other events in the universe as separate events, but to everything else quâ causal system. For of any particular event it would then be true (a) that it and its relation to the system follows from this system, (b) that none of its relations to the system could be different, since what it is and what relations it has are completely fixed by causality, and (c) that it is absolutely dependent on the system for its existence (causally).

To contend, as I have contended, that causality involves a relation of logical entailment between cause and effect and effect and cause is to contend that it is also internal in the tenth [1] sense, and that it would be so in the eighth [2] sense for a being who possessed the requisite insight, if not for the human mind. This would assimilate the whole universe to

---

[1] I.e. such that the nature of one term is *logically* dependent on that of the other, i.e. the events which constitute the cause could not exist and be what they are if it did not produce the effect, and the effect could not exist and be what it is if it had not been produced by the cause.

[2] I.e. cause and effect are so related that determinate characteristics of the one could be deduced *a priori* from the other.

a logical system, though we must indeed remember that the universe is also a great deal more than a logical system.

Besides being internal itself in these senses the relation of causality is a 'generator of internal relations', i.e. wherever C causes E characteristics of C other than the characteristic of being cause of E (namely the characteristics between which the causal relation in question holds[1]), are internally related in the senses in question to E or characteristics of E.

Further, that there are causal relations between all parts of the physical universe is, though not indeed proved with certainty, yet a conclusion which no reasonable man can reject. While the *a priori* proofs of universal interaction (reciprocity) given by Kant do not seem to me satisfactory and I know no other satisfactory *a priori* proof of this, universal interaction when applied to physical objects is at any rate a well-grounded scientific generalisation, if only because light-waves travel from every part of space to every other and so between all physical objects.[2] Even if everything is not completely determined causally, everything physical we know seems in some way to be causally interconnected. It is indeed conceivable that there might be another physical world out of range of and completely unaffected by and not affecting ours, but of such a world we could know nothing, for to know it we should have to be in some way affected by it. It sounds absurd to say that there is a causal connection between my writing this book and the Prime Minister of Australia's breakfast, but it is clear that the physical paper on which I write is causally affected by the surrounding atmosphere, e.g. as regards temperature, this in turn is affected by the state of the ground immediately beneath (if it were converted into an active volcano I should cease to write and in any case the temperature of the ground affects

---

[1] It seems to me in the main a verbal question whether causality is said to be a relation between things (continuants) or between characteristics of things. If we define it as primarily a relation between two characteristics, then 'two continuants are causally related' = 'they have characteristics which are, in the primary sense, causally related'. If we define it as primarily a relation between continuants, then 'characteristic A causally determines characteristic B' = 'any continuant which possesses characteristic A will cause the presence of characteristic B in some continuant (either itself or some other)'.

[2] This is mentioned by Kant himself as an empirical confirmation of his proof. (3rd ed.) It is now questioned by scientists on the ground that some parts of the universe are or will be receding at a velocity greater than that of light. But even if this is true, which is doubtful, these parts will still be causally connected with us through their past history.

the temperature of the air and so in some degree that of the paper), the ground immediately beneath is in turn affected causally by the earth below it, and so on right through the centre of the world to Australia, while there is clearly a causal connection between the state of the ground in Australia and the quality of the pigs, corn, etc., which go to make the breakfast in question.

It is not true indeed that my writing this book is a part-cause of the statesman having his breakfast or *vice versa*. One of the reasons why views such as the coherence theory and the 'internal' theory of relations seem impossible to many thinkers is because they are thought to involve absurd statements of this kind, but it is obvious that two events can be causally connected without one being a cause, direct or indirect, of the other. Two events are also causally connected if both are effects of the same cause, or even only if their causes, though different, are themselves causally connected in some way, direct or indirect. Unless we frankly take the sceptic's position and abandon causality altogether, we can always interpolate between two events on or in this planet a series of causes and effects so that they are causally connected in an indirect way, and if we admit any sort of causal connection between *any* events on the Earth and the other planets and fixed stars, this will itself extend this very indirect causal connection to *all* events on the planets and stars. According to Sir James Jeans, science has made it practically certain that 'every body pulls every other towards it, no matter how distant it may be. Newton's apple not only exerted its pull on the earth, but on every star in the sky, and the motion of every star was affected by its fall. We cannot move a finger without disturbing all the stars'.[1] True, the causal connection may be of no practical or theoretical importance in determining most specific events; but the mere fact that it exists may be of great philosophical importance, however insignificant its actual effects.

Nor would this conclusion be overthrown by the now fashionable indeterminism, though it would be somewhat limited in its significance. Even if indeterminism be accepted the arguments I have given would still hold, for the causal connections I have mentioned cannot be totally denied without altogether breaking with science. Even if everything is not completely determined causally, it is still clear that

[1] *The Stars in their Courses*, p. 74.

causality has a great part to play. The universe would still be a causal system in that everything was causally connected, though it would not be a system which completely in all respects determined its members. This is no unusual feature in a system; a system of professional grading, e.g., determines its members not in all but only in some respects. Indeed, since a concrete thing has most varied qualities, this is the case with most systems at any rate in which existent objects fall. (The case is different when the terms of the system are abstract, such as numbers in a mathematical series.)

I have so far spoken only of the physical world, and we cannot disprove the possibility that there may be things which are neither physical nor mental, or that there may be disembodied spirits, and that such beings may have no causal connection with our world whatever. But of such beings we could know nothing [1]; and, whatever view we take of the relation between body and mind, it seems clear that all embodied minds, at any rate, are through their bodies bound up with and dependent for their existence, at least in their present form, on the physical system. If the relation between body and mind is causal this follows directly from our previous argument, and the only alternative to making it causal is to substitute some other relation which would have to be equally internal in character. Nothing that I have said is intended to imply that the physical is necessarily the only or prior part of reality. For all we know and for anything I have intentionally implied to the contrary, it may be but a small part of a much wider system, or it may derive its systematic character from values which transcend it, or from the purpose of a God.

There is a real sense and importance then in saying that the whole known universe is a system constituted by an internal relation which connects each thing to the rest of the system, though it does not follow that it is such a closely knit logical system as the Hegelians are commonly supposed by their opponents to have held it to be. Causality in general

[1] We may note that believers in God commonly regard God as being the cause of the world or at least as having some relation to the world analogous to causality, while the belief that human beings exist in some future life as disembodied spirits itself involves a causal connection between this life and the subsequent life, and so between these beings in their later state and this world we know.

I indeed look upon as the application to events of the principle of coherence or system, which is a cardinal assumption of thought, whether this principle be conceived as a pragmatic postulate verified by success or as a necessity of logic or as a somewhat dim and confused but nevertheless genuine intuition of the nature of the real world.

§ IV. Conclusions

We have thus as a result of our consideration of causality reached the conclusion that the world known by us constitutes a system in which every particular is linked to the rest of the system by a relation of logical entailment. The presence of this relation is obviously incompatible with the extremer forms of pluralism. It implies that the nature of any one thing taken by itself is incomplete and internally incoherent without the whole system on which it depends. Things by their very essence belong together. But it does not imply that reality has as high a degree of unity as is present in one substance or one mind. Nor does it imply that all relations are internal in the last four senses of the term: some of them are clearly not. Our conclusion is based not on the consideration of the nature of relations as such but on the consideration of one particular type of relation, causality. At least all this will follow if causality is held to be universal, and I must admit that I cannot really think anything as happening without causes sufficient to account for it.[1] If causality is not universal, the world will indeed still be a system, though a less rigorous one, since at the very least causality plays an enormous part in it and in some degree directly or indirectly links all particulars.

It does not follow that every particular event or thing is

[1] I.e. I regard the proposition expressed by saying that every change is caused not as certain but as *prima facie* self-evident, and so to be accepted unless it can be shown to be inconsistent with propositions possessing a greater degree of *prima facie* self-evidence or ' coherence ' or both. (E.g. if it could be shown to be inconsistent with the very possibility of ethics, it might still be justifiable to reject it as being less certain than many propositions of ethics. I should insist that there are different degrees of self-evidence.) I cannot agree with what seems to be Professor Broad's interpretation of the *prima facie* self-evident proposition expressed by saying ' every change is caused ' as being simply that it has a necessary as opposed to a sufficient cause (*Examination of McTaggart's Philosophy*, vol. I, p. 238 ff.).

in these senses internally related to every other.[1] For instance, we need not hold that 'the flower in the crannied wall' is dependent on the planet Mars for its existence, only that it is so dependent on something or other in the universe. Neither are we bound to hold that the true account of its qualitative nature entails all true propositions about Mars so that with sufficient insight we could infer them from knowledge of its nature. But it is by no means unreasonable to hold that its nature could not be understood adequately without bringing in the physical system as a whole. That this is so is the most elementary scientific fact; the flower's growth is dependent on laws of physics such as the law of gravitation and on conditions of temperature which depend on the constitution of the whole solar system, yet the same physical laws and the same physical system are just the factors which have led to the existence of Mars as a planet and to its present state. The point is not that any one thing could be inferred direct from any other, but that the nature of no one thing could be understood without reference to the world system as a whole and that this same world system determines the development of every other particular at least in its general lines. Nor does it follow that all relations are internal. Some, it seems clear, might be different while their terms remained the same, because, even if they must be determined by something, they need not be determined wholly by the nature of their terms, and therefore they might be different without the latter being so, provided only something else in the universe were different from what it in fact is.

There are two further points about relations which go far to modify any thoroughly pluralistic view. In the first place we must remember that experience never gives us relations and terms but a continuum from which relations and terms are abstractions. We must not assume that this continuum can be reduced to a set of terms in relation, indeed I think it true to say not merely that we do not experience it as such but that we apprehend that it is not such, that it cannot be thus exhaustively reduced by analysis to terms and relations. This I mentioned as the element of truth in Bradley's polemic

[1] I have urged above (p. 134) that everything is related to everything else in the seventh sense, but it is obvious that all things are not internally related to each other in the ninth and tenth senses of the term, though everything may well be internally related in these senses to everything else taken together.

against relations.[1] It is, I think, perfectly true and a very important point that, if not all relations, at any rate all relations of which we know between concrete things or states of things (in opposition to relations between universals, of which this is not true), occur in and presuppose a continuum.[2] This is true of spatial relations; it is true of all relations which occur in time; it is certainly true of all relations within the experience of a living mind; it must be true of any relations between qualities of actual existents, because the qualities always qualify things ('substances') which cannot themselves be reduced to a set of qualities in relation. It is not true of relations between abstract numbers or between logical principles, but these numbers and principles are already abstractions that do not exist by themselves.

With concrete things then the idealists are right when they insist that relations between terms can only occur within a wider unity connecting the terms. This view is, I think, also true in the case of universals, but there the wider unity is not a continuum. It is a relational system, by which I mean a set of relations arranged in a determinate order [3] under a given determinable [4] such that some *a priori* inferences are possible within the system. I am inclined to think that it can be shown that all relations between universals fall within some such system or other; however, this is of no particular relevance for our argument here.

Secondly, the advocates of external relations seem to assume too readily that a hard and fast line can be drawn between the

[1] V. above, p. 149.
[2] What is meant by 'continuum' is, I trust, conveyed to some extent at least by my examples. I cannot venture on a definition. What I am giving is not intended to be a metaphysics, which would require such a definition, but a series of suggestions that ought to be taken into account by metaphysics. But my conception of continuum at least involves the negative characteristic of being something which cannot itself be reduced to a set of terms in relation. Note that I only said that any relation presupposes some continuum, not that each relation presupposes a different continuum. Thus it is not legitimate to object that the terms must be themselves related to the continuum within which they fall as part to whole, and therefore require a further continuum, and so on *ad infinitum*. They do not need any other continuum beyond the original one.
[3] I mean that they are in this order objectively. The use of the word 'arranged' is not intended to suggest that they have been put in this order by mind by any process or act of arranging.
[4] It seems obvious that the distinction between determinate and determinable applies to relations as well as qualities.

intrinsic nature of a thing and its 'external' relations. None of them have ever, as far as I know, attempted to work out the distinction in detail and give a systematic account determining which kinds of relations are external and which not, nor have they decided what qualities (if any) are separable from relations. They assume in their philosophy that everything has a qualitative nature of its own to which its relations are logically indifferent, so that it would be logically, if not causally, possible for it to exist without them. Quite apart from any arguments based on the nature of causality, such as those I have used above, is this not a bold assumption which seems to disagree at any rate with the character of the qualities we know, though it may for all we can tell be true of qualities of which we have no idea whatever? Would any qualities of the kind we know be left if we took away all the relations of anything? Consider first the so-called primary qualities of matter. Is the position of a thing logically separable from its spatial relations to other things, or its shape thinkable apart from the relations which the parts of its surface bear to each other and to the objects which bound it? Motion, velocity, mass are in a similar position. I am not sure that I ought not to go further and say that all these so-called primary qualities are reducible to relational characteristics, but even if this is too much to say it is certainly true that they are unthinkable apart from relations. Size and number are left, but these are not characteristics which can possibly constitute any part of a thing's qualitative nature. To know the size of an object is to know the space it occupies or the plurality of its spatial parts but not to know anything about what it is that occupies the space or what its parts are like, and, as for number, it is clear that to say there are e.g. four things is not to say anything about the qualities of the things, if it is to say something about their relational characteristics. The only other characteristics of physical objects recognised by science resolve themselves into causal properties, which are admittedly relational characteristics and not qualities. No doubt if we admit the physical reality of secondary qualities we have characteristics which are neither relational themselves nor bound up with relational characteristics in the same sense as are primary qualities, but the advocates of external relations certainly do not usually hold that the inner nature of matter is constituted by its colour, noisiness, taste, smoothness or hardness, etc.

If we turn to psychological characteristics, we find that the ones we know are again all unthinkable apart from certain specific relations. With the exception of mere sensation or feeling they are all attitudes to something, or awarenesses of something, or dispositions which realise themselves only in such attitudes and awarenesses. This is a commonplace of psychology. They all imply ' objects ' and so relations to objects: in fact from one point of view an attitude may reasonably be said to be just a relation to an object[1] though from another, its qualitative aspect, it is a definite experience of the person who has it. (I am not sure indeed that we might not say that in an important sense it is at the same time both a quality and a relation.) And similarly with an awareness or any cognitive state. ' Feeling ' may seem an exception, as I have said, but feeling as sensing [2] is at any rate relative to the sensum,[3] and feeling as pleasure or unpleasure is always pleasure or unpleasure at something. It always, I think, logically entails something at which we are pleased or the reverse, if only a sensum.[4] In connection with all this a doubt is indeed raised by the fact that a man may feel an emotion or assume a cognitive attitude towards an imaginary object which does not really exist, e.g. he may believe in Zeus or feel amusement at Pickwick. But it is very doubtful whether such cases can be treated without *either* admitting subsistent entities as the objects of his attitude, *or* analysing attitudes to imaginary objects in terms of relations to existent objects or to universals realised in existent objects; and either course would make the attitude ultimately relative to real entities of some sort. And in any case it would be very rash to say that it is logically possible for any mind of the type we know to be a mind at all if it has not at least sensa of which to be aware and an environment of some sort with which to stand

[1] Apart from the organic sensations that accompany it, which come under the heading of feeling.
[2] Sensing is often classed as belonging to the cognitive side of our nature, but it seems to me much better to class it as belonging to the affective side, though it is usually or perhaps always accompanied by some cognition (v. Aaron, *The Nature of Knowing*, p. 19 ff.). Perception, on the other hand, is unmistakably a species of cognition.
[3] Or, if sensa are denied, to the physical objects directly perceived by or appearing to us.
[4] In its other uses the ambiguous word, feeling, I think, stands for either an attitude or an awareness, and is therefore covered by what I have said already.

in relation. That a self implies a not-self is a principle of philosophy not lightly to be set aside, especially by realists.

What does all this prove? I admit that I am none too clear, but one thing seems certain, namely, that it raises very serious difficulties for any philosophy which reduces the world to relations and terms with a nature of their own logically independent of relation. No such philosophy can be accepted till the difficulties have been squarely faced and conquered. The point is not merely that everything of which we know has some relations that are internal in the seventh sense, i.e. such that, if the relation were not present, both of its terms could not be what they are. This must be admitted in any case, since everything is e.g. similar to something else and similarity is such a relation. Nor is it merely that, granted more than one existent in space or time, it is logically impossible for anything to exist in space or time without standing in some relation to other existents, which again must be admitted. It is that all the characteristics we attribute to minds and in science to physical objects seem to be either themselves relational or logically dependent on there being a specific kind of relation between the object to which we attribute them and some other object, without which relation the characteristic is unthinkable, i.e. such objects, or at least all their characteristics of which we know, are internally related in the tenth sense. This is not to say that they are logically dependent on any particular object but that they are dependent on there being some object or other thus related to them. I could not be pleased without being pleased at something, but my pleasure is not thereby shown to be logically dependent on the particular circumstance about which I am pleased at any given time.[1]

As a matter of fact it seems to me that the entities for whose independence of relations the best case can be made out are sensa. Here if anywhere do we find an internal nature separate from relations. But the philosophers who have tried to work out an account of perception have rarely held that sensa were separate entities at all, but have usually come to the conclusion either that they were unthinkable apart from a consciousness which sensed them, or that they were qualities of physical objects, or that they were constituted by the mere

[1] It is, however, admittedly causally dependent on it, and therefore that it is logically dependent on it *among other conditions* follows if what we have said about causality be right, though it could not follow from the present argument.

appearing of qualities which did not really qualify anything, and so they could hardly stand in this proud position of independence according to most views. In any case, unless he comes to the conclusion both that we are justified in believing in physical objects in a realist sense and that these objects are best regarded as groups of sensa, a philosopher can have no ground for asserting the existence of sensa except as perceived by a mind, and even if he adopts the views mentioned he has no ground for asserting their existence except in two kinds of closely interrelated groups, (*a*) physical objects, (*b*) sense-fields of a percipient, or supposing that they could exist in their present form outside such groups. The most he could say is that (*a*) their dependence on these groups may be merely causal not logical, in so far as he distinguishes these two modes of dependence; (*b*) there is a bare possibility, so far as we know, that sensa may also exist apart from any such special group, though there can be no evidence to show that they do so exist or even that it is logically conceivable that they could do so.

At any rate it seems very doubtful whether it is possible to hold the pluralistic view of the world as a set of separate things with natures of their own apart from their relations, and it is certain that philosophers have no right to assume the view without a more effective defence of it against the above objections than has yet been given. On the other hand some idealists have altogether overshot the mark in claiming that *all* relations were internal in some of the senses in which they did claim it, and have created a great deal of confusion by using the term without clear distinction in so many different senses. The advocates of 'external relations' were therefore right in most of their criticisms of the arguments of their opponents, but did not face the three strongest arguments, the argument from causality, the argument that relations presuppose a continuum, and the one based on the difficulty of finding qualities separable from relations. Further, I should agree with almost everything they have said if it is applied only to some and not to all the relations of a thing. There is nothing inconsistent in holding both that most of the relations of a thing are external in the last four senses and that some of them must be internal. Even if the nature of a thing does depend on its relations, this need not prevent some of its relations being quite indifferent to it, because its nature is dependent on other relations. Finally it seems clear that everything is not internally related to everything else taken separately in at least the last three senses of the word (the eighth, ninth and tenth), though the argument from causality seems to show that it is so related to everything else taken together.

The view of the world as consisting of separate terms connected only by relations indifferent to the nature of these terms, which is the main object of Bradley's attack, is in any case quite untenable, though I do not venture to affirm that this is the metaphysics really accepted by most advocates of 'external relations'. Some relations at any rate are not indifferent, otherwise any logical or causal connection would be impossible; and it is not even clear whether things can be said to have a nature of their own apart from relations. The view is also refuted by the previous argument that all relations presuppose a continuum which is not itself reducible to a set of terms and relations. How far the conclusions we have reached go in establishing the 'coherence' view we shall see in the next chapter.

CHAPTER V

THE COHERENCE THEORY

§ I. The Objections to the Correspondence Theory*

WE now pass on to the so-called coherence theory. The connection of this doctrine with idealism is well known. 'Coherence' is held to constitute
(a) a definition of truth, or at least an account of its nature;
(b) an account of the nature of reality;
(c) a criterion of truth.
But since it might well be the case that the theory is tenable in one of these senses without being tenable in the others, we had better treat them separately. As an account of the nature of truth the coherence theory usually starts from a criticism of the 'correspondence theory'. I shall therefore begin by discussing the current objections to this 'correspondence' view so commonly accepted in one form or another by realists and, apparently at least, assumed by the plain man in his ordinary thought about objects. This, however, need not detain us very long, for the view can easily be restated in a form which escapes the objections in question. It may indeed be doubted whether the theory as thus restated should be called the 'correspondence' theory, but at any rate it will certainly not be the coherence theory and will provide a genuine alternative to the latter compatible with realism.

According to most realists as well as to the plain man, a judgment is true when it corresponds to an independent reality and false when it does not, and this is either a definition of truth or expresses at least an essential characteristic of truth. The advocates of the coherence theory object in the first place that no tenable account can be given of this correspondence, for, whether it is regarded as copying or as similarity in structure or as one-to-one correlation, very serious difficulties arise. It seems clear, however, that such criticism cannot be final, for the reason why all accounts of it involve great difficulties may be simply that the relation is unique and unanalysable. In that case we need not be troubled by our failure to give an account of it in terms of other relations, because it is simply not identical in character with any other relation or combination of relations. Our failure to define it may be simply due to the fact that it is intrinsically such as neither to require nor to admit of a definition.[1] If any relation be unanalysable, as some obviously must be if we are to escape a vicious infinite regress, such a fundamental relation as the one between a true judgment and its object is as likely to be so as any, and it seems to be radically different from any other relation of which I can think. We need not object indeed to the attempt to give a further account of it, and I am not trying to show that the attempt must fail, but we certainly need not deny the presence of such a relation if and because it does fail. I cannot imagine any possible way in which it could be proved that if there is such a relation it must be other than unique and simple except by a successful reduction of it to a relation or relations found elsewhere, but the objections which I have mentioned can only disprove the correspondence theory if it is first shown *both* that the relation *must* be thus reducible and that it has not been reduced successfully.

Secondly, it is objected that there are no entities which can stand in such a relation as correspondence to reality when we make a true judgment. Truth has often been defined as the correspondence of our ideas with fact or reality, but there is no psychological warrant for the assumption of any entities ' ideas ', as distinct from (*a*) images, (*b*) thoughts, i.e. acts of thinking or judging, and neither of these will serve the purpose of corresponding. Often the only images we have in thinking are words, but these cannot be regarded as the entities in whose correspondence to reality truth consists. It is not

---

[1] I understand by a definition of something either its reduction to a combination of two or more other entities (whether two relations, two qualities, or a relation and a quality, or a quality and a species of continuant, etc.), or a definition *per genus et differentiam*, not the giving of a mark or property which always accompanies and can be used to distinguish but is not identical with what is defined. E.g. if the copying theory were correct, truth would be definable as the relation of copying (genus) when this holds between a judgment and its object (differentia), or the property in a judgment of standing in this relation. In this sense of definition a unique and unanalysable relation obviously cannot be defined.

the acts of judging or thinking which are held to be true, nor is it the words. It is not judgments in the sense of acts of judging but in the sense of what is judged in the acts of judging and what is meant by the words. Hence arises the view that truth consists in the correspondence of ' propositions ' to reality, these being conceived as non-psychological, non-physical entities which have being but not existence and are independent of being judged. But such a view of propositions has been severely criticised. We need not, however, dwell on the objections to it, for it need not necessarily be involved in the correspondence theory, any more than the view that correspondence consists in copying. It is difficult definitely to disprove the view that propositions have being as separate entities, but at any rate the assumption is one which should be avoided unless facts really compel us to make it. It is, however, not necessary to the correspondence theory, since we may take the position that what corresponds is neither propositions as separate entities nor the acts of judging as a whole but that factor in the acts of judging which, though it has no separate being, we treat separately by abstraction when we speak of propositions. For, even if propositions are not separate entities, we must admit that they can be treated as if they were separate for many purposes. For example, in logic we can say a great deal about them, and even in ordinary life and in science we constantly describe them as true or false, meaning not merely that so-and-so has on a particular occasion judged truly or falsely, but that such-and-such a proposition is true or false whoever judges it. We are speaking of a proposition on most occasions when we make use of a that-clause in ordinary language. The term is technical, but that for which it stands is as common as daylight. Now all this need not necessarily imply that propositions really are entities separate from the act of judging, but it must imply at the least that they stand for real elements in the act of judging which can be abstracted and treated as if they were separate. But if so what corresponds to reality, thus constituting truth, may be this something, whatever it is, for which admittedly they stand. It need not be treated as having separate being by an advocate of the correspondence theory, unless it can be shown by other arguments independent of this theory that it has separate being, in which case any theory and not only the correspondence theory would have to accept the conclusion.

The third objection to the correspondence theory is that we

could not tell whether our judgments [1] did correspond to facts or not unless either the facts to which they corresponded were themselves judgments or we knew directly the facts and not merely judgments or propositions about them. The former alternative is accepted by idealists, the latter by many realists, e.g. Cook Wilson. Either may be declared to be incompatible with the correspondence theory: the former on the ground that it was an essential feature of this theory that the facts to which true judgments corresponded should not be themselves judgments but realities independent of a judging mind, the latter on the ground that there will then be at any rate some true judgments of which the correspondence theory will not hold, namely, the judgments that other true judgments correspond to reality. It is further urged that knowledge cannot be reduced to awareness of a kind of transcription of reality, it must be an awareness of something real or of nothing at all. If we did not have some direct knowledge of reality, however scanty, from the beginning we could never come to know anything.

Such objections are valid against some forms of the correspondence theory. They refute, for instance, a 'representative theory' of knowledge (which must be distinguished from a representative theory of perception [2]), and they refute the view that correspondence is the criterion of truth. We cannot test the truth of a judgment by seeing whether it corresponds to facts without, so to speak, translating these facts into other judgments. Facts can only be reached through cognitive processes, and therefore the results of a cognitive process can only be tested by other such processes. What we call testing by reference to facts is really testing by reference to more elementary cognitions. Sensation as mere feeling must give rise to judgment before it can be used as a test.[3] But correspondence might well constitute the nature of truth [4] without constituting its criterion, and there is a form of the theory which still escapes criticism, as we shall see shortly.

[1] In order provisionally to cover in my account of correspondence both the view which admits propositions as separate entities and the view which does not, I have used the ambiguous term, judgment, which may stand either for 'my judging' or for 'what I judge'.
[2] V. below, ch. VI, sect. 2.
[3] The same objection may be brought against the attempt to make the universal criterion of truth 'verification by experience'.
[4] It is usually in this sense only that the theory is put forward by its advocates.

Fourthly, the correspondence theory is rejected on general grounds because incompatible with the idealist position, as founded on arguments which are treated elsewhere in this book and therefore do not need to be discussed here, e.g. when it is asserted that there are no merely given facts but that all facts clearly show the work of mind in 'truth-making'.[1] We may mention, however, Bradley's assertion that truth must be identical with reality. He bases this on the argument that, if there were a difference between them and this difference were not contained in the truth, the truth would be so far not the truth because defective.[2] His view is that truth is not indeed absolutely identical with reality as a whole in all its aspects but is one complete aspect of reality. This aspect seeks to be and in a sense implicitly is the whole, but like any one aspect of reality, cannot fulfil its nature without self-contradiction, since to fulfil it would be to bring in also all the other aspects and thus cease to be mere truth. For to supplement the nature of truth by the other aspects of reality is to modify it.

Now if truth means what is known or what facts are for cognition in so far as cognition is successful and reality means the facts *per se*, the view that truth and reality are identical may well be accepted. In so far as we know, what we know is identical with reality or it would not be knowledge.[3] But it is not what is known as real fact that is true in the strict sense but judgments about the facts, and there is still surely a distinction between judging, both in cases of knowledge and opinion, and the facts about which we judge. 'Knowledge' is ambiguous, for it may mean both what is known and the knowing of it, and, while in the former sense it would include all the reality known, in the latter sense it does not include and is not even partially identical with what is known. Bradley insists that the boundaries of an object can never be rigidly fixed and that its nature should be taken as including all its relations and all its effects, so that the fact of being known and even the knowing of it by a particular mind would be part of the nature of the substance or continuant known; but the object of knowledge, i.e. of a given cognition, is never, strictly speaking, a substance or continuant as a whole but certain facts about it,

---

[1] E.g. Bradley, *Essays on Truth and Reality*, p. 108.   [2] Id., p. 113.
[3] When I objected to the tendency to make identity the ideal of knowledge, I meant not identity between *what is known* and the real facts but identity between these latter and our minds as *knowing* them.

and these facts, we may reply, cannot include the fact that they are known,[1] though the nature of something which they qualify may do so if we take this extended view of a thing's nature.

Besides, as Bradley admits, he cannot destroy the relation on which the correspondence theory rests. 'Truth, to be true, must be true of something, and this something itself is not truth. This obvious view I endorse.'[2] All he can do is to interpret the view differently. For him the relation does not hold between a factor in our knowing as a particular mental event or a timeless proposition and a real fact, but between a one-sided aspect of reality and reality as a whole, the latter being the harmonious all-embracing experience and the former this experience as it shows itself in one aspect, thought. But we may correctly say that even on his view truth corresponds to reality inasmuch as every element in the whole is supposed to be expressed, though inadequately, in the truth aspect. He holds, indeed, that the internal development of the truth would by inherent logical necessity, if carried to its conclusion, involve complete identity with reality; and at that final stage it would not 'correspond', because it would be identical with reality. But then neither would it be any longer truth according to him, therefore truth might still always correspond to reality. Further, Bradley quite definitely admits correspondence as constituting relative truth in the case of our judgments, while adding that none of our judgments are wholly true and that the notion of correspondence would not be applicable to what was wholly true. Owing to the internally self-contradictory character possessed by the ideal of truth as by all ideals short of the whole, what was wholly true would on his view be more than and therefore inconsistent with truth; but it would seem to follow that all truths, since they are partial,[3] must correspond in so far as they are true. We may further note that correspondence is not treated as indefinable by Bradley but as reducible to 'the possession by truth of a character such as logically to imply the complete reality of which the truth is a partial manifestation',[4]

[1] The fact that they are known may be made the object of a second cognition but not of the one by which they actually are known.
[2] *Essays on Truth and Reality*, p. 325.
[3] I shall shortly criticise his doctrine of degrees of truth. If this doctrine is rejected, the admission that *our truths* correspond is an admission that truth does, for this can no longer be attributed to their falling short of the character of truth.
[4] I am condensing and paraphrasing Bradley's actual words.

but we have not committed ourselves to any particular view as to the nature of the correspondence relation. That Bradley takes the view of it he does depends on his general metaphysics rather than on any specific objections to a realist theory of correspondence.

This illustrates the impossibility of dispensing with the relation described, perhaps very inadequately, as correspondence if we are to give any account of truth that applies to the truths known by us. The strength of the correspondence theory lies in the fact that a judgment is at once different from and yet dependent for its correctness on the object judged about. Whatever metaphysical view we adopt as to the ultimate nature of knowledge and reality we are forced to admit this fact, either openly and consciously or implicitly and unconsciously. Our judgment does not make nor is it identical with the physical fact, the past state of mind, the events in human history, the law of nature, the mathematical or logical principle about which we judge; yet whether the judgment is or is not true is determined by its conformity to or discrepancy with the character of that about which we judge. If a judgment bears a certain relation to its object it is true, if not it is false, and since this relation requires a name it has been called correspondence. The coherence theory, since it describes truth as the coherence of judgments, does not do justice to the fact in question. It tends to ignore the facts that any judgment must refer to something and that a true judgment must be true of something other than itself, that is, while its adherents may admit so much in words if pressed, they define truth in a way which would be quite compatible with a judgment being true and yet true of nothing whatever, for there is no mention of anything but judgments in the definition, and judgments cannot be true merely of other judgments.

Let us then try to restate the correspondence theory in a form which will escape the objections brought against it. In the first place, it will be safest to give up any attempt to explain what correspondence is in terms of any other relation, and simply to treat the relation between a true judgment and its object as unique and unanalysable, at least till a satisfactory analysis has been found for it. We know what it is like, at least partially,[1] in particular cases, because we know what

[1] Its unanalysable character need not prevent it having more than one characteristic, provided it is not reducible without remainder to other relations or relations and qualities.

is meant by holding true beliefs concerning some particular fact, but we are not committed to the view that it can be analysed, or, still less, to any particular analysis of it. In order to give a satisfactory account of truth we must exclude any notion of likeness or copying. Nor need we assume any sort of one-to-one correlation between different elements in a judgment and different facts in reality. Otherwise we are exposed to the objection that judgments must be treated **as a** whole in determining their meaning.

Secondly, while the admission of propositions as separate entities should be avoided if possible, it can only be avoided by an alternative account of what it is that we really discuss under this heading. We might, for instance, make propositions features of or elements in the act of judging inseparable from the latter. The proposition 'S is P' might be described as that which is common to the different mental events which come under the heads of judging that S is P, denying that S is P, doubting that S is P, considering whether S is P, etc., but which is not common to the mental events of judging that S is P and judging that S is Q. What corresponds to reality would be then neither the judging as a whole nor a proposition as a separate entity but a certain factor in the act of judging. False judgments would be judgments in which nothing stood in that relation to any fact outside the judgment. This view would avoid a well-known difficulty about error, for the object of an erroneous judgment would then not be anything real by itself, as it would have to be on most other views, but would only have being as an inseparable element in something else, namely, the mental event of judging. Thus, if X judged that the earth is flat, there would not therefore be a 'real proposition' that the earth is flat. What would be real would be only the complex mental event, X judging it to be flat. The chief difficulty which I can see in the view is that a proposition, e.g. that S is P,[1] cannot be said to characterise a mental event in the way in which a quality or a relational characteristic characterises anything. Propositions cannot be brought, I think, under the heading of qualities, states, events or relations. That is why in stating the view I had to use the vague words, element and factor. However, that is only to say that the cognitive situation is quite unique in character.

[1] By using this symbolism for convenience' sake to represent any proposition I do not mean to imply the view that all propositions are reducible to the subject-predicate form.

Another very interesting alternative is suggested by Professor Stout.[1] According to his view, possibilities and probabilities have objective being as well as actual facts, and in error the object of our mind is an unactualised but still objective possibility. This avoids the necessity of admitting propositions either as separate entities or even as factors in the act of judging, but it is interesting to see that even on this view there is left some relation such as that which advocates of the correspondence theory try to describe, though Professor Stout would himself, I think, not use the word correspondence in connection with his own theory. For, while it is no longer the case that there is a relation of correspondence between the proposition that S is P and the fact S–P, since the first term of the supposed relation has no being on this view either as a separate entity or even as a factor in the act of judging, the distinction between true and false judgments is still constituted by a kind of correspondence between our judging and reality. For a true judgment on this view consists in the adoption towards a possibility of an attitude of belief or affirmation in cases where the possibility really is actualised or an attitude of disbelief or denial in cases where a contradictory of it is actualised, that is, in a correspondence between our judgment and reality in respect of affirmation or denial. We have with profit travelled far from the correspondence theory as usually described at least by its opponents, but we have not eliminated the relation to which that doctrine owes its plausibility.[2]

The third objection to the correspondence theory was to the effect that it cut us off from the direct awareness of reality which is necessary if we are to tell even whether our judgments correspond to reality. As I said, it is valid against some forms of the theory, but it does not alter the fact that the correctness of our judging depends on a special relation to the fact judged

[1] *Studies in Philosophy and Psychology*, pp. 304–6.
[2] The ingenious theory on the subject of propositions put forward by Mr. Ryle (*Proc. of Aristo. Soc.*, 1929–30, p. 91 ff.) has excited considerable interest, but I think I may claim exemption from the necessity of discussing it, as it is hardly a theory that would be held by advocates of the coherence view, and it would on the contrary if correct turn the edge of their objections to the correspondence theory by suggesting another alternative in its place besides coherence. As far as I can see Mr. Ryle gives no substantial argument to support his theory except the objections to the view that propositions are separate entities, but I have mentioned two other ways of avoiding that alternative which in my opinion are preferable for several reasons.

about, which relation need not be incompatible with our being also directly aware of the fact related to our judging by it. It is true that, when we know, we know real facts, not merely ideas or propositions, but there is no difficulty in reconciling this with the other circumstance emphasised by the correspondence theory, namely that when we do know anything there is a special relation between the fact known and a certain factor in our cognitive process, which relation differentiates the latter from error. Whatever else it is, knowing must involve bringing our minds *into accordance with* reality, and this is also the case with right opinion. It is this that the correspondence theory rightly emphasises as the essential purpose of cognition.

It is often supposed in this connection that the correspondence theory is involved in a fatal dilemma. Either we have no direct awareness of reality, in which case we cannot be aware even that what we judge ever corresponds; or we have a direct awareness of reality, in which case the correspondence theory breaks down with some truths at any rate, namely, the truths revealed by that direct awareness. But this argument presupposes that there is no relation of correspondence in cases where we have direct awareness, which is not true. The fact that I am directly aware of a fact at the time of judging does not prevent but is likely rather to ensure my judgment's corresponding to (being in accordance with) the fact about which I judge. We must not indeed suppose, and this is perhaps how the misunderstanding originated, that the judging and the direct awareness of the real which tells us that the judgment corresponds are separate acts and that the second would have to be performed afterwards to test the first. On the contrary, to judge is in the case of a true and justified [1] judgment to see, and in the case of a false or unjustified judgment to think we see, that what we judge corresponds to real facts. If the correspondence theory be right, to know that something is true is just to know that it corresponds, and so its truth need assuredly not be tested again by, so to speak, looking at reality to see whether it does correspond. If truth really is correspondence the recognised methods of obtaining truths will all be methods enabling us to see what judgments correspond to reality. These methods involve at every stage

[1] I add 'justified' because otherwise it might be objected that we sometimes make true judgments on wrong grounds or as a result of mere guesswork.

a direct cognition of reality, and need neither to be replaced nor to be supplemented by a direct awareness radically different from them telling us whether their results correspond.

All successful cognition is in an important sense direct, even when based on inference. For it is the real fact about which our judgments claim to be that we are cognising, and not merely propositions or something else in our mind corresponding to it. At least this is the only sense that I can understand in which it can reasonably be maintained that even all certain knowledge is direct.[1] But, whatever views we hold on this question, they need not prevent us from accepting the correspondence theory, now that we have seen that correspondence and direct awareness are compatible. All judgment is at the same time awareness of the real in so far as it is true and justified, and we do not need therefore any further direct awareness to supplement these judgments, because we already have it in the act of judging itself. It is sometimes suggested that there is a propositional factor only in cases of opinion not in cases of *knowledge*, since, while in opinion we are not, in knowledge we are directly aware of the fact or law cognised, and therefore do not need a proposition as a kind of substitute for it. But (*a*) if there is no propositional factor, what can be said to be true in cases of knowledge? Certainly neither our direct awareness as a whole nor the real known to us. So the paradoxical conclusion would follow that in cases of knowledge the knower knows nothing which is true. We must therefore suppose that there is a propositional factor present in knowledge too, which propositional factor we can in a sense be said to know, though in a sense different from that in which we can be said to know the reality to which it corresponds. (*b*) It seems to me that knowledge and belief shade off gradually into each other in a way which makes it impossible to maintain quite different epistemological theories for the two. (*c*) As I have urged, direct awareness is not incompatible with a relation of correspondence, nor is the propositional factor a substitute which we cognise instead of cognising the real. On the contrary, to know the truth of the propositional factor (in one sense of know) is the same as (in another sense of know) to know the real to which it corresponds. (*d*) We are discussing the nature of truth here, not that of knowledge; and it is surely quite clear that truth in one very important sense of the word,

[1] V. below, p. 265 ff.

the sense under discussion, does not stand for either identity with or direct awareness of the real concerning which the truth holds but for a relation of something else to this, whatever that something is, or a characteristic depending on the relation in question, and it seems to me that, while the relation is unique, 'correspondence' is a tolerably appropriate name when once divested of misleading associations with copying.

As regards the fourth set of objections, they are founded on general idealist arguments which I have discussed earlier. If some of the epistemological theories criticised in Chapter II are accepted it is clear that the correspondence theory falls, but as we have, rightly or wrongly, come to the conclusion that these theories must go this need not trouble us now. And the 'correspondence theory' is confirmed by the fact that no idealist can give an account which makes the slightest sense of our ordinary judgments without admitting a relation of this kind as at least a relative truth. Since we have not found the arguments for an Absolute knowledge of a different kind from ours convincing, we are excused from discussing whether it would be applicable also to this 'absolute truth'. And, unless we accept Bradley's doctrine of degrees of truth, we must admit that the correspondence theory, since it is true of our truths at any rate, holds not only of relative and partial truths but of truths which, as far as they go, are absolutely true though not the whole truth.

The objection that the correspondence theory involves an infinite regress is not, I think, valid. It is the case that, if all true judgments correspond to reality, the judgment that this is so will also correspond and so on *ad infinitum*, but this is no objection unless it can be shown that we could not legitimately make the first judgment without first making the whole infinite series. It only shows what in any case is true and can be shown in various other ways, namely, that an infinite number of potential judgments are true. 'The judgment that the judgment that the judgment that the judgment that all true judgments correspond to reality corresponds itself to reality'[1] is a judgment which is tedious, useless and uninteresting, but then a

---

[1] It may be maintained that this is really no different from the first judgment that 'all true judgments correspond to reality', and that the apparent infinite regress consists only of a set of different possible ways of expressing one and the same judgment. I am not sure whether this is right or not; if it is right, the objection in any case falls to the ground.

great many true judgments, e.g. judgments about the shape and size of each grain of sand on the seashore, are tedious, useless and uninteresting. This is a reason why we should not waste our time making them but no reason why we should refuse to admit a theory which implies their truth, though it fortunately does not oblige us to repeat them. Besides, the objection, if valid, would apply to any universal proposition about true judgments whatever. Not only does a similar infinite regress arise with any rival theory such as the coherence view, but even if we content ourselves with simply denying the correspondence theory we have the very same regress except that each judgment is negative instead of positive, and indeed even if we take the alternative of maintaining that it is meaningless. For 'the statement that all true statements correspond has no meaning' is itself a statement, and so we have 'the statement that the statement that all true statements correspond itself corresponds has no meaning',[1] and so on *ad infinitum*.

On the other hand we ought in thinking of the relation between judgments and their object to rid ourselves of any notion of copying or likeness or one-to-one correlation, and not to make the judgments with which we deal into a screen shutting us from reality or a kind of photograph serving as a substitute for reality. And since in the minds of many these notions are inextricably associated with the correspondence theory, it would be better perhaps to have recourse to a new name and call the view we have outlined the 'accordance' theory of truth. I doubt whether the theory is very different from what the more important advocates of the correspondence theory have meant, but it is certainly very different from what their opponents thought they meant. And there comes a time in philosophical controversy when the meaning of a word has become so obscured by acquired associations and ambiguities that it is a real service to the interests of truth to make a clear cut of the name altogether. The word 'accordance' has several advantages over correspondence. It will not like 'correspondence' seem to imply a set of discrete entities in the judging mind like or parallel to a corresponding set in the

---

[1] If a statement really has no meaning it is presumably a mere set of words or marks on paper and does not express a judgment at all, but the assertion that it has no meaning must then itself have meaning and be a judgment. Consequently it is not possible to reply that the sentences in inverted commas do not express any real judgment.

real world, and it makes it easier to state the theory in terms of our mental acts of judging and not in terms of propositions. We can say ' our judging accords with reality ', but if we use the term ' corresponds ' we have to say that what corresponds to reality is not our judging but our judgments, an ambiguous and misleading word. A person who was most reluctant to admit a relation of correspondence might be quite ready to admit that our judging when true was in accord with reality and that it was this which constituted its truth.

§ II. Degrees of Truth

Besides being a theory as to the nature of truth the coherence view is also a theory as to the nature of reality and the criterion of truth. As an account of the nature of reality it takes the form that everything that is is included in a thoroughly coherent system, and this view is *prima facie* at least compatible with the denial both that truth is best defined in terms of coherence and that for us coherence is the only or main criterion of truth. But it is commonly held both by supporters and opponents that this view as to the nature of reality has an important corollary in regard to the account of truth, which I shall proceed to discuss next, both because it gives rise to some of the principal objections brought against the coherence doctrine as an account of the nature of reality and because it is more closely connected with the subjects just discussed. I am referring to the famous doctrine of ' degrees of truth '. The next subject for discussion after this will be the coherence theory as an account of the nature of reality, and finally I shall say something about it as an account of the criterion of truth.

What I have called the doctrine of ' degrees of truth ' may be summarised as the doctrine that all judgments [1] are both partly true and partly false. This doctrine seems flag-

---

[1] Bradley persistently uses the word judgment without making clear what he means by it, and especially whether he means judging as a mental act or attitude or what is judged (as many philosophers would say, ' the proposition judged '), and as a matter of fact his doctrine of degrees of truth seems to refer to both senses of the word. I suppose he would maintain that they were inseparable. I shall say something later about the relevance of the distinction, but in giving an account of his views I am for the present bound to repeat the word judgment without making the distinction, because he fails to do so himself.

rantly to contradict the law of excluded middle,[1] according to which the only alternatives are absolute truth or absolute falsehood so that a judgment can only be partially true or partially false in the sense that it is analysable into several judgments some of which are absolutely true and others absolutely false. It seems also quite incompatible with the self-evident certainty which we see to attach to many judgments. Surely it is certain that the propositions—nothing can be both black and not black in the same sense of black, in the same respect and at the same time ; I see a black patch now ; if Socrates is a man and all men are mortal, Socrates is mortal—are not only partially but completely true. Surely it is utter nonsense to say that $2 + 2$ equals 4 is partly false, or that $2 + 2$ equals 5 is partly true. And again it is objected that, if all judgments really are partly false, this will apply to the judgment that they are so and to any judgments fixing their relative degree of truth and error, and that if we have no certainty and no absolute truth anywhere even partial truth will be impossible for us.

Bradley, however, is on his guard against such objections. At any rate he repeatedly and expressly recognises the absolute and certain character of some judgments, and has quite definitely formulated a way of reconciling this with his own view.

'If you ask me, for instance, whether there is truth in the statement that $2 + 2 = 5$, I answer that I believe this to be sheer error. The world of mathematics, that is, I understand to rest upon certain conditions, and under these conditions there is within mathematics pure truth and utter error. It is only when you pass beyond a special science, and it is only when you ask whether the very conditions of that science are absolutely true and real, that you are forced to reject this absolute view. The same thing holds once more with regard to " matters of fact ". Obviously the construction in space and time which I call " my real world " must be used ; and obviously, within limits, this construction must be taken as the only world which exists. And, so far as we assume this, we of course can have at once simple error and mere truth. Thus the doctrine which I advocate contains and subordinates what we have called the absolute view, and in short justifies it relatively.'[2]

---

[1] Bradley, *Logic*, I, p. 165 n., admits that on his view the law of excluded middle 'is not true absolutely' but only in a relative and limited sense. It does not according to him have the same degree of truth as the law of non-contradiction.

[2] *Essays on Truth and Reality*, pp. 266-7, cf. p. 276.

Bradley emphatically defends not only the absolute truth but the certainty of the law of non-contradiction, and with greater daring proceeds to ascribe absolute truth and even certainty to his own fundamental metaphysical views.[1] With regard to the main character of the Absolute he holds that his conclusion is certain and 'that to doubt it logically is impossible'.[2] For 'outside our main result there is nothing except the wholly unmeaning or else something which on scrutiny is seen really not to fall outside'. He says that he agrees with his realist and pluralist opponents in refusing to admit that 'every truth can be consistently allowed to be merely relative', and says that he cannot take the opposite of 'Realism' and 'Pluralism' to be 'less than absolute truth, when, so far as I can see, in each case the supposed contrary of my view is, as such, really nothing'.[3]

In order to reconcile this admission of absolute truth in one sense with his doctrine that in another sense no truths are absolute he has recourse to two methods. Firstly, he maintains in regard to some truths, e.g. the law of non-contradiction, that they are absolutely true in the sense of not being corrigible *intellectually*, though corrigible otherwise by the introduction of the sides of experience [4] other than thought. That is, they cannot be refuted or amended as long as we remain within the sphere of thought; we know with certainty that it can never be right to contradict one of these judgments by another judgment. To suggest any alternative inconsistent with them is not to suggest anything thinkable, it is simply meaningless. This view is taken by Bradley of the fundamental principles of metaphysics—the coherence doctrine, the doctrine of degrees of truth and the doctrine that there is nothing in reality but experience. These escape the uncertainty and error which infect all finite truths, because we know that all possible new truths are included in them. We do not know how the principle of coherence will be realised in detail, but we do know that any truth that we may find will be coherent, and we do know, according to Bradley, that it will conform to the principle of degrees of truth and that it will be a truth directly

---

[1] *Appearance and Reality*, pp. 512 ff., 536–7.
[2] Id., p. 518.
[3] *Logic*, II, pp. 681–2 ('Terminal Essay,' added in 2nd edition).
[4] We must remember that according to Bradley there is nothing real but experience.

or indirectly applying to experience. Finite truths are limited by the conditions under which they are asserted, e.g. by the system of the science to which they belong, but these absolute truths are unlimited and unconditioned by other truths, since they are seen to be true of everything.[1]

But, though they attain the highest level attainable by thought as regards truth, even these judgments do not completely fulfil the ideal of thought and truth, because they are still inadequate to the nature of reality. They deal and can only deal in terms of abstractions, and abstractions do not do justice to the nature of the individual real. Reality is more than 'a ballet of bloodless categories'. Truth aims at nothing less than identity with reality, and this is our right and essential aim in knowledge for we seek to know reality as it is, yet it is an aim that can never be fulfilled. This falling short by truth of its own ideal Bradley expresses by saying that no judgment is ever wholly true. Other thinkers would prefer to say that a judgment might be true but must always be incomplete or inadequate, but Bradley refuses to separate the truth and the adequacy or completeness of a judgment.

But, whether he has expressed it in the best way or not, it is difficult to doubt that there is this essential inadequacy in thought. The end of thought, namely complete knowledge, could not be attained by any number of judgments, however true. For, even if it is held, as I think, rightly, that the object of knowledge is not to attain any kind of identity between the knowing self and the reality known, it can hardly be denied that in successful cognition *what we know*[2] must be identical with the reality known and that to have complete knowledge of anything would be to know it in all respects as it is. Now not only are we unable to attain this ideal ourselves, but it seems to be one that from the nature of the case thought can never attain. It seems unthinkable that reality could be reduced without remainder to a set of logically connected universals such as would alone satisfy thought. And this applies not only to reality as a whole or to 'ultimate reality', whatever that may be, but to every and any particular real thing with which we are

---

[1] *Appearance and Reality*, pp. 544–6; *Logic*, II, p. 675; *Essays on Truth and Reality*, pp. 272–3.
[2] Note again the ambiguity of 'knowledge' as meaning both knowing and what is known.

concerned in ordinary life. There is something in it which not only resists complete rationalisation as far as we can see but seems to be intrinsically of such a nature that it never could be completely rationalised. All philosophers are in the last resort driven somewhere and somehow to recognise an irrational element in the real, however hard it may be to determine its relation to the rational.[1]

The problem how to reconcile this admission with the fact that ' to assert this difference seems impossible without somehow transcending thought or bringing the difference into thought' exercised Bradley's mind to such an extent that his solution of it is described by him as the main thesis of *Appearance and Reality*.[2] It consists in maintaining that, while everything real has a truth-aspect which is revealed in thought, there are other aspects without which this aspect is internally incomplete and incoherent, so that the inner nature of thought itself forces thought to go beyond itself if it is to attain its ideal. It can only do this by including all the other aspects of reality, but this is not to attain mere truth, the object of thought, but something more than truth in which truth is included and transcended.[3]

But those judgments which have only the defects inevitable in any judgment as such may remain absolutely true in the sense that they are above criticism as judgments; they have not attained absolute truth, but to be truer they would have to be more true than truth itself, therefore they cannot be replaced by any contrary judgment. The only way in which they could conceivably be amended would be by the incorporation of other sides of experience besides thought, and this would give not truth as such but something higher including it. Since according to Bradley's view there is nothing real save experience, this something is conceived as a harmonious experience in which thought, the truth aspect, plays a part but is so interwoven with other elements (conceived as feeling and will) that its nature is essentially transformed. Thought cannot comprehend this in the sense that it can comprehend how it happens in detail,

---

[1] I realise that my statements in this passage are very vague, but it would be impossible to arrive at a more definite statement of the problem without a lengthy discussion for which I have not the space. Let it suffice then to indicate roughly what kind of considerations moved Bradley here.

[2] Pp. 554-5.   [3] V. especially *Appearance and Reality*, p. 172.

but it can comprehend the general principle that something of the kind must be true. Again this harmonious experience is something which is reached by the internal self-development of thought and not imposed on it from without. For anything less than this whole experience would be logically incoherent in the long run and so would not fulfil the demands of thought itself. We are not therefore left with an 'Other' like Kant's thing-in-itself outside thought.

This is Bradley's main answer to his critics. But, valuable as his suggestions are, they do not remove the main difficulty of the critics. For, though some of our judgments are admitted to be not intellectually corrigible and therefore for us absolute, even these are still stigmatised as false, and if, as Bradley holds, to abstract is to falsify they must be so stigmatised. But it remains incredible that all propositions judged by us can be false, and self-contradictory to assert it if false is used in its ordinary sense, and if it is not used in its ordinary sense it is incumbent to explain in what sense it is used.

Bradley does not apply this solution to judgments such as '$2 + 2 = 4$' or 'I am seeing a black patch'. These truths are finite, and 'any finite truth remains subject to intellectual correction'.[1] For it is not the case that every possible truth can be subsumed under these truths as under the metaphysical truths mentioned above, and therefore there is according to Bradley a theoretical chance of new truths contradicting them.[2] That it may be infinitesimal and so not worth considering for practical purposes is irrelevant. But Bradley would call even such truths absolutely true, though in a sense different from that which he applies to the former class of metaphysical truths. For, he says, a judgment may be wholly true within a special science and relatively to the conditions of that science, or again relatively to 'my real world' in space and time, and yet not be wholly true when taken without qualification, since the conditions of this science or this 'real world' of mine themselves fall short of complete truth and reality.[3] An obvious objection is that in that case the hypothetical judgment that e.g. '$2 + 2 = 4$ *if* the conditions in question are granted' would

---

[1] *Appearance and Reality*, p. 545.
[2] I cannot believe, as has been suggested, that Bradley has simply confused uncertainty and falsity, but I must admit that I cannot follow his transition from one to the other.
[3] *Essays on Truth and Reality*, pp. 266–7, 276.

be absolutely and wholly true, so that we should still have absolute truth. To say that under certain conditions a judgment is absolutely true should mean that if it includes in itself the conditions, whatever they are, it is absolutely true without qualification. But, I take it, Bradley would meet this by replying that if such a judgment could be made including all the conditions it would indeed be absolutely true, but that there could be no such judgment, at least for human beings. For the conditions are partially unknown (no one has succeeded in giving the complete metaphysical and logical basis of any science), and indeed could not be fully known without our knowing everything else, since, as Bradley insists, all truths are interconnected essentially.

But in that case, the objector may retort, it becomes difficult to distinguish those judgments said to be absolutely true within their own sphere from errors or reconcile the doctrine with our knowledge that $2 + 2$ really does equal 4. The true judgment is not '$2 + 2 = 4$ under all conditions'—we indeed seem on his view to *know* this, like all finite judgments asserted without limitation, to be false—but '$2 + 2 = 4$ under *some* conditions,' it being for ever impossible for us to state what the conditions are. This, if Bradley's doctrine be right, would seem to put it in the same position as any other judgment, however false, let alone uncertain, for according to his view all judgments, even erroneous ones, are true under some conditions, the nature of which remains partially unknown.[1] We might, however, still find a way of differentiating it from judgments stigmatised by us as erroneous or uncertain, and thus of setting up a judgment which could claim absolute truth. For we might say that at any rate the judgment that 'the conditions on which the truth of "$2 + 2 = 4$" depends would require much less transmutation in "$2 + 2 = 4$" to make it an absolutely true judgment than would be required to make absolutely true the judgment that $2 + 2 = 5$, or even to make absolutely true probable judgments as to matters of fact', or, more briefly, the judgment 'that $2 + 2 = 4$ is nearer the truth than these judgments', is a judgment absolutely true. Now since Bradley holds that the principle of degrees of truth is itself absolutely true in the sense of not

---

[1] This, the doctrine of degrees of truth or rather one side of it, is affirmed as one of those judgments which are not corrigible intellectually (*Essays on Truth and Reality*, p. 273), and is therefore not liable to the same treatment as the finite judgments of mathematics, etc.

being intellectually corrigible, he may have regarded this last judgment as absolute in this sense, but he gives no clear indication that this is his intention. On the contrary, he denies this expressly of all 'finite judgments' as opposed to general metaphysical principles, and the judgment in question would seem to be finite in character. In any case, however, his view involves the admission that $2 + 2 = 4$ is, strictly speaking, not true, though nearer the truth than most other judgments. Most readers will not find this good enough. We seem clearly to know that $2 + 2 = 4$ is absolutely true if we know anything, and not merely to know that it is true under certain unknown conditions. And if it were not a misnomer according to most of us to speak of it as truer or more certain, since it is absolutely true and absolutely certain, we should say that it is assuredly truer and more certain than the metaphysical principles which Bradley places above it in the scale of truth and certainty.[1] Another objection to his view is that some negative 'finite' judgments at any rate, namely, the judgments that one or other affirmative finite judgment is not absolutely true, must themselves be absolutely true, at least in the sense of being not intellectually corrigible, yet he seems to mean to deny absolute truth even in this sense to all finite judgments.

But, while Bradley's conclusion seems unsatisfactory, we must be very grateful to him for having carried to its logical culmination a serious and instructive difficulty which has not yet been completely removed by his opponents. However, the controversy like so many others is confused by

[1] Professor A. E. Taylor at the time when he was associated with Bradley's point of view gave an account of degrees of truth which is less paradoxical and easier to defend. 'It would not be correct to say that, if our metaphysical interpretation is valid, the view of nature presented in descriptive physical science is *untrue*. For a proposition is never untrue simply because it is not the whole truth, but only when, not being the whole truth, it is mistakenly taken to be so. If we sometimes speak in Philosophy as though whatever is less than the whole truth must be untrue, that is because we mean it is untrue *for our special purposes* as metaphysicians, whose business is not to stop short of the whole truth. For purposes of another kind it may be not only true, but *the* truth' (*Elements of Metaphysics*, p. 214). The author adds in a footnote that the degree of truth and the degree of reality need not coincide, the former being relative to the purpose the judgment is meant to fulfil, the latter to the extent to which the nature of the whole is expressed, thus removing a confusion of which Bradley seems to have been guilty.

ambiguity of terms, for when Bradley and his realist critics respectively speak of judgments they are using the word in different senses. The realists are usually thinking of propositions, whether these be regarded as independent subsistent entities or as mere abstractions from the act of judging; Bradley seems to be thinking rather of the act of judging as a whole indivisible psychical event or, perhaps better, as our whole cognitive attitude to a question, including and inseparable from but transcending the assertion [1] of the proposition. If this is what is meant by 'judgment' it is no doubt a misuse of language to apply the terms true and false to judgments at all, since we do not speak of mental acts or states as 'true' or 'false'; but we can still understand and approve what Bradley meant by calling all judgments both partly true and partly false. For, while there seems clearly to be a sense in which the proposition that $2 + 2 = 4$ as asserted by me is certainly and absolutely true, it is not so clear that my mental state in asserting it contains no element of error at all, either explicitly or implicitly. For it cannot be the mere asserting without grounds or apart from its grounds that constitutes judging, as opposed to statement, but the seeing or thinking we see that what is asserted is true (or at least that it is rendered most probable by the evidence at our disposal, e.g. with assertions based on problematic induction). To judge that S is P is not merely to say that S is P but to be convinced of the truth of this at least momentarily, but the experience of conviction of the truth of an assertion cannot be separated either from our apprehension of the nature of that for which the words stand or from the grounds on which our conviction is founded. Where a judgment is based on inference, it can perhaps as a proposition but cannot as a psychical event be separated from the inference which establishes it, for the person who makes the judgment cannot see the truth of what is judged without at the same time seeing that it follows from the premisses. And, even in cases of self-evidence, the act of judging must be taken to include an awareness of the nature of that for which the words stand and an awareness that this is such as to necessitate the truth of what is judged. Applying these reflections to the judgment that $2 + 2 = 4$, we see that such a judgment, (if as made by a given individual it is a genuine judgment and

[1] I include under 'assertion' the mental assertion to oneself.

not, as often, a mere parrot-like repetition of the words, or an application on fresh occasions of a judgment already made,) must be the seeing that 2 + 2 really must equal 4, and we can only see this through being aware of the nature of two and of the arithmetical system on which the judgment is based. But, whatever the truth as to the nature of two and the arithmetical system, it is quite clear that neither I nor any other human being understands this fully. It is one of the most difficult questions ever considered by philosophers. Hence our cognitive attitude in judging that 2 + 2 = 4 must be in part faulty. It need not include the explicit judging of any false proposition, but we could not say what the judgment really is for us, what the words really mean for us, without revealing views that are partly erroneous.

Likewise if we take 'judgment' in the sense indicated we have no difficulty in seeing what is meant by Bradley's statement that all judgments are at least partly true. For no error, however wild, is totally without some kind of ground, and all errors presuppose some at least partial knowledge. We cannot ascribe a quality to an object, however falsely, unless we have some knowledge either of that quality as occurring somewhere in reality or of simpler qualities in terms of which it could be defined. No cognitive attitude towards a question can be one of totally undiluted error, to consider a question at all we must know some at least partial truth about points relevant to it.

Yet, on the other hand, it seems clear that there is a sense in which the judgment '2 + 2 = 4' is absolutely true and the judgments '2 + 2 = 5' or 'I am in Australia now' absolutely false. This is the case where 'judgment' is taken as meaning not the psychical fact of judging (seeing or thinking we see so-and-so to be true), but what is judged, i.e. the proposition asserted or, on a view which rejects propositions as separate subsistent entities, whatever it holds to be their equivalent for the purposes of logic and ordinary discourse. Now, whatever is the case with our act of judging or cognitive attitude, it does seem obvious that what is judged is sometimes wholly true and sometimes wholly false. Clearly 2 + 2 really is absolutely equal to 4. It is not nearly equal to 4 or only equal to 4 under some unknown conditions or in some slight degree equal to 5. It is because Bradley's opponents are using 'judgment' exclusively in this sense that they can see no strength in Bradley's position. On the other hand the fault rests partly on Bradley's own head, for he never made it at all clear in what sense he was using 'judgment' or in what sense he was using 'partly false', and I should not like at all to commit myself to any definite interpretation of what he meant. All I am trying to do is to point out one important sense in which what he says is true and another in which it is false without committing myself to the view that he was actually using the words in either sense.

If we take 'judgment' as meaning simply what is judged, Bradley's arguments for the view that all judgments are partly true no longer apply. The proposition 'I am in Australia now' is not rendered even partially true by the fact that all its content must fall within reality, for what would be asserted if the proposition were affirmed would be not that all the content fell within reality but that the content was related in a specific way in which it is not in fact related. In other words, the proposition is not rendered even partially true by the fact that there is such a country as Australia and such a person as myself and that it would be physically possible for me to go there. It would not be in any degree partially true even if most of the conditions for my going there had been fulfilled and I had only been prevented from reaching my destination by now through what we call the merest accident. The proposition as a whole is false, since what is asserted is not that Australia exists and that I exist and that I might be there, but that I am there. It is true that it implies and presupposes all these three true propositions, but what proposition the speaker intends to assert must be judged by reference to his purpose, and it would not usually be even part of the purpose of anybody who made this judgment to assert that Australia exists and that I exist and that it would be possible for me to go there. Normally these propositions would be indeed taken for granted but not asserted by anybody who said that I was in Australia.

I am inclined to think this the best view to take; but I believe that very many philosophers, including a number who disagree with Bradley's doctrine of the partial falsity of all judgments, would hold that the proposition 'I am in Australia' should be interpreted as including and not only implying or presupposing the propositions 'I exist' and 'Australia exists', but that would only put the absolutely false proposition further back. For, while the proposition I have cited would then have to be analysed into several propositions some of which were absolutely true, at least one of the propositions into which it was analysed, namely, that giving the relation between myself and Australia, would be wholly false and not even in some degree true. In that case, however, Bradley would have been right in holding that almost all the propositions which we assert in ordinary life by means of a whole sentence are partly true in the sense that each one of them can be analysed into several propositions some of which are true. If we are to regard the propositions 'I exist' and 'Australia exists' as included in the proposition 'I am in Australia', we should have equal justification even for regarding the true proposition '5 is a number' as included in the false proposition '2 + 2 = 5' and the true proposition 'Animals exist' as included in the false proposition 'Unicorns, i.e. animals with specific properties be, exist'. Even this admission would not, however, make truth and falsity a matter of degree but leave a difference of kind outstanding between them. For, in the first place, a compound proposition which is analysable into simpler propositions one or more of which are false, is itself, strictly speaking, absolutely false, even if some of these simpler propositions are absolutely true, since what it asserts is that they are all true, and this is false. And, secondly, at least one of the propositions into which any false compound proposition is analysable would still be wholly false.[1]

The view that all propositions asserted by us are partly false is more difficult to discuss. Bradley argues that anything finite has an infinity of conditions, and that therefore a 'judgment' asserting it must always be conditioned and, what is more, conditional, since the series of conditions being infinite can never be completed and are certainly unknown in their entirety by us. Facts are only what they are in their context and therefore the abstraction necessary for thought must vitiate the truth, according to Bradley, for it consists in taking them away from their context. So much

[1] It is perhaps useful to draw a distinction between absolutely false and wholly false. Any proposition which is false at all is, strictly speaking, by the law of excluded middle absolutely false; but it may be analysable into several propositions some of which are absolutely true, and then it is not wholly false. But in that case obviously some of the propositions into which it is analysable must be both absolutely and wholly false.

is often supposed to be a necessary consequence of the acceptance of the theory of internal relations or of the view of reality as a coherent system. But I cannot see the cogency of the argument. Even supposing we granted that it were logically impossible for any fact to be what it is if any other fact in the universe were different, a view which goes beyond anything that I should be prepared to admit, it would not follow that a proposition asserting any one fact must *include* in itself propositions asserting all the other facts, unless we assume that A cannot logically entail B without including B, a purely analytic view of inference which is itself untenable and which would also render the view of relations suggested completely impossible if it were adopted. It may be impossible for something to be a fact without a vast number of conditions being fulfilled, and yet possible for us to know (or rightly judge) it to be a fact by means of perception or otherwise without our knowing all these conditions. It may be impossible for A and B to be separated in fact, and yet possible for us to know them separately, i.e. to *know* one without knowing the other, though one cannot *be* without the other. We cannot argue, because A is logically inseparable from B, that the assertion of A is self-contradictory unless B is also asserted, but only at the most that it is self-contradictory to assert A and deny B, a very different matter. It does not follow that, because we cannot say 'A is true and B false' without self-contradiction, therefore we cannot without self-contradiction and even with certainty say 'A is true' without specifying or knowing anything about B. This would only follow if it were the case that B was the only possible ground which could justify the assertion of A, but this need not be so. For we may know A empirically by perception, or be able to prove its truth logically from some premiss other than B, or we may be able to establish its probability by inference from its effects. Perhaps we could hardly in practice come to know any fact in any of these ways without knowing a little about its conditions, but it does not follow that we must know its conditions definitely and fully in order to know it. And perhaps in most cases our relative absence of knowledge as to conditions may impair the certainty of our judgment, but it does not follow that, because the truth of a proposition is uncertain, therefore it is only partly true.

I should again admit that we cannot have a complete knowledge of any one thing without knowing everything (meaning by 'thing' particular). For complete knowledge of a particular would comprise a knowledge of all the facts about it, and these include its relations to everything else in the universe and to every characteristic of everything else, since to them all it will have some sort of relation, however indirect. But it does not follow that we cannot know any one fact about it without knowing everything else. I do not see why we should not be able to assert truly that an object is qualified by a universal without knowing everything about that object, still less do I see why the proposition that it is qualified by that universal should be held to fall short of truth just because it logically entailed or was entailed by the whole system of true propositions. It may still be true in the universe as it is, even if it could not be true in any other universe, for the proposition asserting it is a proposition about this universe. To abstract is at the most to introduce a risk of error, not to make it inevitable that the proposition reached by abstraction will be partly false. Hence the doctrine of degrees of truth in the sense under discussion does not follow logically from the theory of internal relations on any interpretation which can with any show of reason be given to the latter, or from the view that the universe is a 'coherent' system logically connected through and through. It only follows if we assume that because a proposition entails conditions on which it depends it must therefore include in itself these conditions. Whether Bradley ever really thought that it so followed in the sense which his realist critics give to the statement is, I think, very doubtful. He did hold that *relatively to its purpose* a judgment may be absolutely true; and what his opponents insist is not that any judgment can constitute complete knowledge of any particular, but that its truth must be estimated by reference to the purpose [1] for which it was made, and that it must not be condemned because it does not do this, since this was not its purpose. Further, and this is more important than a question of mere interpretation, if what I have said is right it follows that the current objection to the coherence theory and the theory of internal relations to the effect that these theories lead to the untenable conclusion that all our propositions are partly false must be abandoned. For they do not lead to any such conclusion.

[1] I do not mean 'practical purpose', but merely that its truth must be estimated by reference to what the person who judges means to assert.

This does not prove their truth, but it removes one of the strongest reasons against accepting them.

Those who use such an argument against the theories in question are in fact employing an argument which would be absolutely fatal to their own views if it were valid. For, if it were the case that membership in a coherent system entailed partial falsity, it would follow that, even if reality is not such a system, all propositions which are in fact members of such a system are partially false. Now, whether the whole be a coherent system or not, it must be admitted that we have 'coherent systems' within the whole.[1] If we take, e.g., the propositions of simple arithmetic, we find a system which comes near the standards of the coherence theory and in which each member is internally related to the system in the sense of logical dependence. Consequently, if the coherence theory really did entail the partial falsity of all propositions, since its opponents would undoubtedly admit that the propositions of arithmetic at any rate, if not all true propositions, form a coherent system in the sense of mutual logical dependence, it would follow that all arithmetical propositions were partly false in any case, and it is just these which are usually taken by realists as the most convincing examples of propositions which are wholly true. If coherence entails partial falsity, then the propositions of arithmetic are partly false, whether the coherence view in general be true or not; if it does not entail partial falsity, the objection disappears. One of the chief aims of opponents of the coherence theory has been to save the certainty and truth of such propositions; but, if this is their aim, to use the argument in question against the coherence theory can only be described as suicidal. But while I think that the doctrine of degrees of truth does not follow logically from the coherence theory interpreted as an account either of the criterion of truth or of the nature of reality, I am more doubtful whether it does or does not follow from the coherence theory if taken as an account of the nature of truth. But then the theory in this sense has already been rejected by us, and so we need not discuss the question.

Bradley also claims to have shown that the notion of relations

[1] (3rd ed.) The coherentist would not admit that any system short of the whole could be perfectly coherent, but it may be argued that such partial systems are coherent at least in the sense of internal logical connection, and it was internal logical connection which was alleged to entail falsity according to the argument I am considering.

is self-contradictory, and can conclude from this alone that all judgments are partially false since all judgments assert some relation. Whether this argument appears to be of any value or not depends on one's attitude to Bradley's view of relations, but that view has been discussed earlier,[1] and I shall just add that the fact that it entails the conclusion that all propositions which we can assert are partly false seems to me the most formidable objection to the doctrine of relations in question, at least if the word 'false' be taken seriously, as I think it must be if all relations really are self-contradictory.

Bradley also argues that the subject and the predicate of a judgment are never identical, and that therefore 'S is P' is never strictly true.[2] The obvious reply is that he has confused the 'is' which expresses predication with the 'is' which expresses identity, but he means that the notion of predication itself involves an unintelligible combination of identity and diversity. I should agree that it is unintelligible if that means 'irreducible to anything else' or 'inexplicable in terms of anything else', but then is there any need to reduce predication to anything else? It seems to me that the notion of attribute and subject must be taken as ultimately indefinable; and even if I be wrong in this the mere presence of both identity and diversity involves no contradiction, unless S and P are asserted to be both identical and different in the *same* respect, which is clearly not the case.[3] There may be other objections to the notion of predication, but if so they have not been explicitly produced. But if Bradley had abandoned the attempt to find direct contradictions, and confined himself to the contention that the nature of no particular could be adequately expressed in terms of universals and by means of a relational mode of thought and that the attempt to do so therefore to some extent always distorts the truth, it would have been perhaps less easy to reply. But I think the conclusion would be better expressed by saying that our assertions are misleading, i.e. suggest false metaphysical views, than that they are partially false.

There remains an argument connected with the question of meaning. It is that we cannot understand fully what is

[1] V. above, p. 147 ff.
[2] *Essays on Truth and Reality*, pp. 228, 255.
[3] I am not, however, prepared to admit that in predication we are asserting the *identity* of S and P in *any* respect, but only their connection.

meant by e.g. $2 + 2 = 4$ without presupposing the whole numerical system. From this consideration it would seem to follow that, since our knowledge of the numerical system and of the nature of number is always very imperfect and partial, the assertion that $2 + 2 = 4$, as made by us, cannot have absolute truth and certainty, because we do not fully know what we are talking about but are in partial ignorance and even error as to the nature of the constituents of the proposition which we are seeking to express. This argument, which does not necessarily presuppose the coherence theory, may be applied, *mutatis mutandis*, to all our assertions, since the words we use always stand for something the nature of which we do not fully know. Now without claiming to provide a complete solution of this problem about meaning I shall contend that it has at any rate been made unnecessarily acute by a confusion between two different senses of 'what is meant by' a word or phrase. 'What is meant by 'two' may stand for (*a*), the number two as an objective characteristic. In that case it is plain that we never know fully what is meant by 'two', since we do not know the full nature of this characteristic. But it may also stand for (*b*), what I or most men intend to express when they say 'two', and this is not the full objective nature of twoness and therefore may be known by us. There are no doubt many cases in which we do not fully know ourselves what we mean even in the second sense, e.g. when we are in complicated emotional states or engaged in difficult philosophical discussions; but this is not so with all judgments. When we assert that $2 + 2 = 4$ or that London is the capital of England, we do know what we mean in this sense, though our knowledge of what number is and what England is may be very incomplete and even mixed with error. (We do not know the full nature of the objective characteristics or continuants involved, but we do know it sufficiently to differentiate them from any other characteristics and continuants of which the propositions would not be true, and we do know that they have e.g. the relation of equality.) Thus, when it is said that the study of higher mathematics throws additional light on what is meant by number and the study of physics on what is meant by motion, this is certainly true if 'what is meant by' is used in the first sense, but not necessarily so if it is used in the second. Such advances in knowledge do throw additional light on the nature of the objective characteristics which are meant by 'number' and 'motion', but they do not therefore necessarily throw additional light on what we intended to express by the terms in statements made before we acquired this knowledge or even in statements of ordinary life made after the acquisition of the knowledge. There no doubt are cases where such an increase of knowledge leads us to understand better not only the objective nature of the characteristics signified by a word but actually also what we ourselves intended to express when we used the word, but I do not see any good reason to hold that this is the case with most definite statements of ordinary life such as 'there are two tables in this room' or 'an aeroplane can move faster than a train'. I must admit indeed that e.g. two presupposes the whole numerical system, and from this it follows that I do not know fully what is meant by 'two' in the first sense. But it does not follow that we cannot know fully what is meant by 'two' in the second sense. To know even this much indeed presupposes some rough idea of the numerical system as a whole, but this we have and, rough though it is, it is quite sufficient to enable us to see with certainty that $2 + 2$ must equal 4. Our cognitive attitude towards two may be mixed with error, as I have suggested above, and yet we may at the same time see the truth of some propositions about two with certainty, provided the error is not such as to invalidate these particular propositions.

It seems to me, therefore, that we can escape the paradox that all our judgments are partly false if we avoid the threefold confusion (*a*) between judgings and what is judged, for it is the latter and not the former which can be true or false, and though the former may always include elements of error the latter may still be wholly true; (*b*) between including and entailing, which leads one erroneously to suppose that the conditions on which a proposition is dependent and which therefore it entails ought to be included in the proposition itself; (*c*) between the two senses of 'what is meant by' something. I must admit, however, that I feel less dogmatic about the question than would seem to the reader from the way in which I have stated my solution. But any arguments that remain in favour of the doctrine of degrees of truth certainly seem to be outweighed by its difficulties.

The doctrine of degrees of truth is true as applied not

indeed to single propositions but to any considerable bodies of opinion or elaborate theories outside mathematics and outside the plain facts of memory and actual experience.[1] It is very easy to forget and very important to remember, especially in politics and theology, that anybody's system of beliefs is in all probability both partly true and partly false, that nobody is quite right and that there is some truth on all sides. As applied in this way the theory is not open to the objections to which it gives rise when applied to single judgments and is of great practical value as a much-needed exhortation to tolerance and caution.

It is also important to remember that it does not necessarily follow that a judgment is of no theoretical value because it is, strictly speaking, false. Although it is the case that in one sense all propositions asserted must be either absolutely true or absolutely false, it is certain that the false ones do not all diverge equally from the truth. That there are degrees of truth in this sense it is most important to remember. The difference between two false propositions may indeed in this respect be far greater and more significant than the difference between a true proposition and a false one, and there may be topics where the best we can do is not to arrive at propositions that are true but to arrive at propositions that are as little false as possible. Such false propositions are not only of practical but of theoretical value: to take a simple case, we are in a much better position even *theoretically* in regard to truth, though we are still making a false judgment, if we think that a mountain is 20,000 feet high while it is really 21,000 feet, than if we think it to be only 5,000 feet high.[2] If we cannot attain the ideal of

[1] A great many statements which appear from the form of the words to represent single propositions obviously do not really do so, e.g. idealism is $\left.{\text{true} \atop \text{false}}\right\}$, and it may even be argued that this is the case with all statements made in ordinary life.

[2] I am assuming that 20,000 feet is given as a fairly exact measurement to a few feet. No doubt when we say ' 20,000 ' we usually mean ' about 20,000 ', and as understood in ordinary speech this might not exclude its being 21,000, but, as understood in e.g. a geography book, to say it was 20,000 feet high would be incompatible with its being 21,000 feet high, though not with its being 20,000 feet 1 inch, since even here ' 20,000 ' really means ' about 20,000 ', only the range covered by ' about ' is diminished greatly. So the same statement might be true in conversation and false in a geography book because it stood for different propositions in the two cases.

truth in a given instance it is best that we should come as near to it as we possibly can, and some false propositions may be far more worth asserting, may be of far more importance for developing a less incorrect view of reality or parts of reality than hosts of true propositions of less range and significance. Thus it might well be the case that almost all [1] affirmative metaphysical [2] and theological propositions which we can assert were literally false [3] (excepting propositions to the effect that one proposition was nearer the truth than another), and yet that these branches of study were of great theoretical value, because, though they established very few true propositions, they might approximate more or less closely to the truth.

To take an example, a believer in God might well hold that the proposition 'God is a person' was false and yet nearer the truth than any other proposition of which we could think in determining the nature of God. To assert that 'God is not a person' would then be true but misleading, since it would suggest the proposition that God is more like an animal or inanimate entity than like a person, which would be a proposition far more divergent from the truth than the proposition that God is a person, or at least would suggest that we could substitute for 'God is a person' some truer affirmative proposition, which might not be the case.

This gives a certain justification to the '*Als Ob*' doctrine, according to which most or all propositions of the kind we are discussing are not true and yet have great value and importance. But I should not regard the importance of false metaphysical propositions as merely or primarily practical but also as theoretical.[4] It is not merely, I mean, that we ought to or are bound to act as if certain false propositions were true, but that they often, though no doubt far from the truth, are really as near to it as we can advance at present. Therefore our provisional acceptance of them improves

---

[1] Note that I have not said 'all', only 'almost all'. I am therefore not liable to the charge usually brought against the metaphysical sceptic of self-contradiction.

[2] As applied to metaphysical propositions this would be a curious reversal of Bradley's view.

[3] It would follow from what I have said that most *negative* theological and metaphysical propositions were absolutely true, but that the assertion of them might be very misleading.

[4] Though no doubt the advocates of such theories commonly use 'practical' in such a wide sense as to cover 'useful for theory'.

our understanding and knowledge [1] of reality and not merely our ability to act, though it should no doubt be accompanied oftener than it in fact is by the recollection that we have no right to say that the proposition is really true but only that it is the best approximation to truth we can make at present. The intellectual position of the man who treats them thus may be sounder than the position of the mere agnostic, who because we cannot reach truth treats all affirmative answers to a particular question as equally removed from truth, and therefore because he cannot attain truth deprives himself of any chance of advancing towards it. 'Half a loaf is better than no bread' in regard to the attainment of truth as in regard to other matters, though we no doubt must not try to deceive ourselves or others into believing that the half loaf is a whole one.

§ III. Coherence as an Account of the Nature of the World

About the topic of this section I shall have less to say. The coherence theory as an account of the nature of the world is derived from three principal sources: (*a*) the argument that coherence is the supreme criterion of truth, and that it could not serve as a criterion if reality were not really coherent, so that the coherence of the real is an assumption on which all knowledge depends; (*b*) the internal relations theory; (*c*) the view that subject and object, judgment and fact, like everything else, are inseparable, which gives its idealist character to the theory. Consideration of the first obviously must await our discussion in the next section of coherence as a criterion of truth, while the other two are discussed *ad nauseam* elsewhere in this book. We shall consequently have little to do here but summarise results. First, however, there awaits us one long-postponed task. It is high time to say something about the definition of 'coherence'.

Coherence must not be confused with self-consistency. Anybody who believed in a thoroughly pluralistic world in which every fact was logically independent of every other would still hold that his view was self-consistent in that the different facts did not contradict each other, but he certainly would not be maintaining the coherence theory but rather its oppo-

[1] In the wider sense in which 'knowledge' is not limited to propositions possessing certainty.

site. What is meant is not merely that the different facts do not contradict each other, which would be compatible with their being all quite indifferent to each other logically, but that they stand in some positive logical relation of entailment to each other.

The easiest way of understanding what coherence means is to consider those cases where the ideal of coherence [1] is admittedly realised or almost realised, though only within a limited sphere. Such cases are provided by the mathematical sciences and perhaps by certain well-knit theories or bodies of doctrine outside mathematics. What are the characteristics of such sets of propositions? In the first place, in so far as they fulfil the coherence ideal, they are so related that any one proposition in the set follows with logical necessity if all the other propositions in the set are true, or, to put it negatively, so that, granted the truth of all the rest, it would be logically impossible for any one of them to be false; and I was first tempted to take this as a definition of coherence. But it is not sufficient without supplementation. For imagine a set of propositions A B C D E F where, writing ent. for entail, we have the relations $A + B$ ent. C, $A + C$ ent. B, $B + C$ ent. A, $D + E$ ent. F, $D + F$ ent. E, $E + F$ ent. D. In such a set every single proposition would be entailed by the remainder, but unless there were some further connection between A B C on the one hand and D E F on the other, it would certainly fall short of the demands of the coherence theory, for it is universally agreed that the latter is incompatible with any admission of the possibility that there might be several different systems of true propositions altogether logically independent of each other. We must therefore enlarge our definition and say that a coherent system of propositions is ' a set of propositions in which each one stands in such a relation to the rest that it is logically necessary that it should be true if all the rest are true, and such that no set of propositions within the whole set is logically

[1] As opposed to comprehensiveness. The absence of comprehensiveness, i.e. the fact that such a system of coherent propositions always covers only a very limited part or aspect of reality, leads advocates of the coherence theory to hold that the coherence in its fullness is only apparent and that there are lurking contradictions. But any definite conception of ideal coherence they have still seems to be derived from those cases where something like the ideal of coherence is apparently, though, according to them at least, not really realised by us.

independent of all propositions in the remainder of the set'.[1] I call two sets of propositions logically independent where no proposition in one set either entails or excludes with logical necessity or belongs to a set of propositions, drawn from one or both of the sets, which conjointly entail [2] or exclude in their own right any proposition in the other set. The view that reality as a whole constitutes a coherent system might be described as the view that the sum-total of true propositions describing all the different facts there are constitutes a coherent system.

Professor Stout says that coherence

' rests on the principle that the Universe contains no *loose* elements. No partial feature entering into its constitution could be other than what it is without correlated difference in other features, which would again involve correlated differences in yet other features, and so on indefinitely. Thus, if anything in the universe is, had been, will be, or could be other than it is, has been, will be, could be, or could have been, the difference would penetrate the whole in its systematic Unity ',[3]

all of which could also be deduced from my definition. Mr. Price describes a coherent system as one such that ' if any one proposition is true, it strengthens the probability of all the rest '.[4] Other possible definitions are (*a*) ' a set of propositions or of facts such that justified inferences can be made from any member of the set to any other,' (*b*) ' a set all the members of which are relevant to each other '. Finally, Professor Joachim has said that

' a system possesses self-coherence (*a*) in proportion as every constituent element of it logically involves and is involved by every other ; and (*b*) in so far as the reciprocal implications of the constituent elements, or rather the constituent elements in their reciprocal implications, constitute alone and completely the significance of the system '.[5]

In this definition part (*a*) goes rather further than the earlier definitions, while part (*b*) adds a new point which will be

---

[1] (3rd ed.) My definition no doubt did not go nearly far enough for the coherentist, but I considered it of use as giving at least the minimum that might be plausibly established.

[2] I say that A and B conjointly entail C where the compound proposition, A and B, entails C, but neither A nor B alone entails C.

[3] *Studies in Philosophy and Psychology*, p. 316.

[4] *Perception*, p. 183.   [5] *Mind*, 1905, N.S., no. 53, p. 9.

discussed later. In regard to (*a*) I should say that, unless we adopt the doctrine of degrees of truth rejected in the last section, this part of the definition does not apply in the least even to the most coherent systems we know. For even in mathematics no proposition taken by itself involves all the rest. It only does so if we add to it others, unless we already assume the view, which I suppose Professor Joachim would hold as at least an approximation to the truth, that every proposition in mathematics really includes as part of its meaning the whole mathematical system by which it is conditioned, from which it would follow that we cannot fully know any mathematical proposition whatever. I do not know which of the above definitions expresses best the usual meaning of coherence as the term is employed by members of the school in question. Very probably it is Professor Joachim's, but I have rather stressed my own, as it seems to me to constitute the *minimum* definition without which a system could not be said to be coherent, and is more capable of establishment.

I think, however, that it is wrong to tie down the advocates of the coherence theory to a precise definition. What they are doing is to describe an ideal that has never yet been completely clarified but is none the less immanent in all our thinking. It would be altogether unreasonable to demand that the moral ideal should be exhaustively defined in a few words, and the same may be true of the ideal of thought. As with the moral ideal, it may well be here that, while formulae are helpful, they can provide no complete stereotyped account, and that the only adequate approach is one for which there is no space in this book, namely, a study of what our thought can do at its best by means of numerous examples.

That the coherence view is true at least on my minimum definition follows logically if we grant the truth of three propositions. They are (*a*) that everything is causally determined; (*b*) that everything is, directly or indirectly, causally connected with everything else, so that there is no series of events in the universe which is causally independent of all events outside that series; (*c*) that the relation of causality involves a relation of logical entailment, so that whatever is causally impossible is also logically impossible relatively to the rest of the causal system. Propositions (*b*) and (*c*) I have sought to establish by argument in the last chapter, at least as regards the world we know (for I do not see how we can disprove the possibility that there are other unknown worlds of some kind, whether physical or non-physical, not causally connected in any way with our world). I am also inclined to hold that proposition (*a*) is true, provided causality is not understood as equivalent to 'mechanical causality',[1] so I am inclined to accept the coherence theory thus defined as an account of the nature of reality as far as it can be known or reasonably surmised by us. It also seems to me that the importance and indeed indispensability of coherence as a criterion of truth makes it reasonable to hold that it or something like it is true of the real world. And I do not think that this can be disproved by any of the arguments against it of which I know. Most of these will, however, be discussed in the next section, when we deal with the question of coherence as a criterion of truth.[2]

But I cannot attribute to the theory the logical certainty which its advocates often claim. It is a reasonable postulate, I think, that reality [3] is a coherent system, but to deny this is not to assert something inconceivable or logically absurd. I have more confidence in accepting coherence as a regulative principle which we have some but not complete justification for believing to be true of reality, than as a proved category.

But I do think that, if coherence can be justified as a principle necessary for all our reasoning, this gives us strong grounds for holding that it or at least something very like it is true of reality. If it can be shown that coherence is the criterion or even an important criterion of truth, this will be the strongest argument for the coherence theory being near the truth also as an account of reality. The other argument most frequently employed by its advocates, namely, the one based on the internal view of relations, does not, however, strike me as valid. For, though it may be true that all relations are internal in some senses in which this term has been employed, I do not see any reason in the nature

[1] V. my first book, *Kant's Treatment of Causality*, p. 216 ff.
[2] It would take us too far to discuss the argument that the coherence theory is inconsistent with human freedom. I do not deny human freedom in any sense in which it is a necessary postulate of ethics, but I do not think that it need or indeed can be analysed indeterministically. (3rd ed.) v. my *Second Thoughts in Moral Philosophy*, ch.V.
[3] I mean by 'reality' our world, not an 'ultimate reality' other than our world, for which there is no evidence.

of relations as such for holding that they *all* are internal in any sense which involves the coherence theory. But I have added above another argument which has been less frequently employed but seems to me much stronger, the one from causality. It should be noted that this is an argument to the effect that everything is internally related to the rest of the world in the sense of being logically entailed by it,[1] not to the effect either that everything is related internally in that sense to every other particular thing or to the effect that all relations are internal.

It would not follow from the view that reality was a coherent system in the sense defined that from any one fact you could infer any other. It is not that we could by any chain of inferences starting from one particular fact reach all other facts in the universe, but that we could not know the grounds of any one fact in full without knowing the general principles governing the universe on which all other facts depend, and that is surely true. We could not understand fully the growth of 'the flower in the crannied wall' without knowing what life as such is and without knowing the general physical state of the earth as a whole, which in its turn depends on the sun, while the latter probably depends on the whole stellar system for its condition and movements. Nor could we understand the numerical or quantitative aspect of any one thing or fact (and everything has such an aspect) without knowing the general mathematical principles which govern the whole of reality.

Again, to say that no one proposition in a coherent system could be false if all the other propositions were *true* is not to say that no one could be false without all the other propositions being *false*. It is true that, given a really coherent system of propositions such as that which constitutes arithmetic, we could by a process of correct inference pass from the falsity of any one proposition in the system to the falsity of any other. Using $\neq$ to represent 'is not equal to', we could if we assumed that $7 + 5 \neq 12$ infer, e.g., multiplying by 20, that $140 + 100 \neq 240$, or, subtracting 6 from both, that $1 - 1 \neq 0$, and could by similar processes reach conclusions contradicting the true result of every arithmetical operation; but this, carried to the extreme, would be a self-contradictory procedure, since we can only prove from this

[1] The tenth sense of 'internal' distinguished, the only one which would yield the coherence view.

premiss that any accepted proposition in arithmetic is false by assuming as true another accepted proposition of arithmetic, e.g. $7 \times 20 = 140$, and so we could only infer from this premiss that all other accepted arithmetical propositions were false by assuming that they were all true. Similarly, I suppose, with any other coherent system of propositions. So we cannot argue that one of the coherent propositions could not be false without their being all false, but only that it could not be false without some of them being so. Thus we need not, as far as I can see, accept coherence in the sense defined by Professor Joachim,[1] though we ought to accept something far more like that than like the opposed pluralist view.

Again, I do not see why one part of a coherent system of propositions taken by itself may not be as coherent internally as the whole system. Granted that it would in that case be logically absurd to assert it while denying the rest, I do not see why there should be any logical objection whatever to asserting it without either denying or asserting the rest or why its internal coherence should be affected by the non-assertion of the rest.[2] To assert separately from the rest is not to deny the rest.

This brings us to a second aspect of the coherence theory, the aspect which Bradley calls comprehensiveness. The advocates of the theory would not regard a system as fully coherent unless it included all its conditions in itself. This would be impossible if there were anything outside itself which either entailed or was entailed by anything in it, and so, if reality is a coherent system, it follows for them that no other system within reality is coherent, since it is not comprehensive. But I do not see myself why its lack of comprehensiveness should affect its internal coherence, just as I do not see why it should make it partially false, unless indeed we accept Bradley's argument that all relations are essentially self-contradictory. If we define coherence in such a way as already to include comprehensiveness,[3] it does follow that nothing short of the whole can be coherent, but in that case I do not see any necessary connection between the first part of the definition, which would have to resemble the one I gave, and the second, which introduces comprehensiveness as well as internal coherence.

[1] V. above, p. 230.   [2] V. above, p. 220 ff.
[3] As, e.g., Professor Joachim does (*Mind*, N.S., no. 53, p. 9).

This may seem to contradict what I have said a little earlier to the effect that we could not 'understand' any one thing fully without understanding the general principles that govern reality, but that is due to an ambiguity in the term understand. 'Understand' may mean 'grasp the meaning of a statement', in a sense of meaning in which it includes only what is actually asserted, not all the implications of the assertion, which may be quite unknown to the person who makes or understands it. In this sense it is, I hold, false that we cannot understand anything fully without knowing the general principles governing reality, and, since we do not in fact know these general principles, the possibility of being able to 'understand' assertions without knowing these principles is presupposed in all the knowledge and opinions we actually possess. But 'understand' may mean 'know the grounds or causes of' or 'know the place in reality of', and in that sense it may be true that we cannot understand any one fact fully without understanding everything else.[1]

One may hold the coherence theory of reality without being an idealist in the sense in which I have used the term, for, while mind and object known are on this view 'internally related' like everything else, it does not necessarily follow that a physical object could not exist without being known by any mind, any more than it would follow that, because the English and the Japanese were on this view internally related, therefore a particular Englishman could not exist without any Japanese knowing of his existence. It would follow, indeed, that no physical object we know could have been what it actually is in a universe in which no minds ever existed or were ever going to exist,[2] but this need not perturb the realist. For he is only concerned to assert that unperceived physical objects exist in *this* universe, not that they would exist in another hypothetical universe different

[1] The first sense of 'understand', I think, is only applicable where we speak of understanding sentences, assertions, propositions; the second where we speak of understanding facts, laws, changes.

[2] Note this last proviso. The view would not imply that no physical objects ever existed prior to minds, but only that, although they existed before mind, they could not have been exactly what they actually were if it had not been the case that minds were to follow. This would be true even if we took the view that changes in matter were the sole cause of the origin of minds, for, granted that C has in fact an effect E, it is clear that C could not have been what it was (in other respects than this causal property) without being such that the effect followed.

from the one in which we live, and in *this* universe there are minds. Idealists have in fact often confused the issue and supposed that because physical objects and minds, like everything else, were internally related, therefore physical objects could not exist unperceived, but this, as I have tried to show earlier, is a mere mistake.[1]

Nor is the coherence theory incompatible with a degree of pluralism. It would be absurd, because everything is thus interconnected into a system, to overlook the circumstance that the connections between different facts are not equally close, that everything is not equally relevant to everything else, and that the relevance may be so slight and the connection so remote that in predicting or describing a process we may be able to ignore most of the other facts in the universe and fix our attention only on a few. If the universe were not, fortunately for us, thus constructed, there would be an end of all science and of all rational practical activity. But, though advocates of the coherence theory have not emphasised this point enough, it would be quite unfair to use it as an objection against their theory, which was never intended to deny the presence of different degrees of relevance.

Again, there is no reason that I can see why the coherence principle should conflict with the infinity of the universe. Even if an infinity of events occur each event may still be determined by others, and they may thus be all directly or indirectly interconnected. Further, provided an infinite series is governed by some law or laws, its infinity need not necessarily make it unintelligible, as can easily be shown with the infinite series of mathematics, and may for all we know be the case with the infinite series of events.

§ IV. Coherence as the Criterion of Truth*

Having considered the coherence theory as an account of the nature of truth and as an account of the nature of the world, let us now consider it as an account of our criterion of truth. Absolute coherence is unattainable by us, but if we are to apply coherence as a criterion at all we must assume that the nearer we approximate to this ideal the more truth we are likely to have attained.

The most convenient method of considering this question will be by attempting to reply in succession to various objec-

[1] V. above, ch. II, sect. 4.

tions that have been brought against the theory. The first is that, even if the criterion of coherence can be applied to subsidiary conclusions, it cannot be applied to the fundamental principles of logic and, in particular, to the coherence principle itself. The reply is that coherence may serve as a test in a twofold sense : subordinate truths may be established by their coherence with other already accepted truths, a fundamental principle by showing that it is a necessary presupposition of any attainment of truth. In both cases we are using the coherence test, only in the one we are working forward with it, so to speak, and in the other working backward. The proof of the coherence principle itself would lie in showing that it was presupposed in all our thinking, and if this could be shown it would be fair to maintain that it had been itself proved by its coherence with all other truths, the attainment of which truths it alone made possible. The circle involved is not vicious in the case of a principle which is necessary to all thought, for if it has really been shown that the coherence test provides the only possible test, it has been shown that the only alternative to its adoption is the impossible one of absolute scepticism. According to Bosanquet, the ultimate argument in proving anything is always the disjunction—this or nothing,[1] the appeal to which is inseparable from the principle of coherence, or is even, we might say, the same as that principle viewed from a different angle.[2]

If the only complete proof is in the last resort by means of the dilemma, Believe this or believe nothing, it is equally the case that, if there is any principle the denial of which without contradicting our whole system of beliefs would contradict the whole of a really important department of belief, we are justified in at least provisionally holding fast to this principle till it can be shown either that we were wrong in our estimate of its importance and may replace it without destruction to the

[1] Ultimately even with subordinate truths, for otherwise the more general truths on which their justification is based might always be themselves questioned.

[2] ' If we ask whether the compelling feature of implication lies in the alternative "This or nothing", or in the connectedness of genuine wholes, the answer must be that the two are inseparable. . . . If there were no connectedness there would be no such consideration as "If I deny this, I must deny that". If the connectedness were not with all we have, we could never reach the final proof, "If I deny this, I must deny everything" ' (Bosanquet, *Implication and Linear Inference*, p. 19).

sphere of belief in question or that its retention would lead to still greater incoherence elsewhere.[1] Many thinkers who are not advocates of the coherence theory have insisted that the justification of even an *a priori* principle may lie in its consequences as well as in its premises or in its self-evidence.[2]

Another more important objection is derived from the empirical character of our knowledge and opinions, the greater part of which seem to be based on experience and not on considerations of logical coherence. The answer given by the advocates of the coherence theory is threefold.

(1) It is admitted that the criterion for us is not merely coherence but coherence with our experience or coherence together with 'comprehensiveness', i.e. to be accepted a system must not only appear coherent internally but must cohere with any empirical data. An advocate of the coherence theory would hold, as Bradley and Bosanquet do, that the two criteria ultimately fall together, since, the Whole being the only fully coherent system, the omission of anything real must lead not only to incompleteness but to internal inconsistency in proportion to the greatness of the omissions; but he may still admit, as these two thinkers also do, that they often fall apart for us.

(2) It is denied that there are any empirical data apart from interpretation, which itself presupposes some kind of systematic ordering of experience into a more or less coherent whole. It would be commonly considered a merely empirical fact that there is a table before me; but in making even such simple assertions I am presupposing a whole system of interpreting sensa in accordance with previous experience. I am implicitly assuming, for instance, that a certain perceived shape under the

[1] I should myself certainly hold this attitude to be justified in regard to any principle which was really necessary to ethics or religion.

[2] E.g. Mr. Bertrand Russell, referring to mathematics and 'mathematical logic', says: 'Some of the premises are much less obvious than some of their consequences, and are believed chiefly because of their consequences. This will be found to be always the case where a science is arranged as a deductive system. With the empirical sciences this is evident. Electro-dynamics, for example, can be concentrated into Maxwell's equations, but these equations are believed because of the observed truth of certain of their logical consequences. Exactly the same thing happens in the pure realm of logic; the logically first principles of logic—at least some of them—are to be believed not on their own account but on account of their consequences' (*Contemporary British Philosophy, First Series*, p. 362). V. also Dr. Schiller, *Logic for Use*.

given conditions, which are very complex though never explicitly formulated by me (—if I were walking in the street or in some place where I did not expect to encounter tables I might interpret the same sensa quite differently—), is an adequate clue to justify the assertion of characteristics which go beyond anything immediately perceived. Also the thought of a table itself presupposes a whole system of classification of objects into animate and inanimate, natural and artificial, etc., besides a reference to human purposes which make intelligible the structure of tables. We are again in all assertions about physical objects assuming the validity of the perceptual criteria we have in use for determining the characteristics of the latter. I am assuming e.g. that the shape I see when looking straight at an object from a distance of a few feet is identical with or very like 'its real physical shape', or that the allowances usually made for shapes and sizes as seen from other positions are correct. I am not conscious indeed of all these assumptions; but they are assumptions in the sense that they would have to be made explicit and defended if my assertion is to be ultimately justified. It might be retorted that, while this is true of physical objects, we can still take perceptions of sensa and of our present state as giving a purely empirical knowledge without any presuppositions, but as soon as we try to state what such empirical data are we have to introduce universals, thus presupposing likeness to remembered previous data and a whole system of classification, etc. The presuppositions are fewer with propositions such as 'I see a yellow patch' or 'I feel a pain' than with propositions about physical objects, but they are still there. Again, analysis itself is a form of inference, from a confused whole as premiss to some distinguished parts of this whole as conclusion, and as such may be said to be tested by its ability to help toward the coherent systematising of the confused whole given. Consequently even the knowledge of such simple propositions is not merely dependent on what is given but requires the employment of the coherence criterion, i.e. we must use that system of interpretation which has been most successful in making previous experiences coherent.

(3) The principle of accepting as fact what one immediately experiences can itself be justified by the coherence theory, for if we did not adopt it we should either have no content for our knowledge at all, which justifies the principle by the This or Nothing argument, or, if we made content for ourselves by

accepting mere fancy as fact, we should have no ground for preferring any one fancy to any other and could not accept them all without self-contradiction. To take what I perceive immediately in myself and my sensa as fact, to accept my memory as trustworthy except where there is special reason for doubt, and to take a similar attitude with more allowance for doubtful cases in regard to my perceptions of the physical world and my reliance on the testimony of others whom I suppose to view the world as I view it—' these are principles by which I construct my ordered world, such as it is. And because by any other method the result is worse ' (less coherent with our experience) ' therefore for me these principles are true.'[1] We use, that is, in interpreting our experience those principles the consistent employment of which leads in general to the greatest coherence, or at least that is the only way in which our use of any principles can be logically justified. The well-known objection that there might be more than one coherent system can be similarly met by a use of the contentions I have marked as (1) and (3).

Another objection to the coherence theory is founded on the existence of truths which seem self-evident without inference. An advocate of the theory would reply that, in so far as we were right and not under some illusion in thinking that we saw them to be self-evidently true, there was implicit in our thinking as real ground our whole previous impression of the system to which they belong.[2] Thus $2 + 2 = 5$ is rejected as self-evidently false because it conflicts with our whole idea of the number system, and $2 + 2 = 4$ is accepted as self-evidently true because it is implied by this system so obviously as to make argument unnecessary. That it is some very rough idea of the numerical system as a whole which is our basis and not a single intuition detached from this is supported by the fact that the meaning of the statements cannot be understood at all except as involving this system.[3] And we may deal similarly, *mutatis mutandis*, with the cases of strong conviction

---

[1] Bradley, *Essays on Truth and Reality*, p. 213. (In making this statement he expressly mentions only memory and reliance on the testimony of others, but the additions I have taken the liberty of making seem to me justified and in accordance with his views.)

[2] Such a proposition might again be true either because it followed from the system or because the very existence of the system presupposed it.

[3] I.e. some rough idea, not a complete knowledge, of the system, v. above, pp. 224–5.

not amounting to certainty which seem underived from argument. If it is rational at all, as indeed it often is, this conviction can be held to be based on our general opinion of the subject-matter as a whole, which is incoherent with the proposition that we reject as probably false or coherent with the one that we accept as probably true, though we may be unable to specify more definitely how it is coherent or incoherent.

It may be objected, however, that this reply only puts the difficulty further back. A proposition is seen to be true, it is said, because it coheres with the rest of the system, but how do we see it to cohere? Surely, even if the truth of the proposition itself can only be discovered by the coherence test, its discovery presupposes that we can see the truth of another proposition independently of the coherence test, namely, the proposition that it does cohere with the system. It cannot be maintained that this is only established because we see that it is more coherent for it to cohere.

This objection shows that the second proposition cannot be related to the coherence test in the same way as the first. If the first (X is true) is a deduction from the coherence principle, the second (X coheres with other true propositions) is not a deduction from it but a particular instantiation of it. The objection is fatal to the coherence theory if the theory means that the truth of every proposition must be based [1] on its coherence with the system, because this cannot hold of the proposition that a given proposition thus coheres. We must suppose, that is, in some cases an immediate insight to the effect that X is coherent or incoherent with the system, which insight is not itself based on a further argument from coherence, otherwise the criterion would not be applicable to anything at all. But such an admission might still leave coherence in the position of the sole criterion, for the immediate insight would consist simply in seeing whether a proposition conforms to this criterion and so is true, or contradicts it and so is false, and the essential force of the coherence theory would not be impaired at all. To use any criterion we must be able sometimes to see whether a given object conforms to it or not.

[1] Most advocates of the theory would say 'identical with' not based on', and thus escape the objection by denying that the second proposition I have mentioned is distinguishable from the first. For they hold the coherence theory not only as an account of the criterion of truth but as an account of what truth is. This view I have, however, emphatically rejected already in sect. 1 of this chapter, and so this way of escape is not available for me.

To know or think something to be self-evident would then be to see or think we see that it 'coheres'.

An interesting and up to a point valid objection is brought by Dr. Schiller, who argues that, even if, which he is unwilling to grant, it were the case that an absolutely coherent system of propositions must be absolutely true, it would not follow that of two imperfect theories the more coherent one must be nearer than its rival to the complete truth.

'We cannot assume that the road to truth runs in a straight line, that we are approaching truth at every step, and that every apparent approach is really on the road to success. . . . One might as well assume that the right route up a mountain must always be one that goes straight for the summit, whereas it may only lead to the foot of an unclimbable cliff, and the true *route* may lead a long way round up a lateral *arête*. This simple consideration really disposes of the assumption that we can declare one theory truer than another, in the sense of coming nearer to absolute truth, without having previously reached the latter; and the history of the sciences fully confirms this inference by furnishing many examples of theories which have long seemed all but completely true and have then had to be discarded, while others which looked quite unpromising have in the end proved far more valuable.'[1]

This argument seems very formidable; but an advocate of the coherence theory might reply that it only proves, what any reasonable person of any school would always have admitted, that of two theories falling short of certainty the one supported by the strongest evidence at a given time may in fact be further removed from the truth. But this fact, as Dr. Schiller recognises in connection with his own theory, does not make it wrong for us to accept whichever theory has the stronger evidence in its favour as the one *more likely* to be true (or at least more likely to be nearer the truth).[2] Except where a proposition is logically necessary, we cannot be sure because it has most evidence in its favour that it is true, or even nearer the truth than any alternative hypothesis which we can frame at the time, but as Dr. Schiller insists we must go by probabilities, and it is universally assumed that the

---

[1] *Logic for Use*, p. 311.
[2] *Other things being equal*, i.e. in the absence of any specific ground to suspect the contrary, we should choose the path that led direct towards the summit of a mountain rather than some other one, as more *likely* to bring us there.

theory which seems most in accord with facts, (this may well be expressed by saying ' which coheres best with our experience '), is most likely to be near the truth. It may not be true, it may even be further from the truth than a theory which now for us has definitely more evidence against it and less in its favour; but in the absence of certainty the best we can do is to take it as a probable hypothesis. If we suspended our judgment when certainty was not available we should have no science outside mathematics and formal logic, and we obviously cannot adopt the principle of accepting a hypothesis which has less rather than the hypothesis which has most evidence in its favour. If we take coherence as meaning mere internal coherence irrespective of experience, then it is inadequate as a criterion, but that is not what is meant by the leading advocates of the coherence theory. They insist indeed that experience *per se* does not give us data apart from systematisation, i.e. apart from the application of the coherence principle; but experience still remains essential for knowledge *in conjunction with* the coherence principle. Further, the principle of accepting our experience as evidence can, as we have seen, itself be justified on grounds of coherence.[1]

The circumstance that a theory includes coherently all the facts we know seems to prove that it is very likely to contain at least much partial truth, for, even if it is not completely true itself, these facts must still be somehow included in the true theory, and it would be too extraordinary a coincidence if a principle from which a great number of detailed facts could be deduced were totally wrong, and not rather a sub-case of or approximation to the true principle. The claims of a particular theory are also often strengthened because there seem to be some grounds [2] for holding that it is the only possible theory which will agree with our experience.

We may, however, accept Dr. Schiller's argument as a stern warning against dogmatism. No doubt, if one assumes, as Dr. Schiller does, that the coherence theory holds up an unattainable standard of absolute certainty and that it does not recognise the problematic and tentative character of most of our actual reasoning, it is right to protest against it; but I can see nothing to justify this interpretation of the theory. I should have thought that the doctrine of degrees of truth,

[1] V. above, pp. 239-40.
[2] Though not conclusive grounds, for we cannot be sure that we have thought of all possible alternatives.

however we may criticise it, quite definitely implied that all our judgments were uncertain,[1] as much as does Dr. Schiller's theory. The theory of degrees of truth errs in attributing to them all not only uncertainty but partial falsity, and in holding that the uncertainty applies even to judgments such as that $2 + 2 = 4$; but these are errors of the opposite kind to those of which Dr. Schiller complains in his very clever polemic against all non-pragmatic systems of logic.[2]

A second objection by Dr. Schiller to the effect that the coherent system would have to include the assertion of a person who denied it and so would not be coherent but contradict itself seems to me more easily refuted. For, while it could not include such an assertion as a true proposition, it could and would include it as a psychological fact, and this is all that is needed. Errors must be included in the real *qua* psychological facts, but they assuredly need not be included *qua* true propositions. If they were, all views and not only the coherence view would be involved in self-contradiction.[3]

Another objection brought against the coherence theory is that it slurs over the vital difference between deduction and problematic induction. Bosanquet replies in *Implication and Linear Inference,*—a book which is as important as any for the understanding of the theory,—that induction resembles deduction in being ultimately based on the principle of:— This or nothing. We may have no insight into the causal laws governing nature,[4] but nevertheless in deciding what these laws are we can only be swayed either by the impossibility of reconciling the phenomena of our experience with any other laws or by the circumstance that the laws which we postulate are such that a number of different actual facts can be deduced from them, thus increasing the coherence of our experience by

[1] Except for a few metaphysical judgments.
[2] In *Logic for Use*.
[3] When we know the truth we can very often see just why particular errors have arisen, i.e. make them coherent with our system. That we cannot do so always is an objection only against those advocates of the coherence view, if any, who claim omniscience. We cannot expect to give a perfect account of all errors any more than of anything else.
[4] The question is separate from the one discussed in ch. IV, sect. 3, as to whether causality involves a relation of logical entailment. Even if that question were answered in the negative it would still remain true that the test for us is coherence with our experience, though it would not be true that reality could be described as a coherent system. I should indeed hold this position to be ultimately inconsistent, but then I do think that causality involves such a relation.

THE COHERENCE THEORY

bringing different elements in it together under the same law. This is the case even with those laws which strike us as the least intelligible and which seem to be based purely on external criteria of *de facto* presence and absence in a way quite unconnected with previous knowledge.[1]

Even in the inductive sciences it is sometimes possible to arrive at an elaborate system of propositions each of which follows with logical necessity from the remainder, though admittedly the foundations of such a system are less secure, since its denial would not destroy the whole of knowledge and it can never be established with logical certainty as the only alternative consistent with our experience. The ideal would be to reach a set of laws which mutually entailed each other and from which all subordinate laws could be deduced so that every fact in the world fell within their range, but this being impossible for us we assume that of two theories the one which brings us nearer to this ideal is more likely to be true. To be successful a theory must not be inconsistent with empirical facts; and on the other hand it must not just enumerate them without connecting them or causally explaining them. It must, if possible, bring them under laws, and the only evidence for the laws is provided by their coherence with experience. For they form the premisses from which many actual facts can be deduced, and thus we bring together into a system what was previously unconnected by deducing different facts from the same set of laws.

It is thus impossible to disprove the coherence theory, for it is impossible to 'get outside' it. Any possible ground of objection can be itself classed as an objection based on alleged incoherence, and therefore falls within the system by assuming that the really incoherent cannot be true. This does not mean that the theory gives anything more than a very bare and formal account of the nature of valid thought. It has

[1] Bosanquet takes as example the law that excision of the thyroid gland dulls the intelligence, and points out that even in a case like this there is 'plenty of justification for the pregnancy or relevance of relation' in a mass of connected knowledge, such as 'that glands are found to possess in their secretions quite specific properties for promoting or arresting organic processes, that the organ to which the thyroid gland belongs has evidently peculiar and profound relations with crises of bodily development, and that in medicinal use the thyroid extract shows a favourable effect on the intelligence correlative to the unfavourable effect of the gland's removal'. Thus the whole theory of hormones and enzymes seems involved (*Implication and Linear Inference*, pp. 89–90).

said something true but it has not said much, and there is endless scope for supplementation by more analytical logicians. But I can see no ground for waving aside the theory as refuted. Any valid detailed logical argument of any sort would be just an example of coherence. No doubt it may be objected that this reduces the theory to the mere uttering of a word, coherence, which can be interpreted so as to cover all arguments, but only by making its meaning so wide as to rob it of almost all significance. To this I can best reply by enumerating what I consider to be the chief contributions of the coherence theory as an account of the criterion of truth and so of the nature of reasoning.

(1) Its insistence on the whole, while it may be overdone and is a poor substitute for detailed argument, is in principle sound, I think. The real criterion for us, the real basis of any conclusions we may draw is our whole impression of the subject-matter under discussion, which alone gives significance to our particular inferences. This is part of the reason why it is so difficult to change even a highly intelligent and broad-minded person's views by a single argument, for a single argument, however strong, finds it hard to stand against a whole system of thought. It is also the reason, I think, why it is so difficult for a person who is not acquainted with a particular science to appraise the value of specific arguments within that science. An argument may appear most inadequate to an outsider, and yet be quite cogent within the context of the science. Even the precise inferences of arithmetic or geometry have only meaning within the numerical or the Euclidean (or e.g. Riemannian) system. But 'the Whole' has been misinterpreted both by some supporters and by some opponents of the theory as standing for a transcendent metaphysical entity, in which case the evidence for its existence would be dubious and its value as a criterion nil. 'The Whole' as a criterion is only the whole of our previous experience, knowledge and belief. This seems a poor criterion owing to our human limitations, but at least it is the best we have. For we obviously cannot on any view use as our criterion experience and knowledge that we have never had. The point that the criterion is the whole seems to me to be admirably developed in greater detail in Bosanquet's *Implication and Linear Inference*, a book that has been unduly neglected, but suffers less than its author's other works from those defects of exposition which, not without some excuse, arouse the ire of more analytical thinkers and

prevent them from profiting by the philosophical insight which the author still abundantly displays.

(2) The coherence theory rightly emphasises the fact that the consequences [1] of a principle may help to justify the principle as well as *vice versa*. This provides a way, I think, of justifying fundamental principles which would otherwise have to be taken either as based merely on an irreducible self-evidence or as arbitrary postulates. Thus to my mind the ultimate proof of causality is constituted by the fact that without it we could have no sort of coherent system of judgments about events in time. The beliefs in physical objects and in other minds, which have given philosophers so much trouble to justify, are likewise established (at least in the case of the latter) if we once grant that we must accept the view which makes the most coherent system of our experience. Our experience is made infinitely more intelligible if we ascribe certain very considerable parts of it to purposive minds outside us (other human beings).[2] (This would not stand as an account of the way in which the beliefs originated, but to make such a circumstance the ground of an objection is to confuse the psychological cause of a view with the real reason why we ought to hold the view.) If we are to aim at giving a rational account of our knowledge we must strive, if possible, to bring it under one principle, and the coherence principle is the only conceivable one which could serve this purpose. Its 'this or nothing' method does seem to me of the greatest importance.

(3) The coherence principle provides the only rational justification for induction. The newer school of logicians admit that they have not succeeded in providing such a justification. They seem to have shown that inductive arguments, if they are to be valid, require several assumptions which it is very unplausible to treat as self-evident in their own right and which cannot be otherwise justified.[3] But, if we assume that in any given case the hypothesis which comes nearest to making experience a coherent system is the one which ought to be accepted, then we have a principle by which we may easily justify the inductive process in general and any subordinate principles which it may require. We have arrived at a single

[1] I do not mean the practical consequences.
[2] For the justification of the belief in physical objects v. below, p. 327 ff.
[3] E.g. the principle of limited independent variety.

principle again and can dispense with a plurality of unjustified assumptions. For obviously any principle really necessary for induction must be *ipso facto* one without which it would be impossible to make any coherent system of our experience, and all such assumptions could therefore be deduced from the principle of coherence alone. Further, we have arrived at a principle which it is reasonable to regard as possessing self-evidence, not indeed in the sense of being absolutely certain, but in the sense of having in its own right a claim sufficient to justify belief.[1] At least in particular cases it does seem self-evident to scientists, historians and practical men that it is reasonable to accept the hypothesis which fulfils this condition rather than another which flagrantly does not.[2] The self-evidence may be explained by the fact that this is ultimately the same principle as is presupposed in all knowledge, though no doubt we are not aware of this as the reason why it seems self-evident to us. Unable to see the intelligibility of nature but still convinced that it is there, men have developed the notion of a causal system of nature as the nearest approach to the fully rational coherent system which is their vaguely discerned ideal, and then made this causal system as coherent as they could.

Differences and difficulties arise because what is coherent with recognised facts may be incoherent with new ones, and because there may be conflicting views as to the kind of system required. Thus men naturally first tried to systematise the facts of inorganic nature on teleological lines, but this ideal because of its inability to achieve its end has been replaced by the mechanical one, and it may be that this too is breaking down now and will be replaced by a third as yet unconceived. From the epistemological point of view at least the coherence theory requires a growing system to meet new experiences and not a rigid, eternally fixed one,[3] and the formula is elastic

[1] I insist later (p. 260) that we ought to regard self-evidence as having degrees.

[2] No doubt they do not accept the coherence principle in words (they generally have never heard of it), but this does not alter the fact that they always choose the hypothesis which strikes them as possessing the characteristic that philosophers call coherence, though they would describe it as ' explaining the facts best ' or use some phrase like that.

[3] From the ontological point of view the answer would be different, in the sense that we cannot possibly regard the change in our views about the system as constituting a change in the system itself. Still I do not see why the coherence theory should be committed to the 'unreality' of time, as is sometimes assumed.

enough to be open to a variety of interpretations. It need not be associated with an unreasonable conservatism or a blindness to new facts, but if it is to avoid this stigma it must be interpreted in a way which stresses adequately the element of comprehensiveness and thus does justice to the empirical.

To insist on coherence as the ultimate justification of induction is not to claim to provide a substitute for the laborious logical analysis of the principles and methods employed. But these principles and methods would all be applications of the coherence principle and justified thereby.[1] They would be necessary minimum conditions without which we could develop no system in science, or in a particular science, that even faintly approximated to coherence. That our science generally must fall very far short of the coherence ideal is no more an objection to the theory than it is an objection to a moral ideal that our practice perhaps falls still more short of it, but we must accept as true those principles without which we could not make any sort of approach to coherence. And it is clear that without assuming some *a priori* principles we could not have any science at all, nay, could not even validly make the simplest judgment of perception, since even that involves a reference to a physical object and so to general laws,[2] the belief in which could not be justified simply by experience but only by arguments which depend on the presuppositions common to all induction.

(4) The coherence theory provides a wider and, I think, sounder view of logic than one which restricts this subject to inferences capable of being put in definite symbolic form. There is a kind of logic also, which is well worth study, in ethics, art, ' rule of thumb ' practical life. This logic is based on a general and indefinite but none the less often highly serviceable and even profound view of the relevant whole. Surely a study of good literature does reveal a rational connection

[1] I do not mean to suggest that people started with the coherence theory and then deduced them from that. Here as elsewhere we can see the validity of particular arguments long before we realise the general principles on which they are based (v. above, p. 159).

[2] If propositions about physical objects are analysed simply into propositions about what human observers normally see or would see under given conditions, then they obviously involve general laws, namely, as to what they would normally see ; if they are interpreted realistically, then we at any rate cannot justify our passage from sense-data to physical objects or our distinction between real physical objects and the objects of illusion or dreams without appealing to inductive or causal arguments of some kind.

of the parts which can rightly be regarded as having a certain logic of its own; and again, to state a quite different point, it is surely clear that most, I do not say necessarily all, morally wrong actions are fundamentally inconsistent (a logical property), because they in the long run defeat their own ultimate purpose, and that this fact is closely connected, though not identical, with their wrongness. I think that the advocates of the coherence theory press this point too much and have been far from completely successful in their treatment of ethics on such lines, but this wider logic is certainly a subject that calls for close philosophical study, though I must admit that I am very much in the dark, no doubt owing to my own philosophical defects, as to what the best way of approaching it would be.

I am thus inclined to accept the coherence theory or something very like it as an account of our criterion of truth, and therefore as an account of the nature of the world. For, even if coherence were not *the* criterion but *only one* criterion of truth, it is difficult to see how we could possibly be justified in supposing that because a proposition fulfilled the coherence test it was true unless we assumed that the real was coherent. If something might be real and yet incoherent, why should a coherent view be more worthy of acceptance, more likely to be true, than an incoherent? But I am not able to accept the theory as an account of the nature of truth; nor is the theory idealist, in the sense defined at the beginning of this book, in any form in which it could be accepted by me. I admit that the view has sometimes been developed in a way which overstressed coherence as opposed to comprehensiveness of empirical fact, and unity as opposed to difference; but then it is impossible to state a theory in a way which will emphasise all sides in due proportion for all readers, and without accepting all Bradley's or Bosanquet's views we may still well raise the cry of 'Back to the coherence theory' in face of the irrationalistic and excessively pluralistic tendencies of the present day.

§ V. Rationalism *v.* Empiricism

Connected with and often underlying the issue between idealism and realism is the still more fundamental one between rationalism and empiricism, and a consideration of the coherence theory brings this second antithesis to a head. With some exceptions most idealists in the positive sense of the term would have to be classed as rationalists rather than empiricists,[1] and this would undoubtedly be true of those idealists who embrace the coherence theory. The association between realism and empiricism is less clear, though in practice the chief modern philosophical realists have been inclined towards an empiricist view. It may, however, reasonably be contended that the logical outcome of the more empiricist types of theory is not realism but that negative subjectivism according to which we have no right to assert the existence of anything beyond the actual and possible sensa of human beings; and it is significant that it is to this view and not to realism that the Cambridge school, which more than any other group of thinkers in this country carries on the empiricist tradition, although it started as strongly realist in outlook, is now inclining.[2]

The most important issue between rationalism and empiricism is not whether our 'ideas' have all been derived from experience, but whether and how far what is often called synthetic *a priori* knowledge is possible. It does not matter if there are no 'innate ideas', provided we are able in some cases to see logical connections by which one characteristic implies another. The idea of number may be empirical in the sense that we could not understand what was meant by 'number' except through having perceived things capable of numeration, but it may still be the case that we can see *a priori* the truth of many propositions about number which yield genuinely new knowledge. What is given in experience may logically imply something that is not so given.

The problem before us has been commonly described from Kant on as the problem of *a priori* synthetic judgments, a synthetic judgment being defined as a judgment the predicate of which is not included in the concept of the subject, but this is ambiguous and misleading. In the first place the question is really one not about isolated judgments but about

[1] By 'rationalists' in general I mean those who emphasise the *a priori* factor, by 'empiricists' those who emphasise more the empirical factor. I do not mean those, if any, who altogether deny one of these factors. Short of declaring either to be the only factor in knowledge there are all manner of shades of view.
[2] This does not apply to Professor Broad.

inferences. Secondly, there is a sense in which the predicate of all true judgments of the subject-predicate form, however empirical and however synthetic, is included in the subject. For, if the judgment S is P is true at all, P must be a real characteristic of S and must therefore in one sense fall within the nature of S. Thirdly, this account presupposes the view that the subject-predicate form is the only ultimate legitimate form of judgment. Fourthly, the word judgment is, as I have said, ambiguous, meaning (*a*) a judging, (*b*) a proposition.

At any rate what seems to me of importance is to maintain the possibility of synthetic *a priori inference*, i.e. inference in which the conclusion is not included in the premisses, and which passes from one or more facts to a different fact not included in these. The word included (or, more commonly, contained) is indeed used of the relation between the premisses and the conclusion as meaning not that the latter is really a part of the former but simply that it follows necessarily from the former, but here ' included in ' or ' contained in ' only means ' entailed by ', and in this sense I have no hesitation in saying that the conclusion of any valid inference is included in the premisses. What I insist is that this sense is quite different from the literal sense of ' included '.[1] Again we must not, because an inference is so extremely obvious that we do not notice that we have inferred, suppose that the conclusion is simply part of the premisses. Nor must we be misled by the fact that in ordinary speech we often use expressions such as ' to say A is to say B ' when we really mean not that A is the same as, or part of, B, but that A implies B.

But, to turn to a more important and dangerous because more subtle point, in cases where it can be shown that the premiss or premisses would be self-contradictory if the conclusion were false (and it may be argued that this is the case with all *a priori* reasoning), it would seem to follow that the conclusion must be itself part of the premisses. For how can anything be rendered self-contradictory by the denial of what falls outside itself? (This line of thought led to e.g. Kant's difficulties in admitting judgments that were both synthetic and *a priori*.) It can easily be seen, it will be said, that e.g. the premisses ' All men are mortal ' and ' Socrates

[1] No doubt, if A includes B, A also entails B, but I should insist that this proposition cannot be simply converted.

is a man' taken together would be self-contradictory if Socrates were not mortal, and therefore 'Socrates is mortal' must be really itself part of the premisses.[1]

But, in the first place, whether or not it be the case that the objective facts to which our premisses refer contain the fact that Socrates is mortal as a constituent, it cannot possibly be that our premisses do so. For our premisses are not the objective facts as such but only what we know about them before making the inference, and in cases of valid inference we do not, when we make it for the first time, know the conclusion till we have made the inference. We do not know the answer to a problem in mathematics before we have worked it out, and syllogistic inferences do not differ in this respect except as regards quickness and simplicity. No doubt the philosopher may say that we knew the conclusion in a sense—a philosopher can always quite simply avoid any objection to his theories by saying that they are 'true in a sense'—or that <u>we knew it implicitly, but this is only to say that we knew something which implied it.</u> This point is so obvious that it would be unreasonable to suppose that prominent logicians have really meant to deny it, but they very often have at least neglected it and as a result often give a most misleading account of the character of inference. Inference, if it is to have any value whatever and indeed if it is to be inference at all, must involve a real progress in thought and not merely a repetition in different words or symbols of part of what we knew already, and if so it is definitely wrong or at the least grossly misleading to describe the conclusion as included in the premisses.

But, secondly, even if we take the view as being simply that the *facts* to which the premisses refer (A and B) always include the *fact* referred to in the conclusion (C), not that the premisses themselves include the conclusion,[2] it is at once confronted with a most serious logical difficulty. For in most cases there are at least two premisses, referring to facts A and B respectively, and C admittedly is not included

[1] I am only taking a syllogism as an example: I do not for a moment mean to imply that all deductive reasoning is reducible to the syllogistic form. Most other forms of reasoning would put the argument which I am going to criticise in a still less favourable position.

[2] How the two positions are to be satisfactorily distinguished I am not very clear, but if they cannot be distinguished that is only another, and indeed a fatal, objection to the view which we are criticising.

in either A or B taken by itself.[1] But if so how can it possibly be included in both taken together? There is no special difficulty about its being entailed by both taken together, if 'entailed' is not identified with 'included' but treated as a synthetic relation not further definable, but how can it be included in them? How can C be a part of A and B unless it is a part of either A or B? The only way in which this could occur would be if part of C were included in A and the other part in B, but that is obviously not the case here. It is not the case that part of the fact that Socrates is mortal is included in the fact that all men are mortal and the other part in the fact that Socrates is a man, or that part of the fact that York is north of London is included in the fact that Cambridge is north of London and part in the fact that York is north of Cambridge. It therefore follows logically that <u>C in cases such as these cannot be part of A + B, since it neither is part of A or B nor consists of a part of A together with a part of B.</u> Consequently there are facts from which we can validly infer facts not included in the former facts. To say that the facts which provide the real premises are not A and B by themselves but the whole 'system' to which they belong only puts the difficulty further back. For C cannot be part of the whole 'system' unless it is part of a fact or facts included in the latter, and the same objections would arise against making it part of any of the facts in the 'system' that we could have known before making the inference to C.[2] If, on the other hand,

[1] It might seem that the fact that all men are mortal obviously includes the fact that Socrates is mortal. But it cannot really do so since if it did the conclusion would follow from one premiss alone which is admittedly not the case. It might still be a fact that all men were mortal though there never had been such a man as Socrates at all, therefore this fact cannot include the fact about Socrates mentioned in the conclusion. There are many other inferences where it would be clearer still that neither of the facts to which the premisses refer by itself included the conclusion, e.g. X = Y, Y = Z, ∴ X = Z; Cambridge is north of London, York is north of Cambridge, therefore York is north of London. Nobody could possibly maintain in these cases that the fact specified in the conclusion was included in the fact specified in either premiss.

[2] That Socrates is mortal is obviously part of the fact that Socrates and Plato are mortal, if it is legitimate to speak of a combination of two facts as 'a fact'; but facts like this clearly could not on any view be said to form part of the premisses for our conclusion as to the mortality of Socrates, for we could not conceivably know them without first knowing what we wanted to prove.

the defenders of the view admit that a fact C could be included in A and B together without being included in A and B as taken separately, they have really given their whole case away. For this is to admit a synthetic relation such that from A and B we can infer a different fact not included in itself, i.e. A + B, since it is now admitted that A + B constitutes a different fact from A by itself and B by itself and that this fact can be inferred from the latter. It must be a different fact on that view, for it includes C while the facts A and B taken separately do not do so; and it must be a fact entailed by A and B taken separately, for otherwise we could not make a valid syllogism by combining premisses which we had come to know apart from each other.

Thirdly, when we say that the premisses (call them a and b) would be self-contradictory if the conclusion (c) were false, we are not really speaking accurately, for it is not that there is a contradiction in $a + b$[1] taken alone if c is false but simply that there is a contradiction in $(a + b)$ + non-c. The proposition $a + b$ itself could not be any more self-contradictory because c was false than it would be if c were true, for it remains the same proposition. The contradiction is not within $a + b$ but *between* $a + b$ and *another* proposition. What is self-contradictory is the combination of $a + b$ with non-c, but this is only to say that there is a relation between $a + b$ and c such that the former entails c and therefore, conversely, is excluded by non-c. But if we look at the position in this way, there is no reason whatever for concluding, because the proposition $a + b$ is contradicted by the denial of c, either that it must include c itself or that the corresponding fact A + B must include the fact C, unless it be already assumed that the relation of entailment is identical with or presupposes the relation of inclusion, and this is simply to beg the question at issue. Most logicians seem, however, not to have distinguished the assertion that ' S is P ' is analytic in the sense that its denial would contradict what we previously knew about S from the assertion that it is analytic in the sense of verbal or tautologous or incapable of giving new knowledge.[2]

The ' rationalist ' philosophers prior to Kant are commonly

[1] E.g. Socrates is a man and all men are mortal.
[2] I do not mean to assume that these last three senses of ' analytic ' are necessarily identical, but I have not space to discuss the distinction between them, if any.

described as having held that all *a priori* knowledge was 'analytic', but what is meant by this is that they held it to be all deducible from the law of non-contradiction, and not that they denied that it was synthetic in the sense of producing new knowledge or of being more than merely verbal. That it was synthetic in these senses certainly was their usual view, though they may not have expressed it very clearly. It is obvious that they all thought it perfectly possible to obtain new and interesting conclusions about the universe by *a priori* inference from data not already including these conclusions. They thought e.g., that they could prove the existence of God by the help of the notions of causation or possibility, and it is quite certain that they did not regard this conclusion as merely tautologous or verbal. On the contrary, the essential part of their opposition to thinkers of a more empiricist tendency lay in their claim to be able to establish by *a priori* reasoning such relatively extensive metaphysical knowledge, of a kind which, while it might be called analytic in one sense, was certainly synthetic in another. (Not that I am prepared to accept the view that all *a priori* knowledge is deducible from the law of non-contradiction.[1] Some excellent arguments against this view are given in Mr. Bertrand Russell's book on Leibniz.[2])

Since the view which makes *a priori* reasoning simply a matter of arbitrary definition seems to be gaining strength nowadays, I should like to stress one further point in opposition to this view, though I could give others also. It is this: supposing even we granted that the primary postulates are always arbitrary, that they are merely 'rules of the game', though I certainly should not be prepared to admit even this much, at least the inference of consequences from them cannot possibly be itself arbitrary. If it were we might, given the same postulates, equally well draw totally different inferences. If Euclid's presuppositions are arbitrary, the hypothetical proposition that, if these are true, e.g. all triangles must have the sum of their angles equal to two right angles, is still necessarily true *a priori*. Otherwise we could, while retaining as valid the whole proof down to the last step but one, still deny the conclusion and assert with equal justification, if we chose, that the sum was equal to a million right

---

[1] Or that the existence of God could be proved in this way.
[2] P. 16 ff. I do not know how far their author would endorse them now.

angles or to none. I do not suppose that the philosophers of considerable reputation who describe all *a priori* inference as arbitrary have really failed to see this simple fact, but they are at least open to the charge of having expressed themselves in a very misleading fashion.

In general I should emphatically reject all the current views of inference which make it analytic in the sense of 'tautologous' or 'verbal'. Such views would reduce all deductive inference to more complicated examples of the type —A is a wooden table, therefore A is made of wood—for they make the conclusion merely a restatement in different words of part of the premisses. What possible value inference could have in that case I am quite unable to see. Mathematicians who are anxious to prove such a theory to be true of their own subject would, if they were consistent, either throw all their mathematical books into the fire or treat the subject as a mere amusement without serious import, like crossword puzzles or chess. If mathematics consisted of such a set of tautologies it would not be thinking at all, and even its worst enemies admit it to be that.[1]

But, if any synthetic inferences are admitted, it follows that there are logical relations of entailment between different facts in the real world, i.e. those facts to which the premisses and the conclusion of an inference respectively refer. For it cannot be right to deduce C from A + B unless C is really *per se* and not only in our thought entailed by A + B. This is rightly assumed by the advocates of the coherence view, and here it is that the problem of this section touches them. For their view of the universe it is absolutely essential that what I have called synthetic inference should be possible and that there should be real relations of logical entailment between objective facts. For this reason and also because of the gross neglect of the synthetic aspect of thought in recent logic and the great intrinsic importance of the ques-

[1] All this would not necessarily follow if mathematics were held to be the working out of postulates not known to be true or even known to be false. For mathematics would then still give *synthetic* knowledge, if only of the truth of *hypothetical* propositions. I am not trying here to criticise the view of mathematics as hypothetical, provided it is admitted (*a*) that, even if the primary postulates are arbitrary, the conclusions drawn from them follow necessarily, (*b*) that the inference used is synthetic in the sense on which I have insisted. (3rd ed.) I should not now go so far as to say that the analytic view would make inference completely useless. As Kant saw, it would make it useful merely for clarifying pre-existing ideas.

tion for philosophy I have thought this digression well worth while, but I am quite aware that I have left untouched many more detailed problems which are very closely connected with the subject-matter of this section. In excuse I may plead not only lack of space but a confidence that the newer school of logicians can handle them infinitely better than I could, which is quite compatible with a strong *caveat* against certain of their general tendencies, at least as expressed hitherto, and a conviction that their general philosophical outlook badly needs supplementation.[1]

Granted that some valid *a priori* synthetic inferences can be made, I do not see any way of determining *a priori* their extent or delimiting in general the circumstances under which they are intrinsically possible. We can no doubt make on the basis of experience of past attempts at inference such generalisations as that we cannot by this means establish new laws of nature, but we are not entitled on such an empirical ground to assert that it is intrinsically impossible to do this, only that this cannot be achieved by human beings at our present level of development. It seems to me that any metaphysical argument must be left standing to be debated on its own merits, and cannot be declared false merely on the ground that it is synthetic where synthetic inference is impossible. I have no doubt, however, that the great majority of those which have actually been put forward in the past would still be overthrown by this debate on their own merits, not because they are synthetic or because they are 'meaningless', but because they are invalid or rest on unjustified premisses.

The more rationalistically inclined philosophers have, however, commonly erred in putting forward extravagant claims to certainty and despising mere probability. It is no doubt true that we cannot attribute probability to assertions based on *a priori* arguments which fall short of certainty in *the same sense* as we can to those based on inductive evidence. The principal difference is that, while a prediction such as that it will rain in London to-morrow must remain merely probable on the basis of the data given, even if we handle our data perfectly, an *a priori* argument which claims to prove a given conclusion can only fall short of certainty because there is a doubt whether we who use it are not guilty of some error ourselves. But, since in philosophy we can rarely, if ever, be certain even after the fullest consideration

[1] For a fuller account v. my article in *Proceedings of Aristotelian Soc. 1939-40*.

that we have not committed some confusion which impairs our argument, it remains true that *in this sense* the conclusions of most *a priori* arguments in philosophy are at the best merely probable. So the common dictum that the *a priori* must be characterised by certainty is misleading. It is even misleading to say that, while we may be uncertain about an *a priori* argument, the argument itself must either be logically certain or a mere fallacy, because an argument, especially in philosophy, may be invalid in the sense that it has not succeeded in establishing what it sets out to prove and yet really prove something *like* the conclusion put forward, and so improve our knowledge by bringing those who accept it at least nearer the truth, though nobody may succeed for centuries in analysing exactly what is proved. I am afraid that there are few philosophical arguments outside pure logic (excepting negative criticisms of other arguments or of particular views) which have done more than this in the past, and I should be happy if in such a difficult subject I should have done as much in the present book.

What has been said applies as much to apparent truths which seem to be self-evident as to conclusions of arguments. 'Intuition' is indeed infallible by definition, since, if we think it wrong, we decline to call it intuition, but this purely verbal point does not imply that what presents itself in the guise of intuition must be either certainly right or a mere valueless prejudice. A seeming intuition may be confused and yet give some truth, and in that case we shall, if we are reasonable, not claim certainty for what we seem to see but only probability, or we may have to be content to say 'I am practically sure that something like this is true'.

This is very relevant to all claims that we can know general truths intuitively in ethics, religion or metaphysics. If absolute certainty is claimed for propositions supposed to be thus intuited, most of such claims quickly become quite untenable and even ridiculous, in view of the enormous difference of opinion between different men and the inability of the person who makes the claim in most cases to define satisfactorily what he does intuit.[1] But it is a very different

---

[1] This is not intended to be applied to formal logic and mathematics, nor to *all* particular propositions in ethics. The view that certainty can be ascribed to general propositions asserting the '*prima facie* rightness' of certain kinds of action seem also defensible (v. Ross, *The Right and the Good*, p. 19 ff.).

matter if we recognise <u>degrees of self-evidence</u>. Then we can admit that there may be non-inferential cognitions which, while not yielding certainty, yet justify belief, and, while not presenting us with any clear definite proposition, yet enhance our knowledge and perhaps form a necessary basis of any advance in a given branch of study at all. It seems to me that such confused non-inferential cognitions form the basis, for instance, of the categories of substance and cause. Anyone who claims that the validity of these categories is self-evident is liable to be challenged to give a precise account of the propositions about them which we do thus know, and he will then probably find that any tenable propositions turn out to be so complicated that it is quite unreasonable or even absurd to suppose them self-evident.[1] But if he admits that our object of knowledge (or, better, cognition, since 'knowledge' implies certainty) is something vague, not stateable, at least by us, in a definite form of words and only capable of being understood progressively if we add to the original non-inferential cognition inference, analysis and testing by its applications, then this position becomes much less easy to assail. That some such non-inferential cognition forms the basis of our belief in induction must be admitted if we are to accept the results of induction as justified at all, and is compatible with the fact that logicians have not yet succeeded in analysing completely and stating definitely what the *a priori* element in induction is.[2] It may strike the philosopher as lamentable that our 'intuitions' should be so vague, but in the case in point and perhaps in others the deficiency in point of theory is not such a handicap in practice. 'Intuition' or (as I prefer to call it, in view of the abuses connected with this term) non-inferential cognition is not a ready-made knowledge of propositions complete once for all, but a developing faculty and one which can only work in conjunction with inference.[3]

[1] Mr. Russell brings this objection against the belief that the principle of causality is *a priori*.
[2] To describe it as the coherence principle, as I did earlier, is certainly not to achieve this.
[3] That there is such a thing as this immediate (non-inferential) cognition at all is sometimes disputed, but, though it has no doubt been very often asserted illegitimately, that it occurs sometimes is proved by the fact that it is presupposed in all inference. To infer we must see the connection between each step and the next *immediately*.

CHAPTER VI

IDEALISM AND THE THEORY OF PERCEPTION

§ I. Introductory Explanation of Terms

WE shall now turn to another set of idealist arguments, those based on our alleged inability to justify the belief in physical objects in a sense in which the latter term denotes objects possessing spatial characteristics that exist even when unperceived by us and is not analysable merely in terms of our experience or of what we actually perceive or would perceive under given circumstances. These arguments differ from those which have been discussed under the heading of epistemological arguments in that they are not drawn from a consideration of knowledge in general but from the particular problem of knowledge (or opinion) concerning physical objects. They do not assume any particular answer to the problem as to the nature of knowing and the relation between knowing and the known object, but simply maintain the impossibility of justifying on the available evidence a particular set of propositions which fall for realists within the realm of knowledge or justified opinion. The arguments do not belong to epistemology, though in their discussion, as in the discussion of any other philosophical problem, epistemological questions may have to be raised by us.

Further, even if valid, they could show only that we have no right to assert the existence of physical objects in the sense indicated, not that there are no such objects. For the arguments do not rest on any supposed contradiction or logical absurdity in the conception of independent physical things, but on the mere absence of evidence justifying belief in their existence. Nor could they be used directly to establish the existence of a universal mind to which these objects would be relative. For we cannot possibly base the conclusion that physical objects exist in God's mind on the premiss that we cannot justify our belief in the existence of such objects. They must therefore be carefully distinguished from other arguments about the physical world which have been used to justify idealism. When it is urged, e.g., that spatial relations imply mind, such an argument is not epistemological in character and yet differs from the arguments discussed in the present chapter in these two respects.

(*a*) It seeks to show not only that we cannot justify the belief in independent physical objects but that this belief is logically absurd.

(*b*) It is quite compatible with the view that physical objects can be shown to be independent of all human (and animal) minds, provided they are dependent on some (presumably superhuman) mind,[1] while the arguments to be considered here show if valid that we have no justification for asserting their independence even of our minds.

In the present chapter and the following one I shall confine myself to a consideration of the evidence for the existence of physical objects independent of our minds (whether or not their nature be ultimately mental or such that they are dependent on a divine or absolute mind). By ' the belief in independent physical objects ' I shall mean ' the belief that there are some entities with spatial properties which exist when not perceived or sensed by any human being (or animal), in a sense in which this proposition is not analysable merely in terms of the actual or possible sensa of observers'.[2] This phrase is intended only as a rough indication of what I mean, not as a precise definition of physical objects. (Under the term ' belief ' I include not only explicit belief but implicitly taking for granted, as we do at the perceptual level ' take physical objects for granted '.) In these two chapters I shall for convenience refer to this belief as realism or the realist view, thus limiting the term realism more than I have done elsewhere in the book so as to cover only the issues of these chapters and not further more general questions as to the relation between knowing and its object or between matter and mind. ' Independent ' I shall

---

[1] V. below, ch. VII, sect. 1.

[2] I do not mean to imply that each such entity is necessarily a physical object by itself. For some realists hold that any single physical object is made up of a whole group of such independent entities (*sensibilia*, or as I call them later unsensed *sensa*), and my account must be worded so as to cover both their view and that of the more orthodox realists. For, though they differ in this, both classes of realists agree that there are some independent extended entities.

use to mean not 'totally unaffected by' but 'capable of existing apart from'. To deny that A was independent of B in my sense would be to assert that its existence apart from B was either causally or logically impossible. 'Secondary qualities' I shall use in the sense in which the term is used by Berkeley and most modern writers, not in the sense in which the term is used by Locke, i.e. 'I shall use it to stand for the actual quality of heat as felt, or colour as seen, etc., and not for the causal property in physical objects of producing sensations of colour or heat in us. By 'direct theory of perception' I shall mean 'any theory according to which some of the immediate objects sensed in perception are physical objects external to our body (in the realist sense of physical objects described) or literal spatial[1] parts of the surface of such objects.' By the term 'representative theory of perception' I mean to cover *any* theory of perception which admits the existence of physical objects in the realist sense but is not a direct theory. I shall draw no distinction between the terms 'immediate perception' and 'direct perception' but use them as synonyms. Nor shall I draw any distinction between 'physical' and 'material', or between 'physical objects' and 'physical things'. 'Object' without the prefix of physical I shall continue to use in the more general sense in which even mental states are 'objects' (of knowledge, etc.), but I shall not use it in this epistemological sense when conjoined with the adjective, physical. '*Sensa*' I shall use to mean 'objects of immediate perception other than physical objects (understood in the sense described) or spatial parts of physical objects'.[2] The terms 'illusion' and 'illusory' I shall use to cover all cases where we should say that a physical thing looks or appears different from what it is, e.g. I shall call all the elliptical shapes we see in looking from different angles at a round penny illusory. This is not the usual usage outside philosophy, but is for philosophy much the most convenient. None of these explanations of words that I have given must, however, be regarded as philosophical definitions, but only as rough ways of indicating in the interests of clarity how I intend to use the words. I doubt whether they could be made completely unambiguous

[1] The words 'literal' and 'spatial' are intended to exclude a view like that put forward by Mr. Price in his *Perception*, which certainly could not legitimately be regarded as a direct theory of perception.
[2] As will be seen, I find it desirable to extend the meaning of the term 'sensa' in the last section of the next chapter.

without a very long discussion, but I hope that at any rate I have removed any ambiguities which might affect the present argument adversely.

§ II. Different Senses of 'Direct Awareness' and their Philosophical Significance

Historically it is perhaps true to say that idealism first developed out of the representative theory of perception. For various reasons it was generally held that we do not perceive physical objects directly but only 'ideas' or 'representations' which they cause in us, and then grave difficulty was and always has been felt in justifying the belief in physical objects at all on these premises. It was partly from these difficulties that sprang Berkeley's theory, Hume's despair of the possibility of defending the belief in physical objects, and much of the idealism and agnostic positivism of the nineteenth century. If we are not directly aware of physical objects from the beginning but only of our 'ideas', it is difficult to see how we can ever deduce physical objects from our data. Consequently the representative theory is regarded by many as an untenable half-way house to idealism; and when there arose at the beginning of the twentieth century a strong school of realists who were determined not to complete the journey they returned to the 'common-sense view' that had been abandoned by most philosophers for centuries and asserted direct perception of physical objects. If we are immediately aware of physical things, they thought, then the idealist cannot deny the existence of the latter. It is therefore necessary for us, before we decide whether the belief in independent physical objects is philosophically tenable, to discuss first whether the representative theory is warranted or whether we can regard as adequate the attempt to justify our belief in the existence of physical objects by saying that we are directly aware of them. It is to be regretted, however, that the assertion that we are directly aware of physical objects has been analysed far less frequently than it has been made, and we must ask the reader not to expect a quick straightforward solution of the problem but to have patience till we have analysed the meaning of the assertion ourselves. Till we have done this we can never be sure that we are not trying to prove direct knowledge or perception in one sense by an argument which really proves it only in another quite different sense of the words.

In the first place the phrase has been used in opposition to a representative theory of knowledge, which must, as we shall see, be distinguished from a representative theory of perception. Some thinkers have either actually held, or been unwise enough or unfortunate enough to use terminology which seemed to imply that they held, the theory either that we can only know our own ideas or that knowing A consists simply in having 'ideas' of A, and the well-warranted rejection of such views gives us one minimum sense in which we must admit direct awareness of any facts that we know at all. Most of those who assert direct awareness of physical objects mean more than this, but they mean this at least, namely, that we know some facts about physical objects (other than facts about the experience they cause in us) in a sense which cannot be reduced merely to having, or to knowing, 'ideas which correspond to them'. They deem it necessary to insist on this because some thinkers have apparently confused the statement that in order to know anything we must have 'ideas' in our mind with the statement that to know anything is only to know our 'ideas' of it,[1] or again with the statement that to know it is to 'have ideas' of it, the ideas being conceived as a kind of mental pictures corresponding to the reality. Knowledge of the physical, as of everything else, may be said to be direct, because it is not a copy in our minds that we know but external reality. So much is clearly true if we know physical facts at all. In general, cognition has not to do merely with something in our minds, it is essentially 'extrospective'.[2]

The same applies if we substitute for 'knowledge' 'belief'

[1] As put this statement sounds self-contradictory. But the view may be interpreted in a way which avoids actual self-contradiction if we understand it as meaning that, where 'A' is something other than an idea of mine, 'I know A', in any sense in which it can be true, is simply an abbreviation for 'I know my idea of A' or 'I know an idea corresponding to A'. In that case there would be a sense of 'know' in which we could not be said to know anything except our own ideas, and another sense in which we could be said to know other objects, the second sense being definable only in terms of the first. The term 'idea' is also extremely ambiguous, like 'concept' (v. above, p. 23 ff.).

[2] 'I have summarily to exclude a supposed sense of the term mediate, which is in reality nonsense. No knowledge, however imperfect, can be mediate in the sense that something is interposed like a screen between the knowing mind and what it knows. If this were so, only the intervening screen would be known, not that which lies behind it' (Stout, *Studies in Philosophy and Psychology*, p. 176).

or 'opinion', a point which is still more important since it is extremely difficult even for a realist to claim absolute certainty for any of our judgments about physical objects. Even if I believe and do not know that 'this table is wooden', what I believe is something about the table and not about my ideas of the table; nor can believing truly, any more than knowing, be reduced to having ideas which correspond to the table, unless we mean by 'ideas' simply beliefs or somehow already include beliefs in the meaning of 'ideas'. The same applies to beliefs about past events, universal laws and minds other than our own. In true belief, as well as in knowledge, we are in direct relation to the object of our cognition and are not concerned primarily with something in our mind at all (except in the special cases where what we believe or know is admittedly a psychological fact about ourselves and not about anything else).[1] This outward reference is as essential in true belief as in knowledge, and at least an attempt to attain it is essential even if we are to have error.[2]

But this is not to say that we perceive material objects directly, any more than the assertion that we have knowledge or true belief about other minds and not only about our ideas of them is an assertion of telepathy. Even if the knowledge of or the belief in physical facts could only be reached by inference, it would still be physical facts which we were knowing or believing in, not only our ideas about such facts; even if we could only perceive directly ideas or sensa, not physical objects, our belief that the latter existed would still be a belief not about the ideas or sensa but about the physical objects. The most that could be granted to the representationist would be that we did not know *by acquaintance* anything physical but only our sensa, but this would not necessarily preclude us from knowing physical facts otherwise than by acquaintance (or at least from having rational grounds for beliefs which were probably true of them). Even if we hold a representative theory of perception we must distinguish it from a representative theory of cognition, and not assume, because when we say that we

[1] And even in these cases the fact known is not by any means always an idea of mine (in any even partially reasonable sense of the word), and it can be known without the help of a representative idea.

[2] Cook Wilson (in *Statement and Inference*) seems to me inconsistent in, on the one hand, stressing this directness of knowledge and on the other treating opinion and belief, even where true, as if they had no such direct relation to reality but were just something that went on in our minds.

perceive a material object we are really only perceiving immediately a representation of it, that therefore when we say we know something we really only know a representation corresponding to it or that cognition always proceeds by taking as its primary object a sort of representative copy of the object cognised.

Neither must we assume [1] that, because and where cognition is direct [2] in this sense, we have a mode of consciousness that is incapable of error. Our minds cannot be directly related to the fact believed in error, because there is no such fact,[3] but this does not necessarily imply that there is any *intrinsic* difference between knowledge and error. The difference may still lie only in the lack of a corresponding fact in error. Erroneous cognition is extrospective just as much as cognition which yields truth, only it fails in its purpose. Even in error we are concerned not with our 'ideas' but with external reality : error consists in thinking that reality is different from what it is, not in merely having ideas which fail to copy reality. If there is no reference to external reality, there is no error about such reality.

Secondly, by the statement that we are directly aware of physical objects we may mean that we do not come to accept their existence as the result of an inference. We do not, it is contended, patiently abstain from believing in physical objects till we have inferred them from our sense-data. On the contrary, we assume their existence from the beginning of life, and most people go through life without ever having *inferred* it at all. This sense of 'direct awareness' must be, like the first, distinguished from what is asserted when we say that we 'directly perceive' physical objects, for even if we did not perceive them directly, we might still, rightly or wrongly, accept their existence as self-evident without inference. Now it seems to be the case that our belief in the existence of physical objects is non-inferential, but this so far is only a

[1] As e.g. Cook Wilson apparently does.
[2] I should hold that all cognition is direct in this sense of the term ; Cook Wilson in accordance with the assumption I am just discussing insists only that *knowledge* is direct, not belief or opinion.
[3] Though they may be thus related to the object cognised, where 'object' is used to signify a continuant or substance, except in cases where we believe that a continuant exists which does not really exist and not merely that an existent continuant has qualities or relations which it does not really have (if indeed these cases are ultimately distinct from the others).

psychological fact. It does not prove that the belief is true; self-evident truths are not inferred, but neither are irrational prejudices. No doubt if we concede that we have non-inferential *knowledge* of physical objects we have been trapped into conceding that physical objects exist, for the term knowledge is not applicable unless the judgments dignified by that name are true. But this is merely verbal: we cannot use the fact that a judgment is non-inferential to prove that it really is knowledge, unless we hold not only that it is non-inferential but that it is self-evidently true.

So, thirdly, when it is said that we are directly aware of physical objects, it is usually assumed that this awareness gives us both certainty and truth, that it is genuine intuitive knowledge. The presence of direct awareness in this sense, if we had it, would undoubtedly be sufficient to justify us in accepting the existence of physical objects as an indubitably certain fact, but it would be quite compatible with holding that what we *perceive* in sense-experience is only our own 'ideas'. It might be that we had an intuitive, certain *knowledge* of the existence of some physical objects even though we did not perceive any such objects directly, i.e. it might be that what we perceived was not the material objects themselves but something else, e.g. ideas in our mind, and yet that we had real knowledge of the objects not based on inference. Non-inferential knowledge is clearly not limited entirely to what we can sensorily perceive and might conceivably extend to the material world. It might also be the case that we had non-inferential cognitions of material objects that fell short of knowledge in certainty but yet justified a belief in their existence.

Direct awareness of physical objects does not therefore necessarily imply the direct theory of perception, and the latter theory, whether right or wrong itself, seems to me to gain an unfair advantage in argument from the assumption that it does. Direct cognition would, in any of the three senses analysed, be quite possible without direct perception; and we cannot therefore argue that, because the former must be accepted, the latter must. But undoubtedly one of the possible senses in which we may understand the statement that we are directly aware of the physical world is as meaning that we directly perceive it, and this sense now comes up for examination.

The question of direct perception is primarily not a question about our cognition at all; it is a question about the nature and identity of certain entities admittedly experienced by us, i.e. whether the something which we by general consent directly perceive when we use our senses is part of the physical world or not. It is admitted that I see, e.g. a square brown patch, in a sense of 'see' which implies presence to my immediate experience; the question between the rival theories of perception is whether this seen patch is physical or not. Some philosophers, the holders of the representative theory of perception, say that it is merely something 'in the perceiver's mind'; others, the holders of the direct theory, say that it sometimes at least exists independently of him and is capable of being perceived by other minds.

Now there is one point which is often overlooked. The judgment that we perceive material objects directly does not necessarily imply that we know directly that they are material objects. We have already seen that we might know of the existence of some material objects directly without perceiving any directly, but the converse is equally true. For it is quite conceivable that what I perceive might be identical with a physical object or part of such an object, and yet that I might have no knowledge of this important fact. Indeed, this would seem actually to be the case, if the direct theory is true at all, and if we are speaking of knowledge and not belief; for clearly representationists and idealists did not *know* that what they perceived was ever identical with or part of a physical object, and it is very unlikely that such a deficiency in knowledge is peculiar to these philosophers Most men may take for granted that what they perceive is a physical object, or part of one, or again they may have an intuitive conviction that this is so which, while falling short of certainty, justifies belief, but can they be said to know it? If we first assume a knowledge of or belief in physical objects we may perhaps then argue that these objects are perceived directly, but this knowledge or belief itself could be based on direct perception only if we included under this term not only the last-mentioned sense of direct awareness, the sense in which it refers to perception, properly speaking, but also the third sense, or the last of the epistemological senses, and said that we have intuitive knowledge (or a conviction justifying belief) that what we perceive is in some cases physical; but these two assertions are commonly not separated or distinguished.

Further, this knowledge or conviction justifying belief,

even if it is present, could not possibly be given by sense-perception as such. We cannot know by sensory perception as such that the immediate object of our experience exists independently of being perceived unless we can perform the impossible feat of perceiving it without its being perceived; nor can we know by sense-perception alone whether other observers see numerically the same things as we see, since we cannot observe their experiences directly. We cannot even obtain by sense-perception an intuitive conviction justifying belief in these or similar propositions. For the question is not whether what we perceive does or does not possess certain observable characteristics. We may perfectly well perceive matter directly without knowing or believing it to be matter, and therefore we cannot use the direct theory of perception to establish the existence of material objects; on the contrary, we can only maintain that theory if we have first established their existence by some other means, or, if that be impossible, seen it to be self-evident by some non-inferential cognition, which may no doubt for anything I have said accompany our perception.

To sum up before going further, we have seen that the question whether we are directly aware of physical objects really covers four different problems.

(1) Is a representative view of cognition true, i.e. is cognition a process primarily directed to our own 'ideas'?

(2) Do we come to believe in the existence of physical objects as the result of an inference or intuitively?

(3) Have we or have we not non-inferential knowledge of the existence of physical objects (or in the absence of this at least an intuition [1], or non-inferential cognition, adequate to justify belief)?

(4) Is what we perceive immediately sometimes a physical object or part of such an object?

---

[1] I am here as elsewhere using 'intuition' to mean non-inferential non-empirical cognition without necessarily implying that the cognition yields truth. A word is needed for this, and I think the common usage of confining the term intuition to cases of knowledge inconvenient, and also misleading because it suggests that there is an internal difference of kind between all true and all false non-inferential non-empirical cognitions and because it leaves no place for the majority of such cognitions, which are neither certain nor completely without evidential value of any kind whatever. Nor do I ever follow some writers in using intuition to stand for perception or a species of perception (e.g. of space and time). That is quite a different sense of

We have further seen that we might have direct cognition of physical objects in all the first three senses without ever perceiving any physical objects directly, and that we might perceive them directly and yet not be directly aware of them in at least the second and third senses. To perceive a physical object directly is not to know directly that any physical object exists, and to know this directly would not be to perceive any such object directly.

It seems to me that the confusion between the question whether we have direct cognition of material objects in any of the first three senses given and the question whether we directly perceive material objects is partly due to the fact that perception is itself a species of cognition. To perceive a fact is to know that fact, to perceive a quality is to know that there is an instance of this quality.[1] But it does not follow that to perceive a material object directly is to know a material object if that implies knowing that it is a material object. For, while we cannot perceive an object directly without knowing that object in the sense of being acquainted with it, it is perfectly possible to be acquainted with an object without knowing all the facts about that object (though not perhaps without knowing some of the facts), and therefore without knowing that it is an independent physical object even if it really is one in fact. Confusion may also be caused by the circumstance that, when we do have the experience of perceiving, we usually also have the belief, explicit or implicit, that what we are perceiving is a physical object, but this, though a usual, is not a necessary accompaniment of the experience,[2] and is in any case a circumstance distinct from, though causally connected with, the perceiving.

If I might make a brief digression, it is very important to note that the confusions pointed out have also had very detrimental effects on the theory of memory and not only on the theory of perception. As in the case of perception of the physical we find the question asked—Are we directly aware

the term, and I am confident that I am in agreement with the more common usage in confining intuition to non-empirical cognition. This makes 'non-inferential cognition' wider than 'intuition' because, as we shall see, the former is sometimes empirical.

[1] These propositions are not convertible, since perception is not the only species of knowledge.

[2] I may perceive something and yet at the same time believe that my percept is totally illusory and does not even represent a physical object.

of the past in memory? Here again philosophers often seem to think that this question can just be answered—Yes or No, but in reality it resolves itself into four separate questions in the same way as the analogous question about our awareness of physical objects. The first question is—Do we know the past directly in the sense that remembering a past event cannot be reduced to knowing our ideas about that event or to having ideas about it? In this sense the direct view of memory is true if we have any knowledge of the past at all.

Secondly—Is memory direct in the sense of non-inferential? Here again the answer is clearly in the affirmative: simple memory is, if not totally unmixed with inference, at least as little inferential as any of our knowledge can be. When we remember a past event, our consciousness of it seems to be its own evidence. We do not believe in the event because we argue that it is needed to account for our present ideas. *Inferences* as to my past actions are not cases of memory, any more than my inferences as to the actions of other people.

The third question is—Does memory give us truth? This is not, indeed, a question that we can ask as outsiders, so to speak, since the truth of a memory judgment, not being inferred, must be cognised in the act of remembering itself and not by means of any external criterion. What purports to be a memory must either be an illusion or its own evidence. But that it is in very many cases its own evidence and not an illusion we can hardly deny; while it is obviously impossible to maintain that there is no such thing as a mistake of memory, it is equally clear that memory does give us truth in very many cases.

But our affirmative answer to these three questions does not necessitate an affirmative answer to the fourth—Is the fact remembered related to us immediately in the sense in which this is the case with an object of present perception? Yet special difficulty has been felt about the directness of memory because it has been supposed that, if we are directly aware of the past in the first three senses, the past must be, so to speak, bodily present to our mind or occupy the same position as our present objects of perception, which it obviously does not do. This has led some thinkers to deny the directness of memory altogether, and others to assert that what are usually regarded as memory images, or some of these, are really identical numerically with the event or object remembered,[1] as it has been

[1] E.g. Professor Alexander, *Space, Time and Deity*, vol. II, p. 197.

asserted that in perception our immediate object is identical numerically with something in the physical world. Hence some have supposed that, since we obviously can know the past directly, such paradoxes are the truth; others have supposed that, since this is obviously impossible, we cannot know the past directly at all. But all this could have been avoided by a simple process of analysis. It is perfectly true that we can cognise the past directly and are not confined to inferring it, but this does not mean that the past is still here as an existent object or that I perceive it as I do what is now given by my senses; it only means that I can make true judgments about it not based on inference.[1] If I actually *saw* the past I might be compelled to hold that it would have to be present while I looked at it, but why should it have to be present now for me to make right judgments about it ? That the past should stand in some relation to the present does not necessarily entail its existence now; otherwise the mere fact that it was past, i.e. related to the present by the relation of antecedence in time, would imply that it was also present. Some relations may entail the contemporary existence of the related terms: this seems to be the case with pure spatial relations, relations like being a friend to, and perhaps the relation of sensing. But there are many other relations which nobody could say implied the coexistence of their terms, e.g. likeness, quantitative relations, causality. In memory I perceive directly my own images or sensations, but these need not and cannot be identified with the event remembered. My relation to them is quite different from the relation I bear to the past event. For I am immediately aware of them as here now, while in knowing a past event I am not immediately aware of it as present but as past. If we doubt the evidence of our immediate experience so far as to say that the images are not really present now but only seem to be so, we might just as well doubt anything.

§ III. The Representative *v.* the Direct Theory of Perception*

To return to the question of perception, the problem here is—Are we to hold that what we immediately perceive is identical (numerically and not only qualitatively) with some

[1] And be aware of their truth.

part of the physical world?[1] It is common nowadays to decry any suggestion hostile to the direct theory as 'subjectivism', but this is partly due to the confusions already pointed out. To deny that what we immediately perceive is a physical object or part of such an object is not, as has sometimes been wrongly assumed, to say that we can only know our own ideas; it is not even to say that our belief in or knowledge of the existence of physical objects must be based on inference, either psychologically or logically. The representative theory is still not free from objection, but, whatever its faults, there are at least some powerful reasons which support it.

The chief of these is the fact of 'illusion' in the wide sense of this term as covering all perceptions which we normally do not regard as veridical. The direct theory holds that what we perceive is identical with physical objects or at least consists of parts of such objects. On this view you and I will sometimes see the same object, e.g. the top surface of a penny, at the same time. But if we are sufficiently removed from each other, the surface of the penny you see will have a different shape from the surface of the penny I see. Therefore, since these two are *ex hypothesi* identical, the same surface of the penny will have or include in its being two different shapes at the same time, and in fact, by an extension of the argument, an infinite, or at least indefinite, number (though this would not necessarily be incompatible with one of the shapes being more important causally than the others). This is not by any means an indefensible view. It has been defended by some of the 'New Realists', and seems to me the most consistent one for an advocate of the direct theory to adopt. We must either put into the physical world every perception (*perceptum*) anybody has, whether well or ill, whether drunk or sober, or admit that in some cases at least perception is representative; and if we once make this concession it is difficult in the extreme to see how we can be justified in asserting the directness of other perceptions. It is certainly inconsistent to maintain both that we perceive material objects directly and that colour

[1] I must ask the idealist who objects that I am here assuming the truth of realism to wait till the next chapter, when I shall try to see what can be said in reply to him. Since the form of idealism discussed in that chapter has commonly been based on the assumption that we could not be said directly to perceive physical objects in the realist sense, it is necessary to consider first what is to be said in favour of and against the assumption in question.

may not be a property of material objects [1]; it is inconsistent to maintain both that we see the mirror itself and yet that the reflection we equally see in the mirror is not there at all; it is inconsistent to say that we perceive physical things directly and yet that their real qualities are quite different from their apparent ones, as is commonly held by physical scientists. Anyone who doubts or denies the external physical reality of even colour is denying that what we perceive immediately is part of the physical world, for what we perceive immediately is obviously coloured. He is denying it even if he only denies the independent physical reality of any of the sensible sounds, tastes or smells sensed by us.

This is the dilemma that confronts the direct theory. We must either admit that perception is non-direct in some cases at least or admit the physical reality of everything that everybody ever apprehends by their senses. The view that physical objects possess all the properties perceived by us but only possess them in relation to an organism or 'from a point of view' is not really a separate alternative, because, if it means that they only appear to a percipient who is embodied in the organism or perceives them from 'the point of view' and are not really present in the object, this resolves itself into a non-direct view of perception [2]; and if it means that they are really present in the physical world as characteristics relative to some other physical object or part of space, this is a form (very possibly the most defensible form) of the alternative view that everything we perceive exists in the physical world as perceived.

It is impossible to avoid the dilemma by saying that illusions can easily be explained by the constitution of our sense-organs and the laws of perspective. This explanation is useful if we hold that what we directly perceive is not a physical object, but if what we perceive immediately is held to be the external physical thing itself (or part of it) we cannot apply the explanation at all unless we are prepared to maintain that the laws of perspective and the constitution of our sense-organs change, not something in our retinas or brains or minds, but the actual physical tables, chairs, trees, etc., and further change them in such a way as to cause them to take an indefinite number of different shapes at the same moment and to give them qualities

---

[1] I am not myself intending to exclude the view that colour is a property of physical objects, but the majority of realists probably do so.
[2] Or into the compromise which I criticise on p. 281 ff.

and positions which they never had at all before. For what we are supposed to explain by the laws of perspective, etc., is why what we directly perceive takes a certain shape, and what we directly perceive according to the direct theory is the physical object itself. That when we look at an avenue we commonly see two converging lines of trees is clear; if what we see is the physical object, that the physical object has this shape follows from the law of identity and cannot be doubted, yet when we walk down it we find that the lines do not converge. Hence either there are at least two differently arranged sets of visual trees there and we have embraced the second horn of the dilemma, or I change the shape of the avenue by walking down it, an assumption of a kind which would not only reduce to chaos the causal laws recognised in science if applied in all cases of 'illusion' but is inconsistent with the fact that somebody else can at the same time still perceive the very same avenue converging towards the end at which I now stand. The case would be different if it could be maintained that when we looked at the avenue we really did not see anything converging but only imagined we did; but if we doubt the verdict of experience here we have no right to believe it anywhere. It is as indubitable a fact of experience as any that under these conditions we do see two lines converging, that what is present to our senses really has this shape. What is shaped thus, since we see it, exists even if it be degraded to the rank of an image in our mind; the question is not whether it is but what it is, whether it is a physical object or an idea or something else intermediate between the two.

One alternative is to hold the representative theory in the case of 'illusions' but retain the direct theory in regard to those cases of perception where there is no reason to suspect illusion. It is sometimes taken for granted that there are no such cases, in the sphere of sight at least, because the laws of perspective always affect what we see. We are always some distance from the object perceived and are never at an equal distance from all its parts; therefore, it seems, we should see those parts of it which are nearer to us as too large relatively to the others, thus distorting its shape and affecting its relations to other objects in the field of perception. But this is not what actually happens, though we should expect it to. If we change our position when looking at objects from only a few feet away, we find it hard to detect any corresponding change in their size and it is at least doubtful whether there is any such change in what we see at all, though we have no doubt about it in the case of remoter objects. This fact has been recently emphasised and investigated by the school of 'Gestaltpsychologists'. It is not merely due, as I erroneously suggested in *Mind*, to our inability to perceive microscopically small differences, because from the laws of perspective alone [1] it would follow that the difference must be quite substantial, sometimes as much as fifty per cent. It is therefore possible to hold that in the case of fairly near objects the direct theory is true and yet that we perceive only a representation in the case of more distant objects. But this, though not impossible, seems very unlikely, for it would involve a total difference between our mode of perceiving relatively distant objects and our mode of perceiving near objects, without there being anything whatever in our conscious experience or in our sense-organs to point to such a difference of kind. It would mean not a gradual transition in respect of degree but an abrupt and complete change in the kind of object I see when I pass the limit where illusion begins; before I saw physical objects, now on that view I see mere representations. Further, even this would not remove the difficulties as to mirror reflections, secondary qualities, etc., and those raised by the contrast between the structure of matter as described by science and as revealed to our eyes. These illusions, if they are illusions, continue, however near we approach to the object. There are ways, more or less plausible, of meeting any one of the difficulties, but together they constitute a formidable barrier. Nor has such a solution escaped the arguments which seem to indicate the dependence of what we see on psychological factors such as interpretation and association.

It has also been suggested that the direct theory might be true of touch and the representative theory of the other senses; but it is difficult to distinguish between the senses in this way and impossible altogether to eliminate illusions of touch.[2] Again there is an equal or greater difficulty in maintaining that we perceive primary qualities directly but not secondary qualities, especially as we never perceive or even imagine one class of qualities without the other. In general, it seems very

[1] I.e. apart from any special physiological or psychological circumstances which neutralise the operation of these laws.
[2] It may be noted that in determining the shape of physical objects we generally prefer visual data (including those obtained by means of a microscope) to data of touch.

difficult to split up our perceptions in such a drastic way as any of these mixed theories do ; it seems arbitrary and unjustified to say that some are direct if most are shown by the fact of illusion to be representative, or to say that some are representative if on general grounds we have established a direct theory. But these views at any rate all agree in admitting both physical objects and sensa, and in admitting that with regard to a great many perceptions the non-direct theory is true.

To turn to other solutions, various, as I think unsuccessful, attempts have been made to reconcile direct perception with illusion. It must in any case be admitted that judgment can be erroneous, and it may be held that we ought frankly to admit the same in the case of perception and conclude that we may perceive an object directly and yet perceive it wrongly. This is the solution adopted by Professor Laird in *A Study in Realism*.[1]

'There is a risk of error', he says, 'in every species of apprehending, and not merely in judgment. That which confronts the mind may or may not be as it seems. An illusory percept, to be sure, claims to be as it seems, and it is verily a determinate appearance ; but that is not to the point since precisely the same thing occurs in a false judgment. Anyone who judges that Caesar died in his bed has a thinkable complex before his mind which is something, appears to be true and is false in fact.'

Now here is, I think, another case where failure to distinguish the different problems involved in the apparently simple question of direct awareness leads to confusion. For the issue is really quite different in perception and in judgment, although at first sight it seems the same. To make this clear let us call the object as it appears to us or is judged by us A x and the object as it really is A y. Now in the case of perception it is a fact that A x exists. It is a fact that converging lines are really there before us when we look at the avenue ; we have as good evidence for that as for almost any empirical judgment. What the direct theory of *perception* says is that A x (the avenue as perceived, that is, the converging avenue) is identical with A y (the real physical avenue) or at least a part of A y, and this is clearly false unless the same physical object can have different shapes at the same time. But no theory of cognition held by anyone asserts that A x (Caesar dying in bed, to take Professor Laird's instance) ever could be identical with or a part of A y (the real state of Caesar), unless

[1] Pp. 41–2.

it were the case that Caesar really had died in his bed. In the case of true judgments there is no difficulty about the identity between A x and A y; in the case of erroneous judgments there are two alternative views held, but neither view implies the identity of A x and A y. Some philosophers hold that, if I judge Caesar to have died in bed, my erroneous belief or judgment indeed exists as a psychological fact, as a state of my mind, but the fictitious object—Caesar dying in bed—has and had no kind of existence or being. But in this case, since it did not exist at all, it could not be identical with the real state of Caesar. Other philosophers, e.g. Meinong, hold that even objects of error have some kind of being, though a different kind from that possessed by ordinary existent objects; but even such a theory would never imply identity between what is asserted in an erroneous judgment and the real state of the object of which the assertion is made. It would maintain that both A x and A y have some kind of being, but not that A x is identical with A y. In the case of perception we have to start by admitting the existence of a certain object, namely, that which we immediately perceive and which we know by the evidence of experience to be two rows converging, and are then asked to say that this object is numerically identical with something, namely a physical avenue, which according to Professor Laird does not converge in this way. In judgment we have a state of mind, certain auxiliary images, that which is judged, and the real fact with which the judgment accords or conflicts; and he would not, I think, imagine that the real fact, the murder of Caesar, could be identical with any of the other three elements in the situation, either with our state of mind in judging, or with the images (probably words) which accompanied the judgment, or with what is judged, namely, that Caesar died in his bed. The position in other kinds of cognition and in perception is quite different. The difficulty in the case of perception is not the mere fact of error, but the demand that we should hold both that what we immediately perceive is numerically identical with a physical object or part of such an object and yet that it is quite different. This difficulty could not be removed unless it were held that we did not really see, e.g. the avenue as converging, and to maintain this would be to contradict the plainest evidence of our immediate experience. If we merely judge that two lines of trees converge they may quite well really not do so; but if what we immediately perceive is two converging lines, what we immediately perceive cannot be identical with the physical lines of trees unless these converge also.

The conclusion seems to be that there is no way out of the dilemma before us. Either everything we perceive is independently real just as we perceive it, or the direct theory is not true in all cases and perception is, at least sometimes, indirect or representative in character. Professor Laird himself, however, seems to give his own case away when he says in the next paragraph [1] : ' It might be otherwise if judgments based on perception referred to the percepts on which they are based, but that is certainly not the case ', a statement which suggests that it is only the inferences which we are tempted to draw from perceptions that are erroneous, not the perceptions themselves. He explains that the judgment based on perception may refer to the object as a whole, not to the ' sign-fact ' qualifying the object, which ' sign-fact ' alone constitutes our percept,[2] provided our percept is thought to ' *mean* ' the object, meaning being on his view an objective relation not necessarily implying a mind or mental in character. But this still leaves him in a dilemma (or trilemma). If he is going to hold that we always perceive the sign-fact correctly and to ascribe all illusion to its not meaning what it seems to mean, he will have to admit that the coloured shapes [3] the drunkard or fever-patient describes as snakes or rats, the bent shape we all see when we look at a straight stick in water, and the duplications we see when our eyeballs are pressed all exist in the external physical world ; if he does not hold this he will have to maintain either that our percept is not always numerically identical with anything physical, or that we do not e.g. perceive anything bent at all when we look at a stick in water but only think we do. The two first alternatives constitute the two horns of the dilemma I have already put forward ; the third, since it has seemed at different times to various thinkers to constitute a possible way out of the dilemma, will now be discussed further.

It has been suggested [4] that what we perceive immediately is

---

[1] P. 42.   [2] I.e. *perceptum*.

[3] ' Shape ' is here used for brevity's sake as equivalent to ' shaped object of immediate perception.'

[4] E.g. by Professor Moore, *Philosophical Studies*, pp. 243–7 ; Professor Prichard, *Kant's Theory of Knowledge*, ch. 4. (In the passage cited, however, Professor Moore is far from committing himself decisively to it, and he has now abandoned the theory, as has also Professor Prichard, I think.)

IDEALISM AND THEORY OF PERCEPTION

not that the immediate object of sense has a certain quality but only that it seems or appears to have such a quality. On that view, when we look at a straight stick immersed in water, what we perceive directly is not really bent but only looks or seems bent. This would no doubt be the best solution if it could be reconciled with our immediate experience, but can it? Clearly what we think we are immediately aware of is not merely something that looks bent but something that is bent; the physical object itself may be straight, but surely, whatever it is that we directly perceive in that case, one fact about it at least is clear from immediate experience, namely, that it is something bent. Therefore to say that there is nothing really bent but that it only looks or appears bent is not merely to deny that we perceive physical objects as they are but to take the much more serious step of asserting that our immediate experience is itself illusory, that we have been quite wrong in the majority of the judgments which we have made as to the data immediately given us, for we have held that they were coloured or shaped in a certain way when they were not coloured or shaped in that way but in another way quite different. Further, this error is not due to bad inference which we had confused with immediate experience, bad inference is certainly not the cause of sensory illusions; it is not due to an over-hasty and superficial analysis of our experience, for however carefully and long we look at the stick we see something that is bent; it is not an extraordinary and occasional illusion but an illusion present in some form in, at any rate, most of our experiences. Most philosophers would hold that we can never be mistaken as to the qualities of what we immediately experience any more than as to the *cogito, ergo sum*, and although I am not myself sure whether this is always the case and there is no possibility of mistake at all, still we surely cannot admit such widespread illusion and error in our immediate experience as is implied by this theory without plunging ourselves into the abyss of an almost total scepticism. If we doubt the verdict of experience here, are we not equally bound to doubt it everywhere?

Two more objections to the theory may be mentioned. In the first place, if it were true, we should in all cases of illusion have a particular instance of a quality which qualified nothing. It is admitted universally that when I look at the stick I at least perceive the quality bentness, and on most other views this bentness qualifies at least a sensum if not a physical object, but on the view we are considering there is nothing really bent for it to qualify. Now I perhaps may be able to apprehend a universal quality which qualifies nothing, but here it is not the universal bentness that we are apprehending but a particular instance of bentness.[1] But can there be a particular instance of a quality without the quality qualifying anything?[2] That seems to contradict the very notion of quality. The theory is still more difficult if secondary qualities are denied physical reality, for in that case there is nothing coloured in existence at all.

Secondly, the theory seems to break down in the cases of double vision and of hallucinatory sense-data. For in these cases it is not only that an object appears different from what it is but that there is no object to appear at all, unless we either postulate a sense-datum distinct from any physical thing, thus giving us a non-direct theory of perception, at least in some cases, or locate the hallucination, etc., in the physical world. The only reply to this would seem to be to say that what we perceive in these cases is space (or space-time) as a substantival entity appearing to have certain qualities, which is a very difficult view to maintain.[3]

But let us now turn to the main argument for the direct theory of perception. It seems to be that, if the direct theory were not true, we should be 'shut up in our own ideas' and could have no justification for our belief in the physical world.[4] Now it is possible that the direct theory of perception may be true, but it is quite impossible that this argument could prove it. For either propositions asserting the existence of physical objects can be rightly inferred or seen to be self-evident without assuming that we perceive some physical objects directly, or

[1] I can only say that this seems to me to be obvious from immediate inspection, though it would apparently be denied by the 'critical realists'.

[2] (3rd ed.) An advocate of the theory criticised may reply that we do not perceive bentness but only something as appearing bent, but I should have thought I could not perceive something as even appearing bent without being conscious of bentness. From the point of view of immediate experience, apart from inference, real and apparent bentness are surely the same thing.

[3] For a criticism of the theory of perception just discussed v. Price, *Perception*, pp. 62–5. (3rd ed.) I suppose, however, that this difficulty might be met, if not very plausibly, by saying that what we perceive as appearing to have these qualities is the atmosphere.

[4] V. e.g. Alexander, *Space, Time and Deity*, vol. II, pp. 199–200.

they cannot. If they can, the argument that we could not attain knowledge of physical objects unless direct perception be a fact falls to the ground. If, however, they cannot—if, as the thinkers in question hold, knowledge of physical objects could not be reached or the belief in their existence justified unless we supposed that we directly perceive some such objects, then we cannot justifiably assert their existence unless we have first judged that direct perception is a fact, and cannot therefore afterwards go on to argue that because we know or rightly believe them to exist the direct theory must be true. Either the belief in physical objects can be justified without first establishing the fact of direct perception, in which case the premiss of the argument disappears; or it cannot, in which case we are trying to prove direct perception from the existence of physical objects and the existence of physical objects from direct perception without having shown that either is a fact. Realists often charge idealists, rightly or wrongly, with having based their conclusions on the fallacious argument:

I want to believe in God.
I cannot justify the belief in God unless idealism is true.
Therefore idealism is true.

I certainly do not admire the logic of this argument, if it is indeed used by any idealists, but it is no worse than the argument:

I want to believe in physical objects.
I cannot justify the belief in physical objects unless the direct theory of perception is true.
Therefore the direct theory of perception is true.[1]

This seems to me the straightforward interpretation of the argument in question, but I will be charitable and take two other possible ways in which it may be interpreted. It may be meant that we in fact know the existence of some physical objects directly from the beginning and could never reach conclusions as to physical objects by inference if we did not. The direct theory of perception would then be just a reflective

[1] The objection here is not to the appeal to intuitive knowledge, which seems a necessary though concealed part of the theory, but to the daring assertion that a theory must be true because a certain conclusion can only be established if it is true. If the conclusion is not self-evident, it cannot be established by means of premisses the truth of which has not itself been independently established; if the conclusion is self-evident, we need no premisses from which to prove it.

statement of the fact that we have this knowledge. In that case the argument would escape being a vicious circle because it would be merely an analysis disclosing a knowledge we already possessed, merely a statement of the fact that we have direct knowledge of physical objects. But after the distinctions made earlier it is now apparent that this involves a confusion between perception and cognition. To say that we have direct knowledge of anything is not to say that we perceive it directly or *vice versa*. We might have non-inferential knowledge of physical objects without perceiving them directly, and we might perceive them directly without knowing that we were perceiving physical objects. Hence anyone who took this line of defence would have to maintain that we knew intuitively (or had an intuitive conviction sufficient to justify belief) not only that some physical objects existed but that a direct theory of perception was true. But it has now ceased to be an argument and become an appeal to an unproved intuition which opponents of the theory reject as a mere prejudice.

To pass to another interpretation of the argument, it is possible that what it means in the hands of some who employ it is simply that the belief in physical objects cannot be psychologically explained unless we perceive physical objects directly. But, even granting that we cannot account for the belief in question by other psychological causes, which may be disputed, the mere fact, if it be a fact, that what we see is sometimes a physical object or part of one could not possibly help to explain the belief psychologically unless in addition to this fact we supposed an intuitive conviction that it is a fact or at least that some physical objects exist. After the exposure of the prevalent confusion between direct cognition and direct perception this ought to be clear. But in that case whether the intuitive conviction was true or false would be quite irrelevant to the psychological explanation of our belief. The belief would be explained just as well if we supposed this conviction to be a mere prejudice due to our innate constitution or to the influence on the evolutionary process of practical needs as if we supposed it to be a genuine veridical intuition. It is a problem in psychology which we are now discussing, and therefore the truth or falsehood of our conviction is irrelevant provided the psychological state is the same.

So I see no good reason for accepting the direct theory

of perception.[1] Further, the adoption of such a view would admittedly involve us in very great difficulties. We have either to locate all our percepts in the external physical world just as we perceive them, or to differentiate and adopt the representative theory for all except a few favoured ones.[2] The former alternative is one that cannot, I think, be conclusively refuted, but the difficulties involved in it are so great that admittedly nobody would accept it unless he thought that there were very strong reasons against any other view, and the reasons that have been given against the representative view seem the reverse of strong. A mixed view, on the other hand, admits the representative theory for most cases of perception, and is also intrinsically very unlikely. For, to quote Professor Broad,

' (i) We are asked to believe that in one special position the physical, physiological, and psychical mechanism produces an utterly different result from that which it produces in all other positions, no matter how close to this specially favoured one. (ii) There is nothing in the nature of any perceptual situation, taken by itself, to reveal to us that it differs in this remarkable way from all the rest. It would have to be discovered to have this property by comparing it and its objective constituent with other perceptual situations and theirs.'[3]

Cases of double vision present a special difficulty, for it is very unplausible to hold that of the two objects seen one is a physical thing and the other a mere sensum, though the way in which either eye is affected is precisely the same and would in either case lead to an equally direct perception of the physical object if only that one eye were concerned. How could it be the case that, when I see a physical thing with my left eye only, I perceive it directly but that this direct perception is prevented and replaced by representative perception just because I see the object also with the margin of my right eye? (Or would the advocate of such a mixed view meet the difficulty by maintaining that we may perceive a physical thing directly if we use the middle of either retina, but that we never perceive more than a representa-

[1] Another set of objections to the representative view is discussed on p. 287 ff.
[2] Or to adopt some compromise which, even if in some respects an improvement, will share in the disadvantages of both alternatives.
[3] *The Mind and Its Place in Nature*, pp. 192–3.

tion of it if we use the margin? This would perhaps be the least difficult way of escape.)

Another serious objection against both the wholly direct theory and any mixed, partly direct theory is constituted by the fact that light has a finite velocity so that, if we perceive physical objects directly, we perceive a past state, which is no longer there, and not a present. The circumstance that in most cases the lapse of time is only infinitesimal cannot remove such a difficulty of principle. However recent, what is seen is still past and therefore not present.[1] It seems to me therefore more consistent and reasonable to adopt a full-fledged representative theory.

But, on the other hand, it is very important to admit readily that the advocates of the representative view have in the past commonly committed a very serious error which made the idealist argument much more plausible than would otherwise have been the case. They have often assumed without any proof that because the immediate objects of perception were not physical objects common to all observers they must therefore be 'mental'. Now if by 'mental' is meant that they are qualities of the mind, this statement is clearly false unless we are prepared to maintain that our mind is blue when we look at the sky and round (or elliptical) when we look at a penny. The immediate objects of sense-perception are far from being mental in the sense in which an act of thought or will is so. They have at any rate far more in common with the physical as usually conceived by us than they have with the mental, at least apart from their causal properties. They may be causally dependent on us, and they may fail to produce the effects that similar physical objects would, but in themselves they seem rather to fall on the physical side of the dividing-line, as is proved by the fact that any idea which we can form of the concrete qualities of matter must be entirely derived from them. But it would be best provisionally to class them as neither physical nor mental, giving them an intermediate position between these two kinds of being. We have no right to assume as a necessary *a priori* truth that everything must fall into one of two classes, the physical and the mental. On the other

---

[1] Similar difficulties could be found in the case of a theory which confined direct perception to perception by touch and did not claim to apply to vision, for the physical process of affecting the sense-organs and brain must take some time, whatever the sense involved.

hand, I should agree that it is reasonable to hold our sensa to be causally dependent on our mind. It is often said that they can only be shown to be causally dependent on the body, but it seems to me clear, as it did to Kant, that they are subject to 'synthesis' by the mind, that they cannot be causally explained without admitting the influence of psychological causes, and that, as they occur when perceived by us, they cannot be altogether separated from 'thought', though I should not hold that it is logically impossible for them to exist unthought or unperceived.

It is objected that the admission of sensa involves the introduction of a new class of entities of a highly peculiar kind whose relations to physical objects are very difficult to understand, and that the production of sensa by the mind or body or both together is 'a very odd kind of causation which is almost creation out of nothing'.[1] I agree with Professor Broad that the alternative views are in various ways in as difficult a position themselves, which cuts away the root of the objection; but there is a further point which is often ignored but seems to me greatly to strengthen the representative theory. It is this: even if we could deny sensa as distinct from external physical entities, it is impossible to deny images, and therefore in any case we shall have to admit a peculiar class of entities which are neither properly physical nor properly mental. Images resemble sensa and physical objects in being extended, they cannot be regarded as qualities or states of the mind, yet they are not external physical things any more than sensa. Images and sensa, if sensa are admitted at all, clearly belong to the same class of being, they only differ in that the latter stand in a peculiar relation to physical objects. Images are usually fainter than sensa, but it is impossible to make of this a difference in kind, and a really vivid image is as clear as many or perhaps even most sensa. True, we can almost always distinguish images from sensa, but, however this distinction is effected, we cannot point to any difference in qualities between the images and sensa themselves to which it is due. Any perceptible quality in sensa [2] may be repeated in images. I know that some realists [3] maintain that, when

[1] Broad, *The Mind and Its Place in Nature*, p. 189.
[2] With the possible exception of pain and pleasure, but obviously the distinction cannot be based simply on these.
[3] E.g. Professors Laird and Alexander.

we do what is usually described as forming an image, we are really apprehending directly [1] the physical thing or past event of which it is an image, but this seems incredible to me, and still less can I accept the analogous explanation they give of images that do not claim to represent anything in the physical world but seem to be mere imaginations. Further, images at any rate, if not sensa, are produced by the mind (or 'mind-body'), and therefore even if we had adopted the direct theory of perception we should still have had to admit in the case of images this peculiar kind of causation resembling creation out of nothing. Hence we cannot gain anything in these respects by denying sensa unless we are prepared also to deny images. The representative theory does not introduce a new class of entity totally different from any other or a new kind of causation, for this has already been admitted by anyone who admits images.

'Occam's razor' is a valuable instrument, but it can only be rightly used to remove entities for the assumption of which there is no good reason; and, while the representative theory accepts a great multiplicity of entities, a purely direct theory such as that of the neo-realists has to accept a great many more. After all it is a commonplace that the world does contain an incredibly great variety of things. The physiological apparatus necessary for perception is by general admission extraordinarily complicated, so we need not be surprised if perception on the non-physiological side also involves much complication.

Advocates of the representative theory have also commonly made the mistake of confusing direct perception with direct cognition and supposing that, because we cannot perceive objects directly, it necessarily follows that we can have no non-inferential cognition of them capable of yielding truth. But more of this later.[2] Here I shall just say that the representative theory would be more correctly expressed as being the view not that we do not perceive physical objects directly, but that we do not perceive them directly *in the same sense* as we perceive directly the sensory data (sensa) which we use in the perception of physical objects [3]; and, further, that

[1] Apparently in the fourth sense of direct awareness (p. 268 ff.), since the 'image' which we immediately perceive is expressly identified with that event or object (or a part of the same).
[2] V. below, p. 317 ff.
[3] I should regard it as correct to say that according to the representative view physical objects or parts of them are not immediately *sensed*.

IDEALISM AND THEORY OF PERCEPTION 289

it *may* still be true that we can in a very important sense cognise them directly in and by means of sense-perception.

One difficult question that arises is whether our immediately perceived sensa and images are or are not situated in a unitary physical space. Here neither alternative is free from grave objections. If they are not in physical space, then it seems that we each have a private space of our own in which our sensa are, or rather a number of different private spaces, one for each sense which gives extended sensa; if they are in physical space there must, it would seem, be a direct spatial relation between, e.g., A's image of Kant and B's auditory sensa or images of words just heard in Cambridge such that one could be, say, 16·364598 inches from the other, which is also hard to believe. But this can be no objection to the representative theory. For on a partly direct view there will still be some extended sensa[1]; and to adopt a completely direct view is not to escape the dilemma but to embrace its second horn. Indeed, the direct theory is in a worse position than the representative theory, for, while the latter can adopt whichever alternative seems better, the former is restricted to one, the second. Further, we should still in any case have to face the same difficulty with images of objects not sensibly perceived at the time or purely fictitious images.

[1] It seems to me inconceivable that sensa could be coloured without being extended, though I must admit that such a distinguished philosopher as Professor Kemp Smith maintains the opposite view.

CHAPTER VII

PHYSICAL OBJECTS

§ I. The Argument from Common-Sense and the Analysis of Propositions about Physical Objects

IN the last chapter I have been speaking as though the belief in the existence of independent physical objects in a realist sense were true. My purpose in this was to see whether the representative theory, which had such a large share in the development of idealism, is defensible or not, and whether the realist could meet the idealist satisfactorily by merely maintaining a theory of direct perception instead. But it remains for us to try to defend the view (*a*) that our ordinary statements about physical objects mean what the realist thinks they mean, (*b*) that some of them are true. Against this many thinkers have maintained that what we call physical objects have no existence apart from human (and animal) experience, or that, while there are things external to us, we cannot be justified in saying anything about them except that they produce such-and-such experiences, or, better, sensa, when we observe them.[1] The name phenomenalism [2] is commonly given to these types of view, and I shall adopt this terminology. According to phenomenalism any statements purporting to be about physical objects can be true or defensible only if they are translated into statements about human experience.

We shall now turn to the argument which, if not *de jure*, is at any rate *de facto* by far the strongest obstacle to the acceptance of phenomenalism, namely, what is usually called

---

[1] Perhaps also that they possess certain formal logical characteristics. It is hardly possible to avoid this admission, as Kant found with his things-in-themselves.

[2] This sense of 'phenomenalism' must be carefully distinguished from the sense in which the word is used by Professor Kemp Smith in his commentary on Kant.

the argument from 'common-sense'. It is not, however, very clear what is meant by the assertion that a particular philosophical view is inconsistent with common-sense. It might mean that all or most people prior to studying philosophy believe that it is false. But it is impossible for anybody to believe that the view, e.g., that there are no physical objects independent of us etc., is false unless the view has occurred to him and been rejected, and the views in question have not occurred to the non-philosopher. He cannot believe them to be false because he has never thought of them. This difficulty might be met by amending our analysis of the assertion in one of two ways. We might say that the statement that a philosophical view is inconsistent with common-sense meant that, though most people prior to philosophical study may not have heard of the view in question and therefore cannot believe it to be false, they hold certain positive beliefs [1] which are in fact logically incompatible with the view. Or we might say that it meant that they would reject the view if it were explained to them in a way which they could understand. I think the statement might stand for either or both of these propositions, and I think that, in the case of the view under discussion, both propositions are in fact true; but it is not so clear why the philosopher should be expected to attach much weight in philosophical questions to the opinion of those who have never studied his subject. If those who have studied philosophy see reason to accept a given view, why should they reject it just because those who have not studied the subject think it wrong? This would only be a reasonable course if the study of philosophy instead of improving impaired one's capacity for making right philosophical judgments, and if so why study it since we could be better philosophers without doing so? But this certainly is not a fair account of 'the argument from common-sense': there is more in it than that.

For, in the first place, it is not the case that views such as phenomenalism seem absurd only to the man who has not studied philosophy. On the contrary, in many cases at least, the appearance of absurdity is not in the least dispelled by study and familiarity. They still seem indeed difficult

---

[1] It is clearly possible in a very important sense, though one extremely hard to analyse, to hold a belief without being able explicitly to formulate it, and it is in this wider sense that I speak of a belief as held by common-sense.

or impossible to refute but also impossible to believe.[1] And, even if we can persuade ourselves that we believe them in the study, we are quite unable to do so in our actual perceptual experience. I cannot speak for all philosophers; but surely it is a very common case, and anyone who feels thus may well be justified in holding that this counts for him as a strong argument against the view in question. He is now appealing not to philosophical beliefs of people who know next to nothing of philosophy, but to a non-inferential but not therefore necessarily irrational conviction which survives the acid test of philosophical study and criticism.

Such a conviction is in the analogous case of solipsism usually sufficient to prevent any serious doubt as to the existence of human beings other than oneself,[2] even though many philosophers have actually admitted, or held views obviously implying that there are no cogent arguments for the belief. This is to the point here, for any philosopher who would not be prepared to discard the belief that other human beings existed even if he found that he could not justify it philosophically ought to ask himself whether he has not the same irresistible conviction (though perhaps somewhat less in degree) in the independent existence of physical objects, when he considers particular propositions about them and does not merely speculate in the abstract, and whether if he is consistent he ought not to accept this here as well as in the case of other minds as a ground for holding the belief or else accept it in neither and become a solipsist.[3]

---

[1] This is the case even with Hume. 'The sceptic must assent to the principle concerning the existence of body, though he cannot pretend, by any arguments of philosophy, to maintain its veracity. Nature has not left this to his choice, and has doubtless esteemed it an affair of too great importance to be trusted to our uncertain reasonings and speculations. We may well ask, *What causes induce us to believe in the existence of body*? but it is in vain to ask, *Whether there be body or not*? That is a point which we must take for granted in all our reasonings' (*Treatise of Human Nature*, bk. I, pt. IV, sect. 2 beginning).

[2] Some philosophers at Cambridge call themselves solipsists, but I cannot believe that they really mean what they seem to me to say (no doubt partly owing to my failure to understand them).

[3] This last argument assumes the falsity of solipsism, but that does not impair its validity as against any philosopher who is not a solipsist. A solipsist (i.e. a philosopher who believed in solipsism) would no doubt be untouched by it, but then if solipsism is true there are no solipsists, since I am not one.

The situation would be different if the existence of independent physical objects could be shown to be logically impossible, but this cannot be done. At the worst all that could be urged is not that the belief in them is untenable but that there are no arguments adequate to establish its truth; but for many philosophers their inability to rid themselves of this conviction may be itself an argument, though not, I admit, a conclusive argument, in favour of its substantial truth.

It is often thought that, while the view that physical objects independent of us do not exist is repugnant to commonsense, the view that, while they exist, we can know nothing about their nature is not nearly so repugnant; but I think that this is only because the latter view is not taken seriously enough. We are ready to acquiesce in the view that we cannot say what matter is in itself but only what it is in its external relations (this has indeed for some time been the orthodox view of science); but, if phenomenalism is to be taken seriously, we shall have to maintain not only that we cannot determine the 'ultimate nature' of matter but that we cannot tell what any of its qualities or relations are at all, except the characteristic of causing certain experiences in us.[1] If the view is to be carried out logically we must deny not only that we *know* the shape and size but that we have the slightest justification for making any statement about the probable shape or size of any independent external objects whatever. We must even deny that we have any reason for supposing them to be in space or time at all. Anybody who holds such a view cannot indeed legitimately be said to believe in the existence of physical objects, for nobody ordinarily means by physical objects totally unknown causes of our experience (these, since we *ex hypothesi* know nothing about them, might equally well be minds), but things with at least a shape and (relatively to other physical objects) a size that can often be specified by us. If indeed the phenomenalist holds merely that we cannot have knowledge in the strict sense of such objects I should agree with him, but when he maintains that we have no right to assert anything about them as even probably true it becomes extremely difficult to reconcile myself to his view.

But, secondly, I should contend, it is not or not only that

[1] And perhaps certain formal characteristics such as conformity to the laws of logic.

phenomenalism contradicts the philosophical beliefs of 'common-sense', but that it contradicts common-sense beliefs on non-philosophical subjects where the philosopher is no more qualified to speak than the plain man. The plain man asserts that the table in his dining-room is square, that Cambridge is just over 50 miles from London, that his fire has burnt out since last he looked at it, etc. Now, except on a certain interpretation of these statements which seems to me quite untenable, they are all flatly contradicted by any view such as phenomenalism; and if we accept phenomenalism we shall have to say that these statements about physical objects are all partially false, and not false in a slight matter of detail but very fundamentally. For they all apply properties such as shape or size to physical objects in a sense which cannot in my opinion be analysed phenomenalistically. And similar propositions are asserted in all the sciences, where the philosopher certainly does not claim to be a better judge than the scientist. If a given philosophical theory does really imply that all these assertions are fundamentally mistaken, it does seem to be a serious objection against the theory in question. And this objection I should bring against all phenomenalists.

The only reply possible for them is to maintain not merely that the only part of any proposition [1] about physical objects which we are justified in asserting as true is a proposition about our sensa,[2] actual and possible, but that such a proposition is all that we *mean* when we make a statement about physical objects, that when we speak of a penny as round we only mean that it appears round under normal conditions, or something of that kind. (A detailed formulation of this interpretation might be difficult and would no doubt not be a matter of universal agreement.) Phenomenalists have in fact rarely made it clear whether they were maintaining that all statements ascribing specific qualities to physical objects

---

[1] Excepting 'formally certified' hypothetical propositions such as '*if* there are physical objects (in a realist sense), any two of them added to any other two will make four'.

[2] Phenomenalists have often said 'experience', but this involves a confusion between 'experiencing' and 'what is experienced'. Kant's 'objects of experience' is better but is open to the objection that, if realism be true, independent physical objects may undoubtedly be said in an important and usual sense to be objects of experience, so that his phrase is verbally compatible with what I have called realism while intended by him to be incompatible with it.

were partially false or that they were true but only *meant* propositions about our sensa or our experience, and in regard to the great majority of those with whose work I am acquainted I am quite unable to say which of the two alternatives they intended to adopt. But the latter is certainly maintained by some. It is held that assertions about physical objects are simply assertions about the way in which they *appear* to human percipients under normal conditions, or about the sensa, actually experienced or possible, of human percipients, i.e. it is held that this is all we *mean* when we make them. This kind of view is now predominant among the so-called Cambridge school of philosophers, though it has not yet been expressed fully in published works by them.

Now the question whether this is so is one as to the usage of words. Such a question might perhaps be settled by argument if it could be shown that the denotation of a given definition did not coincide with the denotation of the term which it claimed to define,[1] though even then the person who maintained the definition might be able to escape refutation by maintaining that in the cases where the two denotations failed to coincide the expression was being used in different senses, i.e. with different connotations, and that his definition only gave the meaning of the expression in one of its senses, not in the other. But, while the denotation cannot be different if the connotation is the same, it may easily be the same though the connotation is different. Wherever two properties of any kind invariably go together, an expression defined in terms of the one will coincide in denotation with an expression defined in terms of the other but not in connotation. Consequently we cannot settle all questions about the meaning of terms by this method, and in the last resort there can be no way of testing the correctness of an analysis of the meaning of a given expression except by observing whether the analysis is of such a character that when we really understand it we can say—' Oh! that is what I really

---

[1] I.e. if it were not the case that the substitution of the *definiens* for the *definiendum* in all true propositions where the latter occurred yielded a true proposition and *vice versa*. For instance, it would be a valid argument against the definition of justice as equal treatment for all that we should not call it just, e.g., to give first-class honours to all the candidates in an examination irrespective of their differing calibre.

meant [1] all the time, though I was not clear about it' or 'though I could not put it so well'.[2] If, when we have come to understand a given analysis, we cannot say this but are convinced that we meant something quite different, even if we are not sure of the correct analysis of what we did mean, we must reject the analysis given. After all the person who really decides what a statement means is the person who makes it. Philosophical capacity is required in order fully to understand a given analysis of the meaning of a statement; but to decide whether it is a correct analysis or not is to decide whether it is identical with what is really meant by the plain man, and the philosopher can only do this because he is also a 'plain man' besides being a philosopher.

It is therefore for each reader to ask himself whether he does mean by an assertion such as 'the table in my dining-room is round [3]' merely that it appears round under normal conditions, or anything of that kind. The only way of deciding is to ask ourselves whether on considering such an analysis we see that this is 'what we meant all along'; and it seems quite clear to me that I do not see any such thing, but am convinced on the contrary that this is not what I meant or at any rate not all that I meant. I must therefore reject the interpretation in question in accordance with the only test available. But I do not see how it can be conclusively proved by argument either that we do or that we do not mean this. All I can do is to state in what respects I think our ordinary assertions about physical objects seem to me incompatible with such an interpretation of their meaning. What I am going to say will seem to many too obvious to be worth mentioning, and I should have thought it was so myself if I had not discovered that some of the ablest philosophers of the present time hold quite different views.

(a) It seems clear to me that, when we ascribe shape or position [4] to a physical object as existing unperceived, when

[1] In that sense of 'meaning', hard to define, in which I can be said in making a non-philosophical statement to be 'meaning' the philosophical analysis of the proposition asserted.

[2] I do not mean to deny that *arguments* may help to put us in a position in which we can see whether this is so and can serve to clear up confusions, etc.

[3] I.e. approximately, not geometrically.

[4] This, I think, is also the case with colour, but I have chosen primary qualities in my examples because there may be some doubt in the case of the former which does not, I believe, arise with the latter.

e.g. we say that a table in a given room where no one is at the time is square, we are asserting a categorical proposition, but according to the phenomenalist interpretation such a proposition must be merely hypothetical, i.e. to the effect that if we touched it, etc., it would appear square. (*b*) Unperceived physical objects, being merely hypothetical entities, could in that case never be correctly said to act as causes except on the regularity view of causation, which I have already rejected, or some very similar view which would be liable to similar objections. It seems to me obvious that by a cause [1] we mean something actual. (*c*) Even in the case of assertions about physical objects perceived at the time, it seems clear that, when we say that they have a given shape, we are ascribing a spatial characteristic [2] to something regarded as existing independently of our experience of it, and that this unformulated belief in independence is a common or even essential part of the normal perceptual experience.[3]

(*d*) On the view to which I am objecting, the statement (i) that ' a physical object perceived by me does not merely *look* e.g. elliptical [4] but *is* elliptical ' only differs from the statement (ii) that ' it looks or appears elliptical ' in that it does not merely refer to my present experience but forecasts the future and implies the past occurrence under given conditions of other experiences (and sensa), and this seems to me clearly not the only point of difference. It seems to me that the assertion that ' A looks elliptical but is not really elliptical ' and the assertion that ' A is elliptical ' differ in that these statements are usually meant respectively to deny and assert the presence of a specific quality of ellipticalness [5]

---

[1] In the sense of the term in which we speak of physical causes, not in the different sense in which we speak of a law of nature as cause.

[2] In a sense in which this cannot be reduced to its effects on human sensa or analysed in terms of actual and possible human sensa.

[3] I do not mean that it is something which can be given by sense-perception as such (v. above, p. 270).

[4] As Professor Moore has pointed out, ' look elliptical ' is ambiguous. It may mean either (*a*) ' look elliptical ' in the sense that its actual sensory appearance is elliptical, or (*b*) ' look as if it were elliptical '. An object which looks elliptical in the first sense often looks round in the second. Obviously ' is elliptical ' is distinct from ' looks elliptical ' in either sense. But I am using the phrase ' looks or appears elliptical ' in the first of the two senses.

[5] Other than the property of causing certain sensa under given conditions or of justifying the inference to certain sensa according to the laws of induction or any relational property of that kind.

in something actually existent at the time, and do not merely differ in what they assert about something that would exist under given conditions but is not actually existing now or about the connection between that and what is actually existing now.

We cannot indeed conclude that, because a sentence is constructed verbally as if it were meant to refer to a present actual existent in the primary literal sense of the word, therefore it is really meant to do so. If a man says 'there is a depression to the south of Iceland' or 'there is a threatened banking crisis', it would be wrong to conclude from the form of his statement that he means that there is one particular thing called a depression in the one case and a banking crisis in the other, which could conceivably be pointed out, that exists as you or I do. In fact 'exists' (or the existential 'is') has more than one meaning, and it is urged by phenomenalists that physical objects only exist in some sense other than a literal one.[1] To this I should reply that the main evidence for the view that 'exist' is used in a sense other than the literal one when we say e.g. a banking crisis exists is our immediate awareness that we are not using it in a literal sense, and the same source of evidence tells us that we are using it in a literal sense when we speak of ordinary physical objects existing. If anyone says that this is no evidence in the second case, it is also no evidence in the first.

(e) It seems to me that terms such as this table, a stone, his hand, etc., as usually employed each stand for a particular continuant, which cannot be the case according to the view under consideration. (f) Propositions about physical things clearly seem to me not to be propositions merely about human experiences and fleeting mental images (our sensa are only mental images which can be correlated in a certain way according to laws of sequence, at least on the view I am discussing). (g) It seems clear to me that we mean to assert in given cases that different people see or otherwise perceive the same thing [2] in a sense quite incom-

[1] Though they are analysable in terms of entities like sensa which literally exist.

[2] This is quite compatible with my own theory of perception, although the latter is representative. For I do not assert that two people cannot perceive the same physical object, but only that they cannot perceive it directly in *the same* sense as that in which they perceive sensa directly. They cannot both sense it, but both can (a) have 'sensa' of it, (b) perhaps have a non-inferential cognition of it (v.

patible with the theory under discussion. (*h*) It is obvious that any proposition I assert about a particular human being implies his independence of any other observers and is not merely a proposition about the sensa of these. But if so it is difficult to avoid holding that this is the case with propositions about his body, since, when I say e.g. that he is in the room or is in good health, I am certainly not usually speaking only of his mind, and in that case it would be senseless to oppose a similar view of propositions about other physical things.

It follows therefore that no analysis of our ordinary assertions about physical objects must be such as to contradict any of the eight conditions just laid down if it is to be equivalent or even similar to the assertion analysed, but a phenomenalist analysis contradicts them all without exception. Finally, I cannot see how the fact that we are so strongly tempted to suppose that we mean something totally different could conceivably be explained if the phenomenalist account of what we mean were correct.

The suggested analysis therefore seems to me not to give an account of what we mean when we make assertions about physical objects. And, since we are only discussing here what we mean, not what is true objectively, this ends the matter for me. Phenomenalists can bring no argument for the acceptance of their analysis except objections to alternative methods of analysis, and these cannot prove that their own method is correct. No one may yet have discovered the correct analysis. This would not be at all surprising, even if there be one, which I doubt,[1] since few philosophers have as yet set themselves deliberately and consciously to the task of analysing what we mean by our statements about physical objects. For the question of the physical world has usually been approached by philosophers from a different angle. But the considerations I have mentioned make it clear enough to my own mind that, whatever the complete account of the matter is, when we assert propositions about physical objects we do mean in some cases to assert at least that they have specific shapes in the sense in which our sensa have them.

below, p. 317 ff.). The position of the theory I am criticising is much weaker, for it leaves no identical particular thing at all of which both you and I can have sensa, while the representative theory does so.

[1] V. below, p. 304.

I think that the chief reason which is liable to lead people to the view that propositions about physical objects are only propositions about our sensa or something of that kind is the belief that, since there is no ground for asserting the existence of physical objects or ascribing e.g. shapes to them in any other sense, if they do not analyse such propositions in this way they will be forced to say that all our ordinary propositions about physical objects are false or at least totally groundless, a conclusion which they naturally and reasonably wish to avoid. But this cannot constitute a legitimate argument in favour of their analysis over against a realist analysis. The premisses are two : (*a*) if a realist analysis of the propositions in question is correct, they will be ungrounded ; (*b*) it is impossible or unreasonable to hold that all the propositions ordinarily asserted by us about physical objects are ungrounded. But if the realist analysis were correct, they would not be ungrounded unless the second premiss is false, for the fact, if it is a fact, that it is unreasonable to hold all the propositions ordinarily asserted by us about physical objects to be ungrounded would itself constitute a ground for them, i.e. (*a*) could not be true if (*b*) is. Hence the two premisses contradict each other, and the argument collapses. This does not prove that a phenomenalist analysis must be wrong, but it removes what has probably been the most strongly felt argument in favour of such an analysis. It would be different if the phenomenalist could show the belief in physical objects in any realist sense to be self-contradictory,[1] but this is not the case. By far the strongest phenomenalist argument against realism is the apparent absence of a legitimate ground for believing it.

But while it seems quite clear to me that a phenomenalist analysis of propositions about physical objects cannot be accepted as giving anything like the meaning our statements bear when asserted in ordinary life, it does not seem to me by any means so clear what the right attitude to the question of their analysis would be. The natural alternative would be to hold that when we say that a physical object is round or red we mean that it is round or red in precisely the same sense as that in which a sensum is round or red; but it seems that the

---

[1] Arguments purporting to show this are discussed elsewhere. But most phenomenalists would no doubt rest their case not on positive arguments to show the falsity of realism but on the alleged circumstance that there is no evidence for it.

question cannot be answered quite so simply and that we could not accept this as it stands without some reservations and qualifications, though not, I think, any of such a character as to be incompatible with the supposition that identically the same determinable [1] qualities as the roundness or redness which qualify them as they appear to us (or qualify their sensa, as a philosopher might put it), also occur in some physical objects independently of being perceived, and that this is often at least part of what is asserted when we assert propositions about physical objects.

The following are examples of the sort of reservations that may still be necessary. In the first place, to say that a sensum is red is to say that the whole of it is red, but when we assert that a physical object is red we do not thereby assert that the whole of it is red but only that its surface is. We are certainly not asserting anything about the colour of its inside or even that its inside has a colour. Secondly, when we assert that a physical object is red we are not implying, I think, that there are no parts of its surface smaller than those visible to the naked eye which are not red. Thirdly, when we ascribe a colour to a physical object at a time when the latter is ' in the dark ', there seems to be some doubt as to whether we mean to say that its surface still has the colour in the sense-given sense [2] even in the dark, and when we ascribe a taste to it and say, e.g., that sugar is sweet we clearly do not mean that it has the taste in the sense-given sense when nobody is tasting it.

Fourthly, it is now widely believed that no physical objects at all possess secondary qualities in the sense-given sense. It is commonly, though quite mistakenly, supposed that this has been proved by physical science. Now a person who, as many people now do, believes that physical objects never have colour in the sense-given sense still speaks of physical things

---

[1] I use the term ' determinable ' here to imply ' not completely determinate '. When we say that a physical object is red we are not specifying what determinate shade of red it has, though, if its surface is red at all in the sense in which sensa are, it no doubt has one or other such determinate shade at any given time, and when we say that it is round we are not usually saying that it is *exactly* circular. (There is admittedly no means of discovering what exact shade of colour any physical object has or whether it is exactly circular.)

[2] The term ' sense-given sense ' is borrowed from Professor Moore. It stands for the sense in which sensa can be said to have the quality (or the sense in which the name for the quality is used with ' appears ').

as red, and so we must suppose that, when he speaks thus, either he has temporarily forgotten the theory that physical objects have no colour, or he does not really believe in the theory but only in his reflective moments thinks that he does so,[1] or he is using e.g. ' red ' as meaning ' appearing red to a normal observer in a normal light ' or some proposition of that phenomenalist type. If the last alternative be accepted, we should have to admit that the meaning of terms like red as applied to physical objects has undergone a change as the result of reflective doubt or disbelief concerning the physical reality of colour in the sense-given sense and that some people use the words with a different meaning from others. This seems strange, but changes of meaning and diversities of meaning between different individuals are very common. In the present case the possibility of it and the fact that it does not interfere with mutual understanding could be rendered comprehensible by two circumstances : (*a*) the denotations of the two meanings approximately coincide though the connotations do not, for, if we believe colour in the sense-given sense to belong to physical objects, we believe that those objects which look e.g. red to a normal eye in a normal light really are red ; (*b*) I think, though I am more doubtful about this, that most of the propositions we assert about physical objects *include*, without being entirely reducible to, propositions as to how an object would look under given conditions, e.g. ' this book is red ' includes, I think, the proposition ' this book would look red under optimal conditions ' besides a proposition ascribing redness to the physical object irrespective of how it looks or would look. If that is so the transition from one meaning to the other is easier to understand, since it consists simply in dropping out part of the meaning which the phrase already had, not in substituting for one meaning another quite different. The fact that in some cases, e.g. at least with taste and perhaps with colour when in the dark, words which often signify certain sensory qualities are used of physical objects without implying that these objects have the sensory qualities in question in a realist sense does, as far as it goes, somewhat support the phenomenalist interpretation of all propositions

---

[1] This is the alternative I should hold to be most likely even in the case of colour. With all due respect to them I should certainly hold it to be true of those who deny primary qualities in the sense-given sense to physical objects. Many of them would no doubt hold the corresponding view about my own position and that of all realists.

about physical objects, because there is a certain antecedent probability that the correct account of all statements applying names of sensory qualities to physical objects will be similar, but this seems to me to have very little weight against the strong positive objections to a phenomenalist account of our meaning in the case of at least some primary qualities.[1]

So it seems to me clearer that people are using terms for shapes in the sense-given sense when they apply them to physical objects than that they are thus using terms for colours, though personally I still think that this is usually at least part of their meaning in the case of colours. But, while I think that when we assert that a physical object is round [2] we are asserting that it is round in the sense-given sense, I do not think that this is necessarily all that we are asserting. We may also at the same time be asserting by means of the same statement that it is round to touch or acts causally like a round physical object or both, propositions which we could not truly assert of a visual sensum; and if this is so it is sufficient to make inadequate the simple analysis of the statement as merely asserting a sense-given quality of a physical object. And there may be and probably are a number of other qualifications which have not occurred to me and which, while not affecting the point of principle that in making assertions about physical objects we are very commonly ascribing to them sense-given qualities, would debar the acceptance of any simple analysis, even in the case of primary qualities. But then our inability to be sure what the exact analysis can be is no argument in favour of a phenomenalist analysis or against the view that in these propositions we are normally asserting the independent physical occurrence of some sense-given qualities. On any view we may be very doubtful or quite in ignorance as to what the correct analysis of a statement is and yet be perfectly justified in believing that of two given

---

[1] The phenomenalist himself will have to admit that the analysis of propositions ascribing colour and other secondary qualities to physical objects will be markedly different from the analysis of propositions ascribing relative size or velocity, for the analysis of the latter will be in terms of measurement and of the former in terms of how things look (or appear to other senses) under optimal conditions. But he will not have to admit such a radical difference as we have had to admit, at least between propositions ascribing taste and propositions ascribing primary qualities, and this is, as far as it goes, a point in his favour.

[2] I am using 'round' to mean approximately round, which is, I think, its usual meaning outside geometry.

modes of analysis one is fairly near what is meant and the other far removed from it.

Indeed, I should go further still and insist that it is highly doubtful whether it is ever possible to give a definite and completely correct ultimate [1] analysis of what we mean by any of the assertions commonly made in ordinary life. For it seems that in such assertions a fully definite and rigid meaning is not commonly attached to all or perhaps to any of the terms employed.[2] It may be important in philosophy to seek definiteness, but here we are discussing what the plain man means, and if what is meant is indefinite any definite analysis of it must be wrong. Or, to put it in another way, a philosophical analysis of his meaning can only be correct if it ends with some words such as 'or something like this'.

In this connection it is most important to avoid the fallacy of supposing that, because Q R is a correct analysis of P, therefore 'S is Q R' is necessarily a correct analysis of what is being asserted when it is said that S is P.[3] The proposition 'S is P' may be asserted by someone who has not the slightest idea that P = Q R or positively disbelieves this, and such a

---

[1] I say 'ultimate' because it is clearly possible to give a definite and correct analysis of e.g. 'brother' in terms of 'common parent', but this is not an ultimate analysis. To be so it would have to analyse 'parent' and so ultimately 'person', a difficult enough matter.

[2] What is asserted is unambiguous not because the words such as e.g. tree or physical object have a perfectly definite meaning to the plain man nor because everybody would agree on a definition if proposed, which might or might not be so, but because usually there can be no doubt that, whatever the exact meaning of the term, it covers the present instance. The plain man has not a perfectly clear idea of the attributes he means by the word animal, as is revealed by the doubts he would feel if asked whether e.g. certain protozoa were animal; but this does not prevent the assertion that 'dogs are animals' from being itself definite in a sense despite the indefinite meaning of the terms used because, though there would be differences of opinion and few people would be clear exactly what the term as used by them covered, everybody is clear that it covers at least the attributes of dogs. Similarly with 'physical', only in this case there happens to be a lack of borderline cases in the world as known by us; we do not come across physical objects which it is difficult to distinguish from minds, or intermediate species between the two (except perhaps sensa and images). Most terms in ordinary use cover whatever varies within certain undefined and only roughly fixed limits.

[3] Unfortunately the word *is* is ambiguous. Where Q R is a correct analysis of the quality P it is correct to say 'P is Q R' in the sense of identity, but this must be distinguished from the predicative copula which is used in attributing the property P, or Q R, to a subject S.

person cannot be said to be asserting the proposition that S is Q R, though he may be asserting something that implies the truth of the latter proposition. For he may know of the presence of P without knowing what are the constituent parts of which P consists. We must not confuse a philosophical account of what physical objects are with an analysis of what we mean when we assert propositions about them in ordinary life. It is true that if, when talking about physical objects in ordinary life, we commonly mean something inconsistent with our philosophical account it will be an objection to the latter, but the philosophical account may simply go further and raise points which are not included in what we meant without being inconsistent with what we meant. This is the way in which I should defend myself against the charge that my theory of perception, being representative, is inconsistent with the truth of such judgments as ' the house you see [1] is the same as the one I visited yesterday '. Such a judgment would still be true even if it be the case that ' see ' must be analysed as ' sense a visual sensum which stands in relation r to a physical object ' [2] and that the person who makes the judgment has never heard of or has rejected this view of perception, for, though this is not what he asserts when he makes the judgment, neither is it denied by him in making the judgment. To analyse ' perceive ' is not to analyse all propositions which refer to perceiving. We can analyse perceiving further, i.e. say in what the process consists as an objective fact, but it does not follow that we can therefore analyse further all propositions in which perceiving is a constituent.[3]

I do not deny that we have a strong tendency to believe that it is a physical object and not a mere sensum with which we are immediately acquainted sensorily, but that is not what we assert when we say ' I see this house '. We do not in this type

[1] ' See ' obviously stands to ' perceive ' in the relation of species to genus.
[2] I do not mean to commit myself to the view that this is a complete analysis. If we, as I shall suggest later, have a non-inferential cognition of a physical object when we perceive, this should be included in the analysis.
[3] On the other hand ' seeing ' can, I think, be further analysed in these propositions as = ' visually perceiving '. For this is what we mean to assert when we say ' see ', though we do not put it in that way; but we do not when we say ' see ' mean to assert anything about the representative theory in any ordinary sense of ' mean '.

of judgment affirm the identity of our sensum with a physical object but merely neglect to distinguish them, therefore my view of perception does not lead to the conclusion that such 'common-sense propositions' are false (even partially), as I think phenomenalism does. The representative view does indeed conflict with a view which the ordinary man prior to philosophical study has a very strong tendency to hold, but it does not conflict with the truth of his ordinary assertions about physical objects, only with the truth of certain philosophical propositions which he is very much inclined to believe, an altogether different matter. For, while it seems very unreasonable to suppose that all the propositions ordinarily asserted by the plain man about physical objects are false, there is nothing unreasonable in supposing that prior to proper reflection he has false philosophical opinions about the general nature of perception.

But, even if no analysis of a common-sense judgment about physical objects can be completely correct, it does not follow that any analysis is as far wrong as any other. Obviously it would still be possible to think of many modes of analysis which would be utterly silly and give nothing in the least like what is really asserted, while others approach much more nearly to the plain man's meaning. And again, of less unreasonable modes of analysis one may rationally be preferred to another, as I have preferred the realist to the phenomenalist, on the ground that it comes much nearer the truth. My contention has been (1) that my mode of analysis gives something very much more like the plain man's meaning than does the phenomenalist mode ; (2) that there is no reason to deny that many judgments about physical objects ascribe shapes and positions to them or at least to their surfaces in the same sense as that in which these can be ascribed to sensa, irrespective of whether anybody perceives the physical objects or not.[1]

We now come to what is perhaps the most formidable objection both to realism in general and to a realist analysis of our ordinary assertions about physical objects, though it is not an objection that has often been advanced, at least explicitly in published works.[2] We may summarise it as follows. If

[1] To say this is not to give a complete analysis of any judgment.
[2] What called my attention to this objection was a lecture by Professor G. E. Moore at Cambridge. Berkeley may have had it in mind when he wrote : 'Again, *great* and *small*, *swift* and *slow*, *are allowed to exist nowhere without the mind*, being entirely *relative*, and

we are to ascribe shape to physical objects in the sense-given sense we must also ascribe size to them in that sense, but this is impossible because sense-given size is absolute while physical size is admittedly only relative. Further, we can ask whether one physical object is larger than another, but we cannot ask intelligently whether its real size is e.g. the size it looks 6 feet away or 1 foot away or how much it differs from either, or make any statement comparing its real physical size to any apparent sensible size whether of it or of other objects. Again it would be nonsense to talk about measuring a sensum or to ask whether the length a line or the area a surface *looks*[1] is more or less than 2 inches, while it is perfectly good sense to make such statements about the measurements of physical things. From this it may be inferred both that size and consequently shape as applied to physical objects have a different meaning from the sense-given one, and that we cannot reasonably suppose that there are any physical objects qualified by size and shape in the sense-given sense of the words.

This objection raises difficulties the solution of which would require a complete theory of space. But it seems quite clear to me that it would not justify an abandonment of realism. It is indeed not contended merely that we cannot in fact determine what the absolute size of physical objects is but that it is absurd to speak of them as having an absolute size, and I am inclined to think that this contention is justified. It is, however, very important to be clear as to the precise sense in which sensa can and physical objects cannot be said to have an absolute size. It is certainly not true that physical objects have only a relative and not an absolute size if by this is meant that the size of such an object is simply a set of relations between it and other objects external to itself.[2] It would be not only false but absurd to say that

---

changing as the frame or position of the organs of sense varies. The extension therefore which exists without the mind is neither great nor small, the motion neither swift nor slow, that is, they are nothing at all' (*Princ.* XI). But it must be admitted that Berkeley's statement is confused.

[1] In the primary sense of ' looks '. We sometimes use ' looks ' to mean ' looks (in the primary sense) as if it were (physically) ', and in that sense we could compare the size it ' looks ' with the size it really is because they are both physical, e.g. we can and do say ' this mountain looks higher than it really is '.

[2] I am thinking of such relations as equal to, about half the size of, bigger by a seventeenth than, etc.

in this sense the size of physical objects was only relative. But this absurdity certainly does not represent Professor Moore's view. What he asserts is that there is often, if not always, a specific determinate size given in perception,[1] i.e. as qualifying our sensa, just as there is a specific determinate shade of colour, whereas no such specific determinate size can be ascribed to physical objects without absurdity. It is impossible to state what is meant quite adequately, because, while we have general names such as large or small, we have no name for exact sizes except those based on measurement, which are useless in dealing with sensa, but the statement given comes perhaps as near as possible to meeting the difficulty. The point is that it is not merely that one sensum [2] is nearly equal to or half as large as another, but that in all or at least some [3] cases it has a quality of size itself in a quite specific degree, just as when it has colour it has some specific shade of colour or other. The fact that what its size is can only be *described* in general terms such as 'very large', or by comparison with other sensa, makes no difference to this.

Now I do not claim for a moment to have a fully satisfactory answer to the objection : that would require a complete theory of space. But I think that the edge of it is much blunted by consideration. I have admitted that in my opinion it would be absurd to ascribe such a specific determinate size to physical objects, but it is not enough to see that this is absurd. What we need is to see why it is absurd, and we can best do this by asking how we should reply to anybody who could not see the absurdity but ascribed absolute size in this sense to physical objects. In the first place we should, I think, ask him whether he thought that a given physical object had the size it appears to have at ten yards distance or the one it appears to have at the distance of a foot, whether it had the size seen by the naked eye or by a microscope, and if the latter by how strong a microscope. In this way we could show him that it was impossible to find out its absolute size or even to conceive any possible means of doing so, but he might still contend that it really had a specific determinate size though we could not

[1] At least in two dimensions.
[2] We do not talk about 'sensa' in ordinary conversation, but we do talk about the way in which things look, which comes to the same thing.
[3] A difficulty is raised by sensa with indefinite outlines. Also it is often held, though in my opinion wrongly, that some sensa do not possess 'extensity'.

determine what this was. So then we should go on further to point out that, however small the size of a physical object, it would contain still smaller parts which were spatially distinct, though perhaps owing to certain causal laws not physically separable.[1] Consequently, if we supposed that its real determinate size was e.g. the size we should see if we looked at it under optimal conditions through an imaginary microscope which could just enable us to see objects one-billionth of an inch in diameter,[2] there would still not be room in it for all its parts since a part a billionth of an inch across would now be an indivisible dot and therefore would have no room for a part of itself one two-billionth of an inch across, and so with any size we chose to ascribe to it *ad infinitum*, which would seem to show that it was actually self-contradictory to ascribe to it any determinate size whatever.

It is thus the infinite divisibility of space which makes it seem impossible to ascribe a specific determinate size to physical objects. If we could hold space to be only finitely divisible the difficulty would disappear. It would indeed then be obvious that a physical object must have a specific determinate size, for it would be divisible into a fixed finite number of minimum spatial parts. But in the case of a sensum this condition is realised, for we obviously cannot distinguish an infinite number of parts in any sensum, and while my inability to distinguish its parts is regarded as irrelevant to a physical object, this is not so with sensa. On the contrary, no part of a sensum A would be regarded as consisting of two parts B and C unless it was possible for the person who sensed the sensum to distinguish B and C.[3] With sensa only distinguishable parts are distinct parts. We now see that the discrepancy between the application of ' size ' to our sensa and to physical objects in this respect is due to the fact that the former are regarded as existing only when sensed and the latter as existing independently of us. But in that case it becomes impossible to be satisfied with this argument for a phenomenalist analysis of our propositions about physical objects. For we now see that it only seems absurd to suppose

---

[1] Whether the electron has or has not physical parts, it certainly has spatial parts. Otherwise it would be a mere geometrical point without any size at all.

[2] Or the size obtained by a combination of the different sensa derived from looking at all the parts of it successively with this microscope.

[3] I do not say that he need actually distinguish them.

that we are using 'size' in a realist sense of physical objects because we presuppose that these objects exist [1] independently of being sensed, i.e. ascribe to them other characteristics in a realist sense.

But I am not prepared to admit what I have so far taken for granted for the sake of argument, namely, that we normally do use 'size' in a phenomenalist sense. The admission that physical objects do not have a determinate size in the sense in which sensa have need not affect the meaning of any of our ordinary statements about them. For these are never about the absolute determinate size either of physical objects or of sensa—for that kind of size we have no names—but always about their size relatively to other objects, and such statements may still well be interpreted realistically as affirming e.g. that A is so much larger than B whether anybody perceives it or not. I see no reason to analyse these assertions in such a way as to include any proposition to the effect that A or B has a determinate size. They may *imply* a proposition of this kind, but it does not follow that they *include* it in themselves.

There remains the difficulty for realism as a philosophical theory of the physical world that on the one hand the proposition e.g. that A is larger than B seems to imply that A and B have determinate sizes, and on the other it is hard to see how they can have these in the sense-given sense, and if not in what sense. For, whatever physical size is, it surely must be possessed in some determinate degree by any object which it qualifies. Also, if the difficulty cannot be met, it would seem to follow that all our ordinary propositions about the size of physical objects are partly false since they *imply* false propositions about determinate physical size, even if they do not include such propositions.

It does, however, seem quite clear that in any case a realist view admits of determinate physical size in some sense, if not in the sense in which sensa have determinate size. It seems clear that the size of any physical object must be some exact ratio of any other [2] and must be theoretically capable of

---

[1] In a primary sense of 'exist'.
[2] Even if we had to add 'relatively to a given point of reference', this would only make the relation triadic and still leave it both determinate, relatively to the point of reference, and independent of a percipient, the point of reference lying in the independent physical world. Again what size an object is will be indeterminate if we are vague as

exactly determinate measurement, even though, as in the case of electrons (the 'indeterminacy' principle), physical laws may debar determinate measurement from ever being carried out. And, as I have said already, it does seem to me that it would be nonsense to maintain that the size of a physical object could be reduced simply to its relations to other objects. Any measurement of it does seem to presuppose that it occupies some definite extent of space itself, the amount of which can indeed only be stated in terms of its relations to other objects but is not reducible to these relations. So much seems logically necessary to me, but at any rate even if I were wrong in this and those who have been led by the latest discoveries of science into thinking otherwise were right, this would not endanger the realist position, since in that case the argument that one physical object cannot be larger than another without having some determinate size would collapse and the whole difficulty disappear. For it is only if relative size is held really to imply determinate absolute size that the objection can be brought at all, and these new theories do not hold it to do so. The fact that a physical object is in a sense infinitely divisible [1] certainly need not prevent it from having determinate relations in respect of size to other physical objects, i.e. those by which it is measured, nor even from having a determinate size itself over and above its relations. The series $\frac{1}{2} + \frac{1}{4} + \frac{1}{8} + \frac{1}{16} \ldots$, for example, is infinite and yet quite determinate. All we can say is that something infinitely divisible and something finite have a different kind of determinateness [2]; but everything that exists at all must have some kind of determinateness. Physical objects may have a determinate size without its being determinate in the way in which the size of sensa is determinate. Also if, as is often held now, space be really finite in extent, a particular physical object would always have a determinate size in the sense that it occupies a determinate proportion of the whole of space.

As to the sense in which we can truly ascribe size to physical

to what constitutes a single object or vary our definition of this to suit our purposes. If we include in a given object its 'sphere of influence', no doubt its extent is indeterminate, but this is only because of the vagueness of the terms we have employed.

[1] I.e. spatially, not physically. As I have said above, the question whether electrons could or could not be split by any physical means has nothing to do with this sense of divisibility.

[2] Perhaps those sensa the outlines of which are indefinite have a third kind of determinateness.

objects if we grant their existence in a realist sense,[1] three alternative possible views suggest themselves.

(1) It seems to me that the correct analysis of propositions ascribing characteristics such as shape or size to physical objects is not just 'that they have shape or size in the sense-given sense', but 'that they have shape or size in the sense-given sense, or something like this'. That sounds unphilosophical, but, as I have suggested earlier,[2] it is difficult to avoid the conclusion that no ultimate analysis of the propositions asserted in ordinary life can be correct unless it ends with a phrase such as 'or something like this'. A definite analysis cannot possibly be correct if what is to be analysed is indefinite. In that case, for our ordinary statements about physical objects to be wholly true it would be sufficient that physical objects should have not size in the sense-given sense but some quality which corresponded to it sufficiently for the purposes of the scientist and the 'man in the street'.[3] 'Size' as belonging to particular physical objects might have most of the characteristics of size as belonging to 'sensa' without having them all. Philosophical realists themselves are by no means committed to the view that there is an exact qualitative likeness between the spatial characteristics of sensa and those of physical objects, indeed such an assumption would be strongly denied by many or perhaps even most. On this view

---

[1] The positive arguments for realism other than the argument from common-sense will be discussed in the next section. At present we are just examining the realist view in order to see whether it need not be ruled out of court at the beginning on the ground of having committed an absurdity in connection with size.

[2] V. above, p. 304.

[3] A phenomenalist might object that his sense likewise corresponded to it sufficiently for these purposes and was therefore covered by the formula 'or something like this'. All I should say in reply is that it seems perfectly clear to me for the reasons given on p. 296 ff. that it is not sufficiently like it to be a tolerable analysis. For even if we cannot give an adequate analysis, we must give one as nearly adequate as possible, and in my opinion a realist analysis approaches much nearer to the meaning of what is asserted than a phenomenalist one. How much difference is compatible with an analysis being acceptable is a matter of degree, but, just as I can be certain that £100 would be too much for me to give to a particular charity and a penny too little, although it would be extremely difficult or impossible to determine the exact, ideally correct amount, I can be justifiably certain that a particular analysis does not correspond closely enough to what is meant to be admissible without being able to give an exact analysis or formulate the exact degree of discrepancy that is admissible.

the reason why physical objects and sensa are not comparable, even theoretically, in respect of size, would be because size in physical objects and size in sensa were different qualities, though they corresponded to each other in some way.

(2) It may be the case that size in physical objects is just the same quality as in sensa but differs only quantitatively in that it is infinitely divisible in the former and finitely divisible in the latter. Indeed, I must remind the reader that no other difference has emerged in the discussion. This difference can easily be admitted by a realist, since it follows simply from the circumstance that our sensa depend on being sensed and physical objects do not do so. On this view we can truly ascribe size to both physical objects and sensa in the same sense but cannot ascribe determinate size in the same sense, or at least ascribe the same kind of determinateness, if what is finitely divisible and what is infinitely divisible cannot be determinate in the same way, as I suppose is the case. Then our ordinary propositions about the size of physical objects may still be true in the sense-given sense, for we ordinarily speak no of the absolute determinate size of physical objects but only of their approximate size relatively to each other.[1] They imply but do not include propositions to the effect that these objects have a determinate size, ' size ' being understood here in the same sense as when applied to sensa, but ' determinate ' perhaps in a different sense.[2]

(3) Size is obviously a very peculiar kind of ' quality ', and I am inclined to think that to say an object has size is simply to say that it has a plurality of contiguous parts differently located spatially.[3] In this sense both physical

---

[1] ' Large ', as applied to a physical object, always means larger than most objects of its kind or larger than we should have expected, etc., and we have no words for any absolutely determinate size.

[2] We should distinguish between (a) a different sense of ' determinate ', (b) a different species of determinateness. If the determinateness of an infinitely divisible object can be said to differ from the determinateness of a finite object as different species within the same genus, (and I do not see why it should not), they are still determinate in the same sense of the word, just as a red object and a blue object are coloured in the same sense of ' coloured ', though they have different species of colour. So I am very doubtful whether even ' determinate ' is being used in a different sense with physical objects.

[3] They need not be qualitatively different : to take an example of a sensum, if I see a uniform patch of white colour, its left half and its right half are still spatially distinct in the sense of being located differently in space, though there is no qualitative difference.

objects and sensa have size.[1] The only difference would be that the number of parts is in some sense infinite in a physical object, but finite in a sensum. Consequently, as in (2), all propositions about the size of physical objects could be interpreted in the sense-given sense and yet be true, except perhaps such a proposition as that physical objects have a determinate size, which would be, if asserted by anybody, a false proposition of philosophy, not of common-sense.

On these last two views the impossibility of comparing the size of physical objects with the size of sensa might be explained on the ground that it is impossible to compare the finite and the infinitely divisible in such a respect, or on the ground that though the characteristic of spatiality in both is the same they belong to spatial systems which are structurally different because the one kind of objects are infinitely divisible and the other only finitely so. Why it would be absurd to talk about the measurement of sensa can be easily seen if we realise that measurement implies juxtaposition to a standard object which can also be used in other cases, and that it is impossible to take up part of a sense-field and thus apply it to something in another field or to another part of the same field.

This is not to say that the old difficulty of infinite divisibility, on which the objection under discussion really depends, is altogether removed. But the difficulty in question has at least been much lessened by the efforts of thinkers like Mr. Bertrand Russell; and we shall in any case not escape it by denying the independent existence of physical objects unless we are prepared also to deny the reality of time, a course which makes all our immediate experience illusory and strikes me not as a conquest of the difficulty but as an ignominious flight from it.[2]

The argument from common-sense therefore remains to my

[1] Obviously, even if size consists in a plurality of parts, we can sense the size of a sensum without counting its parts, but that is because a plurality can be perceived as a whole as well as by counting; and again we can see that one sensum is larger or smaller than another without being able to count its parts, as we can see a crowd as a whole and may be able to tell quite easily that one crowd is larger than another without counting the number of people in each crowd. (Unless we suppose that our sensa are themselves infinitely divisible, in which case they are like physical objects in respect of the quality of size and the whole difficulty disappears, we must hold that the number of parts in them is theoretically, though not in practice, capable of being counted.)

[2] V. above, ch. III, sect. 3.

mind a strong one. It does seem to me that the acceptance of phenomenalism would necessitate the admission that all judgments such as ' the earth moves round the sun ', ' there is a table in this room ', ' the fire is out ' are fundamentally mistaken, and this seems most unlikely. It seems to me more likely that a particular philosophical theory of matter which conflicts with them should be wrong than that they should. Even if we held that some amendment of such common-sense beliefs is necessary, and that it is impossible to fix any definite line beyond which amendment and reinterpretation cannot go, we might yet be quite clear that the phenomenalist goes too far, just as we may be both very uncertain e.g. how much money ought to be devoted to a given purpose and yet quite sure that a penny is too little or a thousand pounds too much. Even if I could see no answer to the arguments used, it would still seem to me more likely that there should be some undetected mistake in these arguments than that there should be no independent physical objects. This belief of mine is much strengthened by my memory of the great number of mistakes that have been made in philosophical arguments by far better philosophers than myself.[1] Phenomenalism is rendered still more paradoxical by the circumstance, often forgotten, that, if true at all, it would refer also to our own and other people's bodies.

At the worst, however, the phenomenalist cannot show that the existence of independent physical objects is impossible but only that the belief in them is ungrounded, and the mere fact that otherwise all the ordinary statements of everyday life (except those of a purely psychological character) and of physical science would be false surely itself constitutes a strong ground for it. After all it is impossible to disprove the possibility that these statements are really based on a kind of cognition which, though not yet successfully analysed by philosophers, is to some extent its own justification. It may be urged that in making such judgments we do really see and are not wrong in supposing that we see them to be justified, and that therefore it is incumbent on the philosopher to analyse the knowledge we really possess and not reject it because he cannot prove it by argument or bring it under any

[1] In view of the disagreement of philosophers, whatever philosophical views are true, the numbers of mistakes made by great philosophers must be surprisingly large, though what a man considers to be the mistakes will differ according to his individual views.

other recognised mode of cognition. However, while this plea deserves the greatest respect, I think myself that realism may be based on argument as well as on non-inferential cognition.

§ II. Is there any Justification for the Belief in Independent Physical Objects?

In this section the question for discussion is how, if at all, we can justify the belief in independent physical objects. By this I mean the belief that there are objects with spatial properties which exist even when not perceived by any human (or animal) mind.[1] Unless this belief be true all our assertions about physical objects in ordinary speech and science will be false in a most vital point, but while I have insisted that this constitutes a strong argument for the truth of the belief no realist philosopher would feel quite satisfied if he could not either produce some other argument for it or give some defensible account of a non-inferential mode of cognition which justified its acceptance.

Now the objections against independent physical things are mainly agnostical, i.e. they mostly claim to prove not that these cannot exist [2] but that we cannot show their existence to be at least probable, and would therefore be adequately met without specific refutation by a counter-argument to show that we can do so. I shall, however, deal with them expressly at the end of the section, but think it better to postpone this till I have discussed various attempts positively to justify the belief in question.

In the first place, can the belief be justified by an appeal to some intuitive insight not founded merely on reasoning or sensation or both together? Difficulties arise when we ask what it is that this intuition or cognition is supposed to tell us, for the proposition that (some) physical objects exist is a proposition of a type which logicians generally admit cannot be known *a priori* and therefore cannot be logically self-evident, since it is existential and not merely hypothetical. It would be generally admitted that we cannot know *a priori* that so-and-so exists.[3] Again, that we could not attain such knowledge by

---

[1] In a sense which is not to be analysed phenomenalistically.
[2] Arguments purporting to show that their existence is logically impossible are discussed and rejected elsewhere in this book.
[3] Except, according to some thinkers, in the case of God or the Whole.

perception in so far as sensory we have seen already.[1] For to say that something is physical is not to say only that it has certain sensible characteristics but also at least that it exists independently of being perceived by us.

We should, however, be committing an error if we confined empirical cognition to the sphere of the senses, as is shown by the case of memory. Our knowledge in memory is empirical not *a priori*, yet what we remember is not sensibly perceived when we remember it. There may indeed be sensible images present in memory, but we only use them as a means in cognising something which is not identical with them. What we remember is often an event or fact quite incapable of adequate representation by the images, and it is always past while they are present. In memory then we have a mode of cognition that is genuinely empirical and yet altogether transcends present sensation. Now it may be suggested that cognition of physical objects is analogous to our cognition of the past in memory. In both cases we do not immediately perceive sensorily what we cognise, in both cases we have sensuous representations (sensa or memory-images) which are not identical with but help us in cognising our objects of cognition, in both cases our cognition is not always veridical but very often justifies a claim either to knowledge or to reasonable belief, in both cases the cognition is partly and indeed in its essential core non-inferential. We cannot validate by argument the evidence of memory against a sceptic who doubts it, yet everyone accepts this evidence not indeed as infallible but as in favourable cases extremely unlikely to be wrong. Should we not take this attitude in the case of perception also?

I do not see any possibility of refuting such a view but am on the contrary very inclined to accept it. The analogy with memory is not perfect, but perception of physical objects may well stand by itself as a unique mode of non-inferential cognition not patterned on any other cognitive process. It would be impossible to maintain certainty for the cognition in question, but this does not prove that it is not under favourable conditions sufficient to justify as reasonable the belief in some independent physical objects.[2] And its probability is greatly

[1] V. above, p. 270.
[2] It would be impossible to maintain that it was nearly as reliable as memory usually is. This seems to be largely because, owing to the elaborate physical medium required, the variety of causes which interfere with its working so as to produce illusions is much greater than in the case of memory.

enhanced by the agreement between the perceptions of different percipients. It may be the case that when we perceive a physical object, at least under favourable conditions, we do cognise some facts about it though without immediately sensing it,[1] as we cognise some facts about our past selves by memory. We do not do so in dreams, but then in dreams our memory and our power of argument are equally impaired or deranged. I should when awake refuse to believe in the existence of physical objects which I seemed to see in a dream unless I could perceive them also when awake, but neither should I when awake regard it as evidence of the occurrence of a past event that I had seemed to remember it in a dream unless I still remembered it as a past event in waking life, nor should I regard it as evidence for the truth of any proposition that I had seemed to prove it by argument completely to my satisfaction in a dream unless I approved the argument in a waking state. We cannot therefore use the case of dreams as a special argument against the reliability of perception unless we are also prepared to use it against the trustworthiness of memory and even of reasoning. Where the cognitive functions of the mind are not seriously impaired, as in dreams or under the influence of drugs, and where there are no special reasons for confusion, it may be that our perception of physical objects, though not capable of yielding certainty, is, even apart from causal or other arguments, a valuable piece of evidence to be taken into account in determining what a physical object is, and the value of these detached pieces of evidence may be greatly heightened by mutual confirmation.[2]

In that case we may, while retaining the representative theory, still insist that in a very important sense we immediately perceive physical objects and not merely sensa. Only we do not perceive these objects in the same sense as we perceive sensa, or perhaps it would be better to say that we do not perceive physical objects directly [3] but cog-

[1] As far as I can understand them, the 'Critical Realists' seem to be maintaining a view of this type in their own terminology, but I differ from them in holding that the sense-datum by means of which we cognise physical objects is not universal but particular. Cf. also Stout, *Mind and Matter*, bk. IV, ch. 4.

[2] Mr. Price has in his book on *Perception* (p. 183 ff.) very effectively defended a similar view as to the evidential character of our perceptions, but it seems to me that the argument really carries one much further away from phenomenalism than he is prepared to admit.

[3] We could not in any case say that we 'sense' them.

nise them directly.[1] This, however, is only a question of terminology.

We cannot indeed maintain that physical objects always have in a literal sense the shape we perceive, for that would be self-contradictory (though possibly tenable in some non-literal sense such as that suggested by Mr. Russell in *Knowledge of the External World*.) But the view I have suggested is not incompatible with the occurrence of illusion and the recognition of certain definite conditions, such as those commonly treated under the heading of 'laws of perspective', which tend to produce illusion. For the view implies only that, other things being equal and in the absence of conflicting evidence, the fact that I seem to perceive certain characteristics in a physical object under favourable conditions creates a strong presumption in favour of the view that it really has these characteristics. We could not claim certain knowledge of the physical but may perhaps claim evidence sufficient to justify belief in the absence of strong arguments on the other side. This represents the ordinary attitude of humanity to the evidence of perception; it is assumed that perception is trustworthy unless and until special reasons, such as incompatibility with other perceptions, arise against accepting its trustworthiness in the particular instance before us or in the class of instances to which that belongs. The fact that perception often yields error is no proof that it can never justify belief. If it were, the same objection would apply to all species of cognition. The argument from illusion does indeed for a reason expounded earlier (p. 274 ff.) make very difficult the view that we are immediately aware of physical objects in the same sense as that in which we are immediately aware of sensa, but this need not necessarily prevent us from sometimes having an adequate non-inferential cognition of them, though we cannot perceive them immediately. For the objection in question only applies to direct sense-perception, not to direct cognition.

As I have remarked, the analogy with memory will not hold altogether. The chief difference is that when perceiving physical objects we only cognise facts about them in and by simultaneously cognising sensa which represent them, while in the case of memory we can be immediately aware of past facts which are not or not adequately represented by anything

[1] I use 'cognise an object' as short for 'cognise facts about the object'.

in our memory images. In the case of memory indeed we are aware of the event remembered and the memory-image as quite distinct from each other, but in the case of perception we are not thus aware of the physical object and the sensum as distinct and only infer their distinctness, if at all, on theoretical grounds. The information we derive from perception, as opposed to inference, about physical objects is thus absolutely dependent on our present sensum in a way in which memory is not dependent on the memory-image. We cannot perceive without sensa, but we can remember without representative images.[1] The rôle of imagery in memory is similar to its rôle in inference, where it is needed to clarify and fix our thought but not to supply information; with perception on the contrary the sole source of information as to the specific character of physical things is our sensum. But the fact that the non-inferential cognition involved in perception is not in all respects similar to that involved in memory is no good reason for rejecting it. On the contrary, if we do have non-inferential cognition of physical things, we should expect it to be a mode of cognition which has characteristics of its own and is not just like the cognition of objects such as events in our past life which are related to us in a different way altogether. Though it is as difficult to prove that any judgments of memory are true as that any judgments of perception are, nobody rejects the evidence of memory because memory is a mode of cognition unlike the apprehension of self-evident logically necessary truths or unlike inference.

We must not indeed lose sight of one element of truth contained in the direct theory of perception, namely, that we are at the time not conscious of any distinction between our sensum and the physical reality which it represents. It is not correct, I think, to hold that our sensum is ever actually identical with the physical thing perceived or even with a surface or part of that thing; but in perception we treat our sensum as if it were so identical, for we can only perceive a physical thing at all by using the really immediate object of sense-perception as a substitute for it in perception, so that to be immediately aware of the latter sensorily is for us equivalent to being sensorily aware of a part of the former. Doubtless we modify that attitude as the result of experience and

[1] Even if it is true that some imagery is always necessary in memory, the imagery may certainly be merely verbal and so not in the least like what is remembered.

inference, but it is essential to perception. This point we shall find to be of some importance later in determining what we can say about the nature of physical objects. It seems to me likely that it is connected with another point of difference between perception and memory. This is that we can only remember what we have first experienced. That fact seems to me to explain, in so far as anything like this can be explained by us, why the cognition of physical objects is only possible through sensa while this is not the case with memory. For a cognition to give us categorical propositions about a particular entity it must be based on some experience, but while we have experienced past events we do not on the representative theory actually experience physical objects in the strict sense. Hence in the case of memory this past experience provides the empirical basis, so that it and not the present sensory representation, if there is one, is the source of our information in memory; but in the case of perception there would be no such basis in actual experience without a sensum.

The cognition of which I am speaking is, if it occurs at all, not a cognition of a general principle but of particular facts in each particular case, as with memory. Nor is it a cognition in virtue of which we can see that the occurrence of characteristics in our sensum *logically entails* the occurrence of similar characteristics in a physical object. Such a claim would be quite unwarranted. It must be a genuine empirical cognition of particular facts in objective space.

We may be rightly convinced that we have some non-inferential cognition of physical objects while being very doubtful what part of our natural beliefs about them are true and quite unprepared to give any definition of physical objects, just as we may be justified in being quite sure that we have some correct cognition of ethical truths and yet be very doubtful how far we ought to trust our ordinary ethical intuitions and quite unable to decide what the definition of good is, if it has one, or whether it is definable at all. Certainly what particular beliefs about the physical world we are to accept must in any case be determined largely by the coherence test, i.e. we must accept those in preference which will render our experience most coherent. All that a person who upholds non-inferential cognition of physical objects need maintain in general is that assurance of a supposed physical fact in the experience of perceiving constitutes *some* evidence for the objective reality of the fact unless it is possible to point to definite grounds which destroy the evidential value of this assurance, and that where the conditions for observation are favourable and the accounts of different observers confirm each other the cumulative force of this evidence may be such as to justify a belief even in the absence of any further positive argument. That we ever have knowledge of physical facts in the strict sense of the term it would be much more difficult to maintain. In view of illusions, etc., the most that anyone could possibly claim to *know* would be the existence of something independent of our mind, and perhaps the existence of an objective space and time. But at the time of perceiving we are, or apart from previous experience and reflective criticism would be, also assured that there is a physical object with the shape and e.g. colour perceived in the place at which it is perceived, and in this we are often mistaken. (Similarly we are often mistaken in other non-inferential cognitions and inferences.) But we find that the illusions in question can in practically every case be ascribed to definite physical causes, and that, if we trust the visual perceptions we have of objects when looking straight at them at an optimal distance, i.e. at the minimum distance prior to the point where the vision becomes confused owing to too great proximity,[1] our trust is not inconsistent with but definitely confirmed by facts. Despite the prevalence of illusion there is no empirical evidence which conflicts with the view that under these conditions our perception of the shape, relative size and position of objects is normally correct, nor even with the view that normally part of their surface really has the colour we then see and that there really are physical objective sounds such as those we hear and smells such as those we sense.[2]

There are, however, two respects in which it would be less easy to defend the non-inferential cognition against the charge of persistent error even under the most favourable conditions.

(1) We seem to be assured in perception not only that there is something in objective space with the shape, etc., which we perceive existing independently of us, but also that the identical object we perceive (sense) so exists, and this, if I was right in accepting a representative theory of perception, is never the case at all. This seems like a positive and invariable

---

[1] A *slight* divergence from this position does not result in any noticeable change in our sensum (v. above, p. 276).
[2] V. below, p. 374 ff.

illusion, and, if it is taken as such, must necessarily lessen our faith in the reliability of the cognition. But might it not rather be said that we merely fail negatively to make a distinction because it is one that is not immediately given but could only be inferred? If my theory be true the plain man is still right in holding that he sees (perceives) something which exists independently of himself, and is only wrong in failing to distinguish the sense in which he perceives this (physical) object from the sense in which he perceives sensa or to distinguish the sensum itself at the time of perception from the object he perceives by means of it. If he infers or assumes that because he cannot distinguish the sensum and the object, therefore they are the same he has committed an error, but this must not be attributed to the non-inferential cognition itself. All that can be alleged against the latter on this score is that it does not reveal a distinction which is there, but then nobody would dream of expecting that it should reveal all the distinctions which it is possible to reach by further inference. (It would also be possible, though, I think, less reasonable,[1] to hold the view that we have direct perception of physical objects in some cases of perception and representative perception in others. To hold that we have direct perception in all cases would be incompatible with the view that space has the nature which we in perception are assured that it has,[2] and is therefore less compatible with our non-inferential cognition than is the representative view.) If physical objects are really cognised in the way I have suggested, it is easy to see that, since the sensum has the same characteristics as the physical object in so far as these are given correctly by present perception at all, we can, where perception is veridical, treat it for certain practical purposes as if it were identical with the physical object.

It is not in any case necessary for us to answer the question as to the specific nature of the relation between the sensum and the part of the surface [3] of a physical object which it

[1] V. above, p. 276 ff.
[2] Because we should then have to suppose that the same physical object had a number of different shapes and that a number of different colours inhered in the same place.
[3] In the case of most physical objects which we ordinarily speak of 'seeing', nobody, whether a holder of the direct theory or a 'plain man', would maintain that we sensed the whole of the object, since it usually has an inside and a back which are obviously not sensed by us (v. Moore, *Philosophical Studies*, p. 230).

represents and resembles. It is, on the contrary, easy to see why we are in the dark as to the nature of this relation. For we are not immediately aware [1] of the two terms of the relation as different at all, only concluding that they are different as a result of inference; and we therefore obviously cannot either sense or cognise immediately the relation between them, since to do so we should have to be conscious in some way at the same time of both the related terms as distinct. Hence the character of the relation is never immediately given to us, and unless it can be reduced to or analysed in terms of some other relation immediately experienced, which seems unlikely, we must always miss its exact nature and can only grope for it by precarious analogical inference. But we can show, I think, that it is impossible to reduce the relation either to resemblance or to causality.

(2) We always, even under the most favourable conditions for perception, seem to be subject to an illusion as to size, since it is impossible to ascribe to a physical thing the size we perceive from any particular point of view.[2] But if, as I have suggested earlier, to say that an object has size is simply to say that it has a plurality of different contiguous spatial parts, then to perceive an object as having a smaller size from one point than from another is not to be subject to the positive illusion involved in seeing an object as possessing a quality in a degree other than that in which it really does possess it, but simply to fail to see from one point as many distinct parts in it as we see from another, and the failure to note distinct parts is not illusion or error but mere absence of knowledge. The trouble is again merely that our non-inferential cognition does not reveal all the distinctions present in physical objects.

I must admit, however, that I am not perfectly convinced of the correctness of the replies I have given on these two points, but in any case it is important again to stress the fact that the occurrence of error or illusion, however frequent, does not prove that we have no non-inferential cognition of physical objects. We may really be in touch with a certain reality in cognition and yet gain only most imperfect information about it mixed with a great deal of error, because our cognitive faculties, though not incapable of attaining truth, are most imperfect intrinsically and are in this case further

[1] In any of the last three senses of immediate awareness (p. 267 ff.).
[2] V. above, p. 307 ff.

hindered by many physical causes. All that the upholder of non-inferential cognition need maintain is the partial correctness of our cognitions, that they give us some imperfect idea of physical objects, and this there is no reason to dispute. All human endeavour is only very partially successful. And this mode of cognition is at least successful enough for the ordinary practical purposes of life, and when developed inferentially has yielded a very considerable body of scientific knowledge (or, rather, justified belief) about physical objects. That non-inferential cognition can only be very successful in eliciting definite judgments if combined with inference is no new theory.

There is another type of view which might admit non-inferential cognition of physical objects, but it need not delay us long. If we hold that the belief in physical objects can be justifiably based on a non-inferential cognition and do not hold that this is an empirical cognition of particulars, the only alternative is to regard it as a cognition of some general principle. But, as far as I know, nobody has yet succeeded in enunciating a general principle justifying the belief in physical objects which seems either clear or logically self-evident. The only alternative left on this view would be to say that we have a confused non-inferential cognition of some truth which nobody has yet clearly analysed but which is at least *like* what is commonly meant by the assertion that there are physical objects in the literal and usual sense of the words. This, as I have suggested elsewhere,[1] is analogous to what occurs in all departments of thought, and it may well be that such a confused but still far from valueless intuition is the real ground of our reluctance to abandon the belief in independent physical objects. This is important as a *caveat* against the subjective idealist and phenomenalist, though obviously no philosopher could be satisfied with it as the last word about physical objects. In passing we should note that such a view would still leave us to determine the particular characteristics of physical objects by reference to our sensa. We can still only reach physical objects through sensa.

Can any positive arguments be given in favour of the view that we have a partially valid non-inferential cognition of physical objects in the realist sense of the term? If the cognition is really non-inferential a proof in the ordinary sense would be needless and absurd; but if it can be shown that

[1] V. ch. V, sect. 5 *ad fin.*

the assumption of it is the only or the best way of explaining the fact that we can make true judgments about physical objects, this may be quite adequate to justify the assumption in question.[1] It may reasonably be retorted to the demands for a proof that

'the ultimate test of any theory of knowledge is its success in answering the question which falls within its province. It sets out to explain how we know [2] what we admittedly do know. It breaks down if instead of this it reaches the result that we cannot know what admittedly we do know. In that case what it has achieved is only to show that the principles on which it has proceeded must be false. . . . A theory of knowledge can accredit itself only by its success—its success in accounting for the knowledge which it finds indispensably presupposed in the ordinary conduct of life and in science. To deny such knowledge instead of analysing its nature and conditions is suicidal. Any theory is therefore self-condemned if it logically leads to the conclusion either that we cannot know the physical world which is essential to Common-Sense, or that we can know it only through a complex and precarious process of inference. It is not the claim of physical things to exist which is on its trial, but only the claim of a certain theory to account for the way in which we know of their existence or are justified in believing them to exist.'[3]

If, therefore, I do not seem to readers to have justified our belief in physical objects, it is to be hoped that they will conclude from this only that I have failed in my task and not that the belief is really unjustified. I think, however, that it is possible not indeed to prove with certainty but to establish by arguments as the most reasonable hypothesis not only that physical objects exist independently but that we have, as claimed, *a partially valid non-inferential cognition of them*.[4]

Let us now turn to these *arguments*. Two preliminary cautions are necessary. In the first place the reader must not suppose that I am giving an account of the way in which the

---

[1] The position would no doubt be quite different if we had not felt ourselves obliged to reject any phenomenalist analysis of our ordinary propositions about physical objects. In that case we could not, as we can now, argue that the propositions of science and common-sense would be false if realism were not true.

[2] I suppose that the word is in this passage being used in the wider sense in which it does not imply absolute certainty.

[3] Stout, *Mind and Matter*, p. 241.

[4] V. especially for this last point pp. 338–9, 343–4.

belief in physical objects actually originated, but only of the way in which we can justify the belief logically. The reasons I shall give for holding the belief are not reasons explaining why the hypothesis of physical objects occurred to humanity, but reasons explaining why, granted that it has occurred to us, it should be accepted. It might not have occurred to us without a ' primitive credulity ' in the physical existence of our objects of perception unjustified by evidence ; but once it has occurred to us it may still be established as probable by evidence not different in kind from that which is used to establish scientific hypotheses.

Further, we must not hope to deduce physical objects directly by a series of steps from the immediate data of sense, but can only attain success in the argument if we treat the existence of physical objects as a hypothesis to be verified by its results and perhaps confirmed further by a negative argument refuting other hypotheses.

The situation is fairly simple. We assume that there is some cause [1] to account for our sensa, just as we assume that, if some money is missing from a room where it was known to have been before, it has not just ceased to exist or moved to another place without any cause whatever. (If we assumed that events [2] could happen without a cause, it would be impossible to convict any criminal.) But only one set of causes to account for them has ever been suggested, namely, physical objects in the ordinary sense of the term and events in these objects. For the subjective idealist and phenomenalist suggest no other way of accounting for our sensa in detail. Even the simplest laws of nature cannot be stated in terms of actually sensed sensa. We do not need to reach this hypothesis by reasoning ; if we could only reach it in that way, possibly we should never have reached it at all because we should not have lived to tell the tale, but by what seems like a heaven-sent stroke of good fortune the hypothesis has occurred to us without reasoning, we have applied it for millennia and it has worked exceedingly well.

It is easy to apply the methods of agreement and difference

[1] I assume that a cause must be something *actual* in the literal sense of the term and not a mere possibility. This seems to me self-evident, but it is also implied by the theory of causation I defended earlier. For the contrary view presupposes some form of the regularity theory.

[2] I do not mean to imply that sensa are events ; but at any rate their coming to be is an event.

and find that no factor in our experience or the experience of other human beings [1] will meet these tests. We are then driven to seek as cause something which is not experienced, but the only characteristics which we can even suggest as belonging to this, since we know no others, are characteristics of the objects of immediate experience. These objects include mental states and sensa. The former or some characteristics like them *may* qualify external objects for anything we can tell, but nobody has suggested or could suggest a way of predicting and ordering our experiences based on the ascription of such characteristics to these objects. There are left the characteristics of sensa, and by ascribing some of these (the primary qualities) to causes of our sensa we are able to fulfil in very large measure the ideal of making our experience intelligible in that sense, whatever it is, in which a scientific hypothesis can be expected to make experience intelligible at all. Some factors external to our experience are required if we are to arrive at any set of general laws systematising our experience and accounting for it in that sense, whatever it is, in which causal laws can rightly be said to account for events.[2] What are these external factors like? If we assume that they have shape, size, motion and velocity, we can connect them by general laws with events in our own and other people's experiences and on the basis of these laws can connect into a system events which could not otherwise be correlated and systematised at all. I should in fact sum up the reasons for accepting the belief in independent physical objects as being that they make an experience *coherent*. Judged by the coherence test it seems obvious that there is no comparable hypothesis. But I shall

[1] In all that follows I am assuming the existence of human minds other than my own and the truth of some of the evidence they give as to their sensa, and consequently my argument will be weaker against those philosophers, if any, who are prepared to accept solipsism. Solipsism can, however, itself be met by the same type of argument, i.e. if no other human minds exist it is immensely improbable that so many details in my own experience should be *as if* the other minds I usually suppose to exist really did so. The argument is strengthened in the case of other minds by the plain evidence of purposes other than my own in the sensa I receive from them, e.g. words which make sense if interpreted according to certain rules.

[2] Even those who disagree totally with what I say about causality in Chapter IV will admit that there is some sense in which causes can be said to 'explain' or 'account for' their effects, and that the final test of any hypothesis as to causes in science is whether an alleged cause can in this sense account for its effect.

be more likely to convince those inclined to phenomenalism if I put the argument in a different form.

We should note here that the most direct type of inductive argument is ruled out by the nature of the problem. When B has been accompanied or preceded by A in all cases where we were in a position to observe the occurrence, it is according to the accepted rules of induction justifiable under certain conditions to infer that B is probably *always* accompanied or preceded by A whenever it occurs, and under far less stringent conditions and with a higher degree of probability to infer that B is *sometimes* accompanied or preceded by A when we do not observe A. Now, if we can argue in this way from the observed correlation of A and B within our experience to the existence of A in cases where A is not experienced but B is, even the more modest second conclusion might be supposed amply sufficient to establish the existence of extended entities which exist when unsensed by any human being. If we are justified in inferring from correlations within human experience that even in some cases one of the factors thus correlated exists unperceived, then we have established the realist case in principle. The objection that we cannot argue in this way from sensa to things of a quite different kind, material objects, might be met if we denied the, as it seems to me, very unnecessary assumption that material objects are things of a quite different kind from combinations of sensa.[1] But unfortunately such an argument from the correlation of A and B in experience could only be used to establish the existence of an unsensed A if that A stood in *the same* relation to the sensed B as the sensed A did to the sensed B within experience.[2] We may argue from an egg to a hen on the strength of past experience but we can only argue on those grounds to a hen which laid it, not to a hen which stood in some relation to the egg other than that of having laid it. Now if from the correlation of A and B in our experience plus the recurrence of B in a particular case where we had not the chance of observing its antecedents we infer that an A existed when we were not sensing it, we have inferred something which does not stand in the same relation to B as the sensed A did in the previous cases of B, at least if a representative theory of perception be true. For the relation between two sensa which follow each other, A and B, is quite different from the relation between the physical

---

[1] V. Section 3 of this chapter.
[2] V. Moore, *Philosophical Studies*, pp. 66–7.

entity of which the first is a sensum and the second sensum, and this being so the argument as it stands can give us no right to infer an unsensed physical A.

But there remains a more effective argument based on the laws of inverse probability, which I shall now employ. It is that countless detailed predictions have been made on the basis of the belief in independent physical objects and have been fulfilled as predicted, which except for a necessary reservation that I shall add later,[1] makes it fantastically unlikely that the belief or something very like it should be false. I am not referring only to the predictions of science, but also to the predictions of ordinary life such as that if I go into a room I shall see (have visual sensa of) a round table, three armchairs, and so on, this prediction being based on the assumption that the table, etc., are there whether anybody is looking at them or not. In view of the vast number of different sensa I have on different occasions, the chance of my having just the sensa which I predict that I shall have on any one occasion by mere coincidence would be only one in very many thousands, yet I may have been in the room hundreds of times and the prediction has been fulfilled each time. Further, every one of the thousands of millions of human beings who live or ever have lived to any age on the earth have had very many such experiences. The fact that many predictions based on the belief in independent physical objects have failed to come off does not much lessen the probability of the belief being true, since their non-fulfilment can always be explained as due to mistakes concerning the particular characteristics of physical objects and does not suggest that no independent physical objects exist at all.

If any hypothesis can be established by verification,[2] it would seem then that the hypothesis that some independent physical objects exist has been so established. This argument has, however, made comparatively little impression because the anti-realist would reply that what has been verified and shown to be highly probable is not the existence of independent physical objects but the truth in most cases of certain general-

[1] P. 340 ff.
[2] Throughout this section I use ' verification ' in the sense in which it is commonly used when it is said that a scientific hypothesis is verified by its consequences. There is another sense of ' verify ' in which the term is used not of the consequences of a hypothesis, the occurrence of which could at the best only make its truth probable, but of the actual observation or experience of the fact assumed in the hypothesis itself.

isations about probable human sensa [1] which may conveniently be expressed by means of the fiction of independent physical objects. But we may apply the argument from inverse probability to the generalisations themselves. For the generalisations about what we shall usually under certain conditions experience, which have been thus admittedly established as probable, can be and were in fact deduced from hypotheses as to the primary qualities of the unperceived causes of our sensa, and hence the verification of the generalisations in its turn verifies those hypotheses on which the generalisations were based. If we make the simple assumption that there are physical objects resembling our sensa and existing even when unperceived (under certain conditions roughly fixed long ago by experience), we are able to deduce from this assumption a vast number of generalisations which have been made first by plain men and then by scientists and which have been verified by their consequences, therefore if these generalisations usually hold without this assumption or something very like it being true we have again a most extraordinary coincidence. Supposing that the probability of any one of the generalisations holding in most [2] cases of human experience, as it does, apart from any assumption about the unperceived physical objects from which it was in fact deduced, were on the average $\frac{1}{10}$, a grotesque under-estimate, for the number of possible alternatives is enormous, if not actually infinite, and supposing again that only a hundred such generalisations had ever been shown to hold, a preposterous under-estimate, even then the probability of all the hundred being true would be $\frac{1}{10^{100}}$, a fraction the denominator of which runs into trillions of trillions. No doubt the generalisations are far fewer than the single predictions mentioned above, so the probability of the former being all true apart from any assumption about independent physical objects is much greater than the probability of the single predictions having being fulfilled without any generalisation being true, but this can be of little comfort to the phenomenalist when even the greater of the two proba-

[1] Or experiences, which he often confuses with sensa.
[2] Note that I say 'most', not 'all'. This is quite sufficient for the argument, since, in view of the vast number of alternative possibilities, the independent probability of a generalisation holding even in two cases out of three is extraordinarily small. And even if it were increased to, say, $\frac{1}{3}$ and the generalisations diminished to 20, the total probability would still be only one over a million million.

bilities is as small as I have suggested. It is no doubt very much more improbable that if I tossed a penny a hundred million times it would come down heads every time than it would be if I tossed it a thousand times, but nobody would on that account seriously consider the latter as a reasonable possibility.

So the argument seems to make it very probable that at least one hypothesis assigning particular primary qualities to some unperceived object is true. And, once we have established the unperceived existence of some extended entities, this greatly increases the probability of any other partially verified proposition ascribing primary qualities to any such entity being true. Experience goes on for thousands of years and always has gone on as if there were independent extended objects resembling our normal sensa of them or complexes of such sensa in respect of primary qualities at least and existing unperceived, but the probability that this would be so if there were not really any such objects, apart from a reservation given later, seems so slight as to provide an almost conclusive argument for the existence of the objects. No doubt some thinkers would reply that what is meant by a proposition about a physical object is not that there is something independent of us extended in the sense in which our sensa are extended, but merely that we have extended sensa and would normally have them under given conditions, but I have already rejected this interpretation of propositions about physical objects.

Further, apart from this question of meaning, it is clear that all the generalisations we can in fact make about our perceptual experiences are deducible [1] from propositions ascribing sensory extension to physical objects [2] as existing unperceived, whether anybody has ever asserted these propositions and made the deductions or not. The argument is thus not dependent on a phenomenalist analysis of common-sense propositions about physical objects being rejected.[3] For it would follow from

[1] In that sense in which one scientific hypothesis is deducible from another.
[2] In the realist sense.
[3] However, if anybody once came to the conclusion that independent extended things in the realist sense existed, I doubt whether he would ever in fact continue to maintain a phenomenalist analysis of propositions about physical objects. For the principal motive for such an analysis is the belief that any other analysis would make most of our ordinary propositions of every-day life false or groundless. But this does not mean that our argument presupposes the rejection of the phenomenalist analysis, but only that if our argument were accepted it would destroy the main reason which (as I think, wrongly) leads people to adopt the mode of analysis in question.

the acceptance of such an analysis only that generalisations about our experience are not ordinarily in fact deduced from generalisations about physical objects in the realist sense of the term, since on that view the propositions in question are not interpreted realistically. It would not follow that they cannot be thus deduced. Indeed, any phenomenalist would surely agree that from propositions about physical objects in the realist sense there *could* be deduced the ordinary generalisations about our experience which he admits,[1] whether the latter have been accepted in fact by people because they were deduced from the former or not. Now if a number of propositions known in fact to be true could all have been deduced from other propositions much fewer in number this constitutes a verification of the latter propositions, unless alternative propositions from which the former set of propositions likewise are deducible can be suggested, and the verification is logically quite independent of whether the deduction has been in fact made by anybody before.

The phenomenalist cannot claim that his hypothesis 'explains' the facts as well as the realist hypothesis does so that it is only a choice between two hypotheses from both of which the known facts can be deduced. For his is not a hypothesis about the causes of our experiences at all but a refusal to account for these experiences. Realists and phenomenalists have the same hypotheses about the general course of experience; realists only add a further hypothesis as to unsensed causes which they think renders our experience more coherent and is verified by the results, while the phenomenalist attitude simply consists in refusing to add this further hypothesis to the hypotheses about experience. Phenomenalism is not an alternative causal explanation of the facts concerning our experience, it is a mere statement of the facts without any such explanation at all. The phenomenalist is not in the position of the scientist who, when e.g. many eclipses have been successfully predicted on the basis of one theory, suggests another which can claim to account for these equally, but of the

---

[1] This does not presuppose his admitting that the former propositions are true. We can see what could be deduced from a false proposition if it were true just as well as what could be deduced from a true one, though I should hold that according to the laws of inverse probability it is very unlikely that the propositions about independent physical objects could be all false and the generalisations deducible from them all true.

scientist, if such a person could be called a scientist, who would not allow any attempt to explain the eclipses causally and refused to admit that it was any argument in favour of any hypothesis that thousands of predictions based on it had been fulfilled.

A complication is introduced by the fact that the probability of a hypothesis does not depend merely on the probability of the facts deducible from it being what they are if the hypothesis were false, but also in some sense on its own antecedent probability. But, while the notion of antecedent probability is a very difficult one, it should surely be clear to anybody that, where the probability of certain events having occurred as if a hypothesis were true without its being true is as one in many millions, it is only reasonable to accept the hypothesis unless either (a) we see it to be logically impossible, or (b) it indisputably contradicts facts as observed and the probability of these having been observed correctly is overwhelmingly great, or (c) owing to a conflict with well-established laws of nature or other well-authenticated hypotheses it is extremely improbable itself. The second and third points obviously cannot be raised against the general hypothesis that some independent physical things exist, and the argument that the existence of these things is logically impossible is discussed elsewhere and rejected by us.[1] Only in accepting any hypothesis we should

[1] If the notion of antecedent probability is admitted as applicable at all, we must grant that the realist hypothesis has a considerable finite antecedent probability. For (1) it is useless to object that for all we know the existence of independent physical objects may be impossible, for the antecedent probability must mean the probability relatively to *our* previous data, and therefore the chance that they might be objectively impossible cannot prevent their having a finite probability unless we have already overwhelming reason to think that they are impossible, which we have not. (2) If it is objected that we cannot allow any antecedent finite probability to the hypothesis because there are always an infinite number of logically possible alternatives, this argument would apply in all cases of scientific hypotheses and preclude us from ever accepting any hypothesis whatever. Further, if the external causes of our sensa had a structure different from what we attribute to physical objects and this structure causally explained our experience equally well, it would have to be at least very like the structure we ordinarily ascribe to such objects, so that our hypothesis would be at least very near the truth, otherwise it would not work so well. (3) But, when we consider the antecedent probability of realism, there are in the last resort really only two alternatives. Either (a) the extended entities we admittedly perceive all cease to exist as we cease to perceive them and nothing like them ever exists unperceived, or (b) some of these entities or some like

add the qualifying words 'or something very like this' to allow for possible amendment, compatible with the facts by which it is verified being still deducible from it in its amended form. This reservation the realist must admit : he must not be dogmatic that the primary qualities of physical things are exactly like those of sensa qualitatively, only at the most that they are sufficiently like to be still called spatial, round, etc., in the same sense or in approximately the same sense as that in which these terms are applied to sensa.

It may be objected that a philosophical theory such as realism cannot be of the nature of a scientific hypothesis and that my argument treats it as such a hypothesis. Without making any dogmatic assumptions as to what sort of arguments can or cannot fall within philosophy, my answer would be that the hypothesis that there are physical objects in the realist sense differs from a scientific hypothesis in that it is a generalised account to which all scientific hypotheses about

them exist unperceived by human beings ; and surely we have no right whatever to assign such a high probability to the first alternative that the probability of the second is reduced to infinitesimal proportions unless positive evidence can be brought against the second. (In the absence of evidence based on illusion, etc., which must not be taken into account in determining antecedent probability, the presumption of probability is definitely against and not in favour of the view that our immediate objects of perception always cease to exist when we cease to sense them, i.e. when another process ceases on which we have no ground yet for asserting them to be dependent. For the arguments I have used against a direct theory of perception are irrelevant here, because we are only considering *antecedent* probability. Further, though I as a result of these arguments hold a representative theory to be more probable than any direct theory, pure or mixed, a direct theory is still clearly less improbable than the view that the predictions made on the basis of the belief in independent physical objects were fulfilled without there being any such objects.)

It may be objected that I have still not established the absolute antecedent probability of the realist hypothesis, since I can say nothing about its probability without making certain presuppositions and therefore the probability always is relative to those. But, if this objection is justified, it will only show that 'absolute antecedent probability' is meaningless or at least does not stand for a notion which we could apply to anything, since we must always make some presuppositions, if only that more than one alternative is logically possible or that the probability of a proposition and its contradictory both being true is zero. But in that case the fact that we could not assign any finite absolute antecedent probability to the realist hypothesis will constitute no special objection to that hypothesis any more than to any other proposition. On this topic v. my article in the Proc. of the Arist. Soc. Supp. Vol. 1945.

physical objects will conform. There is no reason to dispute the place of such an account within philosophy, especially when it is so important for our general philosophical view of the world.

But now we come to certain points which weaken, though they do not destroy, the strength of the case for realism. The argument I have given will only establish with such a great degree of probability as has been indicated not the existence of physical objects possessing spatial characteristics in the sense-given sense, i.e. the sense in which sensa possess them, but at the most the existence of a three-dimensional manifold (or a four-dimensional one including time or rather the set of relations corresponding to temporal relations), for the occurrences said to verify the hypothesis of physical objects are deducible not from the sensory spatial character we commonly ascribe to the latter but from their relational *structure*. That is, experience does verify the hypothesis that there is a set of relations connecting the external [1] causes of our perceptions with each other which is parallel to (i.e. stands in a one-to-one correspondence with) the spatial relations we usually ascribe to physical objects,[2] but not the hypothesis that these unperceived causes are connected by relations which are really spatial or at all like what we perceive when we see e.g. one thing to the left of another. We might perhaps amend our definition of physical objects so as to cover such a view, but if we do so we cannot say in the strict sense that they are spatial or in Space.

It does seem to me, however, a more likely view that the external causes of our perceptions have at least spatial characteristics ('primary qualities') in the sense-given sense. In holding this I am influenced by the following reasons which, though not conclusive, have a very considerable weight :

(a) We must regard the causes of our sensa as in time, and further as in the same time as our sensa, otherwise they could not be regarded as their causes in any sense useful or significant for science ; and if we do not apply causality, we cannot establish the existence of the entities about which we are talking through verification by their effects and the whole argument

---

[1] 'External' is here used not in a spatial sense, but in the sense of 'other than ourselves and our sensa'.

[2] In so far as we have not in particular cases made any mistake according to the established principles of science in so ascribing them.

collapses.[1] Besides, we are in time ourselves, and therefore presumably our bodies are, but if so physical objects in general must be. If, however, they are in time, it seems the most probable view that they are also in space, though I admit that this does not necessarily follow.

(*b*) We may use an argument from analogy. If our previous argument has established with very great probability the view that there are relations between the external causes of our perceptions such that in structure these correspond to physical objects regarded as spatial, it follows by analogy that there is a very considerable probability of their resembling also in their other characteristics these objects as viewed by us. The structure of a relational system must depend on the nature of the relations and qualities of the objects in the system, and it is thus possible to argue from likeness in the former to likeness in the latter.[2]

(*c*) We shall conclude in the next section that the most reasonable view to take of physical things is that they consist of entities the same in kind as those we experience immediately; and in that case there would seem to be some ground for holding that they are spatial in the sense-given sense, or at least have very similar characteristics.

(*d*) If physical objects are not spatial in the sense-given sense but only have relations corresponding to the spatial relations usually attributed to them, we must suppose either that, when we assert a proposition such as 'this book is beside that', we simply *mean* that two unknown somethings are connected by some quite unknown relation corresponding to the sensed relation of 'beside', or that all such judgments are false. But both alternatives seem to me very unreasonable.

It may be retorted that we should analyse our assertions

[1] It may be objected that the fact, if it is a fact, that the assumption that physical objects are in time is necessary to our argument does not prove the truth of this assumption; but if the assumption that they are in time is a necessary part of the hypothesis from which the predictions are deduced, as I think it is, it follows that it is like the rest of the hypothesis verified by the success of the predictions and thus has its probability established.

[2] There are no empirical examples of real sameness of structure combined with radical difference in relations. A map, e.g., is not really similar in structure to the country which it represents, since it is two-dimensional. It is only similar in a certain respect, and it can be similar in that respect only because its parts are linked by spatial relations of distance, etc., which are also held to be really present, though on a larger scale, in the country itself.

about physical objects as being not that it is true that they have spatial characteristics in the sense-given sense, but only that this or something like this is true.[1] Now it would be possible in this way to save the truthfulness of our ordinary propositions about physical objects if they have characteristics very like spatial characteristics, but not if they have only totally unknown characteristics which correspond to spatial characteristics without being at all like them. But, if we say that they have characteristics which are very like spatial characteristics, we are at once saying something very important about their own character and not merely that they correspond to spatial objects. (The statement is indeed vague, but then no realist would claim that we can give their characteristics exactly.)

(e) If the independent causes of our perception are not at least spatial, space and all spatial characteristics are created by ourselves in the act of perception, and this seems at any rate a less likely alternative and one not at all in accordance with the modestly empiricist outlook of those who oppose the assertion of independent spatial objects. It is usually held that we cannot create new characteristics but only combine those which are already given, but unless there really are spatial objects independent of us all the characteristics we perceive are created by us. The circumstance that the creation would be unconscious, not conscious, only makes it all the more miraculous. Surely the best of all reasons why anything should appear in space is that it itself is in space.[2]

(f) Finally we may support our argument by an appeal to the intuitive conviction we have, so strong that we cannot possibly doubt it at the actual time of perception, to the effect that, though we may not perceive them altogether accurately, we are in some way aware in perception of real spatial objects independent of ourselves. I am not claiming that our intuitive beliefs ought to be accepted exactly as they stand just because they are intuitive; but I do contend that this one has a very strong claim to consideration, as has the belief in memory, and that, where there is no evidence against it, we are justified in accepting this mode of cognition as veridical under favourable conditions, as we are justified even without external evidence in accepting a similar view about memory. But the case for this, already pressed above, has now been made much

[1] My exact position regarding this is stated on p. 306.
[2] Laird, *A Study in Realism*, p. 43.

stronger still by the fact that my argument has shown the intuitive conviction to be verified by results in those respects in which we can test it. Where conditions are favourable and there are no specific discoverable causes making for illusion, we find that the predictions based on our belief in independent spatial objects such as we seem to perceive are fulfilled so frequently as to rule out of court as most monstrously improbable the supposition of mere coincidence. Now, though this is logically compatible with the independent object we postulate having only the same relational structure and not the same relations and qualities as we seem to perceive under favourable conditions, the fact that our non-inferential cognition has led us aright thus far surely justifies us in thinking it reasonable to trust it in those respects in which it has not been thus verified, so far as to hold at least that it probably sometimes gives us approximately correct information not only as to relational structure but as to the actual character of physical relations, i.e. in believing on the strength of it that the independent things which affect us in perception are literally in space, literally have shape, literally move and are sometimes literally related to each other in the way we usually think in respect of size, position, distance, etc. It is after all the same indivisible act of perception which seems to inform us both of the ' structure ' and of the actual spatial relations of a physical thing.

At least the arguments which I have specified as (c), (e) and (f) also support the view that not only the primary spatial characteristics but also other sensible ' secondary ' qualities perceived by us such as colour should be ascribed to physical objects, though I should attribute considerably less probability to the supposition that external objects possess such qualities than to the supposition that they possess primary qualities like those we perceive, while still thinking it distinctly more probable than not.

If it were held that any spatial object presupposed a single absolute space or even only a single spatial order, i.e. that everything spatial presupposed the whole of space and that there could not be two or more spaces, propositions which have often been held to be necessary *a priori*, the probability that the external causes of our sensa are spatial would be greatly strengthened, for admittedly our sensa themselves are spatial and those *a priori* propositions would then give us a universal objective space common to all percipients; but there are difficulties about locating all our spatial sensa and images in physical space,[1] and I am not sure that the propositions in question are necessarily true *a priori*.

Further there is one anti-realist hypothesis just as reconcilable with this argument as a realist view. For whatever follows e.g. from the characteristic of roundness in a physical object would follow equally well from the fact, if it were a fact, that some being capable of purpose willed that our experience should proceed *as if* there were a round object existing independently of us although there were no such object, and therefore no argument such as the one we have used could rule out or lessen the probability of the Berkeleian view that our 'perceptions' (sensa) of physical objects are all purposively caused by some non-human mind,[2] though it would make extremely improbable any idealist or phenomenalist view which did not involve such an assumption. Nor do I see any way in which such a hypothesis could be definitely disproved. The notion of a God has been frequently subjected to philosophical criticism, but even those who reject the traditional omnipotent or creative God would admit that it is not possible to bring arguments which disprove the existence of non-human minds; and if so we cannot rule out as impossible the view that these exist and produce our sensa directly. The view *seems* to me false, and I attribute this seeming to a partially valid non-inferential cognition of physical objects, but I may be mistaken in so doing. It is worth while, however, pointing out in this connection that it is likewise impossible to disprove the hypothesis that I am the only person in existence excepting one other non-human mind, and that that mind directly causes those perceptions in me which I regard as caused by other human beings without there really existing any other such beings. I do not see how such a view could be refuted,[3] but I am surely right in rejecting it as unreasonable, and

[1] Though it is on the other hand also difficult to suppose that there are millions of different spaces, one, or rather several, for each observer.
[2] Or minds.
[3] Any argument for the existence of other human minds from analogy, or from successful verification by consequences, or from the apparent presence of a purpose not my own in a great deal of my experience, e.g. the hearing of words which convey an intelligible meaning, would be still compatible with all the sensa which suggest to me the presence of other human minds being the result of a direct purposive act by some single mind such as Descartes' demon or Berkeley's God.

would it not be inconsistent without special reason to admit the tenability of the assumption in regard to physical objects without also admitting it in regard to other human beings? But it might be true in the one case and not in the other for all that. However, even if we did adopt it in the case of physical objects, it would, as has often been pointed out, not make as much difference as one might expect, since the non-human being would then in producing sensa in us still be acting as if there were physical objects and would therefore presumably have a set of 'ideas' of such objects, which would again give a physical world independent of us in a somewhat different form.

Mr. Price has brought the following objections against views which base the existence of physical objects on a causal argument.[1] (*a*) We do not in fact reach the belief in physical objects by causal inference, and if we reach it by some process other than causal inference we cannot merely relegate that process to Psychology as irrelevant for our purpose, since we have no right to assume that it is completely non-rational and exclude the possibility that it may be in some measure its own justification.[2] (*b*) We are more sure of the existence of the physical world than of the truth of the proposition that every event has a cause. (*c*) We can only apply the causal argument at all by presupposing solid objects external to us, and with that 'the whole complex notion of material thinghood, in which causality is a factor, not just the notion of cause alone'. With these criticisms I substantially agree, though I should hold a different view from the author as to what is implied in the existence of physical objects. It should be noted that the process of verification which I have outlined depends indeed on some notion of causality but not on the truth of the proposition that every event has a cause. I have only contended here that when we work out a hypothesis ascribing our sensa to certain causes we have results which make the hypothesis probable, an argument which does not presuppose that they are completely determined by causes in cases where the existence of their causes has not been verified in this fashion, at least unless it be the case that all induction presupposes universal causality. Nor do I contend that the argument is merely causal. Some factors in the verification such as the fact that our sensa can be arranged in series of varying shapes and

[1] *Perception*, pp. 99–102.   [2] Id., p. 90.

sizes all converging on that shape which we ordinarily describe as 'the real shape' of the object are not causal arguments but depend rather on geometrical relations. Again the conception of a physical object presupposes the category of substance in some sense as well as that of cause. But, if this and 'the whole complex notion of material thinghood' is assumed, that notion is verified with the rest by its results. 'Causal' may be too narrow a heading under which to bring the argument. If we require a more general term, I can think of no heading less objectionable than 'coherence'.[1] The postulate of physical objects may be said to be verified by its success in bringing our experience into a coherent system, and this together with our original non-inferential conviction provides some justification for our belief in physical objects. Each by itself would be sufficient to make the truth of the belief much more probable than not, but when they are combined its probability is proportionately increased.

There remains, however, another very strong argument for the truth of the belief in independent physical objects. It is that the awareness of the self presupposes awareness[2] of a not-self, that we can be conscious of ourselves only in opposition to something other than ourselves. It is not sufficient to say that we are conscious of our sensa; for these are not independent of ourselves but only last as long as we perceive them, and we are conscious of a relatively permanent independent background. If we take away the notion of entities external to and independent[3] of it with which it

[1] For physical objects the test of truth is 'the coherence of perceptual data with each other in a system' (Stout, *Mind and Matter*, p. 256). 'So far as what seems to be physical fact in each of several perceptions is a condition or consequence of what seems to be physical fact in the others, each, being founded in its own immediate sense-experience, and so far relatively independent of the others, supports and is supported by them. This is what is meant by saying they cohere. Such coherence is the warrant for our ordinary confidence in the testimony of our senses, which is really confidence in thoroughly verified hypothesis. Procedure by way of hypothesis and verification is thus in principle common to the most rudimentary and to the most advanced stages of our knowledge of the physical world. On the other hand the incoherence of this or that perceptual appearance with its relevant context is the only positive reason we can have for regarding it as illusory' (id., p. 260).

[2] I mean by 'awareness' here direct awareness in the third sense of the term (p. 268), except that I do not attribute to it certainty.

[3] I mean by 'independent' capable of existing apart from, not causally unaffected by.

deals, the whole notion of the self as we know it collapses and must be pronounced illusory. It is not sufficient to say that we are conscious of other human minds and not of independent physical objects, for we are only conscious of the former through their bodies, so that some physical objects at least must exist other than sensed sensa, namely, the bodies of human beings. We must therefore have at least a general consciousness of something independent of us if we are to be conscious even of ourselves, and unless the latter consciousness is an illusion, the former cannot be so either since the two are bound up together. This argument disproves not only other forms of phenomenalism but also Berkeleianism.[1]

Further, such a general consciousness of an independent objective world cannot be separated from the consciousness of some particular physical object or other. We cannot, except at a very advanced stage of knowledge, be conscious of a universal except as realised in particular instances; but the consciousness of which we are speaking was present from a very early stage indeed, long before we were capable of thinking of universals in such complete abstraction. So it seems only possible to hold that we are really aware of an independent physical world if we have a real awareness of some of the independent physical objects in which we believe, and do not merely think we are aware of them, and such awareness is clearly not awareness of a mere x. To be aware of a particular thing is to be aware of at least some of its characteristics in some degree correctly, though perhaps only partially and confusedly. In particular we could hardly after admitting this refuse to accept as genuine and non-illusory such a fundamental factor in our experience as the awareness of independent objective space and to suppose that in some cases our awareness gives us correct information about some real qualities or relations of physical things, to be discriminated from cases of illusion by what I have called the coherence test. (Awareness of space in general cannot occur without awareness of particular spatial objects, any more than, as I have just contended, can the general awareness of a world independent of us.) The argument thus justifies both the belief that there is a physical world in the realist sense and the belief that we have partially valid non-infer-

[1] In the sense explained on p. 340, in which it was not refuted by the previous argument, not in the sense explained in the next chapter in which it is compatible with realism.

ential cognitions of such a world. The cognition must be non-inferential if it is presupposed in our consciousness of ourselves, which is certainly not an inference ; and, being presupposed in the consciousness of our self, it must be partially valid unless the latter is altogether illusory. The non-inferential cognition of physical objects is therefore in a better position than most 'intuitions' which fall short of certainty. For not only are we irresistibly convinced that it gives us some truth when we perceive objects so that even a philosopher can hardly really doubt it, but we find that its claim to be a genuine cognition and not merely a delusion is established by two separate lines of argument. For we have now shown both that it is verified by consequences in those respects in which it can be tested, so far as to establish with extremely high probability its veridical character, and also that our consciousness of our own selves presupposes that we have a real non-inferential cognition of physical things. Surely we are therefore justified in trusting it as a partially valid source of information, while supplementing it by the coherence test, and remembering that to say we cognise physical objects directly is not to say that we perceive them directly in the same sense as we perceive sensa directly and is not incompatible with the occurrence of much illusion.

We may now consider the specific objections of the phenomenalists and subjective idealists to the belief in independent physical objects.[1] They are mostly negative in character, i.e. they could only show at the most not that the existence of such objects is impossible but that we have no right to assert it.[2] As such they are at once refuted if the contention that this assertion can be justified by argument or non-inferential cognition or both combined is correct. Most, though not all, might be classified under the general heading of arguments from illusion.

Now such arguments are themselves commonly based on evidence provided by physical science and on our everyday information about physical objects, and consequently the retort has been made in several quarters [3] that phenomenalists who use such arguments are guilty of a gross inconsistency,

[1] In a non-phenomenalist sense.
[2] Other arguments which seek to prove their actual impossibility are dealt with elsewhere in this book.
[3] E.g. Kemp Smith, *Prolegomena to an Idealist Theory of Knowledge*, p. 41 ff.; Broad, *Perception, Physics and Reality*, pp. 165-6.

for in order to obtain the premises for their arguments they must first be realists, since otherwise they will have no right to assume the facts about physical objects and the physiology of the sense-organs on which the arguments are based and will not be able to refute even the direct theory of perception. How can we know, e.g., ' that the flat sense-datum is not part of the surface of the cricket-ball, unless we know that there really is a cricket-ball and that it really does have a surface which is spherical ? Or how do we know that the reflection of the glove is dislocated as to position and reversed as to right and left, unless we know where the glove itself is and how its parts are arranged ' ? [1] The thinkers in question are ' constantly talking of physical media, of mirrors, lenses and prisms, of drugs and physical diseases, and especially of sense-organs, nerves and brains ',[2] thus presupposing a great variety of knowledge as to the physical world, which world they then on the ground of this very knowledge proceed to deny.

This objection is valid as a criticism of the way in which the contention is usually stated, but, as at least Mr. Price realises, it might easily be restated in such a way as to escape it altogether. For it is generally recognised that we may quite legitimately assume a view we believe to be false for the purpose of effecting a *reductio ad absurdum*. Nobody would say that Euclid was guilty of inconsistency because in order to prove a theorem he assumed its contradictory and then showed that impossible consequences followed. Similarly, it is a strong objection against, though not a conclusive disproof of, a theory if it can be shown that the assumption of it would lead to consequences which are highly improbable though not demonstrably impossible, or that even if it were true there could be no possible ground for believing it; but in order to show this it is necessary to treat the theory you are trying to refute as a premiss to deduce these consequences which will serve as its own refutation. There is nothing illegitimate about this procedure, which is one of the most common in argument. The phenomenalist might therefore reply that he does not assume that his premisses about mirrors, etc., are true but only that they would follow from the realist view, so that the argument runs—*if* realism is true it leads to consequences which are incompatible with itself or at least make it extremely unreasonable to

[1] Price, *Perception*, p. 34.   [2] Id., p. 36.

accept realism, therefore realism ought not to be accepted as true.

The following are the main objections for discussion :

1.—No causal inference can establish the belief in physical objects, for (*a*) a cause need not be and in our experience often is not in the least like its effect ; (*b*) in this case it cannot possibly be like the effect, if the realist view be true, for the cause would be physical and the effect non-physical ; (*c*) the physical object which we are said to perceive is admittedly far from being the whole cause of our perception, and we have clearly no right in any case to single out a particular part of the cause of our perception and say that it is like what we perceive. Further, there is no proof that our perceptions are not caused by something in ourselves or in the common mind of humanity.

Reply.—An inference using causality, though not completely and merely causal, can, as we have shown, provide some justification for the belief. The argument does not depend on the mere ungrounded assumption that the cause must be like the effect, but on the fact that the belief in physical objects provides a way and, as far as we can see, the only way [1] of causally accounting for our experience and making a coherent system of it, and is verified by results. The belief in physical objects cannot be justified to a sceptic who refuses to accept the principles on which all inductive science depends, but if we accept these principles we must give our preference to the hypothesis that there are independent physical objects. The same type of method can be used to determine the particular shape and size of objects, and its applications, while forcing us to differentiate between the physical objects which ultimately cause our perceptions and the media through which they act on our sense-organs, at the same time tell us some of the characteristics possessed by either.

But we must agree with the objector so far as to admit that we can ascribe to physical objects no properties which are not definable in terms of properties of sensa, and therefore that in these respects physical objects resemble sensa. More of this anon.

2. *Objection.*—The realist must admit that what we perceive depends not on the external physical object but very largely

[1] With the exception of Berkeley's hypothesis, which is intrinsically much less likely and would, further, itself involve independent physical objects as ' ideas ' in God's mind if carried out logically.

on our sense-organs. He must further admit that, if a sense-organ is stimulated in other ways, e.g. electrically, perceptions will arise in the absence of any physical objects of the kind of which they seem to be perceptions. Hence he cannot argue that the physical objects we suppose we perceive are necessary to account for our perceptions, since according to the realist himself such perceptions may occur without these objects being present.

Reply.—The fact that our perceptions (perceivings) depend partly on our sense-organs is quite compatible even with the selective theory, according to which our sense-organs and nervous system simply fulfil the rôle of instruments by means of which we can perceive what is there all the time independent of them and us. This selective theory can only be rejected on the ground that the adoption of the coherence test leads us to the conclusion that it is unlikely in many particular cases that the objects perceived by us exist thus independently as perceived, but the same kind of test will also lead us to the conclusion that it is reasonable to suppose that in many other cases there is a physical object having similar primary qualities to those perceived by us. The fact that in some cases perceptions can occur without being caused by objects that resemble our percepts is no proof that they could occur without any physical causes, for the very same reasons which lead us here to deny the existence of corresponding physical objects, namely, that this is the alternative which enables us on the whole to give the most coherent causal account of our experience, lead us in other cases to admit the existence of physical objects such as those we seem to perceive. The fact that we can explain our experience causally best by treating it as illusory in some cases cannot possibly prove that we have no right to assert in other cases, where we can explain it best by treating it as veridical, that it is veridical in fact. In both cases explanation can be effected by means of physical causes. In cases of illusion a causal explanation, as satisfactory as we can have a right to expect, is generally available if and only if we grant the existence of physical objects. The realist can thus explain causally both veridical perception and illusion, the phenomenalist can explain neither the one nor the other.

3. *Objection.*—If Berkeley's hypothesis were true or if life were 'one long dream' our experience might still be just what it is. A god such as Berkeley postulates could make

us perceive what we do in fact perceive without any physical object being there, and any experience that we have in waking life may occur in a dream.

Reply.—Even if the realist had to admit that it was impossible to disprove Berkeley's hypothesis, this would not prove that the hypothesis was true. But, if it is a fact, as I have argued, that we have non-inferential cognition of physical objects, Berkeley's hypothesis is false in any form in which it is inconsistent with that.[1] Also in any case the hypothesis that there are physical objects with at least spatial properties existing independently of being perceived by us seems much more likely to be true. Finally, as I have said earlier, even if Berkeley's theory were right, it could hardly be carried out consistently without positing something like a set of independent physical objects as 'ideas in God's mind', since God would have to be aware of such objects in order to govern our life as if they existed independently of us. As for the suggestion that our life might be a dream, implying that the physical objects we think we perceive might not exist independently of us any more than the objects of a dream, the answer is that such a supposition leaves our experience without any assignable cause, while if we posit physical objects we can do quite as much as could reasonably be expected in the way of causally explaining even dreams and hallucinations.

4. *Objection.*—Since our perceptions are inconsistent with each other, it is not possible to decide what particular properties any physical object possesses. In our ordinary life we assume that physical objects have the shape which we perceive when we are near them and directly facing them, but this is obviously arbitrary and useful only for practical needs. Why should this particular perception be correct if all others mislead us? We cannot trust our senses as regards this shape if we cannot trust them as regards any of the others. Again we assume in ordinary life that physical objects are as we see them with the naked eye, in some branches of science that they are as we see them with the microscope and in others as postulated by the atomic theory. Yet all these appearances are flagrantly inconsistent with each other. It is easy here to multiply examples.

---

[1] I point out later a form of the view, at least suggested by Berkeley, which is quite compatible with a realistic view of physical objects (v. ch. VIII, sect. 1). The other, phenomenalist form I claim to have refuted on pp. 342-3.

Reply.—Even if it be often or mostly very difficult to decide what particular properties a physical object possesses, this can be no argument against the assumption of physical objects, any more than the fact that it is very difficult to come to any conclusive decision about the exact facts concerning a certain empire of ancient history proves that we have no right to assume the existence of such an empire at all. In view of our imperfect knowledge it is inevitable that in any branch of study there will be great difficulty in deciding what the facts are and that in some cases owing to the lack of data we shall be unable to decide at all. It is not as if this were the case with all the supposed facts about material objects, far from it. There is no great difficulty *usually*, for instance, in determining the relative position of two physical objects not very far distant or the order in which two events occurred in time. Two observers may have conflicting perceptions of shape and size, but they (at least if on the same planet) almost invariably agree in perceptions as to time sequence [1] and relative position. Again tactual data almost always agree with each other, and the extent to which visual data disagree has been greatly exaggerated. It is not the case, as is often assumed, that two observers in different positions and at different distances from an object will always see the object as perceptibly different in shape or size. This will, on the contrary, only occur if the difference in position and distance is considerable.

Further, the argument assumes that there is no reason within our experience to distinguish what we usually regard as the real shape of an object from its apparent shapes. This, however, is clearly false. For (1) this shape agrees with the tactual shape while the others do not.[2] (2) It is reasonable to assume that we see an object most accurately where its visual appearance is sensibly clearest and the amount of detail perceived greatest, but as we approximate to this point what we see approximates to the shape usually distinguished as real. (3) This shape can, unlike any of the

---

[1] The much emphasised cases where it is not so constitute only a small minority of our perceptions.
[2] Even though there are illusions of touch as well as of sight, a strong reason for ascribing one shape to a physical object rather than another, granted that we ascribe shape at all, is provided by the fact that the two senses confirm each other.

others, be regarded as the terminus of each of a number of converging series of apparent shapes as we approach it from different sides. It is highly significant that, when Mr. Bertrand Russell tried to construct a theory of the physical world which treated as independently real most of the seen shapes that we usually regard as merely apparent, he was forced to give a very important and quite special position in his theory to what we usually call the real shape, not indeed as an actual existent but as the ideal limit of the series of apparent shapes. (4) All causal laws about the physical object can be successfully formulated in terms of this shape but not in terms of any of the others unless these are in turn defined in terms of what we usually call the real shape, at least as their ideal limit; the object acts as if it had this shape. (5) Granted that it really has this shape we can explain the illusory shapes in terms of laws of perspective. In general, we are justified in accepting one particular shape as the real shape and rejecting the others as apparent because this is the way in which we can best render our experience coherent and causally explain the facts.

Finally, even if we could find no reason to distinguish between the different shapes, it might still be possible to hold that, although physical objects were really shaped, shape did not inhere simply in the object which it qualified but was always relative to an outside point of view, so that it was not legitimate to ask what shape a physical object had *simpliciter* but only what shape it had from a certain point of view, as it is meaningless to ask whether an object is to the left or to the right of another except from a given point of view, or perhaps what its motion is except relatively to other objects. Such a view would be quite compatible with realism as to the physical world. It need not make shape relative to the organism, let alone the mind, of a percipient, but only to some point in space outside the object whose shape we are giving. We must remember, as is pointed out *ad nauseam* in *The New Realism*, that not only perceiving minds but also photographic plates give different views of the shape of the same object from different places. Whether a view like this is to be accepted in preference to a more orthodox view of shape must be decided by asking, firstly, whether we can attach a self-consistent meaning to the view in question, and, if so, secondly, which view gives the more coherent causal explanation of our experience; but these will be questions within realism, and, whichever answer we give, it will not justify phenomenalism or subjective idealism.

The objection based on the discrepancy between an object as seen by the naked eye and the same object as seen by a strong microscope or described in the atomic theory of physics is perhaps more difficult to meet, but I think it may quite reasonably be held that the defects of our ordinary vision here are simply negative, i.e. they consist only in failing to reveal all phenomena which cover less than a certain extension. I see my table as a continuous motionless [1] solid, while scientists say it is not continuous but consists of a set of tiny bits of very dense matter moving very rapidly and separated by relatively enormous gaps of empty space, but this does not contradict any of the characteristics observed through our immediate data of sense. For we admittedly cannot see very small differences, and as far as that is concerned our eyes may still give us faithfully all the differences which exceed the *minimum* we can see. Naturally we can only expect to derive directly from our naked eyes information as to what exceeds, say, a hundredth of an inch; and it is still a fact that, as we should expect from our visual perceptions, no parts of the table more than a hundredth of an inch in area are in motion relatively to the rest of the table [2] and also that there is no empty gap of more than a hundredth of an inch between different molecules composing the table. If we proceed in our ordinary non-scientific moods to assume that because we do not see such gaps or motions they are not present, we cannot blame our perceptions for that.

We may explain similarly the well-known difficulties about colour. What appears as red all over to the naked eye may appear as mainly yellow with only small patches of red when viewed by means of a microscope, but the two perceptions do not really contradict each other, for we cannot in any case claim to see the colour of all the parts of the object with the naked eye but only the colour of some. This is correctly seen as red, but we are not therefore justified in inferring that all parts of the surface are red.

Even apart from these considerations, however, I am very doubtful whether the argument from the atomic theory against the reliability of perception is legitimate at the present stage

[1] I.e. without internal motion and also motionless relative to the floor.
[2] Except again perhaps in an infinitesimal degree.

of science, for physicists now usually seem to have given up the view that atoms, etc., can be represented in perceptual terms at all, and if so I do not see how one could reasonably claim that the atomic theory was inconsistent with our perceptions. It is only if we do what physicists now generally will not allow and claim to make a sort of potentially visual picture of atoms and electrons as little hard balls rotating, etc., in an empty or relatively empty space, that we can even suppose that the theory clashes with our perceptions. It cannot clash with them if atoms and electrons are entities which from the nature of the case cannot be visualised. Finally, even if there were a clash we should still have the coherence test to help us to decide how far we ought to accept either account in preference to the other.

As for definitely abnormal perceptions in a waking state, they can in almost every case be ascribed quite simply to specific causes which account for the illusion; and though no level-headed psychologist or physiologist could claim that we knew the causes of all dreams, causal explanation of dreams has been carried on with very marked success and there is no reason to suppose that explanation in terms of physiological causes, memory of past events, association, suppressed desires, etc., is not always possible on principle. At least there is no ground for supposing that we should be helped in the causal explanation of dreams by positing the physical existence of the objects perceived therein more or less as we perceive them, but this supposition often does help us in the causal explanation of waking experiences, and this is sufficient to differentiate the two.

We can, in short, usually determine the right shape and size of physical objects by what I have called the coherence test. This in almost all cases where we can observe objects fairly closely and clearly provides a perfectly adequate means of picking out one from all the apparent shapes and sizes.

5. *Objection.*—If we ascribe any qualities given by sense to physical objects at all, we cannot ' draw the line ' anywhere without inconsistency, and yet we cannot ascribe them all, for otherwise we should have to say that e.g. when we are cut the pain is in the knife. If we ascribe primary but not secondary qualities, we are confronted with the difficulty that we cannot perceive or imagine the one without the other.

Reply.—We may admit that physical objects must have besides primary qualities some other qualities which are literally extended, but they need not be the secondary qualities with which we are familiar. They may be qualities of a type quite unknown to us. The fact that we can never perceive or imagine visual shape without colour is, except on the direct theory of perception, no proof that these qualities exist together in the physical world, though I think that it is a circumstance which justifies us in ascribing a greater probability to the hypothesis that physical objects are coloured than we should otherwise [1]; and the fact that we can and can only explain causally the perception of primary and even of secondary qualities by postulating primary qualities in physical objects but do not need for a causal explanation to postulate also secondary qualities in these objects provides a reason for the belief in the external reality of shape, etc., which is not also a reason for the belief in the external reality of secondary qualities. I am personally, however, disposed to regard the physical external reality of secondary qualities as more probable than not. In general I must repeat that the fact that it is difficult to determine precisely what qualities belong to material objects is no valid argument against the belief in these objects, and that we must decide between different qualities by the use of what I have called the coherence test. If we obtain a more coherent account of our experience by denying the physical reality of a particular quality and by affirming the physical reality of another quality, this will provide an adequate reason for the distinction between the two qualities, and apart from this coherence test we have no reason to deny the physical reality of any sensible qualities.[2]

6. *Objection*.—All possible propositions about physical objects, whether asserted in ordinary life or in expounding a scientific theory, may be translated without loss of meaning in terms of experience.

Reply.—That I and other human beings would under certain conditions perceive an object as e.g. having a shape is a different proposition from the proposition that it has the shape whether perceived or not. To say that there is some-

[1] I should hold a similar view about the fact that we can never perceive tactual shape without some other sensible quality, usually described as softness or hardness.
[2] Except in those cases, if any, where we can see *a priori* that the quality cannot belong to physical objects as such but is inseparable from our mental state. I think we see this in the case of pain.

thing, S, which has a quality p during the whole of a given period of time is not the same as to say that during this period there *sometimes* (under specified conditions) is something S (a sensum) which has this quality (i.e. when perceived), or that there would be something which had it under conditions which conceivably might be but are not in fact realised. Some people say that the first statement when applied to unperceived physical objects is meaningless, but it seems to me that I can see a perfectly good meaning in it and one palpably different from that asserted in the other two propositions. It is true that we can only describe physical objects in terms of our experience if by this is meant that all the ultimate data by means of which we determine their characteristics must be immediately experienced, but it does not follow that all propositions about physical objects must be reduced to propositions about what we do, or under given conditions should, experience. For, even if we can only ascribe to physical objects characteristics which have been *at some time* given in experience or combinations of these characteristics, it does not follow that we can only rightfully or meaningfully assert that they actually possess these characteristics *when* experienced.

It may no doubt be held that, while both sets of statements are distinct and meaningful, only those about our experience, not those about unperceived physical objects, can be shown to be true; but to this contention the whole discussion of this section has been an attempt to reply. The subjective idealist or phenomenalist usually indeed proceeds to meet the situation by saying that propositions about unperceived objects can be translated in terms not indeed of actual but of possible experiences; but if so they cannot serve to explain our experiences causally, because a mere possibility cannot be a cause. The convenient word, possible, covers a multitude of sins. Finally, I must insist that it is absolutely incumbent on phenomenalists not merely to say in general terms that propositions about physical objects are all to be interpreted phenomenalistically in terms of the experience or sensa of an actual or possible observer, but to show how the process is to be carried out in detail, and to do so without presupposing any propositions about independent physical objects or about the sense-organs of percipients except such as can be themselves thus analysed phenomenalistically without remainder. This more difficult task they have usually shirked, I fear, yet its difficulties must be faced if their view is even to be seriously considered. I, however, do not in my opposition to them lay the main stress on such difficulties but on the objections brought earlier in this chapter.

§ III. The Nature of Physical Objects[*]

Granted that there are independent physical objects, what more, if anything, can we say about their nature? It will be most helpful to start by considering in what respects they differ from and in what respects they resemble the sensa and images immediately perceived by us. When we do this, we at once arrive at a conclusion of considerable significance. We find, on the one hand, that they differ radically from these in their causal properties; but, on the other hand, we are unable to ascribe to them a single positive characteristic, other than logical and causal properties,[1] which is not also either itself present in or at least entirely definable in terms of characteristics present in some of our sensa and images. So much is a commonplace of philosophical argument. Those who suppose that physical objects have none of the sensible qualities given in perception are unable to form any idea at all of what their qualities are except in so far as they are conceived as being analogous to, if not identical with, these sensible properties; and in that case they are still defined in terms of the latter if we say that they are analogous to them, for we are admittedly unable to say anything about their quality *in so far as* it is different. Physical objects very probably have a great many types of characteristics which are not present in any of our sensa, and again it may be the case that we are justified in ascribing to physical objects only a small proportion of the types of characteristics given in our sensa, namely, the so-called primary qualities; but it is certainly the case that we cannot, with the reservations I have mentioned, ascribe to physical objects any characteristic not definable in terms of characteristics given in our sensa. Also the same characteristics may all be found not only in the sensa which occur in external perception but in the mental images which we consciously make ourselves in imagination.

Further, though physical objects may be the *ratio essendi*

[1] I include under these independence relatively to being perceived by us.

of the presence of these characteristics in our sensa, there is no doubt that our sensa are the *ratio cognoscendi* of physical objects. We can only attain any idea of the physical through sensa. For, if we have a non-inferential cognition of particular physical objects, it is certainly a cognition which depends absolutely on our sensa; if we cognise physical objects at all in perception, we only cognise them through our sensa by at the same time cognising our sensa. On the other hand, in so far as we establish what characteristics physical objects possess by argument, again the argument depends on their coherence in a causal system with our sensa, and cannot any more than any causal argument [1] give us characteristics different in kind from those immediately experienced by us, i.e., here, characteristics of sensa. Finally we throughout our ordinary perceptual experience treat our sensa as if they were parts of physical objects and can never except by inference distinguish them from these.

Now if we can and can only discern the nature of A s by observing B s and treating B s for this purpose as if they were A s, and if the only non-causal and non-formal characteristics we can ascribe to A s are characteristics of B s or definable entirely in terms of such characteristics, what should be the conclusion? That the A s, in so far as knowable by us at all, are generically the same as the B s, that their character is modelled on the B s.[2] But then can physical things possibly be sensa? Is that not utterly absurd? Is it not obvious that if they exist at all they must be different from such unsubstantial evanescent entities as these? Well, we must make one concession. I admit that we cannot identify a physical object with a sensum, but it does not follow that we cannot identify it with a *group* of sensa.

[1] The argument is, I admit, not wholly causal, but those elements in it which are not causal are subject to the same limitation. Thus, when we use the argument that our sensa can be arranged in a series of varying shapes and sizes all converging on that shape which we ordinarily describe as 'the real shape' of the object, if we suppose that the last member of the series, i.e. what possesses 'the real physical shape', is something quite different from a sensum, we break the continuity on which the argument depends. (3rd ed.) But v. below p. 446.

[2] If anybody should object that a photograph need not be the same kind of thing as that of which it is a photograph, it is easy to show that the case is not analogous to that of sensa. For we derive information about physical objects from other sources than from photographs of them and therefore can supplement the knowledge we derive from photographs.

This brings me to the theory as to the nature of physical objects which I should put forward as the one that seems most reasonable to me; it may be expressed least inadequately in a few words by saying that they are *groups of unsensed sensa*. This theory disagrees both with the theories prevalent among idealists, who deny any physical objects that can exist when not thought or experienced, and with those usually prevalent among realists, who, if they admit sensa at all, commonly insist on a total difference of kind between physical objects and sensa,[1] and it may seem to realists to have the defects of idealism and to idealists to have the defects of realism; but I would ask those who think it preposterous kindly to wait till I have explained it more fully. I doubt whether, when understood properly, it is even paradoxical, or at least more so than any other proposed philosophical theory of physical objects.

Now, in the first place, I grant that if 'sensa' is used in its strict etymological meaning the statement I have made becomes self-contradictory. But what I mean is that physical objects, as far as known by us, consist of entities which, as far as we can tell, are not themselves sensed immediately by any percipients but are exactly the same in kind as the objects that we do immediately sense in perception. I am realist enough to hold that the fact that one set of sensa are perceived and the other unperceived makes no essential difference between them. They are combined in physical objects in a different way from the way in which they are combined in a percipient's sense-field and they conform to different causal laws; but apart from this I see no reason to assert that they are in any way different, though the wholes which they help to form, i.e. physical objects, may have some properties different from those of any of their parts and different from those possessed by any sensa or groups of sensa immediately perceived by human beings. Certainly they differ greatly from the latter in respect of their power of persistence. The type of view to which I am objecting is the view which sees in physical objects a mysterious order of being quite different from anything given to us in immediate sense-experience. There may be such an order of being, but I do not see any reason to assert its

[1] The theories of Mr. Bertrand Russell and some 'New Realists' constitute an exception. The differences between my theory and theirs are stated below (p. 360).

reality; and if it is real we can know nothing about it, for we can only arrive at legitimate conclusions about physical objects on the basis of sensa.

Secondly, I do not mean to suggest that physical objects may not include in their being all sorts of characteristics such as we never sense or immediately perceive. But this does not imply the presence in physical objects of anything more than different species of sensa. There is no reason, I insist, to suppose a mysterious third kind of being, matter, distinct from the only two kinds of being we immediately experience, sensa and minds, though material objects may well include an enormous variety of sensa beyond anything that we can possibly imagine. There may be and probably are included in them a great number of sensa quite different in quality from any sensed by us, and if so we may still be said to know very little about the nature of material objects; but that is no reason for introducing into the conception of material objects a third type of being generically different from sensa, or for denying that material objects also include sensa almost or exactly like those actually sensed by us. They *may* indeed include besides sensa something else generically different from sensa, but there can be no evidence that they do, and if we suppose the existence of that something the conception of it must be completely empty and useless, indeed it would be more correct to say that it is not a conception at all, for we have nothing to conceive. We can only arrive at a conception of material objects by combining sensa known by us. We must add that they may also include all sorts of sensa unlike those sensed by us, but to postulate a matter in opposition to and distinction from sensa is to assert we know not what for no reason whatever.

Thirdly, I do not mean to cover by the term sensum only that element in our immediate object of sense-perception, whatever it is, which can be ascribed to sensation in the sense in which this is usually contrasted with perception, but everything which we experience immediately in perceiving.[1] I admit that 'pure sensation' is an abstraction which in our ordinary experiences does not occur by itself, and the use of the term sensum is not meant to exclude the possibility that the sensum may be partly due to the work of

[1] And all parts of this which could imaginably be sensed without the other parts. I should call any such part of a sensum itself a sensum.

thought or to commit me to any 'sensationalistic' theory of knowledge or perception.

Fourthly, since I have accepted a representative theory of perception, I hold that the sensa composing physical objects are probably never themselves sensed.[1] What we immediately perceive on my view are sensa grouped differently and numerically different from any sensa in physical objects. But in some cases, those of veridical perception, I suggest, they are qualitatively the same or almost the same as some sensa in these physical things and therefore capable of serving as a counterpart to represent them. But there are sensa, those we call illusory, which have no counterpart in physical objects; and there are in all probability countless sensa composing physical objects counterparts of which never have been and never will be sensed by any human being, nor perhaps by any percipient whatever.

Fifthly, while I should hold that any physical objects whose existence we have a right to assert are groups of sensa, I should not dream of converting the proposition. Mere combination of sensa in any sort of group is not sufficient to constitute a physical object. The last red patch that I sensed yesterday, the sound of the first stroke of Big Ben this year and the taste of the first mincepie ever eaten constitute a group of sensa, but they do not constitute a physical object. And the same would hold if we took all unsensed round shapes. There is clearly some special relation, whether analysable or unanalysable, over and above mere group membership, which constitutes a physical object by relating sensa. I have therefore not given and do not claim to give a *definition* of physical objects in terms of sensa. In order to do that I should have to determine what the further relation is which distinguishes physical objects from other groups of sensa, and it would take me too far afield to investigate this subject.

A theory propounded by Mr. Bertrand Russell in *Our Knowledge of the External World* [2] and some 'New Realists' might be described in terms similar to those used by me. I do not wish to try here to give a detailed criticism of the theory, from which I hope I have derived much profit, since the points of difference between our theories fall largely outside the scope of this book; but it is necessary to mention

[1] At least by human beings.
[2] It must not necessarily be taken as representing Mr. Russell's present views.

what the principal differences are. (*a*) I am not committed to the view that a physical object is a set of all its 'appearances' or that all the sensa anybody senses in perceiving a physical object can be regarded as parts of that object, even if we exclude the extremer forms of illusion. I should be much more inclined to make a distinction and take the view that, e.g., only a round shape and none of the elliptical shapes perceived by us from different positions belong to a penny,[1] except in the less strict sense of 'belonging to' according to which all sensa representing a physical object to percipients might be said to belong to the object.[2] In that case none of the other sensa giving what we consider more or less distorted shapes would have either any existence apart from observers or any exact counterpart in the physical object. Whether this view or one more like the type of view adopted by Mr. Bertrand Russell and some 'New Realists' is correct can only be settled by asking which makes our experience more coherent. (*b*) I am therefore not obliged to accept Mr. Russell's heterodox view of space. (*c*) I do not hold that any of the sensa which we actually sense, even the ones presenting what is commonly held to be the real shape, are independent of us, only that some of them represent 'sensa' similar to themselves in character which are thus independent. In this respect I certainly disagree with the New Realists, but I am not clear whether this view was meant to be accepted or rejected by Mr. Russell. But which view we are to take on all these points is an issue that must be decided by detailed considerations within realism itself. (*d*) I do not mean to suggest that minds also can be reduced to groups of sensa. My metaphysic, in so far as I have one, is dualistic in that it recognises two kinds of entities, minds and sensa, the difference between which is, for us at least, irreducible.

This then is where I stand. The principal reason for my view of physical objects is that if they did not consist of sensa it is impossible to see how we could establish their existence at all. For we can only apprehend them in so far as we apprehend sensa which we in our perception treat *as if* they were parts of them; we can only describe them in terms of characteristics of sensa; we can only determine their position or characteristics either by taking 'on faith'

---

[1] For the reasons for this distinction, v. above, pp. 349–50.
[2] V. Price, *Perception*, pp. 213 ff., 303 ff.

our sensa as giving characteristics belonging to them, or by a mainly causal argument which may justify us in postulating other sensa as causes, but cannot, any more than any other causal argument, justify a transition to a quite different kind of being from any present in the experience on which the causal argument was based and from any experienceable object by which a hypothesis about physical objects can alone be verified.[1] If the existence of physical objects can be maintained at all, then it would seem to follow that they must consist of sensa. Every argument for the existence of a particular material object is really an argument for the existence of a particular independent group of sensa. And I do not see how there can be any possibility of refuting the theory, at least from the realist side, because to do that we should have to establish the existence or characteristics of some physical objects otherwise than by means of the data of our immediate experience which I have called sensa. My view is confirmed for me by the fact that I can find no reason for ascribing any characteristics to material objects which differentiate them generically from groups of sensa. And without some strong positive reason we have simply no right to go beyond the two classes of existent entity which alone we know by acquaintance or immediately experience, minds and sensa, and assert something else which we are not immediately acquainted with and whose nature is totally mysterious to us, matter. Either matter is reducible to sensa or we can know nothing about it and, though it may for all we know exist, it cannot be discussed owing to a total lack of data.

The antipathy that many people will feel to a view which identifies material objects with groups of sensa is due partly to a wrong conception of sensa, i.e. of what it is that we immediately experience. Philosophers and psychologists have often spoken as though nothing were immediately given but a set of fragmentary data falling far short of a complete appearance, unless put together by an act of mind or combined with past memories through a subsequent process of association. This may be true in some important sense, but, if we mean by object of immediate perception what I am actually consciously aware of when I open my eyes and look about, it misrepresents the truth gravely. What I am imme-

[1] But v. p. 446.

diately aware of is certainly not these fragmentary data as they are usually conceived and studied in the psychological laboratory, it is a continuous whole including a fairly complex system of relations within itself as well as terms and a considerable number of perfectly clear distinctions. Such are the entities with which we are immediately acquainted and which we must take as our primary data. I do not mean that all the distinctions and relations are analysed out by us and classified from the beginning, but that we are immediately acquainted with entities which contain them and that we can classify them by subsequent acts of judgment based simply on this primary acquaintance. What is given to me as I look down now in writing is a white plane with the hundreds of grouped black marks that we call letters, it is not merely a set of separate sense-data of black and white. The experience of perception does not consist mainly in combining sensa given separately into wholes but rather in analysing out the chief elements in a given whole. The sensa we perceive immediately are not themselves parts of physical objects, I admit, but they must be at least sufficiently near to them in their appearance to serve as passable imitations. They have at any rate deceived everybody for millennia into taking for granted that they were parts of the physical objects themselves, till people were undeceived by philosophers. If we are to go back, as befits philosophers, to our primary empirical data, we must be true, not sham, empiricists and take our immediate experience as it really is, not as, on the strength of our tacitly assumed philosophical theories, we suppose it ought to be. It is quite irrelevant to point out that what I experience now is very different from what I should have experienced if I were looking at things of the same kind for the first time or if I were a new-born baby. This does not alter the fact that I immediately experience certain objects now, and that therefore these objects exist as experienced, at least as appearances. For we cannot go behind or against the evidence of immediate experience. It is irrelevant how the immediate experience comes about: it is a fact now and its existence proves the existence of its object as I experience it. A history of the development of sense-perception may be very interesting and very important, but it cannot contradict and can indeed in the last resort only be based on the evidence of immediate experience.

Now what is it that we experience immediately when we

use our eyes? It is not a set of universals or mere qualities, but a *particular* existent or existents. It is certainly not a set of unrelated terms; therefore relations, even *if* they be ultimately due to mind, are immediately given as elements in our experience,[1] however they came there. It is not reducible to a set of discrete data of sensation, such as are examined in the psychological laboratory in abstraction from their background, though the study of such abstractions may perhaps be of the greatest value in tracing the historical development of our sense-perceptions. It is not usually a mere two-dimensional plane, even if it be the case, as many psychologists and philosophers have contended, that the sensational elements in this immediate experience can only supply two dimensions, and that therefore originally we could only sense two dimensions [2]; it is on the contrary almost always three-dimensional. Visual sensa are (except for the case of generally admitted illusions, hallucinations and dreams) quite good likenesses of what common sense usually takes physical objects to be, in so far as physical objects can be represented by vision. If our immediate objects of experience had been as different from the common-sense conception of physical objects as many accounts suggest, how could we explain the fact that most people never distinguish them except in obvious cases of illusion and take it for granted that they are immediately sensing physical objects? However, we do not need this argument: all I appeal to is the testimony of immediate experience.

The mistakes I am criticising are no doubt largely due to a confusion between various senses of 'immediately given'. This phrase is sometimes used to mean 'given by sense', in which case it stands (except on certain untenable views) not for our whole immediate experience but only for that element which can be accounted for directly as the result of impressions due to external objects affecting our sense-organs at the time. But we must take as primary the whole of the data of which we are sensibly aware, and these are not limited to what can be directly accounted for in this way. How they are to be accounted for causally is a very interesting question of psychology but is irrelevant here. Needless to say, I do not mean that everything of which we are immediately aware can be assumed to exist externally just as it

[1] Not, of course, as existing apart from their terms.
[2] Not that I believe these statements to be true.

stands, but that its existence must be assumed at least as an immediate object of experience. This is the reason why I have preferred the term sensa to sense-data, because the latter has been commonly used to stand only for what is supposed to be given by present sensation apart from the work of thought, so that the identification of all immediate objects of perception with 'sense-data' would suggest a purely sensationalist view of perception.[1] If we mean to cover by 'sensum' the whole object of our immediate experience when we perceive, it follows that we must regard it as dependent on psychological causes as well as on physical. Sensa are dependent causally on our mind and not merely on our body for their existence.[2]

A difficulty arises as to how much we are to include in the immediate object of awareness. If I perceive a cupboard, I am in some important sense immediately aware of it as a cupboard, i.e. as something with an inside as well as a front, though I do not see the inside, and as something which could be used to store things, etc., but it is obvious that these characteristics at any rate do not really belong to my sensa of the cupboard. But what I meant by my sensa (my immediate object of sense-perception) was what I am immediately sensorily aware of in perceiving, and I am not thus immediately aware of sensa of the interior of the cupboard.[3] Nor can I be said to be aware of the fact that it will be or could be used for a certain purpose in the sense in which I can be said to be immediately aware of present sensa. The right account of the matter is that I *assume* or *take for granted* that it has an interior and can be used as a cupboard. These assumptions may be ascribed to habit, association or rapid inference. That the account given of this is correct is indicated by the fact that nobody would hold that, apart from an inference based on previous experience of such objects and capable of statement as an inductive argument, my perception afforded any evidence at all that the object had an interior or could be used for storing, while everybody in his ordinary daily life and apart from

---

[1] No doubt if 'sensa' were understood strictly in its etymological sense it would be equally open to the objection, but I am deliberately using the term in a sense other than its etymological one, and, as it happens, it is less definitely associated by its past usage with sensationalism.

[2] V. above, p. 287.   [3] I may or may not have *images* of it.

the influence of philosophical scepticism would hold that it provided at least some, perhaps conclusive, evidence for the physical existence of the front of the cupboard itself.

Some people think that sensa cannot be separated from the act of sensing [1]; if so the logical consequence seems to me to be either idealism or the agnostic doctrine of the thing-in-itself. If sensa be mental physical things must be so, for our whole conception of the latter is derived from sensa. If we refuse to use our sensa to determine the characteristics of the external causes of our perceptions, we have no longer physical objects but things-in-themselves about which we know nothing except that they have certain effects on our experience; if we use sensa for this purpose, we cannot say that the characteristics, which in sensa are (according to this view) logically inseparable from acts of perceiving, in material objects are quite separable. We must either deny the existence of material objects in the ordinary sense and maintain that all that science can study is abstracted elements in human experience, or, if we still accept the belief in physical objects independent of us, postulate a superhuman mind, such as Berkeley's God, by which they are experienced. This follows, I say, if we accept the view that sensa are inseparable from an act of sensing, but there does not seem to me to be any adequate reason for holding that they really are inseparable, any more than for holding the analogous view in regard to physical objects. The only sensa we perceive immediately are, I think, directly dependent on some human mind, (though equally, we must add, dependent on physical objects as external causes and on our own body, if realism is accepted,) but it does not follow that all sensa are, unless there is some logical connection between sensa and acts of sensing by which the presence of the former entails the presence of the latter, and this alleged logical connection I cannot detect. No doubt if we define sensa as the objects of immediate experience this verbally entails that they are experienced, but it does not exclude the possibility of objects exactly like them in all or most other respects existing without being experienced at all. Our view is a compromise between idealism and realism: to put it simply, the idealist

---

[1] An example of this view would be the suggested doctrine that it would be a better description of the state of affairs in sense-perception to say, e.g., that we see roundly and redly than that we see a round, red sensum.

is right in holding that we cannot 'get beyond' sensa, wrong in holding that we cannot 'get beyond' experiences; the realist is right in holding that physical objects can exist independently of being perceived, but wrong if he concludes that therefore they must be something quite different from sensa.

If we adopt the view that physical objects are groups of sensa, it seems best first to try the hypothesis which accords most with our usual distinctions in ordinary life between illusion and correct perception, and when tried it seems to me that this hypothesis makes the world more coherent than any other. It may be expressed approximately by saying that we only regard as included in an independent physical object one spatially synthesizable set of sensa and dismiss the remainder apparently perceived by us as illusory, which sensa we include being determined in general by the coherence test and in particular by such circumstances as I have mentioned above.[1] The hypothesis involves a refusal to admit either that two different sensa of the same sense can occupy the same space, or that a physical thing can have more than one shape at the same time. Physical objects are assumed just in order to correlate and unify sensed sensa, and this purpose will only be served effectively by groups of spatially synthesizable sensa. Our hypothesis necessitates the admission that there is an element of illusion in many or most of our perceptions, but on the representative theory this presents no special difficulty. A physical object on our view does not then include all the sensa we perceive when looking at it from all angles and distances.

On our view the sensa forming parts of a physical object will be related in at least two quite different ways. (1) The different spatial parts of, say, a visual sensum forming part of such an object will be interrelated spatially, and likewise with the parts of any extended sensum even of a kind totally unknown to us. (2) Two sensa of different kinds, e.g. a visual and a tactual sensum, which occupy the same space will be related to each other in a different way. It is the presence of this second relation which differentiates those groups of sensa that form one physical object from any other group of sensa.

We must now turn our attention to an examination of the differences between physical objects and our sensa. That there are differences I do not deny, but I think that they may best be explained as differences between two different

[1] V. pp. 349-50.

kinds of groups [1] of sensa. In the first place physical objects can exist unsensed.[2] Secondly, physical objects *persist*, while our sensed sensa are extremely transitory. Thirdly, physical objects and our sensed sensa act according to different causal laws. Fourthly, physical objects are ' perceptible ' by more than one observer at a time, our sensa are (as far as we know) not public in this sense. Fifthly, the same physical object is conceived as capable of having properties belonging to different senses, the same sensum is not. Sixthly, physical objects are ' substances ' while sensa are not. Seventhly, physical objects have not merely a surface but an ' inside '. ' Solidity ' is also popularly regarded as a distinguishing-mark of physical objects as opposed to sensa, but this, in so far as it is applicable to physical objects at all, is either (*a*) identical with the seventh point of difference just mentioned, or (*b*) definable in terms of laws [3] excluding any other bodies from the space occupied by a physical thing, or (*c*) reducible to sensory qualities such as felt hardness, which certainly do not characterise all physical things, if any at all, and are also present in sensa. There are also a great many characteristics which belong to sensa and in regard to which it is at any rate doubtful whether they belong to any physical things, but this does not alter the fact that in so far as we can obtain information about physical objects it is obtained through sensa, though we may not be able to ascribe to them all the characteristics present in sensa.

Let us return then to the other differences. The first, that physical objects can exist unsensed and our sensa cannot, we may grant ; it cannot possibly constitute any essential difference between the two on a realist view. It seems to be connected with the fact that the sensa we perceive are all causally dependent on our body and our mind. There is nothing intrinsically impossible, so far as we can see, in someone perceiving immediately a sensum which is not causally dependent on him, but it seems that the world is so consti-

[1] The sensa we immediately perceive are grouped in specific ways as well as the sensa which make up physical objects. The most important groups they form are those commonly known as sense-fields.
[2] At least by human beings.
[3] In this sense ' solidity ' seems to refer both to certain causal laws governing the resistance of physical objects, or at least their component atoms, to impact, and to the principle that two physical objects cannot occupy the same space, which is commonly held to be logically necessary and self-evident.

tuted that in fact we cannot do so. I think, however, that it would be much wiser to substitute ' unsensed ' for ' unperceived ', the word usually used in this connection. For, since I may well have sensa to which I do not attend and therefore cannot be said to perceive,[1] even some of my own sensa may exist unperceived though not unsensed.

Secondly, the superior persistence of the sensa constituting physical objects may be granted, but mere duration can make no essential difference as far as I can see. I must add that, while sensa are notoriously very short-lived, I see no reason why a sensum should be regarded as merely momentary, unless we start by defining it as momentary. Certainly anything which we can perceive and so identify as a sensum has temporal parts each of which could conceivably have existed by itself. Further, motion within our sense-field is given in immediate experience, and this seems to imply that the sensum which moves in some very important sense continues to be the same sensum while it moves. The notion of the persistent character of physical objects as contrasted with sensa is connected with the notion that they are substances.

Thirdly, material objects certainly follow different causal laws from sensa. It has been asserted that a sensum cannot be a cause at all,[2] but with this I am quite unable to agree. It is true that a sensum cannot be the whole cause of any event, but then it is in the highest degree doubtful, or rather quite impossible, that even anything which could reasonably be called a single physical object is ever the whole cause of any event, and I should have thought it was quite clear that a sensum could be a part-cause of an event.[3] E.g.

---

[1] While I might sense, i.e. feel, something without attending to what I felt, ' perception ' connotes at least attention to it and some notice of its character. E.g., while my mind is occupied with something else, I may have many sensa of surrounding objects and of my body which I do not notice and which therefore, though my sensa, exist unperceived by me.

[2] Price, *Perception*, p. 146; Berkeley (*Principles*, 25) makes the same assertion about ' ideas '.

[3] It may be objected that causality holds between characteristics and so not between sensa, but then, since a physical thing is not a characteristic, the same objection would apply against anyone who ever described a physical thing as a cause or part-cause. Even if causality is primarily a relation between characteristics, there is clearly a secondary sense of causality in which it relates objects possessing the characteristics in question, and it is in this sense that I should apply it to sensa.

if I see a piece of ice, my visual sensum of the ice may be part-cause of my thinking of something cold, or if I hear or think of a word the sensum of that word will be part-cause of whatever is called up by the process which used to be described as association of ideas, and which is undoubtedly a real process, however much it may have been misconceived in the past.[1] But it is certainly the case that the causal laws governing sensa perceived by us are altogether different from any causal laws which, as far as we know, govern physical objects. This suggests an argument against our view. For it may be urged that two things cannot act causally in a different way from each other without being different intrinsically. But the difference in the laws, we can reply, may be due equally well not to differences in the sensa but to differences in the way in which they are grouped. A causal law perhaps always only holds within a given causal system and is dependent on that system. Moreover, the peculiar causal laws according to which the sensa immediately perceived by us act as compared with the sensa in the physical world may be due to the fact that the former are linked with a percipient and are absolutely dependent throughout on the mind and body of this percipient.[2] As combined in a different way independent of percipients they may well act quite differently, and it may be admitted that the peculiar combination of sensa which constitutes a physical object gives them a relative independence, persistence and causal efficacy that they would not otherwise have. Besides, there may be a great variety of sensa in physical objects qualitatively very unlike any that we directly perceive, though we cannot say what they are, and association with these may make a great difference to the causal laws governing also those sensa in physical objects which are like the ones we immediately perceive.

Fourthly, physical objects are held to be perceptible by more than one observer at a time, while the sensa perceived by us are private. This is the usual way of stating the dis-

[1] It is true, as Mr. Price points out, that the relation between a sensum and the awareness of it is not that of causality, but we cannot infer from this that the causal relation in 'association of ideas' merely holds between awarenesses. For it is not the awareness of a visual sensum of ice apart from the visual sensum which forms part of the cause of my thinking of something cold, but the awareness together with the sensum.

[2] E.g. the so-called 'laws of association' seem to depend entirely on this circumstance.

tinction, but a holder of the representative theory will in any case have to modify his language. For, if the representative theory is true, no physical objects can be perceived at all in the sense in which our sensa are perceived, even by one observer. So the difference between them here is rather that physical objects and sensa are only perceived in two different senses of the term, and that in the one sense the same object can and in the other cannot be perceived by two different observers. But again this obviously does not constitute a difference in the intrinsic character of the sensa composing a physical object. It is either a causal or, as we might say, an epistemological property, i.e. the property of being cognisable in one way and not in another.[1]

Fifthly, the same physical object may have properties belonging to different senses, the same sensum cannot. This simply means on my view that a physical object includes in itself sensa of different senses, i.e. it is a difference due to the contrast between a group of sensa and an individual sensum. Other groups of sensa closely united by a specific relation, e.g. all the sensa sensed at the same time by a single percipient, may also belong to different senses. Only they will still not constitute physical objects, because the specific relation which constitutes a physical object is not present.

Sixthly, physical objects are considered to be substances, while it is not usual to regard sensa as substances. The conception of substance is, however, very far from clear. According to one definition, it is that which can have qualities but does not itself qualify anything. On this definition sensa themselves must be substances. According to another view, it is that which is absolutely independent of anything else. In that case nothing short of the whole universe can be a substance. And I do not know how to find anything like a satisfactory account in between the two extremes. The principal reasons why sensa are not held to be substances seem to be these: (*a*) they do not persist, or rather only persist for a very short time; (*b*) they seem to be literally created out of nothing; (*c*) even while they exist they

---

[1] On my view it will be (*a*) *logically* impossible for any physical object as a whole to be perceived immediately in the sense in which a sensum can be, because it is a group of sensa of different senses; (*b*) *causally* impossible, as far as we know, for at least human beings to perceive immediately a sensum which constitutes part of a physical object, though we can see no logical impossibility in it.

seem to be completely dependent for their existence all the time on something else, namely, the body and mind of the percipient whose sensa they are. But most philosophers would, I think, now hesitate very much before affirming that it was logically self-evident or provable *a priori* that, because material objects are substances, the quantity of matter in the world must always remain the same and can neither increase nor diminish, and that if the soul is a substance it follows logically for that reason that it must be immortal. Hence the question seems to become merely one of the degree of persistence and independence. I do not maintain that it is satisfactory to regard the difference in respect of substantiality between sensa and physical objects as one merely of degree, but it puzzles me very much to see what other difference there is. I cannot regard sensa either as qualities of the percipient's mind or brain, or as events, for a red patch is not an event; but we must, I think, recognise that the old dichotomy of everything into substances and qualities, and even the trichotomy into substances,[1] qualities and relations, is not necessarily exhaustive, but may leave outside real entities which cannot be regarded as falling under either heading. We might call sensa *quasi-substances*, as possessing some of the features of substances and not others. But in any case it remains quite possible that, though they are not substances themselves, certain kinds of groups of them are substances. The idea that substances may be composed entirely of entities which are not substances may arouse protests, but I do not see anything absurd in it. It would be wrong to regard substances as ever reducible to sets of qualities, as e.g. McTaggart shows very effectively,[2] but then sensa are not qualities and they agree with substances at least in the characteristic of having qualities without themselves being qualities. This is after all the only sense of substance in which it seems self-evident *a priori* that all qualities actually realised in existence presuppose a substance, or which has been at all well-established or clearly described. My theory is further quite compatible with physical objects as groups of sensa having a persistence and independence which is different not only in degree but in kind from any that could be credited to isolated sensa or to sensa grouped in a different way, e.g. as constituting sense-fields of a percipient.

[1] Or, as they are sometimes now called, continuants.
[2] *The Nature of Existence*, vol. I, bk. II, ch. 6.

Certainly, whatever *a priori* knowledge we may have concerning substance, it is not of a kind that could justify us in positing fresh entities other than those unsensed sensa which we find necessary to explain our experience.

Seventhly, while it is wrong to say that our sensa are merely two-dimensional—what we immediately perceive obviously has three dimensions [1]—physical objects are three-dimensional in a further sense which cannot be applied to our sensa, namely, they have a back and an inside. But they could still be conceived as groups of sensa,[2] though not of sensa which could conceivably be perceived simultaneously by us, if we think of the inside also as consisting of unsensed sensa. This is confirmed by the fact that if we cut or break an object open we normally still perceive sensa purporting to represent what was its inside but is now exposed, and have as good reason as in the case of its outside to assert the physical existence of characteristics corresponding to those of our sensa. It is therefore reasonable and not in the least absurd to suppose that all the time the interior of the object contained unsensed sensa like the sensa we perceive when we cut it open.

I do not think that the view of matter I have suggested can conflict with the atomic theory. For, since science ascribes none but spatial, causal and quantitative properties to atoms and electrons, it cannot possibly be inconsistent with the hypothesis that these are very small groups of sensa. What seems harder to reconcile with the view of physical objects derived from our ordinary sense-perception is the fact, if it is a fact, that what we usually call physical objects consist mainly of empty space, only dotted very sparsely with bits of matter of extreme smallness. In connection with this I must make the following suggestions and then leave it—it is far too complex a subject to be adequately discussed here, and I do not possess the scientific knowledge to make a discussion by me very profitable. (1) Though physicists have now commonly discarded the doctrine of an 'ether' which filled the space between the atoms, they seem to have only done this by treating space itself as if it were a kind of quasi-matter. (2) The fact that physical objects act causally as if the atomic theory were true, which constitutes the only evidence for the theory, need not necessarily be incompatible

---

[1] A surface that is not quite flat or slants is extended in three dimensions, and such surfaces are surely immediate objects of perception.

[2] I should call the parts of a sensum themselves sensa.

with other qualities (e.g. colours, or perhaps many qualities of a kind quite unknown to us) pervading also the space between the atoms and between the electrons within the atom. There can be no scientific evidence against this, for the physical scientist does not introduce qualities of matter other than the primary into his causal scheme at all, and therefore is not in a position to show by scientific arguments that any of those other qualities which may qualify material objects cannot pervade the whole space which appears to us as occupied by the object. When a scientist asserts the atomic theory, he may have really only proved that the agencies responsible for certain effects are concentrated not in the whole volume of physical objects but within certain very small portions of it. (3) At the present stage of science it would require a bold man to dogmatise as to how far the atomic theory is to be taken literally. If it consists, as most physicists now tell us, only of a set of mathematical equations to which the behaviour of physical objects conforms, or something of that kind, it is difficult to see why it should or how it could lead to the conclusion that the material objects we observe do really consist mostly of empty space. Perhaps this is simply a relic of the pictorial literal way of representing atoms which is now being discarded. A far greater variety of possibilities than is usually conceived may be open to us. (4) The suggestion of some physicists that the electron is not an object with definite boundaries but only the centre of a sphere of influence which may extend indefinitely makes in the same direction. If a view like this is taken, there is no reason to hold that the only pieces of real matter in the universe are as extraordinarily small as has been supposed and that there is nothing else but empty space. Electrons, etc., might on the contrary then be merely focal points in a continuous matter.

We are now in a position to say something more about the question of secondary qualities.[1] From the usual realist point of view when combined with a representative theory of perception, though their external physical existence cannot be disproved, there seems to be not the slightest evidence

[1] Under this heading I include all the sensible qualities perceived by us excepting shape, size, motion, spatial position, number, temporal position and duration, and any other characteristics of this spatial or temporal type. I do not mean by ' secondary quality ' a power in a physical object to produce e.g. the sensation of colour or of sound, as Locke does, but the actual seen colour or heard sound itself.

for it, since these qualities are not, like the primary qualities, needed to explain our experience causally, and accordingly the supposition that they belong to physical objects is dismissed as highly improbable, the *onus probandi* being naturally assumed to rest on those who would assert that they do so qualify them.[1] On our view, however, the position is radically altered. For (1) physical objects are regarded by us as consisting wholly of sensa, and sensa, at least as perceived by us, all possess secondary qualities, so that it seems to have become the more reasonable course to ascribe secondary qualities also to physical objects. It may be the case indeed that for special reasons we shall have to deny this status to some secondary qualities, but at least the *onus probandi* rests on the person who would contend that none of the secondary qualities have a physical existence and no longer on the person who thinks that some of them have. (2) We have admitted a partially valid non-inferential cognition of physical objects. But, as we look at them, we are quite as convinced, apart from philosophical doubts of which we do not usually think when engaged in perception, that they have a certain colour as that they have a certain shape, but, if we are justified in trusting our non-inferential cognition as under favourable conditions fairly accurate in the first case, why should we not be so in the second? If, as I have contended, our mere perception of an object does under favourable conditions constitute evidence for the view that it possesses the characteristics we perceive, this evidence supports the ascription to it of colour just as much as that of size and shape. When we are in what seems on other grounds [2] the most favourable position for observation the secondary qualities do not normally tend to disappear but rather increase in intensity, detail and clearness. Further, it seems to me the more probable hypothesis, other things being equal, that we perceive a secondary quality because it, or some-

---

[1] It is logically necessary that whatever possesses the 'primary qualities' must possess some quality other than these, but it does not follow necessarily that it possesses the secondary qualities we perceive. Those of its qualities which were not primary might all be quite different from any known to us.

[2] Such as proximity, maximum amount of detail perceived, evidence to the effect that the physical object acts causally as if it possessed the primary qualities perceived from that position, thus showing that perceptions from the position are correct in those respects in which they can be tested, etc.

thing very like it, is present in physical objects than that in perception we create quite new qualities. Surely the best of all reasons why anything should appear to the normal observer as coloured or noisy is because it really is coloured or noisy.

Of the secondary qualities colour has the strongest claim to physical reality, since all the main sensa out of which people who are not blind constitute physical objects are coloured. Similarly, however, I should argue that the secondary qualities given in touch are probably present in physical objects, so that something in them is soft or hard in a literal sense, either always or possibly only when affected by the impact of another body. Which colour, etc., we should assign to a physical object when there is a clash or apparent clash between different perceptions must be decided by the coherence test in so far as it can be decided at all. It is reasonable to suppose that we are likely to have the most accurate view of the colour of an object when we stand as near to it as possible short of that point where vision becomes confused owing to proximity. ' Illusions ' as to colour are not any more numerous and ' illusions ' as to secondary tactual qualities much less numerous than those relating to the primary qualities. But it does not necessarily follow that physical objects are coloured in the dark, for it may still be that colour is a property which physical objects only acquire when affected causally by the light, or possibly a property which they do not have *per se* but only in conjunction with light. Such a supposition would help to explain many alleged cases of illusion as to colour. We are not, however, debarred from admitting cases of actual illusion, since we have adopted a representative and not a direct theory. Thus I should explain e.g. our perception of mountains at a distance as blue as being an illusion. Again, we must remember that the fact that we perceive a particular physical object as having a given colour all over is still no ground for holding that its surface is really coloured all over in that way, since we cannot perceive all the microscopic parts of its surface. We cannot say on the strength of our perception that it is coloured in the way we perceive it to be, but only at the most that part of its surface is coloured in that way.[1]

[1] Not necessarily even the largest part, as observation under the microscope seems to show, since a part which is spatially much smaller may have a colour sufficiently vivid to overshadow that of the larger part.

Also, there still remains, I think, a sense in which even on my view one would be bound to say that secondary qualities did not and primary did qualify physical objects. For a physical object on this view consists of a group of sensa, and unless we make them all visual we cannot say that colour qualifies the whole group. It does not qualify e.g. the tactual sensa. Hence I do not say that secondary qualities qualify physical objects, but that they 'are present in' them, as qualities of some of the sensa which make them up. On the other hand, since the group as a whole occupies a certain space within certain boundaries and can move as a whole, we may say that it as a whole is qualified by the primary qualities and not only that parts of it are so qualified.

As regards the sensa of senses other than sight and touch, it still seems to me more consistent and reasonable to assume their physical reality unless in a given case there are cogent reasons against it. It seems difficult to suppose that the functions of different senses should be so different that with some we perceive a quality present in the physical world, while with others we just create a kind of quality that is never there at all; and in all cases we are intuitively convinced of the objective physical reality of what we perceive at the time of perceiving. With sound and smell, while the secondary qualities given are not perceived even as *seeming* to belong as qualities to the physical object which we say smells or causes the sounds, I can see no reason to deny the possibility that they may exist in physical space independent of us as qualities of physical entities emitted by the physical objects which cause them. Taste is a sense about which even the man in the street is sceptical. He would hesitate, I think, to say if challenged that sugar was sweet in the sense-given sense when nobody was tasting it, while he probably would not, except in so far as he was affected by a science which is certainly not 'common-sense', hesitate to make the corresponding assertion about sound and colour. Smell is perhaps intermediate in this respect between taste and sound. But I cannot see any logical absurdity even in asserting the physical reality of the qualities given in taste, and I do not see that the variability of taste as between different individuals and the same individual in different states provides any stronger argument against this than do the corresponding arguments against primary qualities, especially as the states where the taste is abnormal are generally states of disease, in which it is natural to expect that the sense-organs will not always function rightly. Of two people one might dislike and another like a taste that was objectively quite the same in quality; and, even if the same kind of food tastes different to different people, that is no reason why in some cases of taste we should not be perceiving a physical quality really present in the object tasted by us. It does, however, I admit, seem to me somewhat odd to suppose that something actually has a certain taste in the sense-given sense when nobody is tasting it, but I do not know why it should seem so. One possible theory of taste is that it is a quality which physical objects only acquire when impregnated with saliva and otherwise affected chemically on being placed in the mouth of somebody, but which still belongs to them objectively when and only when they are thus affected causally. There are also a number of sensory qualities given in the sensations of our own body which may, for anything I can tell, really belong to the latter, e.g. the peculiar qualities of strain present in muscular exertion.

The only felt sensory qualities which do seem to me inseparable from some mental state are sensory pleasure and pain, and this is, I think, because I see them to be qualities of our experiences on the subjective side and not of the objective sensum which we sense when we feel pain or pleasure. The sensum may be pleasant or painful in the sense of causing pleasure or pain, but the pleasure or pain felt cannot themselves qualify it since it is not a living being. But the fact that sensory pleasure and pain are inseparable from the feeling of them is to me no argument for the view that other sensory qualities are, since in their case I can see no logical connection between the sensory quality and the feeling of it. On the contrary, the insight that pleasure and pain cannot exist unfelt is essentially connected with the insight that they are radically different from other sensory qualities, and it is just their difference from these other qualities, and not their similarity, which drives me to classify them as mental or psychical. It seems to me probable, that in all cases of sensory pain or pleasure the person who feels it at the same time senses certain other qualities which (or rather their counterparts) [1] may well belong physically to his

[1] If we are to adopt the representative theory at all, as I have done, we should apply it to perceptions even of our own body.

body.[1] Some of these qualities are primary, such as the size and location of a wound; others of a less definite character and less easy to distinguish from the painfulness itself because of their tendency to blend with it as felt may still be physically real secondary qualities in the body, e.g. there may be some secondary quality present in toothache which belongs to the decayed tooth objectively and yet as felt blends inextricably with and helps to give its specific character to the pain.

Berkeley used an argument based on the psychical character of pain to show that heat also cannot exist unfelt.[2] For, he urged, an extreme degree of heat is felt as pain, but pain can only exist in the mind, therefore extreme heat cannot exist apart from a mind which feels it, from which it would seem reasonable to conclude that moderate heat cannot so exist either. I should be inclined to suggest in reply that the pain is a different sensation from the heat,[3] aroused when the latter becomes so great as actually to injure our tissues, and that our inability to distinguish the two may be due to pain being a sensation of such a character as either to inhibit the other sensation altogether or to prevent us

[1] It has often been pointed out that the term pain is ambiguous, covering both a specific kind of sensation which we call pain and 'unpleasure' in general, which is often due to causes other than physical pain. I should suggest that perhaps pain in the former sense is made up of (a) unpleasure, which cannot exist unfelt, (b) certain sensed qualities which may, for all we can tell, exist unfelt. The same name is commonly applied both to it and to unpleasure because these qualities always or almost always are unpleasant. They are not indeed the only sensory qualities which are unpleasant, (we do not speak of e.g. the taste of ammoniated quinine or the sight of disgusting refuse as a 'sensation of pain',) but they are specially associated with pain in the sense of unpleasure because that kind of sensory quality arouses pain more frequently than other kinds and often in a very high degree. (Even in cases such as that of masochism, where a person for some reason seems to enjoy physical pain, it may still involve an element of unpleasure in his mental state, though this is outweighed by other factors. If it does not, I should hesitate to admit that he can be correctly said to feel 'pain'.) The same ambiguity does not occur in the use of the word pleasure.

[2] *First Dialogue between Hylas and Philonous* (Everyman Edition, p. 204 ff.). For a reply to his and Locke's well-known argument about our two hands feeling the same water as respectively hot and cold v. Professor Broad, *Perception, Physics and Reality*, p. 10 ff.

[3] This is supported by the fact that the physiological sense-organs of 'pain' (here this term does not stand for unpleasure in general but for pain as a specific kind of sensation) are quite distinct from those of heat.

from being conscious of it separately, whether from psychological or physiological reasons or both. The engrossing, attention-compelling character of pain is well known, and may easily prevent us from noting or distinguishing other sensations dependent on sense-organs located very near those which give the pain-sensation. The blending of sensations from different sense-organs does occur elsewhere, e.g. in the case of eating, where something we usually describe as the 'taste' of our food is sometimes found to be analysable as a compound of both true tastes and smells.[1] I consequently can see no insuperable objection to regarding the sensory qualities of heat and cold as physically present in our body under various conditions and perhaps in other objects also.

I find no absurdity in ascribing even beauty to unperceived physical objects. Indeed, if colour and shape are physically real, it seems to me to follow necessarily that some physical objects are beautiful, whether or not they are perceived by any observer. I cannot conceive most or all the mountains I know as having the colours they seem to have and the shapes they seem to have and yet not being beautiful, any more than I can conceive an Euclidean triangle which had a side which was longer than the other two put together. They simply could not have the sensory qualities they seem to have without being beautiful. No doubt there are a great many difficulties in the way of accepting the physical objectivity of beauty, but the discussion of these falls within aesthetics and not within the scope of the present book. Since, however, the argument I have just used about beauty both seems to me valid and also has commonly been overlooked, I mention it and pass on. I do not mean to deny, however, that a good many of the elements which contribute to the aesthetic character of a landscape are subjective (cf. the gloomy grandeur of a dark ravine.)

But the decision as to which particular sensory qualities should be ascribed to physical objects is, at least when we have advanced beyond colour and tactual qualities, very

[1] The fact that it is caused partly by the sense-organs of taste and partly by those of smell does not prove this, but, if on careful introspection a type of sensed sensum A is found to consist of two distinguishable types of sensum B and C, it *may* under certain conditions be justifiable to assume that B and C were present before introspection in all cases of A but were not distinguished. (We may certainly have a sensation, and so a sensum, without expressly noticing that we have it, though we cannot have one without feeling it.)

speculative and one rather of detail than of general principle. It is not necessary to my theory to assert that all the kinds of qualities sensed by us exist in the physical world, any more than it is necessary to assert that each one exists physically as a quality of something external whenever we sense it. The theory, being representative, leaves ample room for illusions, and the fact that it is very difficult to decide in detail what the qualities belonging to physical objects are is not a sufficient reason for casting doubt on their existence. Particular questions of great difficulty arise in every branch of inquiry, and still more in the philosophy behind every branch of inquiry.

There follows from my theory one interesting and startling corollary. It has been commonly regarded, according to the point of view taken, as one of the most incomprehensible mysteries or as one of the most absurd superstitions of theology that it asserted the creation of matter *ex nihilo*,[1] but it seems quite clear in any case that something is created *ex nihilo* not or not only by a God but by mere human beings. So much must be admitted by any theory which allows any sensa or images at all that neither belong to the independent physical world nor are states of our mind. For our actually sensed sensa and images have been thus created; they come into being without ever having existed before and are not merely *changed* but brought into existence by causal action. The fact that images are new creations is obscured by the circumstance that there is a sense in which we can only form them by reproducing or combining what has been previously given in sense-experience. But the actual image itself is still created *ex nihilo*, for the identity with previous images is qualitative not numerical. If I make an image of a centaur by combining that of a man and that of a horse, which have both been given in previous experience, this does not mean that the actual images or sensa produced when I last saw a man and a horse respectively have persisted since then continuously and are now put together by me, as I might put together pre-existing bricks to make a physical wall. All it means is that I make a new image in certain respects like both of them. I must literally create the images of the man's head and the horse's body themselves anew and can-

[1] This does not mean the *uncaused* creation, but the creation otherwise than out of pre-existing material (according to the theologians it was *caused* by God).

not use numerically the same images as I had, say, an hour ago at or just after the time when I saw the objects on which they are modelled, for these images have ceased to exist altogether.[1] Similarly, even if the existence of sensa actually sensed by us is due partly to sensa like them existing as constituent parts of physical things, the actual sensa sensed themselves are still *created* through the interaction of ourselves with our environment and are not identical numerically with these pre-existing (unsensed) sensa external to us.

This much must be admitted in any case; but on my theory of matter it now follows that we have actual experience of the creation by mind not indeed of physical objects, but of entities of the same type as those which form the constituent parts of such objects. With sensed sensa themselves the creation may be attributed more to the influence of external objects and of our physical sense-organs than to that of our minds, but in the case of images we do seem able to produce such entities by a simple act of volition. For images are like sensa in all their qualities,[2] except for the fact that their mode of production is different, and so they must be put in the same class of being as these. This is almost the reverse of what is supposed by the cruder forms of 'naturalism', namely, that we have experience of the development of mind out of matter but not of the production of matter by mind. We must say on the contrary that we have no experience of the former, for to see an entity which showed no signs of the presence of mind at an earlier stage show such signs at a later is not to experience the process of development from matter to mind,[3] but that we have direct experience of the production by mind of members of the class of

[1] The same applies even where an image is an exact reproduction of a sensum which has gone before. Nor can we be saved from the admission of creation by saying that a sensum or image is always part of our whole sensory continuum, for a new sensum or image is still not literally made up of the identical earlier sensa nor only a quality of these sensa.

[2] Mere comparative lack of vividness cannot make any difference of principle. Besides, some images are more vivid than many sensa. The difference between a sensum as presented in immediate experience and an image lies, I think, in the fact that we are conscious of the one as forced on us and of the other as made by our own action.

[3] To do this we should have either to be conscious as matter ourselves at birth, then develop into minds and remember the experience afterwards, or to be immediately aware of the psychological process by which somebody else's mind developed out of matter.

entities of which the physical world is composed. This does not prove that mind could not be produced by matter, nor that mind does or could under any circumstances produce not only sensa such as compose physical objects but such complete physical objects *in toto*, nor would it, if on other grounds we accepted the belief that mind was dominant in reality, necessarily justify us in preferring the hypothesis of a creation *ex nihilo* in time to the hypothesis that matter was logically dependent on mind throughout time; but it remains a point that is well worth noting when we come to weigh against each other the relative probabilities of matter being dependent on mind or mind dependent on matter.

CHAPTER VIII

IDEALIST METAPHYSICS

§ I. Theistic Idealism

IT seems ridiculous to try to discuss in a single chapter such a variety of topics as still lie before us, but this book has already attained such undesirable dimensions that we must now be content with more summary treatment. Nor can I regard the title as anything more than the least unsatisfactory of which I could think to cover the heterogeneous subjects still left over for consideration. I intended to include in it both certain remaining arguments for idealism, which are essentially metaphysical as opposed to epistemological in character, and a brief survey of various types of metaphysical system open to the idealist. The discussion of either will not, I fear, be very satisfactory, for the former always seem self-evident to their adherents and totally pointless to most other philosophers,[1] while there is not much that can usefully be said on the latter without introducing long discussions of subjects which certainly do not fall within the range of this book. But these circumstances provide some partial excuse for the brevity of my treatment of vast issues.

The idealist arguments to be discussed here, even where they concern matter, differ from the arguments discussed in the last chapter in that, if valid, their conclusion would be positive not negative, not to the effect that we cannot justify the belief in matter but to the effect either that it is really mental[2] or quasi-mental or that it implies a non-human experience in which it is an element or a non-human mind on which it depends. The last-mentioned position is specially associated with the name of Berkeley. Like most other idealists he did not rely on such arguments alone but combined

---

[1] *Not* including myself.
[2] ' Psychical ' would be perhaps a better term, if it had not acquired a different sense in connection with ' psychical research '

with them others of a different type such as have been already considered in earlier chapters, but it is certain that, besides holding on epistemological grounds that physical objects because they are ' conceived ' by us must be ' ideas in the mind ',[1] and using arguments based on the representative theory of perception and the difficulty of giving adequate reasons to justify the belief in independent physical objects,[2] he also held that the specific characteristics of so-called physical objects could be seen to imply a mind on which they depended. This last argument has been used by very many other idealists besides Berkeley, and we shall now proceed to consider it.

Before doing so it is, however, meet to say a word in tribute to the father of idealism, a philosopher who has met with much abuse and little gratitude from idealists themselves as well as from realists. Of all the great philosophers of the past Berkeley is the one who in my opinion has been most persistently underestimated alike by friends and foes. I do not deny the inconsistencies and fallacies in his work, but I doubt very much whether as strong a case can be made against him on these grounds as against Descartes, Spinoza or Kant,[3] though Berkeley's clear style, itself a merit, leaves his mistakes much easier to detect. When we remember further that his was pioneer work on a line of thought as new and influential as any that has emerged in philosophy,[4] and therefore just because of its novelty inevitably liable to faults,—(almost all great new advances are first made in a very imperfect, inconsistent form)— and that he practically completed it by the age of twenty-five and then turned his attention to other matters, while other great philosophers have had most of their lives in which to develop their philosophy, we will not be niggardly with our praises. For, repudiate him as the later idealists may, they still use his arguments that to conceive anything is to bring it into relation to mind, that physical things are inseparable from experience, that objects are relative to a subject; and on such arguments the whole character of their philosophy depends. We may not approve of these arguments ourselves, but even

---

[1] V. chap. II of this book. [2] V. chap. VII.
[3] I do not of course mean to suggest that therefore he was a greater philosopher than these, though I should myself be inclined to place him above Descartes.
[4] Though there were no doubt some partial anticipations of it, as of everything else new, which were probably unknown to Berkeley.

IDEALIST METAPHYSICS

if we do not we must admit their importance, seeing that the whole philosophy of the nineteenth century was dominated by such arguments and that they influenced so many philosophers of the highest quality. And Berkeley's philosophy, though not proved, still remains in its main outlines a possibility,[1] since no one has succeeded in refuting it. He has not worked out his system nearly as comprehensively or nearly as fully as most leading philosophers have worked out theirs, and this leaves open the doubt whether he could have done so if he had tried, but the defect may be due less to lack of philosophical capacity than to desire to devote his attention to practical activities and lack of sufficiently keen interest in any except a limited number of philosophical problems.

To return after our digression, we are now to discuss the argument that in virtue of their specific characteristics material[2] objects either logically entail mind or are at least themselves mental in character.[3] It is important to note that, if valid, it would prove not that matter was dependent on our mind or necessarily on any human mind, but only at the most that it was dependent on some mind or other, whereas the arguments discussed in the last chapter, and most, though not all, of the epistemological arguments would prove either that there were no material objects separable from our human minds or at any rate that we had no right to assert their separate existence. Nor do the arguments of the present chapter proceed by showing that physical objects must be *known* by a mind in order to exist, but either that they must be *experienced* by a mind or that they must be themselves of the nature of experience. This is of some importance, even if the mind could not or did not experience them without also knowing them,[4] for it enables these arguments to avoid all the difficulties raised by the fact that knowing, in all cases in which we are

---

[1] V. above, p. 340 for the more phenomenalistic side of it.
[2] It is perhaps desirable to remind readers that I make no distinction between ' material ' and ' physical ' but use the terms interchangeably.
[3] I shall not discuss Berkeley's arguments against the doctrine of an unknowable material substratum, because they could only be valid against Locke's particular view of matter, not against all realist views.
[4] This seems to me clearly possible with human and animal minds, if by ' knowing ' is meant ' explicitly recognising them as having certain characteristics ' and not merely ' being acquainted with them '. No doubt it would not be possible if the mind of which we are speaking is God and if God be omniscient.

acquainted with it, seems to presuppose the independent existence or subsistence of its object.[1] This distinction has, as far as I can see, not usually been realised by idealists, but it is an important one, since the type of idealism which makes matter relative to *experience* can avoid all the difficulties about the nature of cognition which wreck epistemological idealism. It is clear on any view that a mind can know something which is part of its experience or dependent for existence on itself's experiencing it; [2] but it is much more difficult to maintain that everything, or indeed anything, known by a mind is dependent for its existence on that mind knowing it, or that everything is dependent on some mind knowing it.[3] To argue that e.g. colour or heat is inseparable from seeing or feeling is not to argue that colour and heat are dependent on being known. For nobody would contend that, because toothache is admittedly an experience, I must give myself toothache by knowing that I have it. The argument, since it is based on the specific nature of matter alone, would also differ from the epistemological arguments in applying only to material objects and not to all objects that could be known.

An idealism based on these arguments would have another advantage: it would enable the idealist to avoid conflict with common-sense and to retain the advantages of realism in regard to physical objects. Berkeley propounds or at least suggests two inconsistent views. One is that physical objects have no existence except when perceived by us, so that, when we nominally ascribe qualities to them as existing unperceived, we are really only saying what we should perceive under certain conditions; the other, neither clearly developed by him, is that

---

[1] C. A. Strong, replying to Moore's *Refutation of Idealism* in *Mind*, 1905: 'To state the principle in Mr. Moore's own words: " This awareness is . . . of such a nature that its object, when we are aware of it, is precisely what it would be, if we were not aware " (observe that, on any view, this is a perfectly correct and valid principle *as applying to thought*; but the Idealist holds precisely that material objects do not exist for us primarily as objects of thought, or of an intuition assimilated in its character to thought, but as experiences, sensations).'

[2] Otherwise we should be debarred from all psychological knowledge of our own states.

[3] No doubt something which was dependent for its existence on a mind experiencing it might be both experienced and known by that mind, but its existence might still not be dependent on the knowing of it but only on the experiencing of it.

they exist in the mind of God, whether we perceive them or not.[1] The latter is more consistent with common-sense but less consistent with the rest of his philosophy, since it would drive him back to some form of the representative theory of perception, which he repudiates, and would involve the view that God's nature included a quantity of sensuous, inert, extended ' ideas ' (= images), a conclusion very repugnant to Berkeley. It would not agree with many of his own arguments against matter, and it may even be doubted whether it was for long his view at all.[2] And any ideas of physical objects that God may have are in any case never conceived by Berkeley as being either the immediate object of our perception or in direct relation to our perception, for the causes of our perceptions are for him not God's ideas but God's will. Even if there are physical objects ' in God's mind ', according to Berkeley they are not the physical objects which we perceive in any ordinary sense of the word perceive.

But, though Berkeley did not develop it, it is perfectly possible to develop an idealism on similar lines which is quite compatible with a fully realistic view of the physical world relatively to us and with the truth of any of the realistic theories of perception which have been propounded.[3] For physical objects might be as independent of our minds as any realist could desire, and yet be dependent on a divine mind or be part of a divine experience. Such a position would be reached if we both (a) were convinced by the case for realism in any of the forms in which it is presented, and (b) held as a result of an examination of the specific characteristics of material objects that their existence apart from a mind or an experience was logically impossible. For we might well have a right to assert that a material object entailed and so could not exist apart from some mind or experience without being

[1] On the second view the existence of God is proved by the existence of physical objects which are independent of our minds and yet, according to Berkeley, have been shown to presuppose some mind ; on the first view this argument falls to the ground, and Berkeley's proof of the existence of God now depends solely on the argument that there must be a cause of our perceptions and that the only possible cause of anything is ' spirit '.

[2] V. article by Mr. Mabbott in *Philosophy,* Jan. 1931, p. 18.

[3] The clearest example of this type of idealism that I know is provided by Rashdall (*Philosophy and Religion*, ch. 1). But what seems on principle the same view is held by Green and Caird, except that they combine it with the ' absolutist ' doctrine that our true self is to be identified with and has not merely been created by the divine mind.

forced to suppose that it entailed our own or any human mind or experience. A might well logically entail B without its being the case that it entailed any particular instance of B, only some one instance or other. Further, in that case there would be nothing to prevent our holding not merely, as Berkeley suggested, that there existed as 'ideas' for God physical objects like those we perceive, but that the identical object we perceive at the same time existed independently of us in the experience of God. (For even on a representative theory of perception we must admit that we perceive material objects in some sense, and that there is, not indeed identity, but some distinctive relation between the latter and our immediate objects of sensory awareness, in so far as these represent them, and this relation, whatever it is, might equally well subsist if material objects were only 'ideas' of God.) Even if we are immediately aware that material objects are independent of us, we are certainly not thus aware that they are independent of all minds, though they may be so in fact.

The view suggested is usually condemned as crude on the ground that it introduces a '*deus ex machina*', but this seems to me unjustified. There are two views which, whether right or not, have been so widely held by important philosophers that we must suppose them not to be simply silly but to have some reason behind them. They are (*a*) that physical objects exist independently of us human beings, (*b*) that they are only thinkable as dependent on a mind or as parts of an experience. These two views when combined lead with logical necessity to the conclusion that physical objects depend for their existence on a non-human mind or a non-human experience, which must be looked on as at least far superior to ours in metaphysical importance, since the whole material world depends on it. This is not indeed to establish the omnipotent God of orthodox theology but at any rate a God who might be said in a real sense to create and control at least the physical universe,[1] and might indeed be reasonably identified with this omnipotent God by one who like Berkeley saw other reasons for believing in the existence of such a being. The supreme mind on which the world depends is not arbitrarily introduced to remove contradictions in an adventitious theory, but is the logically necessary conclusion of premises the strength of either

[1] What is perhaps the most popular 'proof of God' apart from 'revelation' or 'religious experience', namely, the argument from design, suffers from similar limitations.

of which is attested by its widespread support among philosophers, though they are less commonly combined by the same philosopher. No doubt the introduction of the deity into a philosophical system may sometimes be an essentially unphilosophical move and may be open to the criticisms of those who object to a *deus ex machina*. It may be so under two conditions: (a) where a philosopher faced with a contradiction in his system meets it by merely appealing to the omnipotence of God and saying that with God all things are possible, (b) where an appeal is made to the divine agency to explain particular facts. It is obvious that in these ways the conception may be abused most grossly and employed as a mere excuse for intellectual laziness; but to introduce the conception of God because it is logically entailed by certain well-thought-out premisses is not to introduce a *deus ex machina*. I do not see why the idealist argument for God should be charged with this any more than any other alleged proof of God. All proofs of God must introduce the conception of God in order to meet certain intellectual difficulties; but all proofs of anything else introduce their conclusions for precisely the same reason. It is legitimate to criticise an alleged proof of God and reject it if the premisses are unacceptable or do not really lead to the conclusion, but it is no more legitimate to condemn it offhand as an attempt to make use of a *deus ex machina* than it would be to condemn a proof of matter as an attempt to introduce a *materia ex machina*. No doubt the fact that an argument introduces God is nowadays regarded by many people as a sufficient reason for dismissing the argument at once without consideration, but I cannot see that this is more than mere prejudice.

The view in question would indeed be crude if God were conceived as, so to speak, intervening at odd moments to prevent physical objects from disappearing by looking at them when there was no human being to do so, but this is only a caricature. No doubt physical objects would have to be conceived as dependent on God all the time without interruption, as they are on any ordinary theistic view. Almost the only difference from ordinary theism is that this type of idealism introduces a fresh argument in favour of their being dependent on God and insists against some forms of theism not only that they must have been created by God but that it is logically impossible for them to exist for even a moment without God.

The type of idealism just sketched is the type which attracts me personally most, indeed at one time I definitely accepted it myself. It attracts me because it seems to combine with itself the advantages of realism. Indeed, the realist element is so pronounced that it may perhaps be doubted whether it ought, any more than ordinary theism, to be called idealism. It leaves room for a realistic theory of knowledge and perception, and merely adds that physical objects ultimately imply a mind or experience for which they exist. It does not make physical objects 'unreal' or mere abstractions from our experience, and it avoids all the difficulties of epistemological idealism. The most formidable objections to it are negative, to the effect that physical objects do not really imply a mind or experience and that therefore it is a groundless doctrine.[1] And certainly the majority of the arguments which have found favour with idealists would be impotent to support it, since they would make physical objects relative to *our* minds. If we argue that knowing makes its object or that there is no justification for regarding physical things as separable from human perceptions of them, we certainly cannot reach a conclusion of the kind I have suggested. But we might well hold that unseen colour, unfelt heat,[2] unheard sound, size not relative to an observer, unexperienced or unthought shape[3] were unthinkable without holding that these qualities are all dependent on human beings experiencing them. The argument would only lead to this conclusion if we assumed that the only possible experience was human. If we do not assume

[1] The 'problem of evil' could be met by the assumption that the spirit on whom the physical universe depended was limited in power, (a solution which, whether compatible or not with the demands of the religious consciousness, would certainly be compatible with the use of this idealist argument), or by any other means favoured by the theist.

[2] If the idealist supposed, as Berkeley does, that great heat is inseparable from pain, the absurd conclusion would seem to follow that the divine mind was all the while suffering intense pain from the burning stars, etc., but (*a*) I have suggested a way of escape from the difficulty about the connection of heat and pain (v. above, pp. 378–9); and (*b*) even if my suggestion were not accepted and the two declared inseparable, there would be no difficulty about denying the independence of heat relative to *our* minds (except in the sense in which the term is used in physics), and yet asserting the independence of colour, shape, etc., so that these qualities at any rate had to be regarded as present in a divine mind.

[3] In what, following Professor Moore, I called the sense-given sense of these words (p. 301).

IDEALIST METAPHYSICS

this, all these qualities might still exist in a non-human experience more comprehensive than ours, and must indeed do so if we are still to maintain the view, which it is hard to avoid, that the physical world exists independently of our piecemeal experience of it. Such an argument would not show that everything was dependent on such a non-human mind or experience, but it would show that physical objects were, and would at the same time avoid any taint of subjectivism. I therefore think that those to whom, as to many, it seems unthinkable that physical things could exist unexperienced or unthought should adopt this type of idealism.

It has indeed been argued that physical things might in that case still be relative to several minds and not only to one; but if it were supposed that the several minds each experienced the whole physical world the hypothesis would be superfluous, while, if they each only experienced part, the physical world would not exist as a whole, since its different parts, existing for different minds, would have no spatial relations with each other and therefore would not constitute together the world of common-sense or science. If one mind e.g. experienced the earth and another the sun, the earth and the sun would not be spatially related to each other and astronomy would be false; if one experienced the exterior and another the interior of the earth, it would not be the interior and exterior of the same earth at all. The type of idealism under discussion depends on both (*a*) accepting the existence of the physical world in a non-phenomenalist sense, (*b*) still maintaining that two things can be spatially related only through dependence on a mind or coexistence in an experience; but if we adopt the first view we must include in that physical world in spatial relation all the different parts admitted by well-established doctrines of science, and for one who also adopts the second view this is impossible unless all the parts are present continually to one mind or in one experience. If spatial relation, like everything else in the physical world, depends on presence to a mind, A and B cannot be spatially related by merely being present to different minds.[1]

This idealism should no doubt not be stated in a way which implies that the divine mind postulated is very like ours and that we possess definite dogmatic knowledge as to the nature

[1] For a refutation from the idealist standpoint of the view discussed in this paragraph, in the form in which it is maintained by McTaggart, v. Rashdall, *Philosophy and Religion*, pp. 123–6.

of God. Agreement in the general characteristic of being a mind is compatible with very wide divergencies in other respects, and any experience which could unite in itself the whole variety of the physical world must be unimaginably different from our own, but *some* of its *objects* may still be like ours.

Subjective idealism, if applied to all objects of knowledge at once, involves one in absurdities by making us ourselves create the laws of nature and logic. If it limits itself to impugning the independent reality of the physical world, it is by no means so easy to refute but still leads to a conclusion that will seem absurd to many. These will then hold that it is better to think of the physical world as not merely a product of human minds or an abstraction from human experience, and if they still remain idealists, as they may, will regard it as dependent on or included in a non-human experience or experiences. If they regard this experience as one, their position becomes hardly distinguishable from that of theistic idealism, since they now admit a transcendent being with a rationally ordered experience [1] of wonderful extent, system and variety; if they do not admit *one* experience of the whole world but only experiences, they are open to the objections just stated. I should therefore hold that the strongest type of idealism is theistic, for this type of idealism can alone secure objectivity.

It may be contended that the logical conclusion from the premisses suggested would be not that the physical world is dependent on a mind but that it constitutes or is part of a sentient experience, which for anything we could tell from this argument may not involve intelligence. But this would only be the case if the argument were not that physical things must be objects of awareness but that they must be feelings. Now these two views have often been confused in the past, but I do not see how any idealism can possibly stand which identifies the spatial coloured objects we usually regard as physical with feelings. They are not in the least like feelings (or acts of mind of any sort). Whatever they are, these objects are not sensings, emotions, pleasures or pains, or anything remotely resembling these, and our feelings and acts of mind are not coloured or round, etc. It may indeed be held that physical things resemble feelings or sentient beings in their ultimate

---

[1] A rationally ordered experience either implies or is a mind. For we must *either* hold that any experience presupposes a mind or self to have it which is other than any or all of its experiences, *or* identify the mind or self with its experience.

nature as existing independently of us, though not as perceived or appearing to us, a view which I shall discuss in section 4, but we are now discussing views which seek to save the objectivity of the physical world, more or less as we think we know it, or of that side of its nature (—there may also be many other sides). If we are to think of the spatial objects to which we usually give the name, physical, as existing unperceived by us, while yet not abandoning the idealist view that they are inseparable from some experience, we must think of them not as experiences in the sense of experiencings but as objects of experience, and the only way in which I can do so is by thinking of them as standing in the position of images relatively to a non-human experience. Now, if the hypothesis of a non-human experience is introduced because physical things are conceived as independent of us and it is still thought that they must be relative to some experience, this experience must be conceived as including conscious awareness of e.g. their spatial characteristics as what they are. Otherwise these characteristics do not exist for it, and therefore do not exist at all independently of us, since *ex hypothesi* what existence they have is only for it. But such conscious awareness is not mere feeling or sensation; it is cognitive intelligence. Idealism would be incompatible with its being a fact e.g. that the Earth takes between 365 and 366 times as long to travel round the sun as it does to rotate on its own axis unless this fact be a fact for some experience. It is not merely a fact for human experience, it was indeed a fact long before any human beings knew of it; it must therefore be a fact for some non-human experience. But there would be no sense in saying that such a fact was felt, it must be an object not only of sensation or something analogous but of thought.

This is not necessarily to say that the objects and facts are made by being known, only that they are made by being thought and not merely by being sensed. The plot of a novel is created in the author's mind by his thought and not merely by his sensations, but it does not follow that he makes it by knowing it. But the world is not according to the argument an experience but an object of thought, and to think a complex world as object either implies being a mind or is the same thing as to be a mind. Thus idealism in its least unsatisfactory form seems to me to imply not merely a non-human experience for which the world exists but a mind. Indeed, I can go further and say that it implies a personal God. For a God who can rightly be conceived as a mind would certainly be personal in the most usual sense of the term. But, unfortunately, the truth of the fundamental idealist contention that the *esse* of physical objects does really involve *percipi* has never been established, and for one who is not prepared to accept this as self-evident the whole argument is thus left hanging in the air.

Another point to be noted is that the argument from the specific characteristics of physical objects to a mind implied by these, even if valid, would not necessarily prove that the mind on which the physical world depends created any or all of the finite minds which inhabit that world. In view, however, of the close connection between these finite minds and their physical bodies, it would seem in that case most likely that they also depend for their existence on this supreme mind. It would be difficult to suppose that our body depended all the time for its existence on being continually experienced by a divine mind while on the other hand our mind could exist apart from that mind. (I could not reasonably ascribe the existence of my body to dependence on my own, as opposed to the divine, experience for two reasons : (*a*) I do not experience all the different parts of it all my life but rather only a very small proportion of them at any one time; (*b*) my body is a part of the physical order of nature in close spatial and causal relationship with inorganic matter, and therefore cannot but be regarded as dependent on a divine mind or part of the divine experience if the physical world be so regarded.)

There are certain epistemological arguments such as those used by Royce [1] which do not imply the truth of the doctrine that knowing makes its object or that a mind can only know its own ideas, or any doctrine similar to these, and such arguments would, if valid, well accord with the form of idealism I have just sketched. Only they would prove directly not only that physical things but that all possible objects of knowledge—human minds, psychological facts and relations, universal laws—were dependent on the divine mind. But I have already discussed and found myself unable to accept these arguments. It remains to consider the different argument that the specific characteristics of physical objects imply a mind or experience on which they depend. To this the next section will be devoted. The argument may lead either to theism, or to absolutism, or to phenomenalism, or to the

[1] V. above, ch. I, sect. 5.

IDEALIST METAPHYSICS

view that physical objects though not dependent on any mind are of the nature of ' sentience '.

§ II. Does Matter imply an Experience for which it Exists?

The present section will be shorter than the importance of its subject-matter seems to warrant, because the arguments under discussion, despite the greatness of the issues connected with them, are not arguments about which it is possible to say much with profit. For in discussing them we very soon reach a point at which their advocate can only appeal to their self-evidence and their opponent declare that they are not self-evident to him, and this at once brings the discussion to an end. Nor can I think of any way of surmounting this impasse by intermediate steps. It seems to some thinkers just self-evident without any intermediate arguments that colour, shape, size cannot be separated from the experience of them, and I do not think that this can be explained merely by confusions such as that between ' sensation ' as meaning sensing and ' sensation ' as meaning object sensed, though such fallacies have no doubt played a large part in idealist works. To other thinkers, equally competent, there does not seem to be the least shred of plausibility, let alone self-evidence, in such an assertion. Yet, even if we feel like this, we ought not to dismiss the doctrine too lightly. Its enormous influence in philosophy makes it likely that, though it may not be true as it stands, there is ' something behind it ', to use a colloquial expression. Such notions as that the supposition of a physical object which is not either reducible without remainder to actual and possible experiences or itself of the nature of experience (or ' sentience ') is absurd or meaningless are by no means confined to ' old-fashioned idealists ', but play a part in the philosophies of e.g. Husserl, Whitehead, the ' Cambridge school ', though not developed by any of these in a way which leads to the establishment of a divine mind or an absolute experience by the idealist argument.

But I must admit that what the something true and important ' behind this argument ' is I do not know. During my later student days and for some time afterwards I myself held that it was logically impossible that objects with the characteristics we ascribe to physical things could exist apart from an experiencing mind, and consequently, since I could not help believing that they existed independently of our human minds, I adopted an idealism of the type sketched in the last section,[1] but I do not think I claimed even then to have any further proof of the doctrine that these qualities were inseparable from mind but thought that on careful inspection it could be seen to be self-evident. But before long it ceased to seem so to me, and therefore I abandoned the title of idealist, though in other respects than this my position on the issues which divide the two schools had not yet substantially changed, while naturally it had become more developed in detail. It is thus an argument which, unlike the epistemological arguments for idealism, has always appealed to me somewhat, but I do not see now any real justification for accepting it. I must add, however, that, while I should oppose the view that qualities such as colour or shape in themselves imply a mind to experience them, it does seem to me personally that, quite apart from any specific arguments, such as that from design, the order and system which are so prominent in the physical world we know, even when the utmost reasonable allowance has been made for such new discoveries in physics as the principle of indeterminacy, strongly suggest the presence in some fashion and sense of a mind controlling the physical universe. Whether this is to be called an idealist contention or not I do not know. It certainly has been made by many theists who would not be regarded or regard themselves as idealists, and I have followed the ordinary usage in defining idealism in such a way as not to include all views according to which matter is ultimately dependent on mind but only those which reach this conclusion in certain ways, basing it on the theory of perception or knowledge or on a belief that unexperienced or unknown physical objects are *per se* unthinkable.

It is often contended that it is simply ' meaningless ' to ascribe sensible properties such as colour or shape to objects existing unexperienced, but it seems to me that, whether assertions ascribing these are true or not, they have at least a perfectly good meaning, and, as far as I know, no argument that does not depend on the fallacy of confusing experiencing with experienced characteristics or some fallacy of a similar type can be adduced to prove the contrary view. We cannot

[1] This period covered the production of my first book, *Kant's Treatment of Causality*. But I do not think that my change from what I called idealism to what I call realism affects the arguments used in that book.

indeed experience such properties as existing unperceived, but it is not meaningless to say that a property P which we only experience in conjunction with E can in fact exist apart from E. It is true that we cannot give a meaning to propositions about physical objects except in terms of experience, if experience is used in the wide (I should say loose) sense in which it covers characteristics experienced, that is, it is true that the meaning of any of our significant statements about physical objects must ultimately be interpreted in terms of characteristics which have been on other occasions experienced by human beings, but it does not follow that they are merely statements about what human beings actually do experience or would experience under given conditions.

A statement ascribing sensible qualities to physical objects in the realist sense could, as far as I can see, only be meaningless if ' A is e.g. red or round ' were either identical with or included analytically ' A is immediately experienced as red or round '. Now it seems that the *second* proposition does include analytically the *first*.[1] In that case, however, the first cannot also include analytically the second unless the two are identical; but I really should have thought that sufficient had been said during the early phases of the realist reaction of the present century once for all to put a stop to this fallacious identification, and that there was now no excuse whatever for just assuming its correctness without expressly replying to the realist contention that it does involve a confusion. No doubt, if ' physical ' is defined in a phenomenalist way, it is self-contradictory to say that unexperienced physical things are red or round in a realist sense, but this is obviously only a verbal point. Even if we choose to define ' physical ' in such a way as to include a reference to ' being experienced ', that does not make it self-contradictory to say that something red or round exists unperceived, it only debars us from calling that something a physical object.

There are difficulties about determining what experiencing is as such or observing it introspectively in abstraction from what is experienced, but whatever the account we give of ' experiencing ' we surely must admit that to say that somebody experiences red is not merely to say that something has the quality red, but also at least that that something stands in a

[1] I am using ' immediately experienced ' in a sense in which only sensa are immediately experienced. A physical object some or all of the actually experienced sensa of which were red might not itself be red.

certain relation to something else, which relation is itself distinguishable from the sensible quality (*not* a relation) red. This would be true even if to be experienced were (as on some views it is)[1] nothing more than to be a member of a group of sensa of a certain specific kind, namely, those constituting what we call a person's experience, for the proposition that A is red is clearly distinguishable from the proposition that A is a member of a certain group.[2]

It seems clear to me, therefore, that the proposition ' nothing can be red unless experienced at the time ' is not analytic but synthetic. It might still indeed be the case, if we admit, as I should, the possibility of synthetic *a priori* knowledge, that it is possible on careful inspection to see *a priori* that the predicate, red, is inseparable from, though not identical with, the predicate, being experienced, and similarly with all other qualities applicable to physical objects. That a certain quality given in experience may be seen to be intrinsically (and not merely *de facto*) inseparable from being experienced is made clear to me by the case of pain. I do seem to be able to see intuitively in the case of this quality that it would be a logical absurdity to speak of it as existing unfelt or unexperienced, and I seem to see this also in the case of characteristics which would usually be regarded as more specifically mental e.g. emotions.[3] But I cannot see this in the case of characteristics such as colour, shape, size, motion, velocity, sound, or even smell and taste, nor do I know of any valid argument to prove that they are logically inseparable from being experienced.[4] Therefore I feel bound to reject the idealist contention as not established, though I cannot actually disprove it.

The most I could admit is that in order to think what physical objects are we must think of them *as if* they were objects of experience, or rather of conscious perception, for an imaginary observer. For example, in order to give full intelligibility to propositions about the state of the earth prior to man

---

[1] Not on mine.

[2] Except the group (or, better, class) of all red things, which is obviously not the kind of group the theory has in view, since they do not constitute the experience of any one being.

[3] I do not mean to deny that a person can have a certain emotion without knowing what the emotion is, but only to deny that he can have it without feeling it.

[4] The subtle and detailed argument of McTaggart would require such long discussion that I can only refer you to the criticism by Professor Broad in his new book on McTaggart's philosophy.

IDEALIST METAPHYSICS

we must imagine some mind as contemplating it at the time, when no human mind was in fact contemplating it, and think it as it would have been for that mind. We can make correct verbal statements about it without doing this, but this is the only way in which we can picture to ourselves what the statements really mean. In this sense it may be true that propositions about material objects can only be interpreted in terms of experience, either actual experience or the imaginary experience of an imaginary observer. But I regard this only as a methodological fiction, as a means of making clear to ourselves what they are *per se*, and the fact that we can only determine their nature for ourselves by this means is no proof that they depend for their existence on being observed, though it enhances in some degree whatever probability there is in the assumption that they do so.

I should also admit that, if we assumed on other grounds the existence of a God and the complete dependence of the physical world on God, the suggestion that physical objects might stand to God in some such relation as our mental images stand to us would perhaps provide the most helpful analogy for thinking the relation of the physical world to God. It seems to me that it would at any rate provide a better analogy than the one of the human builder or manufacturer who constructs the products of his art out of material given already. I should further agree with Dr. Fawcett [1] that in that case it would be better to use the analogy of creative imagining than of thought in a more rationalistic sense in picturing the relation between God and the physical world. But we are not discussing the question whether we have a right to believe in God, but the question whether the idealist argument from the specific characteristics of material objects has succeeded in proving the existence of God.

T. H. Green, in order to prove the unthinkability of physical things apart from mind, makes use of an argument from the nature of relations.[2] If A and B are related they are at once separate and together, and for this to be possible ' there must be something other than the manifold things themselves which combines them without effacing their severalty '. Now we can see how this is possible if there is an intelligence which thinks the related things together ; we know that, when we think

---

[1] In *Divine Imagining*.
[2] *Prolegomena to Ethics*, 28, 29. A similar argument is used by Lotze (*Metaphysics*, bk. I, ch. 6, § 80).

two things, they are distinct and not merged in one, and yet also fall within the same unity of consciousness, and so are together. Such a process as comparison involves at once the difference and the union of its objects. They must be different, for otherwise there would be no distinction and therefore no comparison ; they must also be united together, for to think first A and then B is not to compare A and B, to compare them we must hold them together. But it is impossible to conceive how related terms could in any other way be thus at once a unity and separate, therefore the fact of relation implies the existence of an intelligence to which both the related terms are present. This argument is also used by Rashdall for the same purpose.

' Space is made up of relations ; and what is the meaning of relations apart from a mind which relates, or *for* which the things are related ? . . . Relatedness only has a meaning when thought of in connection with a mind which is capable of grasping or holding together both terms of the relation. The relation between point A and point B is not *in* point A or *in* point B taken by themselves. It is all in the " between " : " betweenness " from its very nature cannot exist in any one point of space or in several isolated points of space or things in space ; it must exist only in some one existent which holds together and connects those points. And nothing, as far as we can understand, can do that except a mind. Apart from mind there can be no relatedness : apart from relatedness no space : apart from space no matter. It follows that apart from mind there can be no matter.' [1]

Both thinkers use this argument to establish the view that matter depends on a divine mind, not the view that it depends on our minds. Further, since minds are related as well as physical objects, the argument should, if valid, lead to the conclusion that not only physical objects but also human minds themselves are dependent on the divine intelligence, a conclusion which is, however, not drawn by Rashdall.[2] Someone might no doubt hold that, while spatial relations implied a mind, other relations did not, and in that case the argument would apply only to physical objects ; but the arguments of

[1] *Philosophy and Religion*, pp. 10–11.
[2] He holds the most reasonable hypothesis to be that the mind on which matter depends also created all finite minds, but he does not base it on this argument from relation, which he applies only to material objects. He strongly opposes the ' absolutist ' doctrine that we are in some sense parts of the divine mind.

Green and Rashdall are based on the nature of relation in general, and not only of spatial relations. Green's view seems to be that finite minds are dependent as objects on the divine mind in respect of those relations between different minds and different phases of the same mind of which they are unconscious, but that the divine mind is also immanent in them as knowing subjects.

The view that relations presuppose a combining act of intelligence is also held by Kant,[1] but he gives no reason for holding it. There are indeed distinct traces of the doctrine even in the British empiricists who preceded Kant. Most thinkers in the past have found it very difficult to suppose that any two entities could stand in relation apart from a mind which related them; and it is therefore important to note that the widespread doctrine that relation implies mind, if true, must inevitably involve the conclusion that we and everything of which we can know depend on a single mind. For, even if we are prepared to adopt a phenomenalist view in regard to matter and maintain that it exists only in human (and animal) experiences of it, we must admit at any rate that human and animal minds stand in many relations to each other of which no human or animal mind is conscious all the time or indeed conscious at all. But, if this is so and all relations imply a relating mind, then these relations presuppose some non-human mind, and since everything we know is related in some way to everything else, we could not consistently fall short of postulating that this mind embraces the whole universe (or at least the whole of that part of the universe with which we have the remotest connection or of which we can have the remotest idea). It is even clearer here than in the case of the argument when confined to physical objects alone that it is one and not a plurality of non-human minds which is needed, for if the argument be valid at all it would prove not that everything related to something else must be present to some mind or other, but that any two things which are related must both be present to *the same* mind, and everything in the universe of which we have cognisance is in fact related to everything else. And since the relating is, if the argument is correct, due to the mind, and nothing can exist without standing in relation to other things, it follows that we and everything else are not merely known passively by that mind but depend on its relating action for our very being. But it

[1] *Critique of Pure Reason*, B, 130.

would still not be necessary to hold that we were identical with or part of that mind, only that we depended on it.

This is the argument. It would constitute a proof of God if valid, but I am not convinced of its validity. But it is impossible to refute it since its adherents would claim to possess a kind of immediate insight into the fact that relations imply mind. Unfortunately I do not possess this immediate insight, and many other philosophers are in the same plight. The argument is connected with the prevalent notion that relations cannot just be taken as they stand but require some kind of explanation. They are not ' in ' the terms related, it is felt, but fall somewhere ' between ' them, and there is no place for them unless they exist ' in ' something. But I am doubtful whether this is to do anything more than complain that relations are not qualities. Relations, it is true, cannot be exclusively ' in ' their terms, for otherwise they would not relate, but what right have we to assume that they are ' in ' anything ? If we discard the spatial metaphor, which is useless and misleading here,[1] the only meaning I can attach to ' in ' in this context is ' being a quality or state of ',[2] and that relations must be in something in this sense cannot be regarded as established unless we can establish the view that all relations are really qualities or states. Nor, if we seriously accept the fact of relation as given in experience, does it seem to me necessary or advantageous to introduce a *tertium quid*, namely, a mind, to hold the related terms together, for that is done already by the relation. No doubt the related terms are in a sense apart and in another sense together, as Green says, but if we ask how this is possible I should have thought the only and sufficient answer was to point to the particular relation, and say ' because they are related in this or that way '. This does not indeed remove the possibility that relations imply mind. Some may still hold that they can see a relation between different objects of the same mind to be intelligible and any other relation impossible. But this must be left to the intuitive insight of readers and, as far as I can see, cannot be settled by argument. I have merely sought

[1] Rashdall is thinking specially of spatial relations, but even here the difficulty, I think, disappears, once we clearly realise that even spatial relations do not exist in space in the sense in which things do. The relation of ' being above my body ' is not in my head or in my neck between my head and my body.

[2] (3rd ed.) or thought by a mind.

to remove one or two possible misunderstandings that might obscure the issue.

It remains true, I think, that an idealism of the type outlined in this and the preceding section may plausibly claim one advantage over any form of realism, namely, that, while it is very difficult to frame a realist theory which neither selects arbitrarily nor combines discrepant qualities in one physical object, it is easier to think of the discrepant appearances as combined through being thought by a single mind than as being present together in physical space. But I do not think that this is sufficient to justify the adoption of idealism, and it must be balanced against the well-known difficulties involved in assuming a mind that is conscious without cessation of all the infinite or at least vastly numerous parts of the physical world. I must add, however, that, apart from that apparent conformity to certain purposes which forms the basis of the specific ' argument from design ', the system and order to be found in the physical world suggest to me personally very strongly the view that it is dominated or pervaded by a mind, but I should regard this as an argument rather for theism than for idealism in any ordinary sense in which that term is used in philosophy.

§ III. The Absolute

Many idealists who would scorn to introduce the conception of God into their system do not hesitate to talk of The Absolute or even of an Absolute Mind. One may indeed be permitted to doubt whether in many cases they have any positive notion at all of the Absolute except what is included in the notion of God, and are not merely misled by a prejudice against the introduction of God into a philosophical system and think they have avoided the concept when they have avoided the word. But obviously this could only apply to ' lesser fry '. I would not dream of suggesting that it could be brought forward as a fair criticism of the leading idealists of the ' Absolute ' type. I think the principal points in which the notion of ' the Absolute ' differs from the God of most theology are these. (1) The Absolute is conceived as, strictly speaking, the *whole* of reality, so that it does not merely create but includes in itself all material objects and human minds. (2) At the same time it is not conceived as comprising any consciousness that could remain if all finite minds were removed, but as exclusively realised in these lesser beings. It is not indeed a mere aggregate of them, for reality is conceived as an organic unity, and as members of this unity minds are radically different from what they are as experienced by themselves in their separateness; but, though it is a unity more real than they, it has no existence apart from them as a transcendent mind consciously governing all reality. (3) This usually carries with it the repudiation of the belief in a *personal* God. (4) The Absolute at the same time fulfils the function of the logical system envisaged in the ' coherence theory '. (5) There is, even among philosophers who accept the religious conception of God as valid in its own sphere, a feeling that it is better to use in philosophy a more neutral word so as to avoid undesirable theological associations. The God of religion is from this point of view the Absolute, but the Absolute as viewed from a particular angle and therefore in some degree wrongly viewed, though the error may constitute the nearest approach to the truth we can reach in our practical religious attitude. In regard to the physical world an absolute idealist holds that it, like everything else,[1] is in its full reality very different from what it is as we think we know it, but that it still somehow includes in itself the content of all our judgments about it, though in a transmuted form.

The idealist argument for the believer in the Absolute would be put in rather a different form from that which it takes for the theistic idealist. The former would not argue that matter implies a supreme mind, for the Absolute is not conceived as a mind, though perhaps as ' Mind ', but that there can be nothing in reality save experience, or that physical objects can only be regarded as an abstraction from experience. Thus Bradley lays down as one of the central principles of his philosophy and one of the few truths which we can assert as ' intellectually incorrigible '[2] that ' sentient experience is reality, and what is not this is not real '. How is this sweeping conclusion established? Not by any train of argument, Bradley says, but by ' observation and experiment '.[3] The test is this :—

' Find any piece of existence, take up anything that anyone could possibly call a fact, or could in any sense assert to have

[1] V. the doctrine of degrees of truth. [2] V. above, p. 210 ff.
[3] *Essays on Truth and Reality*, p. 316 n.

being, and then judge if it does not consist in sentient experience. Try to discover any sense in which you can still continue to speak of it, when all perception and feeling have been removed, or point out any fragment of its matter, any aspect of its being, which is not derived from and is not still relative to this source. When the experiment is made strictly, I can myself conceive of nothing else than the experienced. Anything, in no sense felt or perceived, becomes to me quite unmeaning. And as I cannot try to think of it without realising either that I am not thinking at all, or that I am thinking of it against my will as being experienced, I am driven to the conclusion that for me experience is the same as reality.'[1]

Now, since Bradley says that this is not an *argument*, I cannot be expected to refute it by argument. All I can do is to ask the reader to make the mental experiment which Bradley suggests and note the results. But in doing so he must be careful to avoid a confusion which in my opinion makes any contention such as that of Bradley seem much more plausible than would otherwise be the case. There is a sense in which we can maintain that, for us, in Bradley's words, ' experience is the material of existence ', namely, if we mean by ' experience ' experienced characteristics and relations. For it is a fact that we can ascribe to existent objects no characteristic or relation of which it is not true either that it has been experienced itself by us or that it is definable in terms of characteristics or relations which have been thus experienced [2] (though, I should add, objects may really, for anything we can tell, possess millions of such unexperienced characteristics). But it does not follow from this either that physical objects are themselves of the nature of experience or that all physical objects are experienced. For a characteristic that we have experienced in one of the particulars which it qualifies may also qualify countless particulars which have never been experienced. It would be otherwise if we could see that the characteristics which we ascribe to physical objects were all logically inseparable from the experience of them; but I in common with very many other philosophers fail to see this, while Bradley claims to do so. As I said earlier, it is a contention that can neither be proved nor disproved but seems self-evident to some philo-

[1] *Appearance and Reality*, p. 145.
[2] ' Experience ' is not limited to sensation but includes intuitive apprehension of the presence of non-sensuous characteristics and relations in particulars experienced, e.g. causality, mathematical relations.

sophers and totally unjustified to others. If, however, the reader decides that the idealist is right on this point, that will not invalidate for him my criticisms against *arguments* used by idealists. The only difference between him and me will be that he sees or thinks he sees something to be self-evident which I do not see to be so.

But, besides the general point of agreement that the being of a physical object lies in being experienced (and thought), the absolute idealist displays many striking specific points of difference from other idealists. In the first place, since an idealist is commonly thought of as one who emphasises excessively the mental side of the antithesis between mind and object, it is important to note that, while the absolute idealist insists that no object can exist apart from experience, he likewise insists that no ' ideas ' or experience can occur apart from an object.[1] If our knowledge of the object actually constitutes the object realising itself in our minds, this fact may be viewed in two ways. It implies, on the one hand, that there are no objects apart from finite experience ; but it also implies that our so-called mental processes in cognition are not something done by us as minds separate from the world known, but the self-development in us of objects. This view is worked out by Bosanquet in his book on *The Nature of Mind* in a way which suggests ' new realism '.

To turn to another point, absolute idealism assumes that the distinction between different human minds is relatively invalid, that in a very important sense we are all just one and the same mind manifesting itself in different ways. For this view I can see no justification, unless it means simply that the unity between different human beings as manifested in such respects as co-operation and love is *more important* than the difference, though *both* aspects are important. The distinction between different minds remains one of the sharpest of which we know ; no mind, as far as we are aware, can literally share another's experience or be immediately conscious of another's feelings, experientially between them there is no continuity, their experiences do not run together, overlap, have parts (as opposed to universals) in common, they do not and, as far as we can see, could not, without the nature of a finite mind being radically different from what it is in

[1] He might well be copied on this point by a theistic idealist, though some difficulties arise if this conception is applied to God.

fact. There is no more common occurrence in the development of one's thought as one studies philosophy or learns from the experience of life than to find that what one thought originally to be a rigid difference of kind becomes on more thorough investigation or more extended experience one merely of degree in which the contrasted opposites gradually ' shade off ' into each other, so that a point is reached when it is very difficult or even impossible to say where one begins and the other ends. But in this one case we do find a completely clear-cut distinction, an absolute gulf. The experiences of two different human beings remain quite separate. There is no point where they merge into each other so that neither could say whether the experience was his own or the other's at the time he experienced it. No doubt, if we take the nature of a man in a wider sense as including all that the man worked for and purposed, the distinction no longer holds and it may be difficult to set limits and say what belongs to any one man over against any other, as e.g. Bosanquet has so emphatically insisted,[1] but, while it is legitimate for certain purposes to widen the connotation of ' a man ' or ' a mind ' so as to include all this, we must not forget that our experience, at any rate as a psychical process, has these absolute limits. No doubt it is connected in countless ways with the experience of others; but this does not alter the fact that it cannot also *be* the experience of another, and cannot even, as far as we know, be observed (only inferred or guessed) by another,[2] and that there is no gradual transition between two different men's experiences as there is between two things in the physical world so that one can, so to speak, pass from one to the other without a *saltus in aliud genus*. It seems

---

[1] *Three Chapters on the Nature of Mind.*

[2] It is sometimes asserted that direct observation of another's experience is logically impossible. This assertion seems to me ungrounded, and as far as I can see only rests on the old confusion between knowing X and being X. Why should there be any *a priori* impossibility in observing anybody else's experience without oneself having that experience or being that person, any more than there is in remembering my own past experience although I am not having that experience now, or in observing sensa though I am not the sensa I observe ? But, though we cannot say that such observation is impossible, we have no evidence of its occurrence. ' Telepathy ', where it occurs, more probably depends not on direct observation of another but on the communication by unknown means of effects which give an indication of the other's thoughts, etc., just as speech or writing does by more familiar means.

to me fundamentally unreasonable without very strong grounds to slur over in philosophy a distinction that is as sharp as this one.

And the grounds do not seem to me very strong. In the first place it is alleged that the barrier between different minds is broken down in the highest experiences of life, and that it is reasonable to take as a clue to the nature of reality those experiences that strike us as ' deepest ' rather than the commonplace outward facts of everyday life, what we think and feel when we are at our very best rather than what we usually think and feel in our more ' ordinary ' experiences. It is difficult to avoid being unfair to such an argument, because a critic can never be quite sure that he does not fail to appreciate it only because he is lacking in some mode of experience which those who use it enjoy, but I should have thought that the value of such experiences depended as much on the fact that the minds concerned were different minds as that they were in union. Love involves close union, no doubt; but surely it is essential that it should be close union between *different* minds. Love for oneself, in the sense in which one can love another, is either impossible or, if it occurs, an abnormality, the value of which is at least highly dubious. (Self-love, in the sense of devotion to one's own interests, is no doubt common enough, but it is obvious that the word, love, here is being used in a different sense from that in which it is used when we speak of love for another.) And self-sacrifice and co-operation would lose their point if they were not self-sacrifice to *others* and co-operation between different minds, each with its distinctive and unique contribution to bring.

The experience of the mystic gives rather more support to the view, since the accounts of mystics almost all agree in stressing the intense consciousness of a unity which seems to exclude diversities normally taken as ultimate; but even if there is, as the mystic holds, a close unity between everything in reality, it does not follow that the unity is of that type which characterises a single mind. In fact, any such definite assertion about the kind of unity it was would, I imagine, be regarded by most mystics as quite incompatible with its ineffable character, besides not doing justice to its value and closeness. But, however close the unity, it must be admitted that there is also diversity, and the gap between different minds provides one of the most marked diversities we know. Different minds may be one in some sense, but they are not one *mind*. Again, the fact that a society may act as if it were one person only proves that it is in some respects analogous to an individual mind, not that it bears the essential character of such a mind.

Further, there are positive objections to the view of a very serious character.[1] In the first place, it is very doubtful whether it is possible to attach any meaning to the notion either of one mind including another or of *Mind* which is not *a mind*. If it is retorted that 'mind' is being used by the absolute idealists so as to stand not for a self but for the element of form, rationality, wholeness, wherever it occurs, the treatment denies by implication that there is anything to which the term, mind, as used in the sense in which it means a separate, individual self applies, and this seems to me plainly false. It is a fundamental fact of our experience that there are separate selves, though these selves may also be part of a whole to which the term, mind, may be applicable in some other sense, different from the one in which it is originally employed.

Secondly, it is difficult to see how perfection could be ascribed to a mind which really included in itself beings such as Nero or Caesar Borgia or, as far as that goes, myself. For these beings are defective through the presence of some positive evil, greater or less, and not only through the absence of good, and the difficulty is more serious than if these minds had been merely created by, without being part of, the Absolute Mind.

Thirdly, there seems to be a contradiction in holding that the same experience can be both self-contradictory as it stands, as absolute idealism usually holds, and yet through some process of transmutation perfectly harmonious and self-consistent as part of the Absolute. Either the contradiction in my experience is real, or it is merely apparent. If the former, my experience cannot be real even as part of the Absolute, for, if it really contradicts itself, it simply cannot exist, and if it is internally self-contradictory it cannot be made self-consistent by being brought into relation to other things. $B + \text{not} - B + C + D$ must still be as contradictory as $B + \text{not} - B$ was by itself, though no doubt this difficulty was obscured for the absolutist by the views I have

---

[1] V. Rashdall, *Ideas and Ideals* (last chapter), for a very effective criticism of the absolute doctrine from an idealist point of view.

criticised in my account of 'Degrees of Truth'. If, on the other hand, the contradiction is merely apparent, then the absolutist doctrine that all parts of a true whole are, when taken alone,[1] self-contradictory breaks down, and the so-called contradiction is merely a mistake of ours, though perhaps an inevitable one.

If the epistemological arguments for idealism were accepted, the only hope of securing any sort of objectivity would lie in the introduction of God or an 'absolute mind'. If this mind were conceived as immanent, the conclusion would indeed follow that we are really all one mind and not different minds; but, if it were conceived as transcendent, it would not follow that we *are* one mind but only that we *depend* throughout on one absolute mind for our existence (since we all are possible objects of knowledge, and according to that view all objects of knowledge depend on a mind which thinks them). In discussing the subject in Chapter II, however, I came to the conclusion, first, that epistemological idealism was at least ungrounded, secondly, that of its two forms the transcendent was less open to objection, being only incapable of proof while the other is capable of actual disproof. To sum up, I think the common view that idealism, if valid, leads to an immanent and not to a transcendent God unjustified. On the contrary, I do not see how idealism can defend itself at all effectively against attack without postulating a transcendent [2] and even a personal God to secure objectivity. This is not to say, however, that it proves the existence of such a God, unless we accept the positive argument that the *esse* of physical objects is inseparable from their being experienced, and this I have not accepted.

§ IV. Panpsychism

Another form of idealist metaphysics is that commonly known as 'panpsychism' or 'animism'. According to this doctrine, which may or may not be combined with theism

[1] It might still be true that it would be self-contradictory to both affirm them and deny the other parts in the whole, but this is not to say that there is any self-contradiction in affirming them by themselves, i.e. without either affirming or denying the other parts in the whole.

[2] Though no doubt the transcendent God might also be supposed to be immanent.

or even 'absolutism',[1] all so-called physical objects, though existing quite independently of us, are really mental, or, better, to use a more general term not suggesting intelligence or any high-grade life, psychical in character. This is usually combined with the doctrine that they do not really have but only appear to have the physical characteristics which we ordinarily attribute to them, e.g. that they are not really spatial but only appear to be so. (If it were held that they really had both these physical characteristics and certain psychical characteristics such as feeling, as is indeed quite possible, the view would be compatible with realism.) Panpsychism may either be monistic, as when the whole physical universe is regarded as the 'body' of an immanent God, or pluralistic in character as in the case of e.g. Leibniz. The view may be supported by the other arguments for a general idealist position already discussed, or some of them, and then defended as the most reasonable form of idealism, but it also draws upon arguments of its own. In the first place it is contended that, since conscious beings have evolved from inorganic matter,[2] we must attribute to the latter also some faint consciousness or some of the characteristics of psychical life. For it is held to be unthinkable that the conscious could have developed out of what possessed no such quality as consciousness, however faint, out of what had no living experience, however lowly in its development and feeble. Cause and effect must have something in common, and therefore mere unconscious matter, mechanically conceived, could never develop into mind.

It should be noted that this argument could at the best only establish panpsychism if it could first be shown that all other forms of idealism and also realistic theism were either false, or at any rate less reasonable alternatives. For any other form of idealism would avoid the view that mind developed out of unconscious matter as well as panpsychism does; and realistic theism, while asserting as at least probable the existence of matter, would deny that the evolutionary development of minds was due to the matter alone and

[1] One passage in Bradley suggests that he himself is inclined to entertain panpsychism.
[2] This is usually taken for granted by upholders of the view. It is, however, still regarded as very doubtful by some scientists, cf. Dr. J. Gray's address at the annual meeting of the British Association, 1933.

insist that it was only possible because besides the matter there was a mind on which the matter depended, namely, God. The objection given, even if it be valid against the view that our minds have developed out of unconscious matter alone, certainly is not valid against the view that they have developed out of unconscious matter plus (the divine) mind.

In fact, it seems to me that this argument in favour of panpsychism either goes too far or not far enough. For it is not much easier to conceive that minds such as ours could have developed out of beings far lower in the scale of evolution than the lowest animal or even vegetable, i.e. the supposedly psychical beings to which we give the name of inorganic matter, than it is to conceive that they could have developed out of the merely inanimate. Can it be consistent dogmatically to deny the possibility of the conscious having developed out of the unconscious (in the sense of the totally unfeeling), and yet to assert the development of the humanly intelligent out of what is quite incapable of reasoning? *If* we are to reject the former supposition on the ground of unintelligibility, it seems that we ought to reject the latter too and suppose that evolution is only possible because the evolving beings depend on a mind [1] which is at least as highly developed in intelligence and morality as the highest human being, and, since on that view it controls the whole evolutionary process, presumably very much more so. Otherwise we must assume the emergence of new qualities in evolution, e.g. intelligence in the human sense, which were not possessed by anything that had gone before, and this contradicts many notions of causation. But, if we assume such a being, since there is in that case already a consciousness in existence on which depend the material objects from which life and mind seem to have developed, we need not suppose in order to account for the evolution of our consciousness that inanimate objects themselves already possess some form of consciousness. Surely in explaining [2] the evolutionary process the more reasonable course is either to explain it from the lowest we can conceive, or, if this prove impossible, to explain it by reference to the highest qualities towards which we seem in a sense to see it working and which would give it significance, not to take what we only observe in the

[1] Or minds. A polytheistic view is certainly not logically impossible
[2] Whatever is meant in this connection by *explaining*.

middle of the scale, i.e. life without intelligence, and suppose that it is to be explained from that. If we are to deny the emergence of new *kinds* of qualities in evolution we have no course but either to deny in some sense the reality of time or to ascribe the process to a being who already possesses these qualities himself and communicates them to others, the alternative adopted by theism; and, if we do not deny on principle the possibility of new qualities emerging, how are we to justify our denial in the special case of consciousness or experience? I do not wish to lay great stress on this as an argument for theism, but *if* it proves anything it seems to me to tend towards this conclusion rather than towards panpsychism, and theism would render panpsychism unnecessary, at least as far as this argument is concerned.

Secondly, it is argued that it is most reasonable to describe the inner nature of matter in terms of something which we know and experience immediately, or rather that there is nothing else in terms of which we can describe it, and that therefore we should regard matter as psychical or of the nature of experience, while quite independent of our minds or our experience. But this argument can be dealt with very briefly. For, in the first place, it has not disproved the possibility that the inner nature of matter may be quite unknown to us. The fact that the only qualities we know are $a\ b\ c\ldots n$ is no argument whatever for the view that everything which exists possesses varying combinations of these qualities and no others; and, if it be the case, as the panpsychist usually holds, that all the characteristics which we ordinarily attribute to material objects and seem to perceive as belonging to them merely belong to their appearances, there can be no justification for making any assertions about their nature as opposed to their relations to us. If we admit the probability that some of the characteristics we perceive really belong to physical objects the position is different; but to deny on the one hand all the evidence of perception about the characteristics of physical objects, and on the other to assert that they are psychical on the ground that we know none but psychical characteristics seems to me a very unreasonable mixture of scepticism and dogmatism. And, in the second place, the assumed premiss that we experience immediately only what is mental is false. It overlooks the fact that we also experience sensa immediately and the possibility that matter may be described in terms of these. We are conscious of sensa, but the qualities of sensa themselves as we know them do not include any kind or degree of consciousness.

Professor Stout has brought forward several arguments that might be used in favour of what he calls 'animism',[1] but he includes under this term not only panpsychism but also theism, i.e. among the alternatives which he would regard as compatible with the animistic argument is the doctrine that the material world is created by a divine mind.[2] The arguments are, briefly, (1) that the notion of cause must be applied to physical objects, and that causation must be understood as involving something of the nature of will ; (2) the argument from the teleological character of physical processes ; (3) the argument from aesthetic experience, which is thought to imply a certain unity between us and the physical objects we experience as beautiful ; (4) the argument that the widespread belief in animism and the persistent animistic attitude of common-sense would be quite unaccountable if regarded as mere illusion. He also produces various other arguments to overthrow materialism and establish the conclusion that mind cannot have originated merely out of unconscious matter. But none of these necessarily leads or is regarded by him as leading to the idealistic form of panpsychism. They are all of them, as far as I can see, even if valid, compatible with holding, as Professor Stout does hold, that there are objects which possess spatial characteristics independently of the experience or knowledge of them. These objects may indeed possibly have been shown by the arguments in question *either* to possess psychical characteristics also *or* to be dependent on a divine mind, but to hold either of these two views is not to be an idealist.

Keeping to idealistic panpsychism, it seems to me that, as compared with other forms of idealism, panpsychism commits the error of trying to make everything real a subject and nothing real an object, thus destroying the subject-object relation altogether. For it destroys one of the terms between which such a relation could hold by making it unreal. The object must be as real as the subject *per se*, and can only be unreal, or appearance, in the sense that it suggests the existence of something other than itself which does not really exist, or tends to lead us to ascribe to a thing other than itself characteristics which that does not possess. The panpsychist

[1] *Mind and Matter*, bk. I, chs. 2–4.   [2] Id., p. 60.

tends to forget that, though he may say that the physical objects we seem to see are only appearances of mental entities, he has not eliminated the fact that we see them and that the sensa we see are, at least as sensa, quite as real as ourselves and not mental. Strictly speaking, panpsychism is logically impossible unless we deny the existence of sensa,[1] because there at any rate we have non-psychical entities, whether so-called physical objects are or are not really psychical. And, once we admit that some non-psychical entities are given in immediate experience, the assertion that all the physical objects we seem to perceive are really only appearances of psychical entities loses its plausibility. If these entities have sensations or are at all like any psychical entities we can imagine, their existence involves the existence in close connection with them of non-psychical entities, sensa, and these must be treated as equally real. Consequently the appearances we see would be not appearances only of an entity which was purely psychical but of a psychical entity together with non-psychical entities, its sensa. No doubt we can extend the term psychical to cover sensa, but in that case it has lost all its distinctive meaning and no longer implies the ascription to what we call psychical of any sort of feeling or experience, for sensa are only experienced and do not themselves experience or feel. It is not possible to make everything subject since then there would be nothing to serve as its objects; what the idealist should try to establish is the view that everything is either object or subject, the two being correlative to each other.[2]

The view in question also has the drawback against certain other forms of idealism of denying the independent reality of the characteristics ordinarily ascribed to physical objects on the strength of perception. And it ascribes marvellous creative powers to our minds. If there are none but psychical entities without spatial characteristics, it seems strange that these entities should see each other in such an alien

[1] Or unless we hold that, e.g., the blue patch I sense or imagine also itself feels apart from my sensing of it, as we suppose an animal to do, i.e. that the same entity is both a blue patch private to me *qua sensum* and has also the quality of feeling and not merely of being felt by me, a view which has, as far as I know, not been put forward by any thinker.

[2] V. Bosanquet, *The Principle of Individuality and Value*, p. 363 ff., on the objection to panpsychism; also Pringle-Pattison, *The Idea of God*, p. 177 ff.

guise and should create appearances so different from the reality. For, there being on that view nothing but psychical entities, there are no other external causes to which we can ascribe this distortion. It is strange that the appearances should be so radically different from the reality; and if we are so deceived by the appearances as we are on that view, is it reasonable to claim any knowledge or put forward any opinion as justified about the reality?

These objections do not disprove the possibility that the same objects which have the characteristics we ascribe to tables, stones, etc., may also feel, experience and have psychical qualities, the physical qualities and the psychical qualities being equally real. But I do not know of any arguments which convert this bare possibility into a probability, let alone establish it as a fact.

§ V. THE ARGUMENT FROM UNIVERSALS AND MORAL VALUES

There remains the argument which seeks to show not that physical objects but that universals presuppose a mind if they are to have being at all. It has been invoked specially in regard to moral laws and moral ideals and may be summarised as follows:—such laws or ideals have some being, but they do not exist as particular things do nor are they necessarily or invariably present to any human mind, therefore we must postulate a divine mind to which they are present. To give a clear statement of the argument it is perhaps best to quote Dr. Rashdall.[1]

' We say that the Moral Law has a real existence, that there is such a thing as an absolute [2] Morality, that there is something absolutely true or false in ethical judgments, whether we or any number of human beings at any given time actually think so or not. Such a belief is distinctly implied in what we mean by Morality. . . . We must then face the question *where* such an ideal exists, and what manner of existence we are to attribute to it. Certainly it is to be found, wholly and completely, in no individual human consciousness. . . . An absolute Moral Law or moral ideal cannot exist *in* material things. And it does not

[1] *The Theory of Good and Evil*, vol. II, pp. 211-12.
[2] I should much prefer the term ' objective ' to ' absolute ' in order to express what Rashdall means, for ' absolute ' suggests a morality independent of circumstances, which is certainly not his meaning at all.

(we have seen) exist in the mind of this or that individual. Only if we believe in the existence of a Mind for which the true ideal is already in some sense real, a Mind which is the source of whatever is true in our own moral judgments, can we rationally think of the moral ideal as no less real than the world itself. Only so can we believe in an absolute standard of right and wrong, which is as independent of this or that man's actual ideas and actual desires as the facts of material nature. The belief in God, though not a postulate of there being any such thing as Morality at all, is the logical presupposition of an " objective " or absolute Morality. A moral idea can exist nowhere and nohow but in a mind; an absolute moral ideal can exist only in a Mind from which all Reality is derived.[1] Our moral ideal can only claim objective validity in so far as it can rationally be regarded as the revelation of a moral ideal eternally existing in the mind of God.'

I should without hesitation admit the objectivity of values, on which the argument is based.[2] For, while I can give no proof of the kind which would consist in showing that any other view is self-contradictory or logically absurd, it seems quite clear to me both that our ethical judgments are not about merely psychological facts such as emotions of approval and that some ethical judgments are valid. If anybody denies the latter he must maintain that it is a mere illusion to suppose that there is any difference in value between the act of sacrificing one's life to save that of others and the act of murdering them in order to rifle their pockets; if he denies the former and makes ethics a kind of psychology, it must follow that ethical questions could all on principle be settled completely by introspection,[3] or by collection of statistics about men's emotions, etc.,[4] or both,[5] and this seems to me obviously untrue.

Rashdall's argument, if valid, would not, however, apply only to ethical principles but should be expanded into an

[1] He adds in a footnote, ' or at least a mind by which all Reality is controlled '.
[2] V. my *Second Thoughts in Moral Philosophy*, ch. 1 and 2.
[3] I.e. if ethical judgments are held to be assertions about emotions or other psychological facts in the person who makes the judgment.
[4] I.e. if they are held to be assertions about the emotions of most people, or of most people of a certain class.
[5] I.e. if they are held to refer sometimes to the emotions of the person judging and sometimes to those common to most people or to most people of a certain class.

argument from universals in general, though no doubt the argument from those universals which belong to the realm of ethics would have a special importance because it would establish directly not only the existence of some non-human mind, but, what is much more important, of a morally good mind. It seems that, unless the hypothesis of a divine mind is adopted, there will be many universal propositions besides those in the realm of ethics which are true and therefore true of something without being true of anything actual. And, even where a general law is exemplified in particular instances, its meaning cannot be reduced to its particular exemplifications, at least where it is a logical or mathematical and not a causal law. The law that $50 + 70 = 120$ seems to have some kind of being over and above the particular instances of 120 in which it is exemplified, and would still have been true even if there had been in fact no groups of 120 in the universe at all.

Indeed, the argument may be made more general still, since there are many true hypothetical propositions, even about particulars, in which neither the antecedent nor the consequent is realised in fact,[1] though no doubt such propositions while referring to particulars depend on the connection of universals. Further, our ability to assert propositions about the possibility or the probability of X relative to certain data, which propositions may be true though X never exists or occurs, seems also to imply the being of non-existents. Finally, we may note that all *reductio ad absurdum* arguments would be invalid if the truth of a hypothetical proposition depended on the existence of its constituents. For the purpose of such an argument is just to show the non-existence of at least the subject of its antecedent, and the argument must therefore be independent of the latter's existence.

In dealing with the above propositions we are left with three alternatives, none of which seems fully satisfactory as far as I can see.

(1) The propositions in question may be interpreted as giving relations of implication between characteristics in the wide sense of implication in which this term covers both causal and logical implication. If so, the objects to which

[1] The kind of universal propositions we are discussing certainly also fall in the class of hypotheticals, for no non-existential proposition can be categorical.

they refer might still be said always to fall within the existent world on the ground that we are incapable of thinking of any positive characteristic of which it is not true either that it occurs in the existent world or that it is a combination of characteristics which occur in that world, though not in the same combination. The case of negatives might be met either by admitting negative characteristics as realities or by adding the relation of exclusion.[1] Hypothetical propositions in general would then be propositions giving relations between different real characteristics of existent objects, either the simple relations of implication or exclusion between two such characteristics or the more complex non-dyadic relation of ' implying or excluding in conjunction with '. The characteristics in question would be either characteristics of existent objects or conjunctions of such characteristics, and in the latter case the propositions might be taken as ultimately referring to the simpler characteristics to which the conjunctions were reducible, while the relation asserted of implication or of ' implication in conjunction with ' would be a relation which, wherever the hypothetical proposition was true, really held in the existent world between the characteristics in question. Thus the hypothetical proposition that e.g. brakeless expresses would be dangerous would be interpreted as being the proposition that the characteristics of being an express train, being brakeless and being dangerous, which are all possessed by some real objects, though not necessarily by the same objects, are united by the triadic relation of ' implying in conjunction with ' so that the two former imply the latter. The proposition would then still be true of something real, namely, these characteristics, even if no brakeless expresses exist.

This view is exposed to the following great, though possibly not insuperable, difficulties :

(*a*) There are certain propositions which it is difficult to analyse in terms of any combinations of characteristics of existents. Those of geometry provide the most obvious examples, since the characteristics of ' being a point in the geometrical sense ' or ' being a perfect triangle ' do not seem either to be possessed by any existent or to be combinations of characteristics of existents. But there are other cases. It

---

[1] Thus ' if A is B, C is not D ' would become ' A conjointly with B excludes C from being conjoined with D ' or ' implies the conjunction of C and not-D '.

is clear, for instance, that the proposition ' any shade intermediate between orange of a specified shade and red is qualitatively more similar to yellow than red is ' would be true even if there were no existent which had any such intermediate shade, yet we could not then say that the intermediate shade was a combination of any characteristics of existents. Our conception of it would be indeed derived from red and orange, but it could not be correctly described as a *combination* of red and orange.[1] Propositions such as ' perfection is a quality ', to take McTaggart's instance, or ' an omnipotent God either would be omniscient or could become so ', which are undoubtedly true on any view of the universe, would present similar difficulties. I do not dispute that all the characteristics of which we can think are in some way derived from characteristics of existents, but they do not seem to be themselves all either characteristics or combinations of characteristics of existents; and therefore it is difficult to see how all propositions could be *reduced* to propositions about actual characteristics of existents, though I am not prepared by any means to say confidently that there is no possible way out of the impasse.

It seems to me quite impossible to escape the difficulty as McTaggart does by saying that, if nothing has the positive characteristic in question, everything will have the corresponding negative characteristic and the positive characteristic will then still exist as part of the negative characteristic,[2] for I do not see how the characteristic x can possibly be regarded as part of the characteristic not-x. If it were, phoenix-ness would be part of my nature just because I am not a phoenix,[3] and a negative, so far from *excluding*, as it should according to the law of non-contradiction, would always *imply* the existence in its subject of the corresponding positive. We must not be misled by the fact that a negative is commonly stated in *words* which include the *words* that stand for the corresponding positive into supposing that it does really include the latter in itself.

(*b*) The analysis of ' if A is B, C is D ' as equivalent to

---

[1] (3rd ed.) I should now dispute this, but this doubt does not affect my other instances.
[2] *The Nature of Existence*, I, 31.
[3] McTaggart admits this, but surely it is a *reductio ad absurdum* of his theory.

IDEALIST METAPHYSICS

'A B implies C D' still leaves one with propositions, in some cases true, about non-existent entities, for, if A B is to exist, it is not sufficient that A and B should both exist separately. No, they must exist in that combination, and similarly with C and D. Nobody would hold that centaurs exist because men's heads and horses' trunks exist, or that a revolution in England in 1932 was a real event because England exists, there is a time 1932, and there have been revolutions at other times and places. This objection might be met by saying that what was really asserted was that A stood in the triadic relation of 'in conjunction with B implying C D' or in the four-term relation of 'in conjunction with B implying C in conjunction with D'. This answer would enable one to maintain that all the terms of the relation were existents,[1] and that, in all cases where the hypothetical proposition was true, the relation really held between these existents. But what does 'in conjunction with B' mean? It does not mean actually in conjunction with B, for *ex hypothesi* A is not actually in conjunction with B; what it really means must be 'if it were in conjunction with B' or something to that effect, and this only gives us over again the same difficulty of a true hypothetical proposition in which the antecedent or both the antecedent and the consequent are not realised in fact.[2] The only way of escape that I can see would lie in finding some, no doubt very complex, relation between existent characteristics, not necessarily the same in character for all hypothetical propositions, which gave the sense of hypotheticals

---

[1] I include characteristics of existents under the term 'existents'.

[2] I have used the phrase 'in conjunction with' to cover various relations, for the difficulty may occur in several forms. (*a*) If A and B are two attributes, the objection may take the form that the complex attribute A B has no being in the existent world, though A and B may have being separately in different parts of that world. (*b*) If A is conceived as a subject and B as its attribute, then the objection will be that, while A exists as a subject and B as qualifying other subjects, no such thing exists as A with quality B, and therefore we cannot assert any true propositions about it, unless we admit a realm of non-existent entities. (*c*) Many hypothetical propositions have antecedents which consist in 'supposing' that a member of a certain class of events occurred at a time and place where no member of that class occurred, e.g., 'if he had seen the letter first he would not have gone out'. Here the person referred to exists, and the event of his seeing the letter actually occurred, but it did not occur at the time 'supposed' in the antecedent, therefore what is described is still non-existent. In such cases the antecedent conjoins the attribute with a place or time to which it does not really belong.

without having to be itself stated in a way that again presupposed non-existents or hypotheticals.[1] In other words we could only remove the necessity for non-existents on these lines by reducing all hypothetical to categorical propositions about existents. I am again not sure that this is impossible, but it has certainly not yet been achieved.

(c) It seems to me that *a priori* propositions can be seen *a priori* to be true independently of the existence or non-existence of their subject, and that therefore they cannot from the nature of the case be reduced to propositions about what exists; for, though their subjects may in fact exist, they would still be true even if the subjects did not exist. When A entails B we seem to see that it does so whether A exists in fact or not, since in order to establish the entailment we do not need the premiss that A exists. I am not quite sure that it is impossible to explain away this apparent insight or analyse what we really see here in terms of the existent, but I have no idea how this could be done, any more than how it would be possible on these lines to solve the other two difficulties. Even those hypothetical propositions which are based on causal laws and not seen to be necessary *a priori* seem, if true at all, to be true independently of the existence of their constituents, though they could only be reasonably judged by us to be true on the ground of experience of other existents.

It should be noted that my point is not that we can assert or believe what is never realised in fact. We do that also in cases of error, and I should not on that account admit a realm of subsistent objects of error.[2] The difficulty is rather that the propositions we assert or believe about what is not realised in fact are sometimes *true* propositions and it seems clear to me that a proposition can only be true because it 'accords with' (I prefer that phrase to 'corresponds to') something real. If all the hypothetical propositions we assert in which the antecedent does not accord with an actual existent were false, the difficulties would not arise in their present form, but it is quite clear that we know many such

---

[1] The analysis of 'if' as = implying is only possible if we presuppose non-existents; the analysis of it in terms of the relation 'implying (or excluding) in conjunction with', as we have seen, presupposes hypotheticals again, and therefore, as far as I can see, non-existents.

[2] V. above, p. 202.

propositions to be true, that we have rational grounds for believing the truth of many more, and that even where we are altogether unable to decide whether such a proposition is true or false we can see that the question is significant, that it must be the one or the other and that it *may* be true as far as we can tell.

'If P then Q' cannot be interpreted as meaning 'nothing is both P and not-Q'.[1] There is nothing of which it is true both that it is a unicorn and that it is not a whale, but this is not equivalent to saying that if anything were a unicorn it would be a whale. The difference between the two propositions lies in the fact that the latter asserts and the former does not assert a relation of implication in the usual sense in which this word was used [2] until its original meaning was changed so that it might serve as a technical term for 'mathematical logicians'.

(2) It is possible that some form of the view we have just discussed might succeed in overcoming these difficulties, but while not prepared to reject the view with dogmatic confidence I have no notion how this could be done. At any rate the difficulties are so great as to call strongly for an alternative. The usual one adopted is to distinguish between being and existence and admit frankly that there are characteristics which are yet not characteristics of any existing thing. The mode of being they possess is often called subsistence and must on this view be sharply distinguished from existence, both in the sense in which 'existence' can be applied to particulars and in the sense in which it is sometimes applied to the characteristics of such existent particulars. I do not see any objection to this view except that I am not quite sure whether it really solves a difficulty or merely disguises it by the use of a technical term. I am not quite sure, that is, whether I or anybody else really understands what subsistence can mean as opposed to existence, or what can be meant by saying that something can *be* which neither exists nor is a characteristic of an existent. It may be indeed that I am quite mistaken in even asking such a question and really see or could see quite clearly, each time I see the truth of a universal proposition, what this non-existential being is. But I must admit that I am not at all sure whether I do really see any such thing. No doubt the demand for a further explanation may be met by saying that

[1] Or 'everything is either not-P or Q'.
[2] I give a definition of this sense on p. 17.

'subsistence' is unique and indefinable, and this may be the correct answer, since some concepts must be unique and indefinable. Only I am doubtful whether I have really grasped this unique and indefinable mode of being or am merely cloaking my ignorance in words. But the subsistence view is strongly supported by the circumstance that, while, on the one hand, there are strong arguments for the view that universal laws and hypothetical facts have some kind of *being* which does not consist merely in qualifying particulars in which they are realised, it seems, on the other, clearer still that their nature is such as to debar them from any *existence* except as realised in actual particulars. It is not merely that we empirically do not find them existing but that we see it to be logically impossible that they could so *exist*. And, if so, it seems to follow logically that, since they *are* and yet do not *exist*, they must have a mode of being other than existence. But an attempt may be made to explain further this mode of being.

(3) Those who recognise that the being of universals cannot lie merely in actual particulars in the world of finite existents, and yet think that there is no meaning in a subsistence not definable in relation to the existent, may be driven to a solution like that adopted by Rashdall in regard to moral ideas. They may postulate, that is, a divine mind in which these universals and universal laws reside, and maintain that this is the only possible way of making their being intelligible to us. We may note that Leibniz used the argument that we must postulate a supreme mind to think the necessary laws of logic as one of his proofs of God; and universals are certainly commonly regarded as implying in some sense thought or mind even by those philosophers who do not go as far as this, as e.g. by Hegelians. The constant use of 'concept' both for 'universal' and for a mental entity may be regarded as suggesting some real affinity between the two. If we held the view that universal laws depended for their being on being thought by God, we should probably be led also to make the world of particulars thus dependent, since universals are manifested in it and universal laws apply to it.[1]

---

[1] (3rd ed.) I am now less inclined either to the subsistence view or to using the concept of God in order to solve a problem of this sort, but I am no clearer as to what alternative there can be.

The type of view under discussion has the advantage of avoiding the postulation of a quite separate mode of being which must remain indefinable and concerning which doubts arise whether we have really any understanding of what we are talking about when we refer to it. It may seem to some that it provides the only tolerably clear notion of the being of universals that we can form, and I am not certain that it is not clearer than the notion of mere subsistence. But, it may be objected, if we think of these universal laws and hypothetical facts as known by God, does that not imply that they have a being independently of his knowing them? Surely it does if his knowing is really knowing in our sense of the word at all. A possible reply is that they might depend on being thought by God and yet not depend on being known by God, though he would also know them. But the objection remains that, if they are necessary only because God thinks them, he cannot think them because they are necessary or true. Yet we see them to be necessary and true *per se* independently of any direct knowledge of what God thinks. This objection has often been made particularly forcibly against the view that moral laws are created by God. It is sometimes retorted that they are dependent on God but not on his knowing or willing them, or that they are necessities but necessities of God's own nature, so that though they depend on God thinking them God could not but think them without being false to himself. And it may be urged that it is just as unreasonable to expect a definite answer as to the nature of their dependence as it would be to suppose that we could give any kind of account of the mode of thought which God exercised in governing the world. But this weakens the positive argument in favour of the theory, which was that it alone gave a clear account of the being of universals, for the account now is seen to be not clear. It must, however, be admitted that I might see *a priori* that these principles were necessary and true without knowing that they were thoughts of God even if they were so in fact, just as I can know that $2 + 2 = 4$ without knowing the correct analysis of what 2 and 4 are. And if it be objected that we see them to be true *universally*, this implying that they are not true *only* when thought by a mind, the reply may be made that we cannot possibly on any view maintain that they are true where they are inapplicable and that outside the sphere of mind they are not false but inapplicable on this view.

It might be urged, however, that this answer to the problem does not fulfil its purpose of eliminating the notion of subsistence, since, even if thought by God, universal laws still cannot be particular existents without contradicting their own nature and therefore they can only *subsist*. A possible answer to this would be that they may have being in the sense in which propositions have, according to the view of the latter I suggested earlier,[1] namely, that they have no being *per se* but are inseparable elements in an act of thought by which they are entertained, which act exists as a whole. This might, without making them existents themselves, relate them to the existent and enable us to define their being in terms of existents. It may be said rightly that being in our human acts of thought is not enough in those cases where the law really holds, because the propositions we entertain and believe are then true and therefore imply something objectively real of which they are true, and it may then be contended that therefore they must also have a being which is objective relatively to us and that we cannot think the being of a universal law [2] except as being for some mind. In that case universal laws would be viewed, if we may say so without irreverence, as analogous to propositions entertained by God. I must admit, however, that this does not seem to me by any means an adequate argument to establish the existence of God, and I should be more inclined to accept the notion of subsistence as indefinable.

Even granting that to subsist is not to exist, it must be admitted, however, that a philosophy which aimed at a view of the whole could not be satisfied without bringing into relation the subsistent and the existent, and it is sometimes contended that this could not be done except by adopting theism,[3] or by taking a view which, without being theistic, somehow equated the good and the real. Perhaps this may be so, but the arguments in question would take me too far afield from

---

[1] V. p. 202.

[2] Or at least of a law not fully realised in any particulars.

[3] E.g. by Professor Taylor in *The Faith of a Moralist*, and Professor Sorley in *Moral Values and the Idea of God*. It is important not to confuse the latter's argument with that of Rashdall, for Professor Sorley does not simply assume that the validity of moral principles is to be equated with their existence as ideas but only argues that they must be brought *into relation* to the existent, a very different contention, and that this can only be done satisfactorily if we adopt theism.

my main subject to be pursued here, and are no longer specifically idealist in the sense in which I have used the term. No doubt the exact point at which we set bounds to our discussion cannot but seem arbitrary, but it is clear that some bounds are urgently needed and to go further at this point would involve a discussion of the whole question of the relation between ethics and metaphysics.

The attempt to prove the existence of God by a specifically idealist argument seems to me, as it does to most present-day thinkers, to have broken down; but, as I said earlier, it may be that it is not necessary or even rational to base faith in God on a metaphysical proof. In any case I have not in this book attempted to discuss most of the *arguments* for God. Most arguments that have been used cannot be regarded as idealist in character and are quite compatible with most forms of realism. I do not discuss, e.g., the argument from design, or the cosmological and ontological arguments, or again most of the moral arguments that have been used. For idealism is not to be defined as the view that mind is supreme in reality but as a particular way of approach to this view. If it were defined in the former way, all theologians would be ' idealists '.

§ VI. IDEALISM AND VALUES

The preceding section suggests the desirability of considering the relation of idealism to problems of value. It is certainly true that idealists have been very much influenced by considerations of this kind, and it might even be contended that the strongest argument for idealism is that it is only on an idealistic basis that there has been worked out up to the present any really satisfactory philosophical theory of religion, ethics, politics or aesthetics. However, it seems to me that, while most of the philosophers who have developed such theories during the last century have been idealists of one kind or another, this is only because most of the philosophers of the period, or at least most of the philosophers who have been deeply interested in such subjects or have thought that they had positive solutions to offer, have happened to be idealists. It seems to me that their idealism is irrelevant to most of their contentions in connection with these subjects, and that where it intrudes itself it tends to spoil their theories. This is partly confirmed by the fact that, since realism has regained its influence, many and perhaps most philosophical books on these subjects have come from realists.[1] Further, it is quite impossible for me to give any account of the idealist theory on these subjects, because there is no one type of theory belonging specifically to idealism and shared by most idealists. What is commonly called the idealist theory in ethics and politics is the theory only of a particular school, the 'absolute' school, of idealists. We might say in general that idealists have done ethics the service of emphasising and demonstrating the unity between different ethical principles, while not contradicting the plain evidence of our moral consciousness in order to secure a cheaply won unity, as did the utilitarians, and that on the other hand the more special contribution of realists has been to make clearer the issue between the subjective and the objective views of ethics, to define accurately numerous important distinctions, and to provide what are usually much clearer statements as to the principles which should affect our judgments in ethical matters without troubling overmuch about their inability at present to bring all these into a thoroughly coherent system, i.e. they have preferred the criterion of comprehensiveness to that of coherence.[2] Perhaps similar comments may be made concerning the other branches of philosophy which I have mentioned. But in any case no reader who has followed me through all these weary pages would wish that I should add to my book treatises on ethics, political philosophy, aesthetics and the philosophy of religion.

While expressing our great gratitude to the individual idealists who have contributed to these subjects, let us then pass on. It seems to me that the contribution, in so far as it is beneficial, is in the main not a contribution by idealism but by philosophers who also happen to be idealists. In so far as idealism as a theory of metaphysics and epistemology has affected these subjects at all, it does not seem to have affected many answers to particular problems; but it has led to certain misconceptions. The principal that I should cite are these:

(1) There is a tendency in certain Hegelian quarters to speak of all these subjects in formal terms derived from abstract logic, thus failing to do justice to their unique subject-matter.

---

[1] It is my personal opinion that the best work on these subjects has not on the whole been done by idealists.

[2] What I say is only meant to hold on the whole. One of the writers who have contributed most to those ends which I have ascribed specially to realists is an idealist, Rashdall.

It is indeed desirable that thought in these subjects should not be illogical; but it does not follow that goodness should be treated as though it were a species of logical consistency, as it is sometimes by Hegel and Bosanquet, for example. The position that value categories are unique and cannot be reduced to anything else has usually been asserted against the attempt to describe them in purely psychological terms, but it is also valid against the attempt to reduce them to categories of logic.

(2) While many idealists have defended the objectivity of values, certain forms of idealism do imply that we have the power not only to produce a given change but also to give value to the change, that values are a creation of our minds. Such statements are not as bad in the mouth of an idealist as of a realist because where a similar doctrine is held about all objects of knowledge, it does not imply, as it would if maintained by a realist, that value is a kind of illusion or arbitrary convention, any more than is the case with the other objects of knowledge, which are treated in the same way; and it would be recognised that, if creations of ours at all, values are necessary creations which mind could not but produce, which spring from the essential nature of mind; but nevertheless it seems to me a fundamentally false view. When we produce a change we can determine whether it will be a valuable change or not, because we can determine to some extent what sort of a change it will be in its factual characteristics; but given certain factual characteristics its value or disvalue follows necessarily and cannot be determined by us. A man can decide whether to commit a murder or not, but neither he nor society can make the murder a right act or an intrinsically good occurrence. To approve something as good is not to make it good but to recognise or believe that it is good independently of our judgments about it.[1]

Similarly, the idealist influence may very easily be traced in certain widely held aesthetic theories, which conceive the aesthetic experience of the observer of a beautiful object as a kind of artistic creation, and even sometimes go so far as to deny the beauty of nature on the ground that it is not made by an artist or to suppose that its beauty consists merely in an artistic creation on our part by which we express our own

[1] I do not mean to suggest that all subjective theories of ethics are due to the influence of idealism. They are mostly held for quite other reasons, and such theories are often held by realists.

emotions. Much in Croce's aesthetics may be traced to his idealist philosophy rather than to purely aesthetic considerations.[1] But it is important in aesthetics as well as in epistemology to do justice to the fact that we are passive in contemplating the beautiful object as well as active and that its beauty is in a very real sense *given* and not created by us, even with art, at least when we are not ourselves at the very time engaged in painting the picture or composing the poem, and always with nature. This truth is obscured by certain forms of idealism and by the tendency to interpret aesthetics exclusively on the basis of the experience of the artist and not at all of that of the spectator.

(3) One of the most important contributions made by the idealist movement is the development of the conception of an *organic whole*. Idealist thinkers of the Hegelian type have insisted that the ethical criterion cannot be found in anything short of life as a whole; and this is opposed alike to the view which finds it in a summing of different goods that would be good quite apart from their place in the whole, to the view which appeals to unconnected intuitions as the authority, and to that which relies on abstract formal principles said to be known *a priori*. But, having said that the criterion is the whole, this type of idealist ethics is too apt to stop there and leave us without any guidance as to how the principle is to be applied. This is really to fall back again on intuition alone, namely, an intuition as to which action would fit best into a good whole. While intuition has an important place in ethics, reasoning also surely has some share, and not to give any more definite hint as to the principles which should govern the reasoning and the kind of considerations which should be invoked seems to me to be to abandon the task of philosophy

---

[1] 'Croce's contention is clear that to be distinctly aware of any coherently individual shape, sound, colour or other sensible object is the same thing as to have become distinctly aware of *my own* states of repulsion and attraction, whether these turn out to have been mere desires or actual volitions' (Carritt, *The Theory of Beauty*, p. 190). The matter brought to expression in art is according to Croce 'a state of *our own* passions', is 'crude emotionality' (id., p. 188). 'A supposed pure sensation' is according to him, 'really an ideal creation of reality. . . . The assumption of this whole philosophy is clear; it is that the object does not exist unless it is known, that it is not separable from the knowing spirit and indeed the individual spirit' (id., p. 192). These quotations make clear the great importance of the idealist influence in one of the most popular aesthetic theories of the present day.

in despair. Even if we granted that no conclusions could be established with final certainty because their validity might be affected by the fact that they were mere abstractions from a whole which was more than they, it might well seem reasonable, while admitting our results were liable to partial correction, to go on with the reasoning as far as we could. At least we shall come nearer the truth in that way than we should if we had not *reasoned* about particular ethical questions at all. Hence I do not regard the idealist insistence on the Whole as a valid correction of but as a supplement to the various attempts to formulate the chief principles of ethics without introducing this reference to the Whole. The ultimate criterion may be the Whole, but we can only either decide what is right in particular cases or indeed determine any general theoretical principles of ethics by abstracting from the Whole. No doubt, as a leader of the ' realist ' reaction of the time, Professor Moore, has himself pointed out,[1] it is possible to go grievously astray through treating the value of a whole as necessarily always equal to the sum of the values of its parts, but, as Professor Moore has also shown, this admission may be incorporated in an ethical theory which, whether we agree with it or not, is at least far more definite and clear than any that has been produced by the idealism which at every turn invokes the Whole. The idealist may reply that according to his principles ethics cannot be definite; but if it cannot be made completely definite it should at least be made as definite as possible, and this is very far from having been achieved by either Green or Bradley or Bosanquet (to take the three most prominent idealist writers in this country during the last half-century) despite their very real greatness.

(4) The term, idealist theory of ethics, is commonly meant to stand for the ethics of one specific school of idealists, namely, the absolutists. They find the ultimate criterion of the good as well as of the true in coherence, but they are apt to hesitate between two meanings of the word : (*a*) consistency, the good life being the life in which different ends are combined according to a consistent plan, or the only life which can be carried out consistently with that at which we must all aim, namely,

[1] *Principia Ethica*, ch. I, § 18 ff. I do not mean to suggest that Professor Moore would endorse the idealist use of the conception of organic unity. He points out himself that the term as used is very ambiguous and often stands for something which, if thought out, would be seen to be logically absurd (id., § 21–2).

real satisfaction [1]; (b) harmony, this term being a suitable general one to cover love, co-operation, peace of mind, and that union with the real which may be attained in knowledge, beauty, religion. I doubt whether a tolerable coherence theory of ethics could be worked out without using the term in both senses, and I am not clear as to the connection between them. The view according to which the coherence is to be found in agreement with Society or the State I regard as a gross perversion not integral to the theory; but in maintaining that the right act is to be regarded primarily as the *fitting* act, ' fitting ' being understood in relation to the whole concrete situation or even the whole life of the agent, the ' coherentists ' bring out very effectively one important aspect of rightness. Its other aspects as producing good and as (in a sense) unconditionally obligatory must, however, be equally recognised, and there is as yet lacking a theory which combines due attention to all three. Further, I must repeat that insistence on the Whole and on harmony with it does not exempt a thinker who deals with Ethics from the obligation of studying very carefully the more specific principles and methods which we should use to help us in deciding particular cases, a task which has been neglected by advocates of coherence.[2]

(5) The so-called idealist theory of the State has, as far as I can see, no necessary connection with idealism or even with the coherence theory. No doubt the individual ought to be determined by the interests of society, but there would be no society if there were no individuals, and the relation between individual freedom and the authority of the State cannot be settled by appealing to any metaphysical theory. The type of idealism to which we have been referring has unfortunately often been developed in a way which almost deified the State or the nation and did not do justice to the right of individual liberty, but I do not see that this is logically necessary. Indeed it is flagrantly inconsistent with the adoption of the Whole as the criterion, for the Whole obviously includes not only the State of which the particular ' idealist ' politician happens to be a member but the whole human race.

To pass to another quite different point, much stress has been laid in modern German thought on the significance for philosophy of the existence of sciences or branches of study

---

[1] I am not giving this as my own account of the end.

[2] My general views on Ethics are given in *The Definition of Good* (1947) and *Second Thoughts in Moral Philosophy* (1959).

which deal neither with objects that are, properly speaking, physical nor with individual human minds. Unfortunately there is no single word in English corresponding to the term, *Geisteswissenschaften*, which covers these studies in general, but it is easy to see that a great many of the subjects both of serious research and of ordinary conversation are, at least *prima facie*, neither physical things nor minds nor sensa, neither particular existents nor abstract universals, neither substances nor mere qualities, relations or states of substances, and therefore elude orthodox philosophical classifications. When we speak of shares in a certain business, for example, we are not speaking of particular physical objects such as the pieces of paper which represent their value nor are we speaking merely of the psychology of particular human beings. We are speaking of something that cannot be said to exist in the sense in which particular things and persons can be said to do, and yet is essentially a particular and not an abstract universal, since it is quite clear that it is subject to change and can begin or cease to be. The shares in the business have a history and are no more timeless than are the buildings used by the business. The case is the same with many other of the subjects studied in economics. Again, when we seek to outline the history of the literature or art of a particular nation or the thought of a particular school, we seem in some sense to be doing more than giving an account of the artistic productions and opinions or reasonings of individuals.[1] And analogous difficulties arise in determining what is meant by a term denoting a single work of literature. E.g. is 'Hamlet' merely a name for the group of all performances of Hamlet, all particular experiences of reading Hamlet, etc.? It is not at any rate altogether easy to maintain that this is so.

These circumstances have had an important influence upon the idealist movement, especially in the following three respects: (*a*) They have been held to prove that the truth of many judgments at least, i.e. the judgments about the class of objects now under discussion, does not lie in correspondence to anything, since the objects discussed do not *exist*, but in something quite different, which is often called 'validity'. It has even been suggested that perhaps this may be the case with all judgments, or again that all judgments purporting

[1] The word, study or science, which I have used above, itself stands for something which falls within the ambiguous class of entities under discussion.

to be about physical objects are judgments of this type.
(b) It has been contended that the key to the nature of mind is to be found rather in these objective and yet non-physical realities which it produces, acting in human individuals, than in psychical states capable of being revealed by introspection.
(c) Here is the source of the conception of ' objective mind ', as something rational and yet impersonal which is to be found not only in what we call individual minds as such, but equally, or rather more so, in the institutions, cultures, literatures of different social groups.

(d) The subjects of the *Geisteswissenschaften* show the possibility of a *tertium quid* between the individually subjective and the realistically objective.

' To assert, with some forms of realism, that all reality is " out there ", or with some forms of idealism that it is all " in here " dependent on selection and emphasis as guided by passing interest, is to falsify the most elementary convictions of common sense, the constructive work of science and the achievements of the human mind in the worlds of art, morality and social life. These worlds are all real, and, if we are to hold that they embody a higher truth and so possess a higher reality than the world of sensory appearance or instinctive reaction, and again that within them there are differences of level, whereby

In dignity of being we ascend,

our standard must be quite other than correspondence with anything that is given either from without or from within us.' [1]

' It is the peculiar merit of idealism to have led the way in the philosophical study and appreciation of those worlds which the mind not only contemplates but creates and sustains as organs of its own self-realisation. The " Philosophy of the Human Mind ", which in the hands of David Hume and the English Empiricists had remained within the limits of introspective psychology, went out (so to speak) into the world under the leadership of Kant and Hegel and their followers in Germany and England, and drew within its compass the whole achievement of mind in Society and Civilisation. Abandoning the " subjective " point of view of psychology, it acknowledged not only the reality of Nature, but also the reality of the Spiritual Worlds which mind has erected on the basis of and through mastery over Nature.' [2]

No doubt there is a great deal of truth in all this, but while it is obviously the case that propositions referring to the

[1] J. H. Muirhead, *The Platonic Tradition in Anglo-Saxon Philosophy*, pp. 425–6
[2] R. F. A. Hoernle, *Idealism as a Philosophy*, p. 74.

objects under discussion cannot be quite straightforwardly and simply treated as propositions about the psychical states and dispositional properties of individuals, it is not quite clear that they could not be ultimately analysed entirely in terms of these.[1] A really satisfactory analysis in such terms would be very difficult, but it does not seem to me by any means impossible that one could be effected, and I do not know of any discussion of the question of their analysis sufficiently thorough to justify either a positive or a negative decision in this matter.[2] We cannot say, because there is no individual or individuals that we could conceivably point out which the term, industrial depression, as ordinarily used, denotes, that therefore the proposition, there is an industrial depression, necessarily could not be reduced entirely to several propositions of such a type as, e.g., it is hard for most individuals to sell goods at a profit. No doubt there are difficulties in the way of giving any satisfactory analysis of this kind, but I do not see how the objective being of the objects of *Geisteswissenschaften* as specific entities not reducible to characteristics of individual men or their temporary states and hypothetical facts about these men could be established except by an exhaustive discussion of the possible ways of analysis in such terms and a demonstration of their inadequacy. Till this has been achieved, no philosopher is justified in drawing metaphysical conclusions from the objects of study in question.[3]

But, however that may be, I am unable to treat *physical objects* as having being only in a non-existential sense, because, when I speak about a particular physical object, I am just as sure that I am talking about something which I regard as actually existent in a literal primary sense of the term [4] as

[1] And, in some cases, of physical objects also or characteristics of such objects.
[2] Though there may be one. Unfortunately I do not possess any very extensive knowledge of the treatment of the subject in German philosophy.
[3] Perhaps the worst difficulties arise if we attempt the analysis of propositions about states or societies acting as units, e.g. ' Japan invaded China ', but even if it be the case that an analysis of such propositions in terms of individual men is impossible it would only follow that such groups must be themselves treated as individuals, not that the propositions are ' valid ' without being valid of individuals.
[4] The words ' in a primary sense ' must be added because the verb exist is occasionally and the verb to be very often used in a sense in which it is not intended to assert or imply the actual existence of what is denoted by the subject of the verb, in the sense in which a

I am sure that I do not mean by a bank-rate, an industrial depression or a political movement things which could be said to exist in this primary sense. If the negative assertion is justified in the latter case, as it is, by our immediate awareness of what we mean, so is the positive assertion in the former.

All this is not intended to minimise the importance of a philosophical study of the problems connected with the objects of *Geisteswissenschaften*, etc.,—they have been too much neglected in this country—, but to express a doubt whether the ' objective mind ' of which philosophers sometimes talk is not after all ultimately reducible to the minds of particular human individuals. And it still seems to me impossible to eliminate from the notion of truth the notion that all true judgments are true of something, if that something be only a set of laws or a connection between merely subsistent universals. But that we cannot obtain an adequate view of the nature of the human mind if we only consider the psychological states of individuals and neglect human achievements in art, literature, science and social institutions I readily admit. What mind does is more important even for psychology than what it feels like,—and an important part of what it does is to be found in certain achievements which present themselves to us as if they were impersonal and which are in some cases less individual than collective. But this does not apply to what are normally held to be the greatest values of all, the moral values and the values of love in a wide sense of that term, which are essentially and necessarily only realisable in and through the consciousness of some particular individual and which cannot be separated from the mental attitude of that individual, in the way in which works of art or social institutions can be separated from the mental attitude of their author or founders, without destroying their value.

Values have a greater importance for most idealists than for many, I will not say, all realists, because idealists commonly regard existence as in some way dependent on value ; and this brings the idealists face to face with ' the problem of evil '. Many or most forms of idealism [1] are confronted with

particular man or a particular physical thing can be said to exist. This is clear from the examples I have given, e.g. there is or there exists an industrial depression.

[1] No doubt some forms, such as panpsychism and the subjective form which makes the physical world dependent on the human mind, as well as agnostic phenomenalism, are exempt from the difficulty in question.

it as much as is theology. If the world as a whole is 'good' or 'rational' or if it depends on a divine mind, why then all the evil? I have not brought forward this objection earlier because it is not a difficulty peculiar to idealism but shared also by all who believe in God. And if these forms of idealism are weakened by it in comparison with other forms, they are strengthened by their accordance with religious experience and perhaps by the result of other arguments supporting the existence of God.[1] The subject has been discussed in countless works of theology and philosophy, and I do not propose to try to propound a cheap solution in a few pages, but I must say a word about the line of solution specially, though not exclusively, associated with idealist philosophy.

The solution is to the effect that values necessarily presuppose evil for their own full realisation. This certainly seems to be the case with most of the higher values we know. What would become of moral value as we know it without positive defects of character the overcoming of which was difficult, of the value of unselfishness or love [2] as we know it without any possible opportunity for the slightest self-sacrifice or misfortune which called for help and sympathy, of courage without any pain or danger?[3] In general, to have the intrinsic good of conquering evil, we must have real evil to conquer, and the good of conquering the evil may well outweigh the intrinsic disvalue of the evil without which this value could not be obtained, in which case the evil would be 'worth while'.

[1] This must not be parodied as an assertion that idealism is more likely to be true because, if true, it would supply arguments to prove what we want to believe but cannot otherwise prove. All I mean is that, if a theory supports a given conclusion, the probability of the truth of that theory is in some degree increased by the existence of any other arguments or facts independent of the theory supporting the same conclusion, provided any weight whatever, not necessarily a conclusive weight, is attached to the facts or arguments in question.

[2] I do not mean to suggest that there necessarily could not be forms of love and moral action which do not involve this and yet possess higher value than the forms which do, but they would at any rate be generically different from the highest values realised in human life, and therefore evil is at any rate necessary for the realisation of all kinds of goods, even if unnecessary for the realisation of *some*, a distinction which has often been overlooked by the people who adopted this solution.

[3] The connection is not merely causal but seems to be of the type pointed out by Professor G. E. Moore when he lays down his 'principle of organic unities' (*Principia Ethica*, ch.I, § 18 ff.), though no doubt he would object to this application of it.

It may be rightly objected that this does not apply to all values. It does not apply, as far as we can see, to the values of knowledge, since ignorance and intellectual error are not intrinsically evil (unless due to ethical defects such as prejudices or laziness), nor to all aesthetic values since we can have some kinds of beauty at least without presupposing the slightest ugliness or the slightest pain, nor again to all pleasures which, as far as they go, have *qua* innocent pleasures some intrinsic value.[1] And no doubt there may, for anything we can tell, be beings, such as theologians have commonly supposed God to be, who realise values which do not presuppose any kind of evil and yet are far greater than any of which we have the slightest idea. But we might reply that, though not necessary for the realisation of all values, evil is at least necessary for the realisation of some, and this *may* be sufficient to serve as a justification for its existence, since the more values are realised the better. To use theological language, while a perfect God, if such there be, could realise values far higher than ours, he could not realise all the kinds of value possible himself, since some necessarily imply imperfection, and even perhaps in the lower stages of development actual sinfulness which has to be overcome.[2] In that case we might have been created because there was something that even God could not do without us, namely, realise these particular values, which, though very much lower than his values, were still necessary for the full attainment of his purpose, because this must involve the realisation not only of some but of all possible values.

The presence of evil in a rational universe would thus still be capable of justification on principle, provided (1) that evil was necessary for the fullest realisation of some kinds of value, for clearly the more kinds of value there are in the universe the better, provided (2) there was not more evil than is necessary for that purpose, and provided (3) the value of the good attained outweighed the disvalue of the evil involved in its

---

[1] The absolute idealist would, however, urge that these values in their concrete manifestations could not be separated from the whole life of the man in whom they are realised and so from some evil, since a life in which there was no form of evil would be generically and inconceivably different from any life we know. He would say that it is not a piece of knowledge or an experience of beauty or a pleasure *per se* that ever has value but life as a whole, and these only in their context in that whole.

[2] This could not excuse sinfulness, because it is only a means to good as overcome, and nobody sins for the purpose of overcoming his sin.

attainment. The first of these three conditions does seem quite definitely to be fulfilled in fact, since we can see that some kinds of value imply the existence of evil; whether the last two are fulfilled or not we have no empirical ground either to affirm or to deny. There undoubtedly is a vast amount of evil in the world, but then how can we possibly know what amount of evil is necessary for the fullest realisation of values? It is certainly not merely trifling evils but great evils that have called forth the noblest actions of human life, and in general a great victory requires a great obstacle to conquer.[1] No doubt again there are a vast number of evils which we do not see to be conducive to any good which outweighs them, but then we can estimate such a small part of their total effects that no reasonable person could expect to see it in most cases even if they do really always conduce to this. However, this solution does not seem to me to have the least plausibility unless we postulate what Hegelian idealists have very commonly refused to postulate, namely, human survival of bodily death. Nor, whether such views of the fundamental goodness of reality are otherwise capable of establishment or not, can we admit that they may be established by any of the arguments which would ordinarily be called idealist and have been examined in this book.

[1] The reply often made to a person who brings this argument that he could not feel like that about great evils which affected himself personally is irrelevant. The fact that it would be psychologically impossible for me to hold a belief when I was under the influence of a certain strong emotion of a kind to prejudice me against it is no argument whatever against the truth of the belief in question. Further, it does seem from biographical accounts to be a fact that many people have succeeded in feeling like that even about their own greatest misfortunes.

SUMMARY OF MAIN CONCLUSIONS

1. Cognition must be regarded as rather of the nature of finding than of making, though realists have gone too far in asserting that it necessarily implies logically the complete independence of its object. All the idealist arguments from the nature of cognition to the conclusion that Reality is mental or mind-dependent are invalid. The most we can be justified in holding is that we must think of what we know *as it would be* for a knowing mind, and this, though it may justify a kind of methodological idealism as a means to epistemological realism, does not imply that what we know can only exist for a knowing mind (ch. II).

2. But it does not follow that we are unable to draw conclusions from epistemology as to the nature of the real world (ch. III).

3. It is futile to meet the antinomies of space and time by making space and time mere appearances (ch. III).

4. While we must distinguish various senses of 'internal' and 'external' and reject most of the idealists' arguments to the effect that relations are internal in the senses usually maintained by them, conclusions somewhat similar to, though not identical with, theirs are established by a consideration of causality. While causality is not analysable in any simple way, one of the relations subsisting between cause and effect is that of logical entailment.[1] This forces us to return to the view that the world has something of the character of an intelligible system, though we cannot see its intelligibility (ch. IV).

5. Two other important points which have been overlooked by the prevailing pluralism of the present day are (*a*) that relations only occur in a continuum not itself reducible exclusively to a set of relations and terms; (*b*) that, if we took away all the relations of anything, it is doubtful whether it would have any qualitative character left (ch. IV).

6. The view that finds the nature of truth in 'coherence'

[1] (3rd ed.) or, preferably, cause and effect are connected by a relation at least closely analogous to that of logical entailment.

SUMMARY OF MAIN CONCLUSIONS 441

should be rejected and a modified form of the correspondence theory adopted (ch. V).

7. It is possible to hold a 'coherence view' of the world without accepting the doctrine that all propositions are both partly true and partly false. The contrary supposition is due to confusions, (a) between judgments as = judgings and propositions, (b) between entailing and including, (c) between two different senses of 'what X means' (ch. V).

8. The view that 'coherence' is the criterion of truth is not overthrown by the usual objections, provided we either understand by 'coherence' coherence with our experience or add to the criterion of coherence that of comprehensiveness (ch. V).[1]

9. Synthetic inference, i.e. inference from one or more facts to another different fact not included in these, is possible. The views which make deductive inference merely verbal or 'analytic' are untenable (ch. V).

10. The representative theory of perception is preferable to any direct theory. But this does not imply that we cannot have a non-inferential *cognition* of physical objects. This problem as well as that of memory is much obscured by a confusion between different senses of 'direct awareness' (ch. VI).

11. Propositions about physical objects cannot be analysed in terms of actual and possible sensa of human beings. On the contrary, in such propositions we are normally ascribing at least primary qualities to physical objects existing independently of us in the same sense as we ascribe them to sensa. Hence, unless such independent objects with at least primary qualities exist, most or all of the propositions of 'commonsense' and science about physical objects are false (ch. VII).

12. The existence of such independent physical objects cannot be said to be known certainly, but an argument can be given which makes it reasonable to accept it as the most probable hypothesis. We are also justified in holding that we have a partially valid non-inferential cognition of such objects, as we have of past events in memory, though falling below the latter in respect of certainty (ch. VII).

13. The most defensible view of physical objects is that they consist of 'groups of unsensed sensa', representatively perceived but directly cognised, having both primary qualities and at least some of the sensible qualities we call secondary, and including in themselves not all the shapes and colours, etc., seen from different positions but only those which can be

[1] (3rd ed.) But v. p. 444 ff. below.

combined most coherently on the assumption that a physical thing cannot have more than one shape and two sensa of the same sense cannot occupy the same space at the same time. (ch. VII).

14. The view that the specific nature of a physical object implies *percipi* (or experience) cannot be proved by argument and does not seem to me in the least self-evident. For anybody who thinks it to be true the most reasonable form of idealism to be adopted would be the theistic form. Absolutism and panpsychism are open to various objections (ch. VIII).[1]

[1] (3rd ed.) I find to my surprise that 26 years later I can still subscribe to all these conclusions with only a toning-down of 8 and a slight modification in 4.

NOTES ADDED IN THIRD EDITION

Ch. III, § *2*: I have since come to the conclusion that Kant in describing the synthesis was not trying to give a description of a timeless act by which we make the phenomenal world, and consequently that the side of Kant's view which I have, like many other commentators, criticised is not really there, but only the side which I on the whole approve, v. my *Short Commentary on Kant's Critique of Pure Reason*, p. 88 ff.

Ch. IV, § *1*: I shall not add to the intricacies of the chapter on relations, though I could have done so. In particular I overlooked the fact that a relation may also be said to be internal not relatively to a particular it relates in its whole nature but relatively to it quâ member of a certain class. Thus the relation of having written is internal relatively to the class of authors in the sense that an author logically must have written something, but it does not follow that I logically must have written something, only that I could not have been an author if I had never done so. But this distinction is not very relevant to the theory that reality is a closely knit system based on the internal theory of relations. Nor have I covered *all* the senses in which Bradley uses the phrase 'Internal relation'.

Ch. IV, § *2*: I have spoken on p. 147 as if Bradley himself assumed that a relation was a sort of third term, when in fact what he is doing is criticising this very view as one of the alternatives to his own. Thus interpreted, it seems to me that his argument must succeed unless we admit, as I should, that the notion of relation is unique and irreducible. For his argument consists in showing that a relation cannot be reduced to anything else, either to a third term or to some quality or qualities, for if so it would not relate, and then assuming that this destroys the chance of giving any defence of the concept of relation at all.

Ch. IV, § *3*: I should now prefer to say not that logical entailment is one of the relations which make up causation, but that causation is closely analogous to logical entailment. I still do not understand how we can defend induction or avoid leaving the empirically given regularities as mere monstrous coincidence unless we admit that cause and effect are necessarily connected (at least unless we adopted an occasionalist or Berkeleian view, which would be even less palatable to modern thinkers). But I made a mistake in speaking as if we could never infer B from A unless A entailed B. This is of course not the case; the inference may be only probable, or it may be valid only on unstated assumptions, so that it is not a case of A entailing B but of A plus conditions CD . . . N entailing B. But what I should still contend is that no such inference could validly be made without the covert assumption that there are some *necessary* causal connections, though these may not directly connect A and B. For otherwise we cannot pass from what has happened in some cases to any generalisation (even only probable) about what will happen in others, on the basis of which we can alone make forecasts. There is no ground for supposing that the same cause will be followed by the same effect in the future unless we are justified in supposing a necessary connection between cause and effect. The circumstance that has perhaps been most influential in leading people to reject my view is that causal inferences are, commonly at least, only probable, whereas *a priori* inferences are not, but this can easily be explained provided we remember that, if entailments hold between the physical cause and the effect, we cannot discern them *a priori* and therefore in finding causes have to use just the same arguments as anybody who does not believe in my theory of causation. I do not want to justify induction in a way which would make it a species of deduction, but I do not think that this would be the effect of my argument, since I regard the general proposition about causation presupposed not as a premiss but as a principle of reasoning; and I do want to be able to maintain that induction is *rational*. I think that much the most defensible alternative view to mine would be one which admitted causal necessity but denied that this involved the conclusion that a being who knew what the cause was and could see logical entailments would be in a position to infer the effect *a priori*. For a further defence and development of my view v. my article in the *Journal of Philosophical and Phenomenological Research*, June 1952.

Ch. V, § 1: My views on the correspondence theory have changed in the following respects since I wrote *Idealism*. (*a*) I now admit that, when it has been reduced to a form in which it can meet all criticisms, the correspondence theory really tells one remarkably little, hardly more than that truth depends on some relation to a reality which is itself not just a set of judgments. Even this much is however needed as a reminder to ardent coherentists (or pragmatists). (*b*) I should now hold that there is not just one relation of correspondence. True categorical descriptive judgments correspond to reality in one sense, hypothetical judgments in another, evaluative judgments in another.[1] (*c*) I do not now regard facts as ultimate entities, as I possibly did in *Idealism*. Propositions ultimately correspond to things or events, facts just being abstractions from these. (*d*) But it now seems not inappropriate to me to speak of correspondence as a criterion of truth in cases where we are judging about our present state of mind or immediate objects of perception. Here we surely know our judgment to be true just because we are directly aware of the reality about which we judge and see it to accord with that.

Ch. V, § 4: The complaint has been made that I and others have put the coherence criterion to two radically different uses. We assumed that, whenever we make correct deductive or otherwise *a priori* inferences, we are using the principle of coherence, but we also conceived the principle as underlying inductive arguments on the ground that these are

[1] On this v. my *Second Thoughts in Moral Philosophy*, ch. 2.

attempts to make a coherent system of our experience as far as possible. The one type of argument proceeds from premisses to a conclusion deduced from them, the other contends that a proposition is justified because other propositions known to be true can be deduced from it, i.e. because it provides an ' explanation ' of known facts. It has been replied that it is a point of the coherence theory that induction is not a fundamentally different type of reasoning from deduction, and however this may be—I myself think that the truth on this matter lies somewhere between the typical coherentist view and the fashionable modern view which exaggerates the difference—it must certainly be remembered that we can argue backwards from conclusion to premisses as well as forwards from premisses to conclusion. When p entails q, we use the relation to establish q if we are fairly sure of p, but if we think q false we can equally well argue back and use this to refute p, and further, if q is true, the fact that it follows from p may under certain conditions, as every scientist knows, undoubtedly constitute an argument for the truth of p. Now the conditions under which this is so seem to be just those which lead one to say that, if we accept p as true, it will make our beliefs approach closer to a coherent system. Certainly on anybody's view it is an argument for a theory that its consequences are true and fit into a system with other established truths. Now if we take the general ideal to be a coherent system, we are clearly going against it if we deny q while asserting p when p entails q; but we are also going against it if, other things being equal, we accept a theory which gives a number of independent *ad hoc* explanations for particular facts in preference to one which brings them all into the same system. (I think this is in the main what is meant when it is said that we ought in science to accept the simplest hypothesis.) They are very different faults, but they are both violations of the spirit of rationality.

At the same time I should want to insist that all knowledge and rational belief are not just a matter of finding or making coherent. Not only is sense experience absolutely necessary, so that the criterion cannot possibly be just coherence but at least coherence with sense experience, but we have also to supplement the coherence criterion by other modes of non-inferential cognition. In the first place we are dependent throughout on memory, and to remember is not just to find a past fact coherent with the present. Secondly, we shall have to admit another kind of non-inferential cognition in moral and evaluative judgments unless we can be content with an ethics that is either completely *a priori* (a deductive system) or at the other extreme entirely naturalistic in which case it would be based simply inductively on empirical facts. Finally, as I insisted in the first edition,[1] the application of the coherence criterion itself requires ultimately an immediate insight into what coheres and what is incompatible, which cannot always itself be justified by saying that it is coherent with our other knowledge to suppose that the propositions do or do not cohere. In view of these considerations my formula for the criterion of truth would not be coherence alone, or even ' coherence with experience ', but ' coherence with our non-inferential cognition ' or ' non-inferential cognition as tested by coherence '. Once this line is adopted, it might indeed be argued that I am as much an adherent of the correspondence as of the coherence theory, for non-inferential cognitions are insights into what is true, i.e.

[1] v. above p. 241.

what corresponds to the real. However, even if this is so, it does not alter the fact that, while the correspondence theory in any tenable form tells one very little, the coherence theory does to my mind enhance one's understanding of the nature of knowledge and reasoning greatly (if somewhat one-sidedly).

Ch. VI, § 3: The contemporary hostility to sense data has not persuaded me to change my views. Unfortunately in discussing the topic two questions commonly seem to have been confused. One is the question discussed here as to whether physical objects are directly perceived, the other is the question what, if anything, can be sorted out as immediately given by our senses in distinction from interpretation. The difficulties raised by the latter question seem to me irrelevant to the former. If the content of what we immediately perceive (are sensibly aware of prior to any conscious inference) is never or rarely just the result of sensation but includes a great deal of mental interpretation,[1] this is to me only an additional argument against the view that we perceive physical objects directly and for the view that what we directly perceive is dependent on our mind. Incidentally it seems to me the chief argument against the view of Lord Russell that what we actually perceive is always our brain (though admittedly not actually perceived *as* such).

The popular philosophical view that the sensa theory and the direct theory are just two different languages expressing the same facts really assumes that the direct theory is true and that we cannot regard sensa as actually existing entities but as a mere linguistic device for speaking about cases where our perception is not veridical. If so, the section as a whole is an argument against this view.

Ch. VII, § 3: I must now admit a gap which I had overlooked in the arguments for my view of matter. I assumed too readily that there could be no way of justifying the belief in physical objects, interpreted realistically, unless they were ' groups of unsensed sensa '. In defence of my point of view I used the argument that a causal inference cannot enable us to conclude to the existence of anything different in kind from what we experience, and I am still convinced that we cannot prove or make it probable by any causal argument that physical things are thus different. But it does not follow that we cannot use a causal argument to establish the probable existence of physical things if in fact they are thus different. The causal argument I gave for their existence rested on the contention that it is very unlikely that the predictions based on the belief in them would have turned out true so frequently if they did not exist, and this argument does not use the premiss that they are like what we experience otherwise than in respect of structure. But I still think that the notion of physical objects as groups of unsensed sensa remains a plausible and interesting possibility. It is certainly very dogmatic to assume, as holders of the representative theory have generally done, that matter is necessarily generically different from the sensa we experience.

[1] v. above p. 361 ff.

INDEX

Aaron, Professor R. I., on sensation, 191 n.
Absolute Mind, 19 ff., 28, 50 ff.; Absolute not conceived as a mind, 59 ff. 210, 403 ff.
Accordance, as new name for correspondence, 207–8
Activity, as feature in causation, 164, 172
Aesthetics, idealist influence in, 429–30. See *Beauty*
Agnosticism, 105 ff., 228
Alexander, Professor S., on causation, 154 n.; on images, 287; on memory, 272; on perception, 282 ff.
Als Ob school, 115, 227
Analysis, in philosophy, 8–9, 260; of propositions, in general, 219, 295–6, 304–5; of propositions about physical objects, 296 ff., 305 ff., 312 ff., 332 n., 337–8, 354; of hypothetical propositions, 418 ff.; analysis a form of inference, 239
Analytic, as opposed to synthetic, judgments and inferences, 31–2, 67–8, 173–4, 220, 251–7
Animism, 410 ff.
Antinomies, in Kant, 84 ff., 110
Appearances, argument that our knowledge is limited to, 64 ff., 76 ff., 84 ff.; in Hegel, &c., 93; in Kant, 85 ff., 94 ff., 101–2, 106, 110; reality of, 88 ff., 94 ff.
A priori knowledge, 40, 57–8, 144, 159, 422; Kant's view of, 64 ff., 67 ff., 72 ff., 112; *a priori* connection in causation, 173 ff., 179–80. See *Entailment*
Arithmetic, involves an empirical element, 72; Kant's view of, 66, 70. See *Mathematics*
Atomic theory, the, its apparent discrepancy with our perceptions, 351–2, 372–3

Beauty, physical objectivity of, 379, 429–30
Being, as opposed to existence, 37 n. See *Subsistence*
Berkeley, George, 340, 347–8, 383 ff.; his arguments for idealism, 12 ff., 306 n., 378
Bosanquet, B., on coherence, 237, 244–5, 246; on ethics, 429; on mind, 406, 407; on panpsychism, 415; on relations, 123, 126, 130 n., 145, 146, 152; on time, 93
Bradley, F. H., on relations, 44, 120 n., 123, 133, 143, 144, 145 ff., 151, 194; on time, 93; his theory of truth, 25, 199 ff., 208 n., 209 ff., 234, 238, 240; his view of reality as experience, 404 ff.
Braithwaite, R. B., on causation, 155 n., 162, 165
Broad, Professor C. D., 9, 36 n., 398 n.; on the *a priori*, 73 n.; on causation, 155, 187 n., 251; on perception and physical objects, 285, 287, 344, 378 n.

Caird, E., 21, 60, 387 n.
Cambridge School, the, 1–2, 8–9, 247, 251, 295, 395
Campbell, Professor C. A., on Bradley, 150, 151 n.
Carritt, E. F., on Croce's aesthetics, 430 n.

Categories, Kant's treatment of, 64 ff., 71, 77 ff., 97, 103, 104–5, 112, 114

Causality, nature of, ch. IV. sect. 3, 47, 117 n., 128–9, 260, 327 n.; implies coherence, 231–2; in Kant, 68, 71, 77, 95 ff., 103, 104, 110, 112, 113; mechanical, 182; proof of, 77–8, 95, 112, 247; in sensa, 368–9; universality of, 181 ff., 185–6, 187; causal argument for physical objects, 327 ff., 341–2, 346, 356, 361; causal argument for theism or panpsychism, 411 ff.

Certainty, of judgments, 209, 220 ff., 258 ff. See *Knowledge*

Change, reality of, 41–2

Characteristic, definition of, 120 n.

Cognition, my use of term, 17 n.; idealist theory of, ch. II, ch. III sect. 2, 112 ff.; relation to its object, 15–16, 27, 44 ff., 53, 122, 129, 137 ff., 144, 200 ff.; non-inferential cognition, 259–60, 260 n., (see *Intuition*); non-inferential cognition of physical objects, 267 ff., 284, 292, 316–26, 338–9, 342–4

Coherence, definition of, 228 ff.; as criterion of truth, 236 ff., 328; does not entail doctrine of degrees of truth, 220 ff.; in ethics, 250, 431–2; as theory of nature of reality, 148, 175, 185, 228 ff., 250; as theory of nature of truth, 201, 222, see *Correspondence*; uncertainty or certainty of, 210, 232, 242; view founded by Kant, 112

Coincidences, arguments from, 152, 169–70, 330 ff.

Colour, physical reality of, 274, 282, 301 ff., 339, 351, 353, 373, 375

Common-sense, argument from, 291 ff., 306, 314 ff, 326, 386 ff.

Comprehensiveness, as opposed to coherence, 229 n., 234, 238

Conceive, ambiguity of word, 13–14, 24

Concept, ambiguity of word, 14, 23–4, 61, 62

Construction, mental, 23 ff., 37. See *Synthesis*

Content, as opposed to form, 108

Continuum, 188–9; sensory, 381 n.

Contradiction, nature of, 150–1, 255; law of, 67, 76, 210

Copying theory of knowledge, 29–30, 41, 195–6

Correspondence, relation of, 49–50, 53 ff., 137 ff., 196, 200, 201–2, 203, 204; correspondence theory of truth, ch. V sect. 1, 266, 433 ff.

Creation, of characteristics, 338, 375, 415; of physical objects, 381–2; of sensa, 287–8, 380 ff.; of values, 429

Criterion, of truth, 236 ff.

Critical Realists, the, on perception, 282 n., 318 n.

Critique of Pure Reason. See *Kant*

Croce, Signor Benedetto, 13 ff., 23; aesthetics of, 430

Cunningham, Professor Watts, 3 n.

Davies, Dr. S. H., 34 n.

Definition, meaning of, 196 n.

Degrees of truth, ch. V, sect. 2

Determinable, 128 ff., 189

Determinateness, different senses or species of, 311, 313 n.; of size, 310–11, 313–14

Determinism, not provable by science, 181

Difference, relation of, 134–5

Dimension, third, in sensa and physical objects, 363, 372

Direct awareness, 198, 203 ff., 264 ff., 284; direct theory of perception, 263, 264, 268 ff., 274 ff., 320–1, 323, 335 n.

Dreams, as source of argument against realism, 318, 348, 352

Electrons, in relation to a philosophical view of physical objects, 309 n., 352, 373

Emergence, in evolution, 412–13

Empiricism, 251 ff.

Entailment, logical, how we arrive at notion of, 73; involved in causation, 166 ff., 171 ff., 180; synthetic, 252 ff., 257 ff.

INDEX

Epistemology, idealist arguments based on, ch. II, 64 ff.; 141–2, 386, 410; realist epistemology, 33 ff., 58, 216 ff., 265 ff.; epistemology still important for metaphysics, 79–80
Error, 202, 203, 244, 267; in perception, 278 ff., see *Illusion*; Royce's explanation of, 50; view that all judgments are partly erroneous, 145 ff., 209 ff., 219 ff.; no absolute errors, 217 ff.
Essential, meaning of term, 121 n., 122, 131 n.
Ethics, 73, 249–50, 417; idealist influence in, 428–9, 430 ff.; certain knowledge in, 259 n. See *Values*
Evil, problem of, 436 ff.
Excluded Middle, law of, 209, 219 n.
Existence, different meanings of term, 298, 435–6
Experience, as part of definition of idealism, 3–4; Kantian argument that knowledge is limited t 67 ff.; as opposed to mind, 392–3; propositions about physical objects interpreted in terms of, 95, 294 ff., 353 ff., 397–9; view of reality as, 210, 212, 404 ff., 413; empirical element in knowledge, 72 ff., 156 ff., 238 ff., 251, 317, 321; experiencing as opposed to knowing, 33, 385–6

Fact, as opposed to theory, 25–6; as object of knowledge, 43 n.
False propositions, value of, 226 ff.; all judgments held to be partly false, 145 ff., 209 ff., 219 ff.
Fawcett, Dr. D., on imagining, 399
Feeling, meaning of term, 191; in Bradley, 145, 212; physical objects wrongly compared to, 392–3
Fiction, idealism as, 22, 56 ff.
Form, as opposed to content, 72, 108
Future, the, judgments about, 34–5, 37 n., 92 n., 158

Geisteswissenschaften, philosophical significance of the, 433 ff.
Gentile, Signor Giovanni, 13 ff., 23, 29, 38 n., 41
Geometry, 29, 419; Kant's view of, 65, 68 ff., 73, 75–6
Gestaltpsychologie, 277
Given, the, ambiguity of term, 363 ff.
God, as opposed to the Absolute, 403 ff.; Berkeley's view of, 387; creation by, 380 ff., 399; and problem of evil, 437 ff.; idealist arguments for, 365, 387 ff., 399 ff., 403, 411–13, 416 ff., 424 ff.; Kant's view of, 103 ff., 115; personality of, 227, 393–4, 404; as regulative principle, 103, 115
Good. See *Ethics* and *Values*
Green, T. H., 21, 387 n., 399 ff.
Ground, relation to cause, 154, 168, 174

Heat, objections to physical reality of, 378–9, 390 n.
Hegel, 7–8, 60 ff., 434; on ethics, 429; on time, 93
Hegelians, 119 n., 125, 186, 424, 428–9, 430–1, 439
Hobhouse, Professor L. T., on relations, 147
Hoernlé, Professor R. F. A., on idealism, 434
Hume, David, on causation, 163, 164, 173, 175; on physical objects, 292 n.
Hypothetical propositions, analysis and metaphysical status of, 418 ff.

Idealism, definition of, 2 ff.
Ideas, 196; innate, 251; in knowledge, 54 ff., 265 ff.; regulative, 105 ff. See *Concepts*
Identity, as supposed aim of knowledge, 44, 50, 60, 61–2, 65, 199–200, 211; and predication, 150, 223
Illusion, meaning of term, 263; idealist arguments based on, 344–5, 347 ff.; in immediate experience, 89, 281; as opposed

IDEALISM

to veridical perception, 95 ff., 113, 275 ff., 285 ff., 322, 324, 359, 366, 375
Images, mental, 287 ff., 320, 380–1
Imaginary objects, 191, 202
Immanence, of Absolute Mind, 19, 41, 50, 51, 410
Immediate experience, the real object of, 361 ff.
Imply, meaning of term, 17 n. See *Entailment*
Important, meaning of, 121–2 n.
Independence, definition of, 262–3 ; of object of knowledge, 33 ff., 37 ff., 57–9 ; logical, 230 ; of physical objects, 297 ff., ch. VII sect. 2
Indeterminism, 232 n. ; not provable by science, 181–2
Induction, intuitive, 177 ; problematic, presuppositions of, 156 ff., 166 ff., 175–6, 244–5, 247–9, 260
Inference, implies causation, 163 ; judgment inseparable from, 216 ; synthetic as opposed to analytic, 67 ff., 74, 173–4, 251 ff.
Infinity, problem of, 84 ff., 236, 309 ff. ; infinite regress, 123, 143, 147 ff., 206–7
Interaction, universal, 184 ff.
Introspection, knowledge by, 34, 36 n., 89 n. ; mental events not all objects of, 39
Intuition, meaning of term, 270 n. ; in ethics, 430 ; in Kant's sense, 65 n., 68 ff. ; non-perceptual, 73 n., 259–60. See *Cognition, non-inferential*

Jeans, Sir James, on universal interaction, 185
Joachim, Professor H., on coherence, 230–1, 234 ; on relations, 121 n., 143, 144, 152
Judgments, ambiguity of term, 197, 198 n., 216 ff. ; alleged partial falsity of all, 145 ff., 209 ff., 219 ff. ; alleged partial truth of all, 217 ff. ; synthetic, 251 ff. See *Cognition, Propositions*

Kant, ch. III ; on appearances, 85 ff., 94 ff., 101–2, 106, 110 ; on *a priori* knowledge, 64 ff., 67 ff., 72 ff., 112 ; on the categories, 64 ff., 71, 77 ff., 95 ff., 103 ff., 110, 112, 113, 114 ; on causality, 68, 71, 77, 95 ff., 103, 104, 110, 112, 113 ; on coherence, 112 ; on experience, argument that knowledge is limited to, 67 ff. ; on God, 103 ff., 115 ; on infinity, 84 ff. ; on intuition, 68 ff. ; on mathematics, 65, 66, 68 ff., 73 ; on objectivity, 94 n., 95, 97 ; on physical objects, 78 ff., 85, 94 ff., 99 ff., 113 ; on psychology, 94, 96–7, 114 ; on reciprocity, 78 n., 95 n., 184 ; on regulative principles, 105 ff., 114 ff. ; on science (physical), 94, 114–15 ; on self, 65, 94, 96, 100, 103, 111, 112, 113–14 ; on sensation, 83 ; on space, 68 ff., 73–4, 84 ff., 94 n., 99 ; on substance, 71, 78 n., 99 ; on synthesis, 69 n., 81 ff., 108, 112–13 ; on synthetic judgments, 67 ff. ; on thing-in-itself, 65, 99, 100 n., 101 ff. ; on thought, as opposed to knowledge, 102 ff. ; on time, 68, 71, 84 ff., 94 n. ; realism of, 64, 93 ff. ; scepticism of, 105 ff. ; subjectivism of, 63 ff. ; transcendental method of, 79 ff. ; distinguishes consciousness and its object, 32 n. ; his *Opus Postumum*, 98
Kemp Smith, Professor N., on definition of idealism, 2 ; on Kant, 63 ff. ; on perception and physical objects, 282 ff., 289 n., 344
Keynes, Dr. J. M., on probability, 35 n., 170
Knowledge, different meanings of word, 14, 36 n., 43 n., 73 n., 199, 271 ; as opposed to opinion, 27 n., 37 n., 139, 142, 205, 210 ff. 220 ff., 259, 265 ff., 322. See *Cognition*
Köhler, Professor W., on causation, 176 n. See *Gestaltpsychologie*

INDEX

Laird, Professor J., on images, 287; on perception, 278 ff., 338; on relations, 124, 125–6
Laws, of thought, 26, 28, 64; certainty of, 212–13; of nature, see *Causality, Induction*
Leibniz, 123, 424
Logic, 72, 73, 249–50; inductive, 159–60; logical connection between cause and effect, 166 ff., 171 ff., 180
Lotze, Hermann, 25 n., 399 n.

Mabbott, J. D., on Berkeley, 387 n
McTaggart, Dr. J. E., pluralism of, 391; on relations, 119 n., 132; on subsistence, 420; on substance, 371; on time and space, 89 ff.
Mathematics, 68 ff., 73, 256–7; certainty in, 209, 213 ff., 222, 224–5; coherence in, 229, 231, 233–4, 238 n.; relations in, 126
Matter. See *Physical Objects*
Meaning, ambiguity of term, 224–5, 235; questions about, how answered, 295–6; meaning of common-sense propositions may be indefinite and yet unambiguous, 304
Memory, 271 ff.; compared to cognition of physical objects, 317, 319–20; implies causation, 162–3; relation to epistemological idealism, 17 ff.; validity of, how vindicated, 240
Mental, as opposed to physical, 60, 286, 411 ff.
Metaphysics, certainty or uncertainty of, 210, 227, 259–60; possibility of, 91, 258
Mind, as opposed to experience, 392 ff.; held to be implied by material objects, 385–6, 390 ff., 400–3; relation to matter, 381–2; held only to know what is mental, 26–7, 60, 413; 'objective mind,' 434 ff; view that all minds really one, 18, 125, 406 ff. See *Absolute*
Monism, 153; mistaken arguments for, 124–5, 146
Montague, Professor W. P., on causality, 169

Moore, Professor G. E., on ethics, 431; on idealism, 32, 33, 386 n.; on perception and physical objects, 280 ff., 297 n., 301 n., 306–7, 323 n., 329; on relations, 131, 132
Motives, causation by, 161–2
Muirhead, Professor J. H., on idealism, 434

Naturalism, 2 n., 381
Nature, of a thing, meaning of expression, 119, 123, 199
Necessity, causal, 164, 167 ff., 172, 180; in Kant, 95 ff.; logical non-causal, 168 n., see Entailment; in mathematics, 70
New Realists, the, 33, 274, 350, 359–60

Objectivity, of ethics, 416–17; in Kant, 94 n., 95, 97; of universals, 50, 61, 418 ff. See *Independence*
Objects, of cognition, &c., 44 ff., 51 ff., 137 ff., 144, 191, 199 ff., 406, 414–15; argument that all knowable objects imply a mind, 14, 20 ff., 31 ff., 61–2, 112. See *Physical Objects*
Organic unity, 430–1, 437

Pain, 32 n., 377–9, 390 n.
Panpsychism, 410 ff.
Passivity, immediate awareness of, 164, 165
Past, the, being of, 37 n., 45, 272–3; not changed by cognition, 38, 42; problem of infinity of, 84 ff.
Perception, ambiguity of word, 14; immediate data of, 362 ff.; may involve non-inferential cognition of physical objects, 267 ff., 284, 292, 316–26, 338–9, 342–4; representative *v.* direct theory of, 263, 268 ff., 273 ff., 305, 322–4; as opposed to sensation, 191 n., 362 ff., 368 n.; involves synthesis, 112–13
Percipi, supposed to be implied by *esse*, 31 n.
Personality, of God, 227, 393–4, 404

Perspective, laws of, 275–7, 319
Phenomena. See *Appearances*
Phenomenalism, discussion of, ch. VII sect. 1 and 2
Physical Objects, ch. VI and VII *passim*; meaning of term, 262, 294 ff., 435–6; arguments that they imply mind, 21–2, 57–8, 235–6, 385–6, 390 ff.; arguments for independent existence of, 113, 291 ff., 315, 327–44; Kant's view of, 78 ff., 85, 94 ff., 99 ff., 113; nature of, ch. VII sect. 3; necessary connection implied in, 77–80, 95, 165–6, 249 n.; non-inferential cognition of, 267 ff., 284, 292, 316–26, 338–9, 342–4
Pitkin, Professor W. B., 33
Plato, 67
Pleasure, 377
Pluralism, objections to, 125, 183, 187, 193, 210; moderate pluralism true, 236
Possibilities, being of, 38 n., 203, 418
Predicate and Predication, 122–3, 150, 223, 252
Price, H. H., on coherence, 230; on perception, 282 n., 318 n.; on arguments for and against realism, 341, 345; on sensa, 360, 368; on synthesis, 113
Prichard, Professor H., on perception, 280 ff.; on theory of knowledge, 33
Primary qualities, inseparable from relations, 189; physical reality of, 297 ff., 302 n., 303, 328 ff., 336 ff., 348 ff.; as opposed to secondary qualities, 190, 352–3, 373–4, 376
Probability, notion of, 35 n., 73, 170; antecedent, 334–5; arguments from probability or improbability, 169–70, 330 ff.; different senses of, 258
Propositions, 197, 202–3, 205, 216 ff.
Psychology, 436; *a priori* element in, 176 ff., 179; Kant's view of, 94, 96–7, 114; psychological explanation, 284

Purpose, in relation to judgment, 49 ff., 221

Ramsey, F. E., on causation, 157 ff., 168; on vagueness and precision, 9
Rashdall, Hastings, ethics of, 428 n.; idealism of, 387 n., 391 n., 400, 409 n.; his argument for God based on moral values, 416 ff.
Rationalism and Rationalists, 251 ff., 255–6, 258 ff.
Realism, in general, as opposed to idealism, 8–9, 58–9, 251, 428; epistemology of, 33 ff., 58–9, 216 ff.; in Hegel, 59 ff.; in Kant, 64, 93 ff.; realist view of physical objects, 262, ch. VII sect. 1 and 2, 365–6, 387 ff., 403
Reality, meaning of term, 60 n., 93, 232 n.; degrees of, 215 n.; knowledge of, 74 ff., 91, 103 ff., 110, 173, 198, 204 ff.; truth held to be one aspect of, 199 ff., 212–13
Reasonable, different senses of, 157 ff., 168
Regularity view of causation, 152 ff.
Regulative principles, 105 ff., 114 ff., 232
Relations, abstraction from continuum, 149, 188–9; between cognition and its object, 15–6, 27, 44 ff., 53, 122, 129, 137 ff., 144, 200 ff.; between past and present or future, 38, 42–3; Bradley's argument against, 145 ff.; different kinds of, 273; given in experience, 363; held to imply mind, 81, 399 ff.; internal as opposed to external, ch. IV *passim*, 43 ff., 221, 232–3; as opposed to qualities, 121 n., 122–4, 147, 148, 190 ff.; as opposed to relational characteristics, 119, 120, 147, 190
Religion, 7, 92, 106–7, 238 n., 259–60, 404. See *God*
Representative theory, of knowledge, 198, 265 ff.; of perception, 263, 264, 269 ff., 273 ff., 298 n., 305–6, 322–4, 359

INDEX

Ross, Dr. W. D., on ethics, 259 n.
Royce, Josiah, 49 ff., 394
Russell, Earl, on causality, 153, 161 n., 260 n.; on 'imply,' 17 n.; on inference, 238 n.; on infinite divisibility, 314; on law of non-contradiction, 256; on physical objects, 350, 359-60; on relations, 119 n., 123, 143, 149; on time, 93
Ryle, G., on propositions, 203 n.

Scepticism, 27, 105 ff. See *Agnosticism*
Schiller, Dr. F. C. S., on coherence, 242 ff.; on relations, 147
Science, physical, encroachments on philosophy in the name of, 181-2; idealistic method in, 56; Kant's view of, 94, 114-15; presuppositions of, 122 n., 152, 166 ff., 173 n., 176, 236, 248-9; recent developments of, 182, 311, 352, 372-3; relation to philosophical theory of physical objects, 335-6, 351-2, 372-3; truth of, 90, 106-7, 294 ff., 315
Secondary qualities, meaning of term, 373 n.; question of their physical reality, 282, 301-3, 339, 351, 352-3, 373 ff.
Self, causation in, 161 ff., 166, 176 ff.; implies relations to other things, 191 ff., 342 ff.; Kant's view of, 65, 94, 96, 100, 103, 111, 112, 113-4
Self-evidence, on coherence theory, 240-1, 248; degrees of, 177, 187 n., 260; scepticism about, 27, 65, 260 n.
Sellars, Professor R. W., 45
Sensa, meaning of term, 263, 357, 358; as opposed to sensing, 32 n., 365; nature of, 192-3, 286 ff., 308, 309, 361 ff., 368 ff., 371; ours dependent on mind, 287, 364; relation to space, 289, 339-40; view that physical objects consist of unsensed sensa, ch. VII sect. 3. See *Representative theory of perception*
Sensation, ambiguity of word, 14; Kant's treatment of, 83; as opposed to perception, 191, 362 ff., 368 n.
Shand, A. F., 176 n.
Shape, nature of physical, 190; real, as opposed to apparent, 348 ff., 360
Similarity, relation of, 117 n., 126, 128, 131, 133, 134, 135
Size, nature of physical, 190, 307 ff., 324
Smell, 376, 379 n.
Solidity, 367
Solipsism, grounds for rejecting, 247, 328 n.; implied by certain views, 18, 54, 91, 292
Sorley, Professor W. R., argument for God, 426 n.
Space, in Kant, 68 ff., 73-4, 84 ff., 94 n., 99; physical, 336 ff., 360, 372, see *Size*; reality of, 88 ff., 92-3; relation of sensa to, 289, 339-40
Spinoza, monism of, 124
Stace, Dr. W. T., on Hegel, 60, 61, 62
State, the, absolute idealist theory of, 432
Stout, Professor G. F., on 'animism,' 414; on causation, 163, 176 n.; on 'cognition', 17; on coherence, 230; on error, 203; on knowledge of physical objects, 318 n., 326, 342; on mediate knowledge, 265 n.; on propositions, 203; on relations, 147
Strong, Professor C. A., on Moore's *Refutation of Idealism*, 386 n.
Structure, justified beliefs about physical objects held to be limited to, 336, 337
Subject, of proposition, 122-3, 252
Subjectivism, use of term deprecated, 6; in Kant, 63 ff.
Subsistence, as opposed to existence, 423 ff.
Substance, 124, 165-6, 260, 342, 370 ff.; in Kant, 71, 78 n., 99
Syllogism, synthetic character of, 253 ff.
Synthesis, in Kant, 69 n., 81 ff., 108, 112-13. See *Construction*
Synthetic, as opposed to analytic, judgments and inferences, 31-2, 173-4, 251-8; in Kant, 67 ff.

System, in Hegelians, 59 ff.; involved in all judgments according to Kant and Bradley, 78, 95–6, 115, 150; reality viewed as a, 136, 182 ff., 187 ff., 231 ff.; relational system, 189; suggests mind, 396. See *Coherence*

Taste, 301, 376–7, 379 n.
Taylor, Professor A. E., on degrees of truth and reality, 215 n.; on God, 426 n.; on relations, 126, 130 n., 133 n., 147, 151–2
Telepathy, 407 n.
Theism, arguments for, 365, 387 ff., 399 ff., 403, 411–13, 416 ff., 426–7; how distinguished from idealism, 3 ff., 7, 33 n., 389, 427. See *God*
Theology, propositions of, 227
Theoretical, as opposed to practical, 226 ff.
Thing-in-itself, defence of, 107 ff.; idealist criticism of, 12, 16, 61, 102 ff.; Kant's view of, 65, 99, 100 n., 101 ff.
Thought, as 'objective' in Hegelianism, 59 ff., as opposed to feeling, 393; as opposed to knowing, 102 ff.
Time, in Kant, 68, 71, 84 ff., 94 n.; reality of, 38 n., 88 ff., 93, 336–7
Touch, 277, 286 n., 349 n., 353, 375
Transcendence, of Absolute Mind or God, 19–20, 23, 41, 51, 410
Transcendental method, the, 79–80

Truth, Bradley's theory of, 199 ff., 208 ff.; coherence theory of, 201, 220; copying theory of, 29–30, 41, 195–6; correspondence theory of, 195 ff., 266, 433 ff.; theory of degrees of, ch. V sect. 2·; relation to reality, 137 ff., 196, 200 ff., 212–13; timelessness of, 38

Uniformity of Nature, principle of, 156, 161 n.
Universal laws or truths, knowledge of, 17 ff., 39. 40, 43, 57–8, 65, 75; subsistence of, 418 ff.
Universals, objectivity of, 61, 72 n.; relations between, 131, 189; subsistence of, 418 ff.

Vaihinger, Professor H., on Kant's *Refutation of Idealism*, 100. See *Als Ob*
Values, 416–17, 436, 437–9
Verbal, view that inference is merely, 255–7
Verification, as criterion of truth, 198 n., 330 n.

Whitehead, Professor A. N., 165, 395
Whole, the, as criterion, 238, 240, 246; in ethics, 430–1, 432
Will, causation by, 161–2, 164, 178
Wilson, Professor Cook, on God, 3 n.; on knowledge, 198, 266 n., 267 n.; on relations, 125 n., 147
Words, their influence on thought, 149